# THE CAMBRIDGE HISTORY OF
# ENGLISH LITERATURE

VOLUME VIII

THE AGE OF DRYDEN

# THE
# CAMBRIDGE HISTORY OF
# ENGLISH LITERATURE

EDITED

BY

SIR A. W. WARD

AND

A. R. WALLER

VOLUME VIII

THE AGE OF DRYDEN

CAMBRIDGE UNIVERSITY PRESS

CAMBRIDGE

LONDON · NEW YORK · MELBOURNE

Published by the Syndics of the Cambridge University Press
The Pitt Building, Trumpington Street, Cambridge CB2 1RP
Bentley House, 200 Euston Road, London NW1 2DB
32 East 57th Street, New York, NY 10022, USA
296 Beaconsfield Parade, Middle Park, Melbourne 3206 Australia

ISBN 0 521 04522 3

First published 1911
Reprinted 1920
Cheap edition (text only) 1932
Reprinted 1934 1949 1952
1962 1964 1968 1976 1979

Printed in Great Britain at the
University Press, Cambridge

# PREFATORY NOTE

*The Cambridge History of English Literature* was first published between the years 1907 and 1916. The General Index Volume was issued in 1927.

In the preface to Volume I the general editors explained their intentions. They proposed to give a connected account of the successive movements of English literature, to describe the work of writers both of primary and of secondary importance, and to discuss the interaction between English and foreign literatures. They included certain allied subjects such as oratory, scholarship, journalism and typography, and they did not neglect the literature of America and the British Dominions. The History was to unfold itself, "unfettered by any preconceived notions of artificial eras or controlling dates," and its judgments were not to be regarded as final.

This reprint of the text and general index of the *History* is issued in the hope that its low price may make it easily available to a wider circle of students and other readers who wish to have on their shelves the full story of English literature.

CAMBRIDGE
1932

# CONTENTS

# CHAPTER I

## DRYDEN

'THE Age of Dryden' seems an expression as appropriate as any description of a literary period by the name of a single writer can be, and yet, in one sense, it is a misnomer. On the one hand, in the chapter of English literary history which more or less covers the forty years between the restoration and the opening of the eighteenth century, not only is Dryden's the most conspicuous personality, but there are few literary movements of importance marking the period of which he did not, as if by right divine, assume the leadership, and which did not owe to him most of what vitality they proved to possess. On the other hand, as has been again and again pointed out, Dryden, of all great English writers, and, more especially, of all great English poets, was the least original, the least capable of inspiring his generation with new ideas, of discovering for it new sources of emotion, even of producing new artistic forms. Many currents of thought and feeling suggested to him by his age were supplied by the power of his genius with an impetus of unprecedented strength ; more than one literary form, offering itself for his use at an inchoate, or at a relatively advanced, stage of development owed the recognition which it secured to the resourceful treatment of it by his master-hand. Whether or not the debt which his extraordinary productivity as a writer owed to the opportunities given him by his times can be taken into account as against the transformation of his material by his genius may be regarded as a question open to debate. There cannot, however, be any doubt at all that neither can Dryden's own achievements be appreciated apart from the influences of his age, nor is any judgment of the literary produce of that age, as a whole, to be formed without an estimate of his contribution to it being regarded as the dominant factor in the result. Thus, in an attempt to sketch, once more, the course of his literary endeavours, it would be futile to detach their succession from the experiences of his personal life, largely determined, as these were, by political reaction and revolution, and by other changes in the condition of the country and in that of its intellectual centre, the capital.

John Dryden (he wrote his name thus, though, before him, the spelling was varied both by his kinsmen and by his parents) was born 9 August 1631, in the parsonage house of Aldwinkle All Saints, near Oundle in Northamptonshire, of which his maternal grandfather, Henry Pickering, was rector[1]. His parents were of good county descent; but his father, Erasmus Dryden, was a younger son with many brothers and sisters, and his estate at Blakesley, on the other side of the county (near Canons-Ashby, the family seat), which afterwards descended to the poet, considerably burdened, was valued at sixty pounds a year in the money of the time. He appears to have resided generally at Tichmarsh, the chief seat of his wife's family, near Oundle. On both the father's and the mother's side, the future laureate of the Stewarts was connected with the parliamentary side; his mother's cousin-german, Sir Gilbert Pickering, was one of the judges of Charles I (though he did not sit on the final day), and, afterwards, became chamberlain at the protector Oliver's court and a member of his House of Lords[2]. After receiving his early education either at Tichmarsh or (as is the more usual tradition) at Oundle grammar school, Dryden—at what precise date is unknown—was admitted as a king's scholar at Westminster, where he was trained under the redoubtable Busby. In a note to a translation of the *Third Satire of Persius*, published by Dryden in 1693[3], Dryden states that he remembered translating this satire at Westminster school 'for a Thursday-night's exercise.' The direct influence which exercises of this kind, vigilantly supervised, must have had upon the formation of his style as a writer of English verse is obvious; but, though Dryden surmises that copies of his translations were preserved by Busby, none is extant, and the sole poetical relic of his Westminster days is his contribution to *Lachrymae Musarum* (1649), in memory of his schoolfellow, Henry Lord Hastings— a small volume, whose black-bordered title-page heralds not less

---

[1] See a valuable article in *The Saturday Review*, 17 April 1875, entitled 'The Birthplace of Dryden,' which, besides summarising what is known as to the localities of his birth and childhood, gives an account of most of what remains on record concerning his kith and kin.

[2] It would seem to be this Sir Gilbert, who, in *The Medal of John Bayes*, and elsewhere, is held up to scorn as a committee-man or sequestrator.

[3] The translation of the *Fifth Satire* is inscribed to Busby.

than thirty-three elegiac pieces, by Herrick, Denham, Marvell and others. About Dryden's juvenile elegy, much that is superfluous has been written; it was not wonderful that a schoolboy poet should exaggerate the bad taste into which the followers of an artificial school of poetry frequently lapsed[1]; but the verses also give proof of that rapidity in connecting thoughts (the very essence of wit) and that felicity in expressing them which were among the chief characteristics of the formed style of Dryden.

In May 1650, he was admitted as a Westminster scholar at Trinity college, Cambridge, whence he matriculated in the following July. Of his college career, nothing is known, except that, quite early in his third year of residence, he underwent a not very serious disciplinary punishment[2]. He took his B.A. degree in January 1654, but did not proceed to M.A., which degree he only obtained in 1668, when it was conferred on him at the king's request by the archbishop of Canterbury (Sheldon). It appears, probably on his own authority[3], that he continued in residence at Cambridge till 1657; but there is no evidence as to the date when he began his life in London, though he may be concluded to have done so before the death of the protector Oliver (September 1658).

Cambridge would not seem to have fascinated the imagination, or to have enchained the sympathies, of an *alumnus* destined to hold a prominent place in her long list of poets. In the earliest years of the second half of the century, the university had much to suffer from the ascendancy of the army, and may even momentarily have trembled for its existence. During Oliver's protectorate, however, when the university was represented in parliament by his son Richard, it began to revive under a more tolerant *régime*. Dryden's family connection was, as has been seen, with the party in power; nor was his a nature into which the iron of political tyranny was likely to enter very deeply. But it is quite unnecessary to seek for explanations of the preference which, a quarter of a century later, in one of the several prologues[4]

---

[1] See, besides the notorious allusions to the small-pox, the concluding apostrophe to the young lord's betrothed.

[2] There is no evidence to support the assertion of Shadwell (in *The Medal of John Bayes*) that Dryden, having 'traduced a nobleman' and suffered castigation, narrowly escaped expulsion from his college in consequence.

[3] In *Notes and Observations on The Empress of Morocco* (1674), cited by Malone, *Life of Dryden*, p. 27, Dryden is spoken of as 'a man of seven years' standing at Cambridge.' He had himself a hand in this pamphlet.

[4] The date of the particular *Prologue*, first printed in 1684, is safely conjectured by Christie to have been 1681.

addressed by him to the university of Oxford, he avowed for it, as
'Athens,' over his own mother-university, 'Thebes'—nor need this
preference be taken very seriously[1]. And, in any case, it is quite
out of keeping with his usual indifference to such attacks to suppose that his coldness towards Cambridge was due to a captious
'Cambridge' pamphlet (which, by the way, was published at
Oxford), *The Censure of the Rota on Mr Dryden's Conquest
of Granada* (1673); while equally little importance attaches, in
this connection, to the statement of Dennis (a Caius man) that,
about the same time, not only the town (London), but, also, the
university of Cambridge, was very much divided as between
Settle and Dryden, 'the younger fry,' in both places, 'inclining
to Elkanah[2].'

In 1654, soon after Dryden had taken his bachelor's degree,
his father died, and he became the owner of the small paternal
estate. From the time of his residence at Cambridge, either
before or after this event, hardly any literary remains have come
down to us. Dryden, as Malone points out, had no share in any
of the collections of contemporary Cambridge verse printed during
his period of residence. On the other hand, from the first year
of his undergraduateship date the pleasing lines, proudly signed
'J. Dryden of Trin. C.,' prefixed to a volume of *Epigrams* (1650)
put forth by his friend John Hoddesdon, who, unlike Dryden
himself, was moved to seek reputation as a poet

> before the down begin
> To peep, as yet, upon [his] smoother skin.

And a more personal interest attached to a copy of verses
forming part of a letter written by him, in acknowledgment of
the gift of a silver inkstand, to his cousin Honor, the daughter
of Sir John Dryden, the head of the family. They are, as Scott
points out, in Cowley's fantastic and farfetched style, and are not
altogether pleasing. For the superstructure of a supposed attachment and blighted hopes which has been raised upon the evidence
of this letter, there is not a tittle of proof[3].

---

[1] As Christie points out, the poet, in transmitting to Rochester another *Prologue*
addressed to 'Athenian judges' six months earlier, and asserting, *inter alia*, that
> poetry which is in Oxford made
> An art, in London only is a trade,
observed to his patron 'how easy 'tis to pass anything upon a University.'

[2] Cited by Saintsbury, G., *Dryden* (English Men of Letters), p. 65.

[3] To be sure, one of the two heiresses of Dryden's second acted play, *The Rival-
Ladies*, is named Honoria, and one of the stories included by Dryden in his last
important work is Boccaccio's tale of *Theodore and Honoria*. To be sure, too, Honor
Dryden, though she inherited a large portion, never married.

When, in 1657 or 1658, Dryden took up his abode in London, to which, with the exception of occasional visits to Northampton-shire and other easily accessible parts of the country, he remained faithful during the rest of his life, Cromwell's rule had, for some years, been firmly established, and Sir Gilbert Pickering was in full possession of the great man's favour. That the young Dryden actually became 'clerk' or secretary to his influential kinsman rests only on the late evidence of Shadwell's lampoon[1]. But no special connection of the kind with the protector's court or person is needed to account for Dryden's first public appearance as a writer with *A Poem upon the Death of His Late Highness, Oliver, Lord Protector of England, Scotland and Ireland,* first published separately early in 1659, and reprinted in the same year, in company with an ode on the same subject by Thomas Sprat (afterwards dean of Westminster and bishop of Rochester) and some lines by Waller *Upon the late Storme and Death of the Protector.* Sprat's is a not undignified effort in a style in which he acquitted himself so well as to become known as 'Pindaric Sprat,' and contains a daring figure afterwards appropriated by the master of the species, 'the incomparable Dr Cowley[2].' Waller's lines, as usual with him, beat out the gold of a single thought into very thin leaf. Dryden, on the contrary, whose poem was again reprinted in 1659, revised, and under the title of *Heroick Stanzas consecrated to the Memory,* etc., surveyed his theme with not less circumspection than ardour, and chose his topics of eulogy not only, as Scott says, with attention to truth, but, also, with a manifest desire to avoid hyperbole. Even the fine passage

> Such was our Prince, yet owned a soul above
> The highest acts it could produce to show

cannot be censured as an exaggeration, except by those who deny that Cromwell was a great man and, as such, necessarily greater than his deeds. The poem, though still studded with farfetched and not always appropriate conceits (*e.g.* 'War, our consumption,' st. XII; 'Bolognia's walls,' st. XVI; the death of Tarpeia, st. XXXIV), shows Dryden already controlling the form chosen by him with a certainty not to be found in his juvenile efforts, and master of an overpowering directness which was to become

---

[1] In *The Medal of John Bayes* (1682).

[2]        He brought them to the Borders, but a Second hand
            Did settle and secure them, in the promis'd Land.

The passage shows that Sprat's tribute, like Dryden's, was intended to meet the eye of Oliver's successor.

one of his most notable characteristics[1]. Thus, the *Heroick Stanzas*, though, necessarily, they attracted little attention at a time when the immediate future absorbed public interest, and though their author, naturally, was willing to allow them to be forgotten, hold a permanent place among his poetical achievements.

Dryden's working days in the service of the muses had now begun. With his very modest income, and without any family interest that could be of use to him, he can have looked the world in the face in no very sanguine mood; and, indeed, a certain reserve and lack of satisfaction in life and in the work which he had to do in it is noticeable in his writings, as it seems to have been in his personal bearing. Shadwell's sneer that Dryden had 'turn'd journeyman to a bookseller' probably applies to a rather later period of his career, and may be an illnatured perversion of an insignificant fact[2]. But, in any case, Dryden, till he had studied his brief and taken up his pen, was devoid of the political, and, still more, of the religious, enthusiasm which might have sufficed to inspire him as a writer; and few poets have ever been less manifestly moved by spontaneous lyric impulse. What he wrote in the earlier part of his literary career was, as it were, automatically suggested by the great changes in contemporary public life, to which his literary powers, growing surer of themselves in each successive trial, responded without any apparent hesitation.

As there had not been any signs of ardour or strong personal conviction in the *Heroick Stanzas*, so, when the restoration of the Stewart monarchy had been accomplished as the only feasible termination of the crisis, and when Dryden, once more, went with the times, he went with them in his own temperate and reasoning way. This may certainly be averred with regard to the substance of the paean sounded by him on the occasion of the return of Charles II. For, although, in *Astraea Redux* (1660), he did not shrink from any extravagance in picturing the popular joy, and the hopes in which, 'now Time's whiter series is begun,' the subjects of Charles II indulged, yet, the royal qualities on which he enlarged as warranting these emotions were those which the king actually

---

[1]      His grandeur he derived from heaven alone. (St. vi.)
        When absent, yet we conquered in his right. (St. xxiv.)
        He made us freemen of the continent. (St. xxix.)

[2] The bookseller is stated, in a note, to have been H. Herringman, 'who kept him at his house for the purpose.' Dryden seems to have lodged over Herringman's shop in the New Exchange, Strand, and Herringman was the publisher of the poems of Sir Robert Howard, Dryden's future brother-in-law. The combination was irresistible.

possessed, or, at least, was anxious to display—prudence in adversity, and clemency in the day of success. At the same time, he abstained from personal abuse, either of Cromwell (for the comparison to 'the bold Typhoeus' cannot be set down as abuse) or of any other leader of the rebellion. There is, of course, much audacious misuse of the classical and Scriptural illustrations in which this poem abounds; but that was part of the 'noble' style which is essential to courtly panegyric. The general spirit of the poem is merely that of frank timeservice ; though the shameless apostrophising of the rechristened Naseby, which had earned some of the naval laurels celebrated in the *Heroick Stanzas*, as 'now no longer England's shame,' must be allowed to call for severe censure. The genius of the poet shows itself not only in magnificent aberrations, like the comparison to the star of Bethlehem of the star that had shone at Charles II's birth and now shone again,

> Guiding our eyes to find and worship you ;

but, also, in exquisitely graceful turns of expression, to which the metre suits its music with inimitable ease, such as the tribute to May, the month in which the king was born :

> You and the flowers are its peculiar care[1].

Nor are characteristic strokes of wit wanting, like that on the grief inflicted by Charles II's departure to the Dutch (against whom Dryden was beginning to cultivate an irrepressible dislike[2]):

> True sorrow—Holland to regret a King!

On the occasion of Charles II's coronation (1661), Dryden was ready with another 'panegyric,' again in heroic couplets, *To His Sacred Majesty*, congratulating him on his pacific intentions in convoking the Savoy conference (not yet a declared failure), and on his improvements in St James's park, where

> the mistrustful fowl no harm suspects,
> So safe are all things which our King protects,

as well as on his approaching marriage. With this piece of pure adulation—*merum mel*—may be mentioned the lines *To My Lord Chancellor*, offered to Clarendon on New Year's day 1662, in which the conceptions of derived greatness and original merit are skilfully mixed, but, as is perhaps explicable, without any great

---

[1] The emphasised use of the pronoun *you* became one of the notes of Dryden's verse.

[2] See *Satire on the Dutch written in the year* 1662, which, ten years later, Dryden frugally utilised for the prologue and epilogue to *Amboyna*.

expenditure of personal sympathy[1]. The *Verses to Her Royal Highness the Duchess* (Clarendon's daughter) belong to a later date (1665) and, apparently, were not known till printed with the preface to *Annus Mirabilis*, in which poem are sung the praises of 'victorious York.' As might be expected, they show a marked advance in concentrated vigour of phrase, though not rising anywhere to the beauty of the passage, justly singled out for praise by Saintsbury, which then seemed to summarise the fortunes of Clarendon[2].

The whole of the first group of Dryden's poems may be said to be brought to a close by *Annus Mirabilis, or The Year of Wonders* (1666); but, before the production of this work, he had already brought out several plays. It was, not improbably, in this way that he was brought into contact with Sir Robert Howard, a younger son of the earl of Berkshire, who had long been connected with the Stewart court and whose wife was a daughter of the great lord Burghley. On 1 December 1663, Dryden married lord Berkshire's daughter Elizabeth, then twenty-five years of age. The marriage took place with her father's consent, and lady Elizabeth seems, sooner or later, to have brought her husband some addition to his estate. She was, no doubt, his superior in rank, but not in any unusual measure. That Dryden was not, at this time, leading the life of a bookseller's hack is shown, *inter alia*, by his election, in November 1662, as a fellow of the Royal Society, in its early days often as much of a social as of a scientific honour[3]. The circumstances of Dryden's marriage and wedded life, whether actual or fictitious, were an inexhaustible fund of scandal to the malevolent. One story ran that lady Elizabeth's brothers had bullied Dryden into the match; another, that it was made up to cover a *faux pas* on the part of the lady with another man. It is clear that she had led no cloistered life; but Dryden seems to have been throughout on easy terms with Sir Robert Howard, even during their literary controversy, and sufficiently acknowledges his personal goodwill[4]. The general

---

[1] Clarendon's 'early courtship of the Muses' is mentioned at the outset of these lines; but there is no reason for suspecting a reference to poetical compositions, of which we have no knowledge.

[2] 'Our setting sun from his declining seat,' etc.

[3] The immediate cause of Dryden's election may have been the lines addressed by him in this year, *To my Honoured Friend Dr Charleton, on his learned and useful Works, and more particularly this of Stone-heng, by him Restored to the true Founders*, which may be summed up as a rather shallow eulogy of Bacon and some later English scientific luminaries at the expense of Aristotle.

[4] See letter prefixed to *Annus Mirabilis*.

character of Dryden's long married life remains obscure; it has been freely described as unhappy, and, in its last period, cannot but have been darkened by his wife's mental decay; on the other hand, there are indications in their correspondence of pleasant relations between them. That the husband provoked or requited the wife's infirmities of mind or temper by infidelities is a conjecture resting on an assumption; for the assertion that 'Dryden was a libertine' remains unproved[1].

*Annus Mirabilis*, though not written in the heroic couplet with which Dryden had already familiarised himself in both dramatic and non-dramatic composition, offers unmistakable proof of the ease and self-confidence which by this time he had already acquired as a writer of verse. The stanza form of decasyllabic quatrains here adopted had already been used by Sir John Davies in his philosophical poem *Nosce Teipsum* (1599), where it well suits both theme and treatment[2], and had been revived by D'Avenant in *Gondibert* (1656), where the poet, in order to satisfy his principle that each quatrain 'should contain a period,' often becomes prosy in consequence. For the rest, *Gondibert*, though composed under the critical eye of Hobbes, and compared by him to the *Aeneid* and the *Iliad*, notwithstanding the advantage which accrued to these as dating from 'what is called old time, but is young time,' contained little that invited imitation; while the long and not uninteresting critical *Preface*, though it may have helped to suggest the writing of those critical essays of which Dryden composed the earliest in the year before that in which *Annus Mirabilis* appeared, clearly did not serve as a model for them[3].

Like *Gondibert*, *Annus Mirabilis* was the fruit of exile; but, while part of the former was written at the Louvre, Dryden had been driven from London, by the great plague and the great fire commemorated in his poem, to take refuge at his father-in-law's country seat at Charlton in Wiltshire. In *An Account of the Ensuing Poem, in a letter to Sir Robert Howard*, dated

---

[1] The unknown 'W. G.,' whose letter in vol. xv of *The Gentleman's Magazine* for February 1795 (p. 99), mentioning that he remembered seeing Dryden with the actress Anne Reeve at the Mulberry gardens, has been repeatedly cited, makes the further observation that 'in company' he was 'the modestest man that ever conversed'—not a common characteristic of libertines in general, or of those of Charles's days in particular.

[2] See vol. iv, pp. 162—3. As to the metre, cf. *post*, chap. ix.

[3] As to *Gondibert*, see *ante*, vol. vii, chap. iii. Hobbes's praise of the story of Gondibert and Birtha, the great magician's daughter, as an 'incomparable description of Love,' is discounted by its resemblance, in its opening passages at all events, to the scenes in *The Tempest* between Prospero, Miranda and Ferdinand.

November 1666, Dryden, although he utters some heterodox opinions about Vergil, declares that 'he has been my master in this poem,' which, indeed, is distinguished by a masculinity of tone and a richness of imagery that lend force to the assertion. The admirably chosen title was not original, though the application seems to have been new[1]. Dryden describes *Annus Mirabilis* as a historical poem, apparently implying that it does not make any pretensions to being an epos, for which it lacks both the requisite unity and the requisite length of action. On the other hand, it treats its twofold theme, the Dutch war and the fire of London, with great skill, both in the selection of topics, and in the management of the transitions which give coherency to the whole. As for the war, its final cause lay in the commercial jealousy between the two nations, which made itself felt wherever English mercantile enterprise was seeking to compete with that of a more successful rival, and which, of course, came home most nearly to the city of London. But it was also due to a general antipathy on the part of the English against the Dutch, as of the naturally stronger, to the actually wealthier, community. Dryden, accordingly, takes care to dwell on the strength of England, as contrasted with the meanness, baseness and so forth, of Holland. Moreover, the upper class of English society was offended by Dutch burgherism and republicanism, while the court resented the act excluding the house of Orange from the stadholdership. When, therefore, war was declared, a good deal of enthusiasm (of a kind), especially among the gentry, hailed the event; and Evelyn gives an amusing description of the outbreak of a universal passion for taking service in the fleet. Dryden, in his preface, describes that part of his poem which treats of the war as 'but a due expiation' on his part for 'not serving his King and country in it.' The navy, as the favourite service of both the king and his brother the duke of York, was, at

---

[1] See *Somers Tracts*, vol. VII, pp. 644—5, for a notice of pretended prophecies as to the fire of London, stated to have been printed in 1661 or 1662, in the nonconformist interest, under the title *Annus Mirabilis primus et secundus*. For a full account of the proceedings against Francis Smith and others, supposed to be concerned in the printing of *Mirabilis Annus, or the Year of Prodigies and Wonders*, printed 1661, see *Index Expurgatorius Anglicanus*, pp. 183—8. The expression 'The Wonderful Yeere' had, however, been used more than half a century earlier, and, curiously enough, of the plague year 1602, when more than 30,000 persons were said to have fallen victims to the epidemic in London. See Dekker's *The Seven Deadly Sinnes of London* (Arber's edition), p. 5. Burnet, in his *Life and Death of Sir Matthew Hale* (1682), p. 102, mentions that, 'in the year 1666, an Opinion did run through the Nation, that the end of the world would come that year.' Though Burnet says that this belief was possibly 'set on by Astrologers,' and Dryden had a *penchant* for astrology, he does not seem to make any reference to it in his poem.

this time, extremely popular ; and Dryden's confessed anxiety to have his sea terms correct was pedantry in season.

Altogether, his account of the progress of the war—from the dearly-bought victory[1] of Solebay to the barren triumph off the North Foreland[2]—is full of fire and spirit; and it was not any part of the poet's business to expound how, when the campaign of 1666 came to an end, the feeling began to spread that, with or without further naval victories, the situation of the country, against which France was intriguing in every part of the king's dominions, would, before long, become untenable. Thus, when Dryden represents the terrible visitation of September 1666—the destruction of the far greater part of London by fire—as having befallen England at a season of undiminished confidence, and as a nemesis of this national pride—he is putting a gloss of his own upon the actual sequence of affairs. He had, moreover, omitted any account of the plague, whose ravages were at their height at a date considerably earlier than that of the events described in the introductory part of his poem, and had thus made it easier to represent the fire as a calamity which overtook the nation when 'palled' with the long succession of its 'joys.' The fury of the fire at its height is depicted with splendid energy, and the daring figure of the witches' sabbath, danced by the ghosts of traitors who have descended from London Bridge[3], is not less apposite to the wild scene than that of the divine extinguisher by which the fire is put out is preposterous. The poet's prophecy that a 'greater and more august' London would arise 'from her fires' was fulfilled; but the companion political prophecy had a lamer ending in the peace of 1667, which was all that England gained from the glories of the 'wonderful year.' Yet the literary achievement itself was wonderful. Without the assurance to be derived from any great previous success, Dryden had undertaken a task so full of pitfalls that nothing but a most extraordinary impetus could have carried his course past these to its goal—and this, though he had hampered himself with a metrical form which, as he knew and confessed, had made a far more exacting claim upon his ingenuity and skill than the couplet

[1] The laments of ' sea-green Sirens ' for the death of admiral Sir John Lawson are of a piece with ' the mermaid's song ' at the end of *The Battle of the Baltic*, and must be censured or extolled in its company.

[2] This was the occasion on which de Ruyter (whom Dryden compares to Varro at Cannae) saved his ships, as has been observed, in order to sail up the Medway with them ' another day.'

[3] That they then seated themselves on the roof of Whitehall is a supposition due to a persistent misprint in st. 224, pointed out and corrected in Sargeaunt's edition of Dryden's *Poems* (1910).

already familiar to him. The courage and dash of the whole performance, which cast into the shade its lesser features, its far-fetched conceits and other reminiscences of poetic schools that were nearing their end, could not but apprise the critical world, including king and court, that a combatant had descended into the arena who was unlikely to find an equal there.

Meanwhile, like most of his would-be rivals, he had formed a connection with the theatre, and continued to maintain it. In his thirtieth year, on the very morrow of the restoration, Dryden made his earliest known attempt as a playwright. His dramatic productivity slackened very much during the latter half of his literary life; but he cannot be said to have ever wholly abandoned this form of production; indeed, in his very last year, he contri-buted some new matter on the occasion of the revival, for his benefit, of one of Fletcher's plays. Within this period, he tried his hand at most dramatic forms in actual use, and, for a time, iden-tified himself with the most conspicuous new development. In view, however, of the assertion deliberately made by him in his later days[1], that 'his genius never much inclined him to the stage,' and of the general course of his literary career, which shows him rather falling back from time to time on play-writing than steadily attracted by it, the fact that he was the author, in whole or in part, of nearly a score and a half of plays, would be surprising, were it not for the extraordinary promptitude and adaptability of his powers. It will be most convenient, before returning to his other literary labours, to survey briefly his dramatic work as a whole. Its fluctuations were largely determined by influences which he could, indeed, sustain and develop, but into which, except in the instance of one transitory species, he can hardly be said to have infused any fresh life; so that his plays, as a whole, remain, after all, only a subsidiary section of his literary achievements.

The principal currents in what, according to a rather loose terminology, it has been customary to call the restoration drama, will be discussed in other chapters of the present volume; and what is said here is only so much as is necessary to make the general course of Dryden's productivity as a dramatist intelligible.

Inasmuch as the primary object of the London stage, when re-established with the monarchy, was to please the king, his court and its surroundings, and, inasmuch as, in that court, many besides the king himself had acquired a personal familiarity with the

---

[1] See *A Discourse concerning the Original and Progress of Satire* (1693) (*Essays*, ed. Ker, W. P., vol. II, p. 37).

French stage and its literature which, at all events in his case, dated back to the earlier years of his exile, French influence upon the English drama in the restoration age was, almost as a matter of course, both strong and enduring. But it is equally certain that the basis from which the English drama started on the reopening of the theatres was no other than the old English drama, at the point which it had reached at the time of their closing. Beaumont and Fletcher, and the drama of tragicomic romance which, through them, had, for a generation before the closing of the theatres, established their supremacy on the English stage[1], were the favourites there when the theatres reopened; nor had either Jonson or Shakespeare been forgotten, and the former was still, though the flow of humour among his followers had begun to run dry, regarded as the acknowledged master of comedy. The dominant power on the French stage down to about the middle of the fourth decade of the seventeenth century had been that of Hardy, whose most celebrated play, *Mariamne*, dates from 1610, and whose *vogue* did not begin to give way till after his death in 1631[2]. Now, Hardy, like the dramatists who gave the tone to English dramatic literature in the generation before the closing of the theatres, kept the French stage popular by means of the mixed species of tragicomedy, and thus prevented it from falling back on the academical lines of Senecan tragedy represented by Garnier. It is true that he was warming in his bosom the great reformer of both French tragedy and French comedy, who said of himself that, in his earlier plays, he had no guidance 'but a little commonsense and the examples supplied to him by Hardy'; but Corneille's epochal production of *Le Cid* did not take place till 1636 (*Médée* appeared only a year earlier); and *Le Menteur*, which stands in much the same relation to the development of French comedy as that held by *Le Cid* to the progress of French tragedy, was not produced till 1642. Thus, though Part I of *Le Cid* was brought out in an English translation (by Joseph Rutter) in 1637 and Part II (in a version in which Richard Sackville, afterwards earl of Dorset, is said to have had a share) in 1640, both being republished in 1650, it seems clear that the main influence exercised by the French upon the English drama was due to Hardy and tragicomedy, which dominated all the French dramatists—including Rotrou,

---

[1] As to the long life of romantic tragicomedy, and its survival after the restoration, see the lucid exposition in Ristine, F. H., *English Tragi-Comedy, its Origin and History* (New York, 1910), chaps. v and vi.

[2] See Rigal, E., *Alexandre Hardy et le Théâtre Français à la fin du XVI^me et au commencement du XVII^me siècle*, Paris, 1889.

whose work synchronised with Corneille's earlier dramatic labours
—rather than to Corneille in the maturity of his creative genius.
When, however, the perennial conflict was renewed under new
conditions and on reasoned principles by Corneille, a loftier and
more logical conception of tragedy approved itself to the French
critical public; and, perfected in practice by the singularly refined
and sensitive genius of Racine, French classical tragedy reached its
consummation as a distinct species of dramatic literature. The
beginnings of Molière (though more than one of his plays have an
earlier date) may, for our present purpose, be placed in 1658, when,
both as actor and writer, he first appeared before Louis XIV and
his court. It was not long before the English drama, in the hands
of Dryden and others, revealed the impression made on it by these
new developments, the effects of which, whether direct or indirect,
will be summarised in later chapters[1]; but they should not be
regarded as what in no sense they were, the starting-points of our
post-restoration drama.

Of special importance for the progress of the English drama,
both before and after the closing of the theatres, was the influence
of prose fiction, operating either directly or through plays for
which it had furnished material. The two literatures which here
particularly come into question are the Spanish and the French
—of popular Italian fiction, the heyday seemed to have passed
away, as, in the seventeenth century, artificiality of taste established its rule. Concerning Spanish influence, more will be said
below[2]; while it is not unfrequently difficult to substantiate a
traditional derivation from a Spanish play, the direct indebtedness
of English dramatists to Spanish prose fiction was, beyond doubt,
considerable in extent, both before and after the restoration.
French prose fiction, on the other hand, in the course of the
seventeenth century, passed through an entirely new phase in its
history; and, inasmuch as this very directly influenced an English
dramatic species with which Dryden was, for a time, identified,
reference must be made to it here[3]. With the *Astrée* of Honoré
d'Urfé (1610—2) began a literary movement representing, in the
first instance, a reaction towards a refinement of sentiment and
expression which had been incompatible with the turbulence of a
long epoch of civil war. This movement culminated in the school

---

[1] See *post*, chaps. v, vii, and xvii.   [2] See *post*, chap. v.
[3] See also *post*, chap. xvii; and cf. Ward, *Hist. of Engl. Dr. Lit.* vol. iii, pp. 307 ff.
For other authorities, see Hill, H. W., 'La Calprenède's Romances and the Restoration
Drama' in *University of Nevada Studies*, vol. ii (1910), p. 3.

of romance associated with the name of La Calprenède and, still more largely, with that of Madeleine de Scudéry, the authoress of *Le Grand Cyrus*. Gomberville and the comtesse de La Fayette belong to the same group, but that lady's last and most celebrated novel, *La Princesse de Clèves*, is already differentiated from the creations of Mlle de Scudéry by being, to some extent, based upon historical fact, towards which, as a writer of memoirs, the authoress had a leaning. The romances of this school invariably turned on the pivot of 'heroic' love, or love in more than the usual number of dimensions, and, though dealing with the deepest of human emotions, they never fell out of the tone of elaborate conventional formality. They were, in some instances, translated into English or imitated by English writers, from the commonwealth times onwards, when, no doubt, they had been welcomed, in many quarters, as alternatives to the drab dulness of everyday life[1]; and, after the restoration, as will be seen, they supplied themes to dramatic writers whose object it was to heighten and intensify the characteristics of stage romance. While prose fiction, of this class, continued to attract English readers to within the last quarter of the century, in France, a reaction had already set in towards simplicity, on the one hand, and satire, on the other; but, in these directions, English dramatists were not, at all events at this time, prepared to follow.

It was, then, under these influences, that Dryden gradually settled down to the particular forms of dramatic composition which he chose from time to time, and in no regular succession, to make his own, and which he frequently illustrated by signally suggestive prose commentaries, written with consummate grace and ease in the form of dedications, prefaces or essays, thus bringing his dramatic productions into harmony with rules of good sense and good taste evolved from established theory and, still more largely, from approved practice. Dryden's plays would often lose much, if not most, of their interest if read without reference to their prefaces and other critical apparatus; neither, however, is it advisable, except in a few special instances, to detach these from the texts which gave rise to them.

In the actual year of the restoration, or, at all events, within a few months from that date, Dryden, perhaps stimulated by the use

---

[1] See Dorothy Osborne's *Letters* (chap. III), 1653, from Chicksands, where *La Cléopâtre* and *Le Grand Cyrus* appear to have been her habitual companions, and Pepys's *Diary*, 7 December 1660 (when he sat up till midnight reading Fuller's *Abbeys*, while his wife, whose devotion to these romances he did not share, was immersed in 'Great Cyrus') *et al.* As to the chief English translations and imitations of these French romances, see *post*, chap. XVI.

made in the commonwealth period of quasi-dramatic dialogue as
a vehicle of political satire or invective[1], proposed to himself to
read a political lesson to the public by means of a historical
tragedy, *The Duke of Guise*, applying the doubtful parallel of the
Catholic league to the recent memories of puritan ascendancy.
But the attempt was not thought successful by judicious advisers,
and what had been written of the play was left over to be utilised
by the author in the tragedy which, many years later, in 1682, he
produced in conjunction with Lee. Thus, the first play by Dryden
produced on the stage was *The Wild Gallant*, first acted in
February 1663. It has no further claim to be singled out among
the comedies, at the same time extravagant and coarse, in which
the period of dramatic decline abounds; though there are some
traces of the witty dialogue, often carried on by a flirting couple,
in which Dryden came to excel. The statement in the prologue
that the author was 'endangered by a Spanish plot' (*i.e.* a rival
'Spanish' play) has been perverted to the direct opposite of
its meaning, and the most humorous incident in the piece is
conveyed straight from Ben Jonson[2]. The play did not find favour,
except, apparently, with lady Castlemaine ; and, in the sequel,
Dryden only intermittently returned to comedy proper. He wrote
of himself, early in his dramatic career[3], that he was 'not so fitted
by nature to write comedy' as certain other kinds of drama; 'he
wanted,' he confesses, 'that gaiety of humour which is required to
it[4]'; and he also wanted, as he might have added, the facility of
invention—whether of situations or of characters—which relieves
the productions of a comic dramatist from the sameness which is
noticeable in this class of Dryden's plays. He consoled himself
with the notion that 'a reputation gained from comedy' was hardly
worth the seeking; 'for I think it is, in its own nature, inferior to
all sorts of dramatic writing[5].' Thus, he only returned to it from
time to time, and wholly eschewed 'farce, which consists principally
of grimaces[6],' and from which he naturally shrank, devoid as he

---

[1] As to these political squibs in dramatic form, cf. Ristine, F. H., *u.s.* pp. 151—3.

[2] Cf. *post*, chap. v. The 'Spanish plot' in question was that of Tuke's *Adventures of Five Hours*. Cf. *Modern Language Notes*, vol. xix (1904), p. 166. Fitzmaurice-Kelly, *History of Spanish Literature*, p. 263, had already pointed out that *El Galán escarmentado*, which was supposed to have suggested Dryden's plot, could hardly have reached Dryden before it was published. The borrowing from Jonson's *Every Man out of His Humour* is in act i, sc. 3.

[3] *A Defence of an Essay of Dramatick Poesie* (1668) (*Essays*, ed. Ker, vol. i, p. 116).

[4] See, also, the dedication to *Aureng-Zebe*, where he freely confesses that some of his contemporaries have, even in his own partial judgment, outdone him in comedy.

[5] See preface to *An Evening's Love* (*Essays*, ed. Ker, vol. i, p. 135).

[6] *Ibid.*

may generally be asserted to have been of any inclination to what was grotesque, or even merely odd or quaint. And, in the critical essays and excursuses which illustrated his practice, he discusses the comic drama with comparative rarity[1].

*The Wild Gallant* was written in prose, as was *Sir Martin Mar-All, or The Feigned Innocence* (1667, printed 1668), an adaptation by Dryden, whose name was not attached to it till thirty years later, of the duke of Newcastle's translation of Molière's early comedy *L'Étourdi*, with certain touches suggested by two plays by Quinault. The translation is not close, nor the treatment refined; but the play was very successful. In prose is also the main portion of *The Assignation or Love in a Nunnery* (1672, printed 1673), worthless, except where in some blank verse passages it rises to a higher literary level. *Marriage-à-la-Mode* (produced at the same dates), which, unlike *The Assignation*, greatly pleased the town, thanks to the admirably drawn coquette Melantha, presents the same mixture of prose and blank verse. Of Dryden's remaining comedies, *Limberham, or The Kind Keeper* (acted in 1678), which is entirely in prose, has unmistakable dramatic merits; but it was speedily withdrawn, having been judged a gross libel on a well known public personage, generally supposed to be Lauderdale[2]. Dryden's last comedy, *Amphitryon* (produced so late as 1690), for which both Plautus and Molière were put under contribution, is, again, a mixture of prose and blank verse; none of Dryden's plays more brilliantly attest his literary gift, and none have more of the wantonness to which he afterwards pleaded guilty.

In Dryden's second acted play, *The Rival-Ladies* (acted 1664), he had already passed from comedy into tragicomedy, where his genius was more at home. Its complicated plot (two ladies disguise themselves as pages in order to take service with a gallant whose affections are set on a third) caused it to be supposed, rightly or wrongly, to have a Spanish origin; its dialogue falls into the stagey antithesis which, though it was as old as Shakespeare, *The Rehearsal* and Butler[3] were to ridicule without mercy. What, however, is most noticeable in this play is the first, though still tentative, use of

---

[1] See, however, *A Defence of the Epilogue* (*Essays*, ed. Ker, vol. I, pp. 172 ff.), where Dryden criticises Jonson, not without a certain severity; the comparison between French and English comedy in *An Essay of Dramatick Poesie, passim*; and preface to *An Evening's Love*, already cited.

[2] Scandal was very busy with Lauderdale's private as well as his public morals; but there is nothing 'convincing' in the caricature. Others thought it intended for Shaftesbury, who was attacked in similar fashion by Otway.

[3] *Repartees between Cat and Puss at a Caterwauling.*

rime as a proper feature of dramatic verse. This use is defended in a dedication to lord Orrery—the earliest of Dryden's critical excursions. It should be remembered that, since Fletcher's short preface to his *Faithfull Shepheardesse* (printed 1609 or 1610), such discussions of dramatic problems as these had fallen out of use, and that the public was now neither 'railed into approbation,' as it had formerly been by Ben Jonson, nor gently led on to acquiescence in the precepts of its critical guides. Following the example of Corneille[1], Dryden took advantage of the revived interest in the stage to address its patrons, as it were *ex cathedra,* but without any assumption of academical solemnity or rigour. To the subject of the dramatic use of the heroic couplet which he here broached, he afterwards returned at greater length, both in his *Essay of Dramatick Poesie* and in his *Essay of Heroick Plays*; but he did not claim the innovation as primarily his own, and he recalled the fact that the rimed five foot couplet, in a form approaching as near as possible to that which it owed to Waller, had been first applied to its 'noblest use' by D'Avenant in the quasi-dramatic *Siege of Rhodes* (1656, enlarged 1662). Dryden, however, was the first to employ the rimed couplet in the dialogue of an ordinary stage play, though he, too, only introduced the innovation tentatively. Etherege went a step further, and, in *The Comical Revenge, or Love in a Tub* (acted and printed 1664), put the whole serious part of the play into heroic couplets. Inasmuch, however, as, in the same year 1664, lord Orrery's *Henry V*, which is entirely in heroic couplets, was performed, Etherege and he must be left to 'divide the crown' of having introduced the innovation with Dryden and D'Avenant. If it could be proved that Orrery's 'first play,' mentioned in king Charles's letter of 22 February 1662 was *Henry V*, there would be no doubt as to Orrery's priority over Etherege[2].

It does not seem to be necessary here to enter into a re-examination of the question of the suitableness, or unsuitableness,

[1] See *post*, p. 23.

[2] See Siegert, E., *Roger Boyle, Earl of Orrery u. seine Dramen* (*Wiener Beiträge zur Engl. Philologie*), Vienna and Leipzig, 1906, p. 19. Orrery claimed to have written his tragedy *The Black Prince* 'in a new way,' by which he means the rimed couplet; but this play was not acted till 1667, or printed till 1669. *Henry V*, however, and *Mustapha*, which were likewise in rime, were first performed in 1664 and 1665 respectively. See *post*, p. 22, note. As to Etherege, for whom Gosse (*Seventeenth-Century Studies*, ed. 1883, p. 238) claims that he was the first to carry out, though Dryden was the first to propose, the experiment of writing ordinary plays in rime, see *post*, chap. v.

of the heroic couplet as a form of dramatic verse. Not only in certain kinds of romantic comedy, for which it has been claimed as a suitable vehicle, but, also, for various eccentric species which have been or may be invented—such as pantomime, burlesque or extravaganza—it may readily be allowed to be both well fitted and effective. As to its use, however, for the purposes of the regular tragic or comic drama, the case is altered. Partly, of course, the objection lies in the tendency of the couplet, as treated by Dryden and his successors, to make against continuity of flow, to shut up the sense within fixed limits and, because of the consequent demand for precision of statement, to impart to dialogue or soliloquy a didactic rather than dramatic colouring. And, further, with regard to the use of rime itself in English dramatic verse, the *caveat* of Taine cannot be put aside, that 'rime is a different thing for different races': the Englishman being transported by it into a world remote from the actual, whereas, for the Frenchman, it is nothing more than a conventional costume[1]. The heroic couplet, as used in Dryden's plays and those which followed their example, therefore, operates against, rather than in favour of, theatrical illusion and the sway of the imagination on the stage, and helps to urge the dramatist who employs it in the direction of conventionalism and artificiality. Against this general result, it is useless to argue that passion, and even mere eloquence, at times gets the better of the outward form, and, by its driving force, moves and disturbs the hearer in spite of himself.

No sooner had Dryden, in *The Rival-Ladies*, produced a tragicomedy, containing an element of rimed verse, in which he had made successful use of his gift of poetical rhetoric, than he was characteristically ready to take a leading part in evolving an ulterior dramatic species not precisely new, but with features of its own so marked as to differentiate it from tragicomedy proper. The tragicomedy bequeathed to him and the restoration dramatists in general by their predecessors was wont to possess a double plot, consisting, to use Dryden's own phraseology[2], of 'one main design,' serious in kind, executed in verse, and 'an underplot or second walk of comical characters and adventures subservient to the chief fable, yet carried along under it and helping to it'; although, in point of fact, the connection between the two was frequently very slight. At different stages of his career, he produced three more

---

[1] *Hist. de la Littérature Anglaise*, bk. III, chap. II, sec. IV.

[2] *A Discourse concerning the Original and Progress of Satire* (*Essays*, ed. Ker, vol. II, pp. 102 f.).

plays[1], of various merit, which belonged to this class. *Secret Love, or The Maiden Queen* (acted 1667), of which—probably because of the frank gaiety of Nell Gwynn's scenes in it—Charles II approved so greatly as to dub it 'his play,' is founded, as to its main plot, on *Le Grand Cyrus*, and, as to its comic underplot, partly on that romance and partly on the same novelist's *Ibrahim, ou L'illustre Bassa.* The interest in the serious plot is impaired by the quite unheroic character of Philocles (intended, as Dryden says, to represent queen Christina of Sweden's favourite Magnus de la Gardie); and the chief attraction of the play consists in the 'discoursive' passages between Celadon and Florimel. In *The Spanish Fryar, or The Double Discovery*, again (acted and printed 1681), which seems certainly to have been designed as a tragi-comedy by Dryden, the comic effect preponderates over that of the serious plot, though the latter cannot be said to be without interest. The interweaving of the two has been praised—perhaps overpraised—by more than one eminent critic[2]. The comic dialogue of this play is excellent, and the character of the friar by no means a *replica* of Fletcher's *Spanish Curate* (though there are points of resemblance in the two plays), but a new variety of an unctuous type which, from Chaucer to Dickens, has afforded unfailing delight to the public, and which it must have given Dryden, who hated priests and parsons with a consistent hatred, much satisfaction to elaborate. His last tragicomedy, *Love Triumphant, or Nature will Prevail* (acted 1694), in which there is a large admixture of rime, merely repeated in its main plot that of *Marriage-à-la-Mode*, and the play justly proved a failure.

Dryden, as already noted, had not brought out more than two plays, in the second of which he had made occasional use of the rimed five foot couplet, when he was found ready to assist his brother-in-law Sir Robert Howard in the composition of what may be described as the first heroic play[3]. The shortcomings in the

[1] *Marriage-à-la-Mode*, of which the main interest lies in the comic action, has been reckoned above among the comedies. Scott suggests that it may have been at first designed as a heroic play, but that one effect of *The Rehearsal* was to induce the author to recast the piece.

[2] Dryden himself, in *A Parallel of Poetry and Painting* (1695), refuses to defend *The Spanish Fryar* on this score, and declares its faults to be those of its genre, which is 'of an unnatural mingle' (Ker, vol. II, p. 147).

[3] Sir Robert Howard, who was also a politician and a placeman, figured both as a historical and political writer, and among the poets and playwrights of the age. His comedy *The Committee* (1662) satirised *ex post facto* the doings of the puritan party when in power. Of the tragedies for which he was solely responsible, the most

versification of part of this play, which was printed as Howard's, suggest that it was submitted by him for revision to Dryden, whose superior skill in the handling of the couplet he freely confessed. Though devoid of any kind of interest except that which this and later heroic plays sought in the remoteness and consequent strangeness of scene, *The Indian Queen* was successful; and Dryden was thus encouraged to write a 'sequel' to it under the title *The Indian Emperor, or The Conquest of Mexico by the Spaniards* (acted 1665), by which the success of the new species was established and his own reputation as a playwright definitively assured. His other plays, which, both in form of verse and in treatment of subject, fall under the same designation, were *Tyrannick Love, or The Royal Martyr* (acted in 1668 or 1669), the two parts of *Almanzor and Almahide, or The Conquest of Granada* (1669 and 1670) and *Aureng-Zebe* (1676). It will thus be seen that the number of heroic plays by Dryden was small, and written at considerable intervals. The earlier of these breaks (1665—8) was largely due to the closing of the playhouses in consequence of the plague and the great fire. The later (1670—6) interruption was, no doubt, partly caused by the appearance of *The Rehearsal* (1670). Although that celebrated burlesque cannot be said to have killed heroic plays, there can be no doubt that, notwithstanding the brilliant features which some of these plays displayed, the elements of vitality were wanting in the species. The list of plays which, as written partly or wholly in the rimed couplet, have any claim at all to be reckoned as heroic, is small in itself, and, if reduced by certain obvious omissions, contains, with the exception of Dryden's, few works of even secondary significance[1]. In a word, Dryden completely dominates the English heroic play.

interesting is *The Great Favourite, or The Duke of Lerma* (1668), of which the matter was taken from recent historians. Sir Robert Howard, who had kept himself as prominent as he could in life, was buried in Westminster abbey. He is the Crites of *An Essay of Dramatick Poesie*; Shadwell ridiculed him under the less courteous appellation Sir Positive Atall. His brothers Edward and James likewise wrote plays; the former was author of *The Usurper* (1668), a tragedy in which Oliver Cromwell was represented in the character of Damocles, and Hugh Peters appeared as Hugo de Petra; the latter perpetrated a version of *Romeo and Juliet* (1662), with a 'happy ending,' which was performed on alternate nights with the catastrophe. James Howard's comedy *All Mistaken* (printed 1672) was acted before Charles II at Trinity college, Cambridge, in October 1667.

[1] See the list in appendix D of Chase, L. N., *The English Heroic Play* (New York, 1909). Besides Otway, Crowne and Lee (for certain of their plays), only lord Orrery, Sir Robert Howard, Elkanah Settle and Banks seem to call for consideration. Of the latter two, something will be said elsewhere (see *post*, chap. VII); as to Orrery, a note may be subjoined in this place. Roger Boyle, earl of Orrery, who, as lord Broghill, played a part of some importance in Anglo-Irish relations, is, in literature,

Like *The Indian Emperor*, *Tyrannick Love* treats with much freedom a theme out of the common track—in this case, the persecution of the Christians by Maximin and the martyrdom of St Catharine. The argument of *Aureng-Zebe* deals, again quite freely, with a notability of the writer's day, though largely following the course of Racine's *Mithridate*, and borrowing the matter of one scene from *Le Grand Cyrus*. On the other hand, the most important and the most typical of Dryden's heroic plays, *The Conquest of Granada*, is essentially based on Madeleine de Scudéry's *Almahide*, while one of its episodes is taken from her *Le Grand Cyrus* and another from her *Ibrahim*. But the important point is that these subjects, as treated in the plays in question, all resemble one another in their substance, and, more or less, in its adjuncts. The plays are all of them 'heroic' plays, and the metre which they employ is called the 'heroic' couplet, because they follow and imitate the example of 'heroic' romance, as set forth by Ariosto himself[1]. Their themes, like those of heroic poetry and fiction in general, are the 'emprises' and conflicts of absorbing human passions—love, jealousy and honour—all raised to a transnormal height and expressed with a transnormal intensity[2]. Their men and women are, if the term may be thus applied, 'supermen' and 'superwomen,' and their master passions are superlove and superhonour. From these out-of-the-way premises flow a number of out-of-the-way results. The actions must be suited to the motives; their conditions must be unexpected changes and chances and tumultuous backgrounds, their complications must be insoluble except by violent means, and deaths as numerous as

most notable as the author of the romance *Parthenissa* (1654—65). As a dramatist, he is frigid and uninteresting, though his subjects were unusually varied and treated in the approved heroic style, and though he was not unskilful in the use of the couplet which he claimed (not very distinctly) to have first used on the stage. His most effective play was, perhaps, *Mustapha* (1665), taken from an episode in Georges de Scudéry's *Ibrahim* (founded on his sister's romance); his most interesting drama, *The Black Prince*, like all Orrery's plays, in heroic verse, was not acted till 1667. *The History of Henry the Fifth*, which ends with an act of heroic renunciation on the part of Owen Tudor, was the earliest produced by Orrery on the stage, and, probably, the earliest written by him. According to Pepys, when Orrery's 'heroique plays could do no more wonders,' he turned to comedy. But it was too late. (For a full account of him, see Siegert, E., *u.s.*)

[1] See the magnificently audacious passage in *An Essay of Heroick Plays* (*Essays*, ed. Ker, vol. I, p. 150): 'I opened the next book that lay by me, which was an Ariosto in Italian ; and the very first two lines of that poem, gave me light to all I could desire :

Le donne, i cavalier, l'arme, gli amori,

Le cortesie, l'audaci imprese io canto,' etc.

[2] 'When I invent a History,' says one of the characters in *Clélie*, 'I think I should make things much more perfect than they are. All Women should be admirably fair, and all Men as valiant as Hector.' (Cited by Hill, H. W., *u.s.* p. 29.)

leaves in Vallombrosa. Furthermore, the personages of these dramas must conduct themselves in a manner wholly unlike the usages obtaining in the daily round of life; it must be a manner appropriate to spheres into which the imagination alone can transplant us—ancient Rome, Jerusalem, or Troy, or, still better, because still less familiar, Mexico or the east Indies. Finally, the verse, as well as the words, must be suited to the action, and the 'heroic' couplet must serve the purpose of a sort of 'cothurnated,' which is interpreted 'stilted,' speech[1].

It was inevitable that a succession of plays of this type should soon pall upon the spectator, because of the sameness of their method (one of Dryden's most persistent assailants, Martin Clifford, accused him of 'stealing from himself'), unless each new production sought to force the pace, and to outvie its predecessors. The interest in the action, cut adrift, as it was, from probability and from the sympathy which probability begets, had to be sustained by all sorts of adventitious expedients—supernatural apparitions and magic processes, with fantastic songs, serenades and dances. But, notwithstanding the resources of Dryden's rhetorical genius, and the wonderful mental buoyancy with which he carried out any task undertaken by him, the species was doomed to self-exhaustion, nor can its master long have deceived himself on this head.

Dryden's apologetic *Essay of Heroick Plays* was preceded in date of publication by his *Essay of Dramatick Poesie* (1668), written in reply to Sir Robert Howard's preface to his *Foure New Plays* (1665). The earlier essay is in that dialogue form which had preserved its popularity in the literatures of Europe since it had been revived by Erasmus and others in the renascence period, with which Dryden's age was familiar from both Spanish and French precedents, and which was practised by many contemporary English writers, including Clarendon and Burnet. But there can be little doubt that Dryden derived the most direct impulse to the composition of the essays in dramatic and other literary criticism with which he enriched the library of English prose from the three *Discours* severally prefixed by Corneille to the three volumes of the 1660 collection of his plays, and the *Examens* which, in the same edition, preceded each drama[2].

---

[1] All this is put at length in some valuable papers entitled 'Dryden's heroisches Drama,' contributed by Holzhausen, F., to *Englische Studien*, vols. x—xvi (1889—92).

[2] See Ker, *u.s.* introduction, p. xxxvi, as to Martin Clifford's charge against Dryden of pilfering from other French critical writers.

Dryden's famous essay is written with great spirit, and with a fusion of vigour and ease altogether different from the vivacity by which literary critics appealing to a wider public at times strive to hide their thoroughness, or the want of it, as the case may be. The dialogue form is employed with Platonic grace, the *venue* being laid under the sound of the guns discharged in the battle of Solebay, and audible in the Thames 'like the noise of distant thunder or swallows in a chimney.' The conclusions reached may be described as eclectic and, at the same time, as based upon experience, albeit the latter was, necessarily, of a very limited range. As a matter of fact, Dryden's opinions on most subjects—and not the least on dramatic theory—were sufficiently fluid to respond without reluctance to the demands of common-sense ; nor did he ever take pride in a *doctrinaire* consistency—even with himself. The arguments, in this *Essay*, of Neander (who represents Dryden's own views) lead to the conclusion that observance of the timehonoured laws of dramatic composition, as reasonably modified by experience—in other words, adherence to the principle of the unities as severally interpreted by Corneille—is reconcilable with the greater freedom of treatment assumed by the masters of the English drama; while the plea for the use of the rimed couplet, based on its dramatic capabilities, especially in tragedy, comes in as a sort of corollary[1].

The immediate occasion for Dryden's *Essay* had been the confession of a doubt by Sir Robert Howard (who, as Crites, reproduces it in the dialogue) with regard to the appropriateness of the use, in which he had formerly taken part, of the rimed couplet in dramatic verse. Howard having replied to Dryden's answer in the preface to his play *The Great Favourite, or The Duke of Lerma* (1668), without losing his temper—as why should he have done, except to give grounds for the persistent misrepresentation of a literary difference as a personal quarrel ?—Dryden wound up the controversy by *A Defence of an Essay of Dramatick Poesie* (1668), prefixed to the second edition of *The Indian Emperor*, from later editions of which, however, he omitted it. This piece, which is an admirable example of light raillery, though with just a suspicion of a sting, adds little to the previous force of his argument; but the incidental remark that 'poetry only

---

[1] As Ker says, the substance of the *Essay* is aptly summed up by the triplet in Dryden's *Prologue* to *Secret Love* (1667) :

> The Unities of Action, Place and Time,
> The Scenes unbroken, and a mingled chime
> Of Jonson's manner and Corneille's rhyme.

instructs as it delights' explains the failure of many attempts made in defiance of the truth conveyed by the saying.

*The Conquest of Granada* (1669—70) may be justly described as the heroic play *par excellence*, and exhibits Dryden as exultantly carrying through a prolonged effort such as only the splendid vigour of his peculiar genius could have sustained throughout at so tremendous a pitch as is here essayed. The colouring of the whole is gorgeous, and the hero, Almanzor, combines, on Dryden's own showing, the imposing features of the Achilles of the *Iliad*, Tasso's Rinaldo and the Artaban of La Calprenède's *Cléopâtre*. Dryden had now reached the height of his popularity—it was in the year 1670 that he was appointed poet laureate[1]. With an arrogance which Almanzor himself could hardly have surpassed—though it is hidden behind the pretence that

not the poet, but the age is praised—

the *Epilogue to the Second Part* declares the dramatist superior to all his predecessors, including Jonson, in 'wit' and power of diction. The poets of the past could not reply; but, among the critics of the day who took up the challenge, Rochester, for one, retorted with a rough *tu quoque* which is not wholly without point[2]. Other protests may have ensued; at all events, Dryden did not allow the hot iron time to cool, but followed up his rodomontade (for it deserves no other name) by *A Defence of the Epilogue, or An Essay on the Dramatick Poetry of the last Age* (1672), which cannot be called one of the happiest, and is certainly one of the least broadly conceived, of his critical efforts. Finding fault with a series of passages in the chief Elizabethan and Jacobean dramatists was not the way to make good the general contention on which he had ventured. He appealed once more to his own generation against its predecessors; but he was wise enough not to appeal to posterity.

Meanwhile (in December 1671), the nemesis provoked by the arrogance of success had descended upon Dryden, though in no more august shape than in that of a burlesque dramatic concoction by a heterogeneous body of wits. *The Rehearsal*, as the mock play with its running commentary was called, had gone through a period of incubation spread over nine or ten years, and among the contributors to the joke were the duke of Buckingham, Thomas Sprat (already mentioned), Martin Clifford, master of the

---

[1] See, as to the date, Malone, *Critical and Miscellaneous Prose Works of Dryden*, vol. i, part i, p. 87.

[2] Cited in Scott-Saintsbury edition, vol. iv, p. 244.

Charterhouse, a very learned and foulmouthed writer[1], and, it is said, though without proof, Samuel Butler. They included in their ridicule anything which seemed to offer them a chance in any of Dryden's plays; but they also impartially ransacked the productions of other dramatists; indeed, it would seem that, before Dryden, D'Avenant and Sir Robert Howard, had, in turn, been thought of as the central figures of the farce, and that it was only the triumphant success of *The Conquest of Granada* which had concentrated the attack upon its author. The recent appointment of Dryden to the poet laureateship, of course, suggested the name Bayes, which the lampooners continued to apply to him for the rest of his literary career.

*The Rehearsal,* which, if the long line of its descendants, including Sheridan's *Critic,* be taken into account, proved an important contribution to the literature of the stage, is an amusing *revue* of now for the most part forgotten productions, diversified by humorous sallies of which the spirit of burlesque always keeps a store for use. Its satire against heroic plays is incidental, except in so far as they carried artificiality, exaggeration and bombast further than had any other of the species of plays ridiculed. Its satire against Dryden himself glanced off, practically harmless, from a personality in which there was nothing to provoke derision, and from a genius to which no adversary could seriously impute poverty of invention or sameness of workmanship. Thus, he was able to treat the satire, so far as it concerned him personally, with more or less goodhumoured contempt[2]; and his *revanche* on Buckingham, when it came, was free from spite. As for heroic plays, he certainly did not leave off writing them because of *The Rehearsal*; nor did it deter him from publishing a reasoned essay in defence of the species. But he could not expect to outdo his chief effort of the kind; and no other playwright was likely to seek to surpass him in a combination of treatment and form which he had made peculiarly his own.

In 1672, *The Conquest of Granada* was published in company with a prefatory essay *Of Heroick Plays*. The essay opens with the assertion—the latter half of which Dryden was afterwards himself

---

[1] 'Sprat and Mat' afterwards assisted Settle in his *Absalom Senior, or Achitophel Transpros'd*. Cf. Malone, *u.s.*

[2] He even made occasional use of the fun of the piece by way of illustration; but, when, in his *Discourse on Satire* (1693), he sought to depreciate the force of the satire, he was not very happy, or, at least, remains rather obscure (vol. ii, p. 21, Ker's edition). It is curious that, in the scene cited by Chase (*The English Heroic Play*, appendix C) from Arrowsmith's *Reformation*, a comedy (1673) satirising rimed tragedy, there should not be any apparent reference to Dryden.

to help to refute—that heroic verse was already in possession of the stage, and that 'very few tragedies, in this age' would be 'received without it.' For the rest, this essay only develops propositions previously advanced, besides fearlessly engaging in a defence of the *non plus ultra* of the heroic character-type, Almanzor, the Drawcansir of *The Rehearsal.*

It was not till three (or four) years later that Dryden took a final leave of heroic tragedy with *Aureng-Zebe, or The Great Mogul* (acted 1675, and printed in the following year). As the prologue, one of the noblest of Dryden's returns upon himself, confesses, he was growing 'weary of his long-loved mistress, Rhyme,' and, while himself abandoning dramatic for other forms of composition, inclined to 'yield the foremost honours' of the stage to the early masters on whose want of refinement he had previously insisted[1]. The play itself, while already less rigidly adhering to the self-imposed rules of the species, is visibly influenced by the example of the refinement and restraint of Racine.

Between *The Conquest of Granada* and *Aureng-Zebe,* Dryden had produced, besides two comedies already noted, a tragedy *d'occasion,* of which the plot is, indeed, as in a heroic play, based upon amorous passion, but which was thrown upon the stage to inflame popular feeling against the Dutch (with whom the country was now at war). *Amboyna, or The Cruelties of the Dutch to the English Merchants,* a production unworthy of its author, was hastily written in prose, with an admixture of blank verse. On the other hand, in the opera *The State of Innocence and Fall of Man* (printed in 1674, shortly after the death of Milton) Dryden had, no doubt, taken his time in 'tagging the verses' of *Paradise Lost*; for his dramatic version of the poem was meant as a tribute to its great qualities and not intended for performance on the stage, any more than Milton's own contemplated dramatic treatment of his theme would have been. *The Author's Apology for Heroick Poetry and Poetic Licence,* which accompanies the published 'opera,' does little more than vindicate for the treatment of sublime themes the use of a poetic diction from which convention shrinks; but it is valuable, if for nothing else, for its opening definition of true criticism, which they wholly mistake 'who think its business is principally to find fault.' The 'operatic' version of *Paradise Lost* must be pronounced a failure, not the least in

---

[1]
> —Spite of all his pride, a secret shame
> Invades his breast at Shakespeare's sacred name.

A more magnanimous literary confession was never made.

what it adds to its original[1]; its chief interest in connection with Dryden's literary progress lies in his skilful handling of certain celebrated argumentative passages.

With Dryden's *remaniement* of Milton's greatest work may be compared his handling, before and after this well meant attempt, of two Shakespearean dramas. In the case of *The Tempest, or The Enchanted Island* (acted 1667, but not printed till 1670), Dryden's own preface, dated 1 December 1669, shows that the workmanship was mainly D'Avenant's, who, as Dryden, with his habitual generous frankness, declares, 'first taught him to admire Shakespeare.' To D'Avenant was owing the grotesque notion of providing a male counterpart for Miranda, a sister for Caliban and a female companion for Ariel; and he would appear to have generally revised the work of his younger partner[2]. Quite otherwise, Dryden's *All for Love, or The World Well Lost* is not an adaptation of *Antony and Cleopatra*, but a free treatment of the same subject on his own lines. The agreeable preface which precedes the published play, written in a style flavoured by the influence of Montaigne, which was perceptibly growing on Dryden, takes the censure of his production, as it were, out of the mouths of the critics, and then turns upon the poetasters with almost cruel ridicule, which may have helped to exasperate Rochester, evidently the principal object of attack. In *All for Love*, Dryden, with as little violence as might be, was reverting from the imitation of French tragedy to Elizabethan models. The dramatist seems as fully as ever to reserve to himself the freedom which he claims as his inherent right; if he pays attention to the unities, especially to that of place, it is with more exactness 'than perhaps the English theatre requires'; and, if he has 'disencumbered himself' from rime, it is not because he condemns his 'former way.' His purpose was to follow—we may probably add, to emulate—Shakespeare, treating the subject of a Shakespearean tragedy in his own way, uninvidiously, but with perfect freedom. In the result, Dryden has little to fear from comparison in the matter of construction; and, though, in characterisation, he falls short of his exemplar, at all events so far as the two main personages are concerned, there is much in the general execution that calls for

[1] So, in act III, sc. 1, the vision suggested to Eve by the whisperings of Satan.

[2] In 1673, *The Tempest* was turned into an opera by Shadwell, who shifted the scenes, and added, besides at least one new song, an entirely new masque at the close. It is this version, and not D'Avenant and Dryden's, printed in 1670, which was printed in the 1674 and all subsequent editions of the restoration *Tempest*. This rectification of a longstanding blunder is due to the researches, conducted independently in each case, of W. J. Lawrence and Sir Ernest Clarke: see bibliography, *post*, p. 398.

the highest praise. He was conscious of his achievement, and declared that he 'never writ anything for himself but *Antony and Cleopatra*[1].'

Once again, in *Troilus and Cressida, or Truth Found too Late* (printed 1679), Dryden concerned himself with a Shakespearean play, this time, however, adapting his original plot with scant piety—in his own words, 'new-modelling the plot, throwing out many unnecessary Persons; improving[2] those characters which were begun and left unfinished, as Hector, Troilus, Pindarus and Thersites, and adding that of Andromache.' It cannot be gainsaid that Shakespeare, for whatever reason, failed to carry through the action of his *Troilus and Cressida* with vigour and completeness; but what he left was marred rather than mended in Dryden's adaptation, the catastrophe being altered and the central idea of the play, the fickleness of the heroine, botched in the process—and all to what end[3]?

With this attempt, which must be classed among Dryden's dramatic failures, was printed the remarkable *Preface concerning the Grounds of Criticism in Tragedy*, which, although not actually the last of Dryden's contributions to dramatic criticism, may be said to complete their cycle. Here, at last, we find a plain and reasonable application of the fundamental Aristotelian theory of tragedy to the practice of the English drama. Shakespeare and Fletcher—the former in particular—are set down as deficient in 'the mechanic beauties' of the plot; but, in the 'manners' of their plays, in which the characters delineated in them are comprehended, the two great masters of the English drama are extolled at the expense of their French rivals. Although exception must be taken to the distinction between Shakespeare and Fletcher as excelling respectively in the depiction of the more manly and the softer passions, 'to conclude all,' we are told, 'Fletcher was a limb of Shakespeare'—in other words, the less is included in the greater. Thus, though neither of much length nor very clearly arranged, this essay signally attests the soundness of Dryden's critical judgment, with his insight into the fact that the most satisfactory dramatic theory is that which is abstracted from the best dramatic practice. It was not given to him to

---

[1] See *A Parallel of Poetry and Painting* (*Essays*, ed. Ker, vol. II, p. 152).

[2] *I.e.* working them up for stage purposes. Betterton played Troilus, and spoke the prologue in the character of the ghost of Shakespeare (*Thomas Betterton*, by Lowe, R., p. 123).

[3] Cf. Delius, N., 'Dryden und Shakespeare,' in *Jahrbuch d. deutschen Shakespeare-Gesellschaft*, vol. IV (1869).

exemplify by his own dramatic works the supreme freedom claimed by the greatest masters of the art; but he was not to end his theatrical career without having come nearer than he had as yet approached to his own ideals.

From this point of view, two tragedies may be passed by in which the unbalanced, but not wholly uninspired, powers of Lee cooperated with the skill and experience of Dryden[1]. *Oedipus* (acted 1678), though provided with an underplot, threw down a futile challenge to both Sophocles and Corneille. In *The Duke of Guise* (acted in December 1682), Dryden's share seems to have been mainly confined to the furbishing up of what he had written many years before[2]. Whatever he might say in the elaborate *Vindication of the Duke of Guise* (printed in 1683), the political intention of the play, as a picture of the now discomfited intrigues of Shaftesbury in favour of Monmouth, was palpable, and not disproved by the fact that the authority of Davila had been more or less closely followed, or by the other fact that the parallel might, in some respects, have been pressed further than would have been pleasing to king Charles[3].

In *Albion and Albanius*, Dryden committed himself to a still lower descent—hardly to be excused by the 'thought-depressing' quality of opera mentioned by Dryden (who, on this head, agreed with Saint-Évremond) in the interesting preface which gives a short account of the early history of musical drama. After many delays, the chief of them being due to the death of Charles II, in compliment to whom the opera had been first put together, it was at last performed on 3 June 1685. Ten days later, the news arrived of Monmouth's landing at Lyme, and the unlucky piece, with its jingling rimes, music by L. Grabut and all, was finally withdrawn. Saintsbury describes it as, to all intents and purposes, a masque; but it lacks all the beauties of which that kind of composition is capable, and which are not made up for by the grotesquely ridiculous supernatural machinery to which here, as in *The Duke of Guise*, the author condescended to have recourse. Dryden was not, however, deterred from carrying out his intention of writing the 'dramatic opera' of *King Arthur or The British Worthy*, to which *Albion and Albanius* had been designed as a prelude. It was produced in 1691, with music by Purcell; but, notwithstanding the claim put forth in the preface, little or no proof is

---

[1] As to Lee, see *post*, chap. VII.    [2] See *ante*, p. 16.
[3] The not very skilful passage in honour of the king's 'brother of Navarre' (act V, sc. 1) must have been foisted in as a tribute to the duke of York.

furnished of Dryden's familiarity with Arthurian romance ; and, in spite of the magic, there is not much fire in the piece, while the figure of the blind Emmeline is an unpleasing experiment. Perhaps, as the tag suggests, the poet was, for once, almost losing heart.

After the close of king James II's reign, however, two plays were produced by Dryden, which may be regarded as a worthy consummation of his dramatic development. Yet *Don Sebastian* (acted 1690) is incorrectly regarded as marking his emancipation from the traditions either of tragicomedy or of the heroic play, though it is blank verse which, in this piece, alternates with prose. On the contrary, the serious action of *Don Sebastian* is a romantic fiction—an attempt to account by a love-story, ending with a most astonishing recognition, both for the well known disappearance of Don Sebastian in the battle of Alcazar and for the rumour that he lived for some time afterwards as an anchorite. The comic action of the mufti is repulsive, though noticeable as illustrating Dryden's *animus* against all kinds of clergy[1]. The only real attempt at drawing character is to be found in the figure of Dorax, particularly in a scene which has met with universal praise[2].

Although the tragedy *Cleomenes*[3], *the Spartan Hero* (acted 1692) is not usually deemed equal to its predecessor, it is finely conceived, and, on the whole, finely carried through on the lines of French classical tragedy, without any comic or other adventitious admixture. The character of the hero (performed by Betterton), though probably modelled on Hengo in Fletcher's *Bonduca*, is drawn with vivacity, and, in the earlier part of the rather long drawn out catastrophe, with pathos. Plutarch's abundant material is supplemented from other sources ; and, though, viewing Dryden's dramatic work as a whole, it is impossible to regret that he should not earlier have engaged in a wholehearted imitation of French tragedy, his one complete attempt in that direction must be pronounced a noble play. With it, our survey of his career as a dramatist may fitly end ; for it is unnecessary to do more than refer to the *Secular Masque* written by him, together with a prologue and epilogue, to grace the revival, for his own benefit, of Fletcher's *Pilgrim*, which actually took place in June 1700, little more than a fortnight after the beneficiary's death. The

---

[1] 'Priests of all religions are the same,' *Absalom and Achitophel*, part I, v. 99.
[2] Act IV, sc. 3.
[3] Dryden, with Corneille and Racine in his ear, accentuates *Cleoménes*.

tone of gentle pessimism audible in the masque recurs in the
epilogue, where, without the acrimony with which he had assailed
'Quack Maurus' (Sir Richard Blackmore) in the prologue, he
defends himself against the censures preferred against the contemporary drama in Jeremy Collier's *Short View of the Immorality
and Profanity of the English Stage* (1698).  Dryden's defence—
truthful so far as it goes (which is not very far)—is the evil
influence of ways of thought and life brought over by a 'banished
court'; a far nobler attitude than this of uneasy apology had been
the open avowal of shame made by him many years earlier in the
ode *To the Pious Memory of Mrs Anne Killigrew* (1686)[1].

Dryden's association with the stage was not a source of pride
to himself, and can be regarded only with qualified satisfaction by
the admirers of his poetic genius.  That he attained to a very
notable degree of success in almost every branch of dramatic
literature which he essayed cannot be held surprising ; but it
was only in the heroic play, in which he strained every nerve to
'surpass the life,' that he distanced all his rivals and followers.
Although, at times, carried away by the impetus of his own genius,
Dryden could not often put his heart into his dramatic composition, least of all into the comic side of it.  He wearied of play-
writing from the outset—frequently passing from one kind of play
to another, and back again, but rarely satisfied with any phase of
his endeavours.  When, after a long interval of absence he returned
to the arena in whose contests he had taken a prominent part,
about whose theory and practice he had speculated widely and
written at length, but which, at times, like Ben Jonson he was
led to call the 'loathèd stage,' it was with a sense of fatigued
unwillingness which even the most overworked and *blasé* of
modern playwrights, 'still condemned to dig in those exhausted
mines,' would be slow to avow[2].

This, of course, is not to say that Dryden failed to enrich
English dramatic literature by much magnificent writing—more
especially in his heroic plays—or to deny that at least one comedy

---

[1] Dryden's best balanced utterance on the subject is, perhaps, that in the preface
to the *Fables* (*Essays*, ed. Ker, vol. ii, pp. 272—3) ; but neither does this ring true.
As to Collier's attack (and as to previous invective against the stage) see Ward, A. W.,
*History of English Dramatic Literature*, etc., vol. iii, pp. 509 ff., and cf., for an account
of the controversy, 'The Life of Jeremy Collier' in vol. i of the 1845 edition of
his *Ecclesiastical History*, pp. xv ff.  Of Collier, something will be said in vol. ix of
the present work.

[2] See the account of the reasons which had made him utterly weary of the theatre,
in the preface to *Don Sebastian* (*Works*, ed. Saintsbury, vol. vii, p. 307), where he
applies to himself the phrase cited above.

(as we may call *The Spanish Fryar*) and one tragedy (*All for Love*) from his hand permanently hold their own among dramatic masterpieces of their respective kinds. It is of greater importance that, in Taine's words, Dryden's work as a dramatist 'purified and clarified his own style' by teaching him closeness of dialectics and precision in the use of words; that, in it and by it, under the guidance of Corneille, he learnt the art of political oratory and debate, and, at the same time, attained to that mastery of the heroic couplet of which he was to make superb use in his satirical poems. Dryden, who, in these poems, was to show an unsurpassed power of drawing character, rightly recognised in its presentation the supreme function of the dramatist; but, the secret of exhibiting the development of character by action he was not able, unless exceptionally, to compass, and it was thus that he came to fall short of the highest dramatic excellence.

Reserving, for the moment, a reference to the lyrics in Dryden's dramas, we must not take leave of these without a word as to his prologues and epilogues. There was no species of composition in which he more conspicuously excelled, or in which those who came after him more decidedly failed to reach his eminence; but many circumstances help to account for the signal success with which, in the present instance, he exerted his innate power of 'improving' every literary opportunity that came in his way. The age which preceded Dryden's was, above everything, a pamphleteering age; and his own generation had retained at least a full freedom of unlicensed allusion—whether political or other. When we further remember that the mode of the day was a frankness of tongue in which dukes and duchesses did their utmost to imitate linkmen and orangewomen, it is not difficult to understand why the prologue and epilogue, instead of adhering to their humbler task of commending to attention and favour a particular play, became accepted vehicles of political praise and blame, intermixed with current social satire of all sorts. In the relatively small area of restoration London, of which the court was the acknowledged centre, these sallies were always transparent and always welcome. The licence which the prologues, and, still more, the epilogues, allowed themselves was, consequently, wide, and was duly reprehended by censors of the stage like Jeremy Collier. Their delivery was generally entrusted to stage favourites, who were assured of a hearing and 'might say what they liked.' Very frequently, as in the case of many of Dryden's, these addresses were composed by leading authors for less known writers, or, again, by personages who wished to remain free from direct responsibility. Their importance may, perhaps, have been exaggerated; but, printed as broadsides, they must often have added to the attractions of a performance, and have been carried home as an enduring remembrance. Thus, the composition of them was assiduously cultivated, and remunerated by a handsome fee[1].

The examples of this kind of composition remaining from Dryden's hand amount to nearly one hundred. They attest his inventive powers in the way of conception and arrangement—including the variety of 'prologues made to be dialogues,' burlesqued in *The Rehearsal* in the 'prodialogue' between Thunder and Lightning[2]; they also attest his power, both of more playful sarcasm (as in his multiform jests against the critics) and of condensed invective or admonition. Among them may be included three prologues spoken on definite political occasions, unconnected with the production of particular stage-plays; one of these, the *Prologue to the Duchess* [of York] *on her return from Scotland* (1682) is a charming example of reckless flattery.

We now resume our general summary of Dryden's life and literary work from the time of the beginning of his labours as a dramatist, which it seemed most convenient to survey continuously. His simultaneous appointments in 1668 as poet laureate (in succession to D'Avenant) and as historiographer royal (for which latter post his qualifications, doubtless, were found in *Annus Mirabilis*) imposed no duties 'hereafter to be done,' nor were any performed by him in either of his official capacities; for his translation of Maimbourg's *History of the League* (1684), at the request of Charles II, can hardly be regarded as a service to English historiography. Thus, he went on writing for and about the stage, adding to his modest income by dedications, prologues, introductory essays and prefaces. But, though criticism often meant controversy, and a constantly growing reputation drew the eyes of Londoners and strangers on the famous man of letters, as he sat in his accustomed seat in Will's coffee-house, at the corner of Russell street and Bow street, Covent Garden, everything seems to show

---

[1] The usual fee was five guineas, till Dryden charged Southerne ten for a prologue and epilogue to *The Loyal Brother, or The Loyal Prince* (see Scott-Saintsbury's edition, vol. I, p. 245). Both are very hard on the ' Whiggs,' and Dryden scarcely ever wrote anything coarser.

[2] Cited in *A Study of the Prologue and Epilogue in English Literature from Shakespeare to Dryden*, by G. S. B. (1884), to which the reader may be referred for a careful treatment of an interesting subject.

that, by disposition, and in his ways of life, he was a quiet and retiring man, plain in his habiliments, and averse from the broils which disgraced the republic of letters.  Those in which, in his earlier days, he was implicated do not seem to have been of his own seeking; but the existing methods of literary, and, more especially, theatrical, competition, and the consequent necessity of securing the patronage of leaders of society and fashion, made it all but impossible to be in 'the town' and not of it.  Noblemen of Rochester's stamp, and others of a more sober sort, took pride in displaying their more or less arbitrary patronage of men of letters. This condition of things may almost be said to have culminated in the 'Rose-alley ambuscade,' one of the most shameless episodes in English literary history.  On the suspicion of his having assisted John Sheffield, earl of Mulgrave (afterwards duke of Buckingham-shire) in a passage in his *Essay on Satire* reflecting on Rochester's 'want of wit,' Dryden was brutally assaulted by hirelings of that patron of letters, who had recently transferred his favours, such as they were, to other writers (1679)[1].

It would not serve any purpose to dwell upon the general mori-geration of Dryden, who, in this as in other respects, was 'hurried down' the times in which he lived, to the leaders of politics and fashion, to the king's ministers, favourites and mistresses, or upon the flatteries which, in dedications and elsewhere, he heaped upon the king himself, and upon his brother the duke.  The attempts, however, which have been made to show that his pen was 'venal' —in any sense beyond that of his having been paid for his compli-ments, or, at least, for a good many of them—may be said to have broken down; and the fact that he may have received payment from the king for writing *The Medal* does not prove that he was inspired by the expectation of personal profit when he first attacked the future medallist in *Absalom and Achitophel*.

In undertaking the composition of this great satire, whether or not at the request of Charles II, Dryden had found his great literary opportunity; and, of this, he took advantage in a spirit far removed from that of either the hired bravos or the spiteful lampooners of his age.  For this opportunity he had been uncon-sciously preparing himself as a dramatist; and it was in the nature of things, and in accordance with the responsiveness of his

---

[1] There is small comfort in a parallel; but, in noting the light thrown by this incident upon the relations between society and letters in Dryden's age, it may be added that the date of a not dissimilar brutal insult to Voltaire by a member of the house of Rohan was 1725.

genius to the calls made upon it by time and circumstance, that, in the season of a great political crisis, he should have rapidly perceived his chance of decisively influencing public opinion by an exposure of the aims and methods of the party of revolution. This he proposed to accomplish, not by a poetic summary of the rights of the case, or by a sermon in verse on the sins of factiousness, corruption and treason, but by holding up to the times and their troubles, with no magisterial air or dictatorial gesture, a mirror in which, under a happily contrived disguise, the true friends and the real foes of their king and country should be recognised. This was the 'Varronian' form of satire afterwards commended by him, with a well warranted self-consciousness, as the species, mixing serious intent with pleasant manner, to which, among the ancients, several of Lucian's *Dialogues* and, among the moderns, the *Encomium Moriae* of Erasmus belong. 'Of the same kind is "Mother Hubberd's Tale" in Spenser, and (if it be not too vain to mention anything of my own) the poems of "Absalom" and "MacFlecknoe[1]."'

The political question at issue, in the troubled times of which the names 'whig' and 'tory' still survive as speaking mementoes, was that of the succession of the Catholic heir to the throne, or of his exclusion in favour of some other claimant—perhaps the king's son Monmouth, whom many believed legitimate (the Absalom of the poem). For many months, Shaftesbury, who, after serving and abandoning a succession of governments, had passed into opposition, had seemed to direct the storm. Two parliaments had been called in turn, and twice the Exclusion bill had been rejected by the lords. Then, as the whig leader seemed to have thrown all hesitation to the winds, and was either driving his party or being driven by it into extremities from which there was no return, a tremor of reaction ran through the land, the party round the king gathered confidence, and, evidence supposed sufficient to support the charge having been swept in, Shaftesbury was committed to the Tower on a charge of high treason. It was at this time of tension, while a similar charge was being actually pressed to the gallows against a humbler agent of faction (the 'Protestant joiner' Stephen College), that Dryden's great effort to work upon public opinion was made. Part I of *Absalom and Achitophel*, which seems to have been taken in hand quite early in 1681, was published on 17 November in that year. Shaftesbury, it is known, was then fearing for his life.. A week later, in spite of all efforts to the contrary, the bill

---

[1] *A Discourse concerning the Original and Progress of Satire* (*Essays*, ed. Ker, vol. II, p. 67).

was ignored by the Middlesex grand jury. Great popular rejoicing followed, and a medal was struck in Shaftesbury's honour, representing the sun emerging from the clouds, with the legend *Laetamur*. But, this momentary triumph notwithstanding, the game was all but up; and, within a few months, Monmouth, in his turn, was under arrest, and Shaftesbury a fugitive in Holland.

Without a mention of this well known sequence of events, the fact might, perhaps, be overlooked that part I of *Absalom and Achitophel*[1] is complete in itself, being intended to help in producing a direct result at a given moment, and that it is in no sense to be regarded as a mere instalment of a larger whole, or as an introduction to it. Part II was a mere afterthought, and, being only to a relatively small extent by Dryden, should, in the first instance, be left out of consideration.

*Absalom and Achitophel* veils its political satire under the transparent disguise of one of the most familiar episodes of Old Testament history, which the existing crisis in English affairs resembled sufficiently to make the allegory apposite and its interpretation easy. The attention of the English public, and, more especially, that of the citizens of London, with whom the decision of the immediate political issue lay, was sure to be arrested by a series of characters whose names and distinctive features were borrowed from the Old Testament; and the analogy between Charles II's and David's early exile and final triumphant establishment on the throne was a commonplace of restoration poetry. Indeed, the actual notion of an adaptation of the story of Achitophel's wiles as 'the Picture of a wicked Politician' was not new to English controversial literature; in 1680, a tract entitled *Absalom's Conspiracy* had dealt with the supposed intentions of Monmouth; and a satire published in 1681, only a few months before Dryden's poem, had applied the name Achitophel, with some other opprobrious names, to Shaftesbury. For the rest, Dryden, with the *grandezza* habitual to him, was careless about fitting the secondary figures of his satire exactly with their Scriptural *aliases*, or boring the reader by a scrupulous fidelity or even consistency[2] of detail.

*Absalom and Achitophel* remains the greatest political satire in our literature, partly because it is frankly political, and not intended, like *Hudibras*, by means of a mass of accumulated detail, to convey a general impression of the vices and follies, defects and extravagances, of a particular section or particular sections of the nation. With Dryden, every hit is calculated, and every stroke

---

[1] It was not, of course, when first published, called 'part I' at all.

[2] *E.g.* in the allegorical use of the names Hebron and Jordan.

goes home; in each character brought on the scene, those features only are selected for exposure or praise which are of direct significance for the purpose in hand. It is not a satirical narrative complete in itself which is attempted; the real *dénouement* of the piece falls not within, but outside, its compass; in other words, the poem was to lead up, as to an unavoidable *sequitur*, to the trial and conviction of its hero. The satirist, after the fashion of a great parliamentary orator, has his subject and his treatment of it well in hand; through all the force of the invective and the fervour of the praise, there runs a consciousness of the possibility that the political situation may change. This causes a constant self-control and wariness in the author, who is always alive to his inspiration and never unmindful of his cue. Instead of pouring forth a stream of Aristophanic vituperation or boyish fun in the vein of Canning, he so nicely adapts the relations of the more important of his characters to the immediate issue that the treatment, both of the tempter Achitophel and of the tempted Absalom, admitted of manipulation when, before the appearance of the poem in a second edition[1], the condition of affairs had changed.

Chapter and verse could, without difficulty, be found for every item in Johnson's well known panegyric of *Absalom and Achitophel* in his *Life of Dryden*. The incomparable brilliancy of its diction and versification are merits which, to be acknowledged, need only to be mentioned. Still, its supreme excellence lies in its descriptions of character, which, no doubt, owed something to his dramatic practice, and more to the development which this kind of writing had experienced during a whole generation of English prose literature, reaching its full height in Clarendon. Dryden's exquisite etchings cannot be compared with the finest of the full-length portraits from the hand of the great historical writer; but, thanks, no doubt, in part, to the Damascene brightness and keenness into which the poet had tempered his literary instrument, and thanks, also, to the imaginative insight which, in him, the literary follower of the Stewarts, was substituted for the unequalled experience of their chosen adviser, Clarendon, the characters of the poem live in the memory with unequalled tenacity. How unmistakably is the preeminence of Achitophel among the opponents of the royal government signalised by his being commissioned, like his prototype[2] when charged with the temptation and corruption of mankind, to

---

[1] The story according to which the tribute to Shaftesbury's merits as a judge was inserted because he had presented one of Dryden's sons to the Charterhouse was a fabrication as baseless as it was stupid. See Malone, *u.s.* pp. 148—9.

[2] We remember who, according to Johnson, was 'the first Whig.'

master the shaken virtue of Absalom! Yet, when the satire proceeds
from the leader to the followers, what composite body of malcontents
was ever analysed, even by a minister driven to bay, with surer
discernment and more perfect insight? The honest whigs, the utili-
tarian radicals, the speculators who use party for their private ends,
the demagogues and mob-orators who are the natural product of
faction—all are there; but so, too, are the republicans on principle,
headed by survivors of the fanatics who believed in their own
theocracy. Of course, the numerical strength of the party is made
up by the unthinking crowd that takes up a cry—in this case, the
cry 'No Popery.' Of the chiefs of the faction, for the most part, a
few incisive lines, or even a damning epithet, suffice to dispose;
but there are exceptions, suggested by public or by private considerations. In the latter class, Dryden's own statement obliges
us to include Zimri (Buckingham)—a character which he declares
to be 'worth the whole poem[1].' What he says of his intentions in
devising this masterpiece of wit, and of his success in carrying
them into execution, illustrates at once the discretion with which
he applied his satirical powers, and the limitation which his nature,
as well as his judgment, imposed upon their use. Moral indignation
was not part of Dryden's satirical stock[2]. Even the hideously true
likeness of Titus Oates (Corah) preserves the accent of sarcasm
which had suited the malicious sketch of Shimei, the inhospitable
sheriff of the city; it is as if the poet's blame could never come with
so full a tone as the praise which, in the latter part of the poem,
is gracefully distributed among the chief supporters of the crown.
The poem ends with a speech from king David, only in part reproducing the speech of Charles II to the Oxford parliament (March
1681), of which the king is said to have suggested the insertion.

Though, as has been seen, the Middlesex grand jury was proof
against Dryden's satire, which provoked a number of replies not
calling for notice here, the reaction with which he had identified
himself was not long in setting in—so much so that, in March 1682,
the duke of York was not afraid to show himself in England.
It was about this time that Dryden, it is said at the king's
suggestion, published *The Medal, or A Satire against Sedition.*
Into this poem, which, likewise, called forth a variety of replies
attesting its effectiveness, the didactic element enters more largely

---

[1] See *A Discourse concerning the Original and Progress of Satire* (*u.s.* p. 93).

[2] Buckingham may not have wholly disliked the lines, though he retorted on them
clumsily (if Wood is right in ascribing to him *Poetical Reflections*, etc., *by a Person
of Quality*, 1681). Pope's verses on Buckingham can hardly be said to have bettered
Dryden's; for the added pathos is really hollow.

than it had done in the case of its more famous predecessor; but
the principal point of attack is again selected with great judgment.
Shaftesbury's hypocrisy is the quality for which the hero of the
puritan citizens is more especially censured; while his worshippers
are derided, not because they are few, but because they are many.
The inimitable apostrophe to the *mobile*, metrically, as well as
in other respects, is one of the most magnificent mockeries to be
found in verse:

> Almighty crowd! thou shortenest all dispute;
> Power is thy essence, wit thy attribute!
> Nor faith nor reason make thee at a stay,
> Thou leap'st o'er all eternal truths in thy Pindaric way!

Among the whig writers who came forward to reply to *The
Medal* was Thomas Shadwell, whose contributions to the dramatic
literature of the age are noticed elsewhere[1]. Dryden and the
'True Blue Poet' had been on friendly terms, and the former had
written a prologue for Shadwell's comedy *A True Widow* so
recently as 1679. But, in *The Medal of John Bayes*, the source,
as has been seen, of not a few longlived scurrilities against
Dryden, and (if this was by the same hand) in *The Tory Poets*,
Shadwell contrived to offend his political adversary beyond
bearing. Johnson and others have, however, blundered in supposing the whig writer's appointment to the poet laureateship,
which was not made till 1689, to be alluded to in *Mac Flecknoe;
or, A Satire on the True Blue Protestant Poet, T.S.*, which was
published in October 1682. Unlike *Absalom and Achitophel* and
its offshoot *The Medal*, *Mac Flecknoe* is a purely personal satire
in motive and design. Richard Flecknoe was an Irishman, formerly
in catholic orders, who (if a note to *The Dunciad* is to be trusted)
had 'laid aside the mechanic part of priesthood' to devote himself
to literature. It is difficult to understand why (except for the fact
that he had been a priest) Dryden should have determined to
make this harmless, and occasionally agreeable, writer of verse
a type of literary imbecility[2]. Flecknoe must be supposed to
have died not long before Dryden wrote his satire, in which the

---

[1] See *post*, chap. VI.

[2] See, also, *A Discourse concerning the Original and Progress of Satire* (*u.s.* p. 27)
where the collocation 'from Spenser to Flecknoe' appears as an equivalent to 'from the
top to the bottom of all poetry.' Some curious early lines by Marvell entitled *Fleckno,
an English Priest at Rome*, describe him as reciting his verses in a lodging, 'three
stair-cases high' (Grosart's Fuller Worthies edition of *The Complete Works of Andrew
Marvell*, vol. I, pp. 229 ff.). They first appeared in 1681, and may, possibly, have
suggested Dryden's choice. Though he reprinted the poem with corrections in 1684,
he does not appear to have acknowledged it as his before 1692.

'aged prince' is represented as abdicating his rule over 'the
realms of Nonsense' in favour of Shadwell. This humorous fancy
forms the slight action of the piece, which terminates with a mock
catastrophe suggested by one of Shadwell's own comedies. Thus,
with his usual insight, Dryden does not make any attempt to lengthen
out what is in itself one of the most successful examples of the species
—the mock heroic—which it introduced into English literature.
Pope, as is well known, derived the idea of his *Dunciad* from *Mac
Flecknoe*; but, while the later poem assumed the proportions of an
elaborate satire against a whole tribe of dunces as well as against
one egregious dunce, Dryden's is a *jeu d'esprit*, though one brilliant
enough to constitute an unanswerable retort upon unwarrantable
provocation. Slight as it is, *Mac Flecknoe* holds a place of its
own among Dryden's masterpieces in English satirical poetry.

This cycle of Dryden's writings is completed by his share in the
*Second Part* of *Absalom and Achitophel*, published in November
1682, a few weeks after *Mac Flecknoe*, and in the same month as
*Religio Laici*. Dryden could therefore hardly have had time for extensive collaboration with Nahum Tate, a painstaking and talented
writer who, with enduring success, adapted *King Lear* and took part
in a version of the *Psalms* with Nicholas Brady[1], and who, in his
turn, was poet laureate (from 1692 to 1715). Tate, who had the
gift of being able to accommodate himself to diverse styles, not un-
skilfully copied Dryden's—here and there taking over lines bodily
from part I; but it is clear that, apart from the characters of Doeg
and Og (Settle and Shadwell) and the powerful lines preceding
them, which include the denunciation of Judas (Robert Ferguson
'the Plotter'), the masterhand added not a few touches, from the
opening couplet onwards. Elkanah Settle, whose reputation was
greater in his own day than it has been with posterity, had invited
the lash by a long reply to *Absalom and Achitophel* entitled *Absalom Senior, or Achitophel Transpros'd*, in which others are said
to have assisted him[2]. The characters of the two lampooners remain
the *non plus ultra* of haughty satirical contempt. Instead of
the wary assailant of political and social leaders like Achitophel
and Zimri, we are now confronted by the writer of genius spurning,

[1] The scornful reference in part II, v. 403 to Sternhold and Hopkins's version is by
Dryden.
[2] Cf. *ante*, p. 26. It is in this that occurs the curious charge, which, however,
Dryden declared false, that, at one time, he
   would have been his own loath'd thing, call'd priest.
A second reply attributed to Settle seems not to have been his. See Malone, *u.s.*

with ruthless scorn, the brotherhood in letters of a Doeg or an Og; what is best and strongest in the satirist seems now up in arms.

*Religio Laici*, which, for reasons easily guessed, was not reprinted by Dryden in his lifetime after the third edition (1683), is classed (by Scott) among his political and historical poems; but its primary interest is personal, as must have been his primary motive in composing it. He wished to know where, in the matter of religion, he stood. Now, for Dryden, there was but one way of realising any position which he held or any line of conduct on which he had determined. This was to place it before himself with the aid of his pen, at whose bidding, if the expression may be allowed, his thoughts at once fell into lucid order, ready for argumentative battle. Though Johnson's wish may, in some degree, be father to the thought, when he declares *Religio Laici* to be almost the only poem by Dryden which may be regarded as a voluntary effusion, Saintsbury has rightly insisted on the spontaneous character of the poem. This spontaneity is, indeed, all but essential to the conception of the work; nor was there any possible motive or reason for simulating it.

The title, of course, was anything but original. Lord Herbert of Cherbury's treatise *De Religione Laici* had been published in 1633, Sir Thomas Browne's *Religio Medici* ten years later. With Dryden, though not with Browne, the emphasis rests on the second noun of the title. Amidst the disputations and controversies of learned theologians, a plain word seems not uncalled for from one who can contribute nothing but commonsense and goodwill, unalloyed by self-opinionatedness. Thus, the layman's religion is expounded with the requisite brevity, and with notable directness and force, lighted up by a few of the satirical flashes which had become second nature to the writer, but not by any outburst of uncontrollable fervour. He takes his stand on revelation, but is careful to summarise the natural proofs of the truth of Christianity. The old objection to supernatural religion, that it has not been revealed to all men, he is content to answer by a pious hope, expressed in words both forcible and beautiful. He puts aside the difficulty of the damnatory clauses of the Athanasian creed by conjecturing a very human explanation of their origin, and, after citing a liberal French priest[1] in support of the contention that the authority of the Bible is weakened by mistakes of transcribers

---

[1] Father (Richard) Simon (author of *Histoire critique du Vieux Testament* (1678) and other works), for the benefit of whose young English translator, Henry Dickinson, the poem had originally been composed.

and commentators, approaches the crucial question: what authority, then, is to decide? An infallible authority it must be, and the only church which makes such a claim fails to satisfy the tests of infallibility or omniscience. Better, therefore, accept authority where it is ancient, universal and unsuspected, and leave aside matters which cannot be thus settled—

> For points obscure are of small use to learn,
> But common quiet is the world's concern.

*Religio Laici*, it is needless to demonstrate at length, represents merely a halfway house on the road which Dryden was following. Reverence for authority was an instinct implanted in his nature; his observation of the conflicts of public life had disgusted him with the contrary principle of resistance, and, at the same time, had impressed upon him the necessity of waiving minor difficulties for the sake of the things that really mattered. If the layman's simple creed should fail, in the long run, to satisfy the layman himself, it could easily be relinquished; for, as the designedly pedestrian conclusion of the poem avers, it was meant merely for what it was—a plain personal utterance.

And, thus, the reader of Dryden's writings in their sequence is not startled on reaching the passage in his biography which has given rise to much angry comment and anxious apology, without, in truth, calling for anything of either. In February 1685, Charles II died. Dryden's literary services had materially contributed to carry safely through some of the most dangerous stages of the conflict the cause of the legitimate succession, on which Charles had gone near to staking the stability of his throne. The poet's efforts against the party which he had again and again denounced as revolutionary had estranged from him old literary associates— some of them more pliable than himself—and had left him, more than ever, a reserved and, probably at least, a lonely man. But, whatever the king's personal interest in Dryden's literary activity, the royal bounty flowed but very intermittently, and neither the three hundred a year due to the poet laureate nor an additional pension of one hundred (granted some time before 1679) was paid with any approach to regularity. Not until 1684, after he had addressed a letter of complaint[1] to Rochester (Laurence Hyde) at the treasury, was a portion of the arrears paid, while he

---

[1] This is the letter containing the celebrated passage: ' 'Tis enough for one age to have neglected Mr Cowley, and starved Mr Butler.' In *The Hind and the Panther*, part III, vv. 247 ff., the abandonment of Butler is absurdly laid at the door of the church of England.

was appointed to a collectorship of the customs, with a minute
salary but (probably) a more substantial amount of fees. In these
circumstances, Dryden, whose play-writing had usually been a
labour of necessity, and for whom, as a political satirist, there was
no opening in the period of reaction following the *esclandre* of the
Rye House plot, had to do such taskwork as came to his hand—
prefaces, like that to a new translation of Plutarch; prose translations of his own, like that of Maimbourg's *History* already
mentioned; and verse translation, from Ovid, Vergil, Horace and
Theocritus, inserted in the first volume of *Miscellany Poems*
printed in 1684 and 1685 (the latter under the title *Sylvae*[1]). The
hope long cherished by Dryden of writing an epic poem for which
he had already been in search of subjects, receded more and more
into the background[2]; and, of the muses whom he was constrained
to serve, we may well believe that—

> little was their Hire, and light their Gain[3].

When, early in 1685, Charles II died, Dryden honoured his
memory with a Pindaric ode, *Threnodia Augustalis*, to which
the poet gave a semi-official character by describing himself as
'servant to his late Majesty and to the present King.' The ode,
which has some fine turns, without altogether escaping bathos,
treats a not very promising subject (which baffled Otway[4]) with
Dryden's usual skill in the selection of qualities warranting
praise; the inequalities of the metre, on which Scott wittily dwells,
are less violent than those to be found in the far more celebrated
*Alexander's Feast*. Dryden's other effort as poet laureate,
*Britannia Rediviva: a Poem on the Prince born on the* 10*th of
June*, 1688, is written in the couplet of which he was master; but
the occasion—for surely never was the news of a royal birth
received as was that of the prince to be known in later years as
the Old Pretender—could not be met without artificiality of tone.

Before the publication of this poem, in which are to be found

---

[1] Collective publications of this kind had gone out of fashion since the early days
of Elizabeth, and the practice was thus revived at a time when translation ran original
composition hard in the race for popularity. Altogether, four volumes of this
*Miscellany* were published in Dryden's lifetime; but they were carried on by the
publisher Tonson, by whose name they were sometimes known, till 1708. The fashion,
which contributed materially to keep alive a taste for poetry, continued into the
middle of the eighteenth century, and reached its height with Dodsley's celebrated
collection (1748).

[2] See *A Discourse of Satire* (*Essays*, ed. Ker, vol. II, p. 38).

[3] *Threnodia Augustalis*, v. 377.

[4] See his *Windsor Castle*, and *The Beginning of a Pastoral on the Death of his late
Majesty*.

many allusions to the doctrines of the church of Rome together
with a reference to the 'still impending Test,' Dryden had himself
become a Roman Catholic. As already hinted, the supposition
that this step was, or might have been expected by him to be, to
the advantage of his worldly interests is not worth discussing.
The intellectual process which led to it, and to the ultimate
completion of which *Religio Laici* points, was neither unprecedented nor unparalleled; moreover, whatever they may have
expected (which nobody can tell) neither Dryden nor his wife or
eldest son (if, as is supposed but not proved, they had become
Roman Catholics before him) gained anything by their conversion[1].
That he should have chosen a time for joining the church of Rome
when the prospects of her adherents in England seemed bright
was in keeping with his disposition; for he had, as an acute critic[2]
says, 'a sovereign intellect but a subject will.' But there is no
single known fact in his life to support the conclusion that he
changed his faith for the sake of gain. Nor can his consistent
adherence to the church which had now received him be explained
away by the insinuation that another change would not have been
of any use to him. It is sometimes forgotten that his political
was consistent with his religious loyalty, and that, under the new
*régime*, he declined to take the oaths which might have secured
to him the continuance of at least a measure of royal favour.

The effect of Dryden's conversion upon his spiritual life lies
beyond the range of literary criticism. It is, however, certain
that, to the aspiration 'good life be now my task[3],' there corresponds,
at a time very near that of his change of faith, a confession which,
in depth of feeling, and in severity of self-judgment, stands almost
alone in his published writings. The spring and force of by far
the most beautiful among his longer lyrics, the ode *To the Pious
Memory of the Accomplisht Young Lady, Mrs Anne Killigrew*
(printed in 1686, the year after that of her death), are characteristic
of Dryden's genius; but, in the spirit of the poem, especially of
the well known fourth stanza[4], we recognise that it was composed
at a time when his whole nature was moved by unwonted impulses.
A fainter recurrence of these may, perhaps, be traceable in some

[1] Even the recognition by the new king of the additional pension granted by
Charles II to Dryden preceded his conversion, whether or not he had, before that date,
been seen at mass.

[2] Skelton, John, *John Dryden. In Defence* (1865), p. 22.

[3] *The Hind and the Panther*, part I, v. 76.

[4]     O Gracious God! how far have we
    Prophan'd thy Heaven'ly Gift of Poesy, etc.

passages of his later writings; on the other hand, it cannot be averred that, in these writings, as a whole, there is any indication, as there is certainly no pretence, of a change which purifies what is intentionally impure, or refines what is intentionally gross[1].

The new king was not in a position to disdain the aid of any fresh ally; and the services of Dryden's pen were speedily claimed by the side which he had joined. But the desired version of the *Histoire de l'Hérésie* (1374 to 1569) by Antoine Varillas, never saw the light—hardly, as Burnet contended, because of his criticisms of the French historian and publicist[2]. Dryden's assistance was also engaged in defence of a paper written by Anne Hyde, duchess of York, giving reasons for her conversion to the church of Rome, which James II had published with two statements found among his deceased royal brother's papers, acknowledging the authority of that church. Stillingfleet had commented on the publication as a whole, and now replied in a *Vindication* on which, in his turn, Dryden, denounced by Stillingfleet as a 'grim logician,' commented in an *apologia* of an altogether novel description.

*The Hind and the Panther* was published in 1687, and is said to have been written at Rushton in Northamptonshire, a sylvan neighbourhood. If Dryden's conversion does not present any psychological difficulties, it also seems natural that he should have speedily proceeded to explain to the world a position not new to it, but strange and, therefore, in a sense, new, to himself. That *The Hind and the Panther* cannot be harmonised with *Religio Laici* is, of course, part of the situation, although the two poems are not inconsistent with each other as stages of a mental evolution. To suggest that the later work was written to ensure the favour of James II (from whom it does not appear what Dryden had to expect beyond punctuality), is to ignore a very plain historical consideration. In April 1687—a fortnight before the publication of the poem—James II put forth the declaration for liberty of conscience, which extended to nonconformists in general, and was, in fact, the catholic king's bid for the support of the protestant dissenters in his struggle with the establishment. On the other hand, the convert Dryden's personal confession of faith was, at the same time, an *eirenicon* to the church of England from

---

[1] See, on this head, Beljame, A., *Le Public et les Hommes de Lettres en Angleterre au 18me siècle* (Paris, 1883), p. 219.

[2] As to Varillas's work, see the chapter on Historical Writers in vol. IX (*post*) (Burnet).

the catholic side, and a summons to her to join hands with the church of Rome against the protestant nonconformists. Inasmuch as a similar royal declaration had been issued in Scotland two months earlier, and the dispensing power had received a solemn judicial affirmation in the previous year, Dryden could not have been taken by surprise by the king's recent action. He could, therefore, hardly have put forth a 'libel of policy' less likely to commend itself to the king and those who advised him in accordance with his wishes, or have given a more palpable proof either of obtuseness—a quality not characteristic of him—or of candour.

The poem is far the longest of Dryden's original productions in verse; but it is carried on with unmistakable vigour to its somewhat abrupt close, and, in its concluding, as well as in its opening, part, displays the reverse of a falling off in power of either invention or expression. Criticism has chiefly directed itself against the plan of the work, which Johnson, for instance, terms injudicious and incommodious, rather than to the conduct of the arguments, which cannot be described as inadequate or uneven[1].

*The Hind and the Panther* (as would be obvious, even were it not made additionally clear by the first lines of part III) does not pretend to be more than a fable, a product of an artificial stage of poetry, which confines its attention to human nature and introduces animals merely in a parabolical way: so animals would have spoken or acted, had they been men. All references, however interesting, to the beast-epos, an independent literary cycle, into which satirical meanings and types were not introduced till a comparatively late date, are, therefore, more or less out of place in this connection. Still less can there be any question here of the transfer of a whole world of human sentiment and character into the outward conditions of animal life—as in Edmond Rostand's *Chantecler*—not for purposes of analogy, but in order to read a poetical significance into the whole system of animated nature.

---

[1] How a theological argument may be carried on in verse without the skill and effectiveness to be found in *The Hind and the Panther*, is exemplified by *A Poem on the Real Presence and the Rule of Faith*, printed as an appendix to Henry Turbervil's *Manual of Controversies clearly Demonstrating the Truth of the Catholic Religion, with several Sentences out of the Fathers* (4th edition, 1686). The sentences are stated to be collected 'by J.D., the Author's Friend.' It does not follow that the poem is by 'J.D.'; and I cannot, in any case, think that the latter, though it is chiefly directed against Stillingfleet, shows signs of Dryden's handiwork. The composition is extremely uneven; and, while it is just possible that Dryden may have turned Turbervil's unadorned prose into verse, leaving the file to do its work later, the probability is the other way, for 'the numbers' did not come to Dryden in this halting fashion.

*The Hind and the Panther* is allegorical only in its *mise-en-scène* and distribution of characters; as a fable, its fault is that it falls short of the moderate amount of imaginary verisimilitude required by this literary species. On the face of it, therefore, Prior and Charles Montague, the authors of *The Hind and the Panther Transvers'd to the Story of the Country Mouse and the City Mouse* (1687) were justified in ridiculing in the preface to their squib the incongruity of animals indulging in theological controversy and Biblical criticism, as was Johnson in repeating the same cavil in different words[1]. But Dryden had often, in regard both to the drama and to other branches of literature, defended the cause of 'English freedom'; and, in his free use of the machinery of the fable for satirical and didactic purposes, he was following the examples of Chaucer and Spenser. Still, poetry and theological controversy are illmatched associates, and Dryden was at little pains to mitigate the harshness of the union, dropping the fabulous vestment which he had cast round his disputants so soon as he chose, in order to resume it at his convenience.

Of the two justly celebrated 'fables' proper included in part III of this poem, the earlier—that of the swallows—attests the independence of Dryden's attitude towards the court, where the censure of father Petre (the Martin), though supposed to be delivered by an adversary, cannot have been welcome. In the story of 'the Pigeon's and the Buzzard's love,' the character of Burnet (the Buzzard), ranks with the most powerful of the poet's satirical efforts. Unlike Stillingfleet, who is dealt with earlier in the same part of the poem, Burnet, though he is called 'invulnerable in his impudence,' lay broadly open to attack, and, according to his wont, had voluntarily descended into the arena with his *Reasons against Repealing the Test*[2].

*The Hind and the Panther*, for reasons which have been made apparent, could not bring the poet into favour with any party; and critics like Martin Clifford and 'Tom' Brown could fall upon him as they pleased. When, in contravention of the hopes uttered

---

[1] Much of the ridicule in this burlesque, which revived the methods of *The Rehearsal* on a much less appropriate occasion, is trivial, and some of it is so vulgarly personal, that Dryden, if the story be true, may very well have taken offence at it. The preface was said to have been by Montague.

[2] Burnet, who seems originally to have had a friendly feeling towards Dryden, revenged himself when mentioning the proposal, in 1669, of a tax on playhouses, by describing 'the great master of dramatic poesy' as 'a monster of immodesty and impurity of all sorts' (*History of his own Time*, edition 1833, vol. I, p. 495). Burnet did not cultivate precision of style; but it seems clear, even without the note in the edition of 1754, that he referred to Dryden as a play-writer only.

in *Britannia Rediviva*, the change of *régime* ensued, and William and Mary held sway in her father's stead, Dryden's places and pensions were taken from him, and Shadwell wore the laurel. It seems to have been about this time that Dryden became indebted to Dorset for substantial support; but he manifestly continued to add to his income by literary labours. That the vitality and freshness of his powers still remained undiminished is shown by the variety of his productions in these years. Not long before the end of James II's reign, he had written the playful *Letter to Sir George Etherege*, which alone among his complimentary epistles and addresses (extending over many years of his life) is in Hudibrastic metre. In 1690, as has been seen, he successfully resumed work for the stage. There does not seem to have been any indisposition on the part of the new court to show goodwill to him as a playwright; but, in commanding *The Spanish Fryar* to be performed on one of her first appearances in public, queen Mary chose more fortunately for him than for herself. Meanwhile, the connection between the publisher Jacob Tonson and Dryden was productive of much literary work, though, when there was a pecuniary pressure upon Dryden, the relations between them frequently tried his patience and, at times, roused him to wrath[1]. Besides the translations from classical poets already mentioned as included in the earliest volumes of the *Miscellany*, Dryden, with the assistance of his two elder sons, brought out, in 1693, a complete translation of Juvenal and Persius, prefaced by one of the most delightful of his essays. In its earlier portions, *A Discourse concerning the Original and Progress of Satire* may, after the manner of such *prolegomena*, have been put together so as to suit the amount of information to the appetite of the reader; but the comparison between the three Roman satirists contains some admirable criticism, and the easy and graceful style is enjoyable from beginning to end. The essay prefixed to Dryden's translation (1695) of Du Fresnoy's *Parallel of Poetry and Painting* (the French prose version printed by the author with his original Latin poem *De Arte Graphica*) is, perhaps, more obviously written to order. It contains an elaboration of the theory that the true imitation of nature consists of the pursuit of the ideal in art—a view on which Dryden had insisted in his early disquisitions on dramatic poetry[2], but which, though it might have commended itself to Goethe, has until recently been regarded as out of date.

---

[1] Witness the triplet under Jacob's portrait, perhaps the ugliest of all Dryden's 'word-pictures.'

[2] This is clearly put by Ker, introduction to *Essays*, vol. I, pp. lxviii—ix.

In the third and fourth *Miscellanies* (1693 and 1694) appeared Dryden's version of book I, and of certain other portions, of the *Metamorphoses*, with the parting of Hector and Andromache out of the *Iliad* as well as a translation of the third *Georgic*[1]. In 1694, the idea of a translation of the whole of Vergil seems to have suggested itself to Dryden; and the completed work was brought out by subscription in 1697[2]. The enterprise and its success made much talk in the world of letters, and, from still remote Hanover, Leibniz commented on the prize of £1000—Pope was told that it was £1200—which had fallen to the fortunate 'Mr Dryden's' lot. But, though Dryden, without pushing his interests unduly, was not forgetful of them, he did himself honour by steadily refusing to dedicate his *magnum opus* to the king, to whom he had declined to swear allegiance[3]. The actual dedication of the *Aeneis* to Normanby (Mulgrave) is one of Dryden's longest, but not one of his most interesting, efforts of the sort[4].

The longlived favour shown by the English reading public to translations from the classics was largely due to the fact that the intellectual education of boys belonging to the higher classes was still largely carried on by exercising them in translation from the classics into English prose or verse; Dryden himself, it will be remembered, had been trained in this way at Westminster. This practice must have encouraged freedom of rendering as well as elegance of composition in translation; and Dryden, possessed of a genius singularly open to suggestion and facile in execution, was of all translators most certain to excel in the art thus conceived. From the point of view of exact scholarship, nothing can be said in favour of a method which does not show any reverence for the text, and very little for the style, of the original author. But Dryden's contemporaries were perfectly willing that the glorious rush of his poetic style should dominate the Vergil of the *Georgics* and the Vergil of the *Aeneid* alike, as it had the Roman satirists before them; and the breadth and boldness of some of the finest Vergilian passages lent themselves readily to reproduction by the

---

[1] In the *Miscellany* of 1694 also appeared the epistle *To Sir Godfrey Kneller*, a painter to whom Dryden must have been attracted by his success in seizing the distinctive features of a quite extraordinary number of sitters. The reference to the 'Chandos' portrait of Shakespeare, of which Kneller had sent Dryden a copy, is commonplace in thought.

[2] See Appendix to second impression.

[3] He had been pressed to dedicate the work to the king by his publisher, who caused the engraved representation of *pius Aeneas* to be provided for the purpose with a hooked nose, still visible in certain of the extant copies.

[4] It contains, however, some valuable observations on metrical form; and it is in this essay that Dryden speaks of having 'long had by me the materials of an English *Prosodia*' (*Essays*, ed. Ker, vol. II, p. 217).

English poet, although others remained, whose majesty and depth of sentiment he could not infuse into his couplets[1].

The freedom which Dryden had assumed as a translator of the Roman poets he carried a step further in the reproductions of Chaucer and of Chaucer's frequent source, Boccaccio, which were not published till two months (or rather less) before his death. They were accompanied by versions of the first book of the *Iliad* and of certain parts of the *Metamorphoses*, and some original poems ; and the whole volume, with a preface dated 1699, has the curious title *Fables, Ancient and Modern.* Dryden earned the gratitude of all lovers of English literature, when, near the close of his brilliant career, and after recurring to the classical exemplars of his youth, he turned to 'our old English poet,' Chaucer. He describes himself in the preface as having been moved by the thought that there was much in Chaucer (it was certainly not the noblest or the raciest elements in his genius) in which he resembled Ovid[2]. But he also observes that, of the great English poets who had found no immediate successor in their insight into the poetic genius of our language, the *catena* Milton—Spenser—Chaucer was closely linked, and that, in going back to Chaucer, he went back to one whom he accounted the first great writer in English poetical literature. For the sake of the spirit of this tribute, worthy alike of him who paid and of him who received it, Dryden may readily be forgiven some of the blemishes (if they be justly deemed such) in the execution of his task. In a few instances (far fewer than are to be found in the earlier translations), effects are heightened which there was no reason for heightening, and turns of phrase are introduced incompatible not so much with the dignity as with the natural simplicity of thought (*naïveté*) characteristic of all that Chaucer wrote. (Curiously enough, this criticism, if just, is not applicable to the tales from Boccaccio, who was anything but *naïf.*) It has been cleverly said that Dryden 'scrubbed up' Chaucer— a process which suits fine old plate, but not the total effect of a beautiful old house[3]. The amplifications which Dryden openly

---

[1] The attack upon Dryden of Luke Milbourne (1698) was, probably, the result of jealousy, as he had issued a version of book I of the *Aeneid*, said to be now lost. His *Notes*, for which he paid dear, contain some other specimens of his translations from Vergil.

[2] *Essays*, ed. Ker, vol. II, p. 247 ; see, however, pp. 254 ff.

[3] Of this, Dryden was perfectly aware ; nor could the case against his own method be better stated than it is by him (preface to *Fables* in *Essays*, ed. Ker, vol. II, p. 266) on behalf of the earl of Leicester, 'who valued Chaucer as much as Mr Cowley despised him.' (So, in his turn, Mr Pope enquired 'Who now reads Cowley,' though condescending to own a *tendre* for 'the language of his heart.')

permitted himself it would be begging the question to condemn as
such; on the other hand, they are not necessarily to be regarded
as additional beauties. The most extraordinary, as it is the most
extensive, addition is the tag to the version of the exquisite
'Character of a Good Parson,' which seems to have been made
with the twofold purpose of proving him a nonjuror, and of pointing
out that he was the reverse of a type of parsons and priests in
general[1]. The prose *Preface to the Fables* is one of the most
delightful and one of the most unconstrained of all Dryden's prose
pieces; nor can it be doubted to whose example the fascination
which this essay has exercised upon many generations of readers
must, in part, be ascribed. 'The nature of a preface'—he might
have said, the nature of half the prose writing that commends
itself to that large proportion of the public that are not students,
and, at times, to some who are—'is rambling; never wholly out of
the way, nor in it. This I have learnt from the practice of honest
Montaigne,' whose influence, indeed, is progressively perceptible
in Dryden's later prose writings, though it was nowhere emphasised
by too close an imitation[2]. For, in truth, there are features in
Montaigne—his quaintness, for example, and his playfulness—
which are foreign alike to Dryden's directness of manner and to
his reserved disposition. In referring, as he does in different parts
of this *Preface*, to the accusation of 'loose writing' brought against
him by Blackmore[3] and Collier, he cannot be said to plead with
much success, unless it be in mitigation of the offence charged
against him; but he makes amends, not only by the modesty of
his defence, but, also, by the practice into which he puts his regrets.
The selection of 'Fables' from Chaucer, and, still more so, from
Boccaccio, would have been of a different kind had Dryden desired
'more to please than to instruct'—in other words, had the last
fruit from an old tree been designed, like some of its earlier
produce, to tickle palates pleased only by over-seasoned cates.

The last period of Dryden's literary labours had also witnessed
his final endeavours in lyrical verse—a species of poetry in which

---

[1]
      In deference to his virtues I forbear
      To shew you what the rest in orders were.

[2] See, on this subject, *post*, chap. xvii.

[3] Dryden's quarrel with Sir Richard Blackmore seems to have arisen, not (as
Johnson thought) out of the 'City Knight or Knight Physician's' virtuous preface
to his *King Arthur* (1695), but, rather, from the reflection, in his *Satyr on Wit* (1699),
on Dryden for the 'lewd alloy' in his writings. The retorts on Blackmore and
Collier in the prologue and epilogue to *The Pilgrim* have been already noticed
(*ante*, p. 32).

he achieved a more varied excellence than is always placed to his credit. The *Song for St Cecilia's Day*, designed for performance on that festival in 1687 by a recently founded musical society in London, must have been written within a year after the beautiful ode *To the Pious Memory of Mrs Anne Killigrew* already mentioned. Though, of course, devoid of any personal note, and so short as to be of the nature of a *chorale* rather than a *cantata*, it solves its technical problem with notable skill, and the commanding power of the opening, upon which the close solemnly returns, is irresistible[1]. Yet neither in this ode nor in its more famous successor, *Alexander's Feast; or, The Power of Musique*, written for the same festival in 1697, has Dryden escaped the danger inseparable from arbitrary variety of length of line and choice of rhythm. In a lyric on a solemn, and, to all intents, religious, theme—for music was drawn down from heaven by the inspired saint—any approach to an ignoble or lilting movement jars upon ear and sentiment; and this is not wholly avoided in *Alexander's Feast*, while, in the earlier ode, it occurs, so to speak, at the height of the argument. The example which both these odes attempted to set, of making 'sound an echo to the sense,' was not one to be easily followed; nor can they be themselves regarded as more than brilliant efforts to satisfy the illdefined conditions of an artificial form of lyrical verse.

Dryden's lyrical endowment shows itself without ostentation in the songs scattered through his plays. These products of an age distinguished by a very strong and carefully cultivated sense of music often possess considerable charm, even when divorced from their natural complement, and seem, as it were, to demand to be sung[2]. But, for the most part, they are wanton in thought, and, at times, gross in expression, and there were probably few of his productions for which their author would have been more ready to cry *peccavi*.

His contributions to a directly opposite class of lyrics—hymnody—were long supposed to have been extremely few; and the question whether their number admits of being very much enlarged may be said to be still awaiting final judgment. The only hymn known to have been published by Dryden himself or in his lifetime is the well known 'paraphrase,' as it calls itself, of the

[1] Granville (Lord Lansdowne) directly imitated it in *The British Enchanters*, act I, sc. 1 (1706).

[2] Of this sort are the songs in *An Evening's Love*, *The Indian Emperor*, *The Conquest of Granada* (Part I), *Cleomenes*, etc.

*Veni Creator Spiritus*, and is a composition of simple, and even severe, dignity. Together with this hymn, Scott, on evidence which, so far as it is known, cannot be held conclusive, admitted into his edition of Dryden two others—one, a translation of *Te Deum*, the other (erroneously called by Scott *St John's Eve*) a translation, in an unusual metre, of the hymn at evensong on St John's day, which forms part of a sequence. It has now been discovered that these three pieces are included in a collection of 120 hymns printed in a book of Catholic devotions dated 1706; and internal evidence of metre and diction, coupled with the (late) tradition that Dryden wrote a number of hymns by way of absolving a penance imposed on him, has been held to warrant the conclusion that he was the author of all. Saintsbury can hardly be mistaken in the view that, if *St John's Eve* be Dryden's, other hymns with which this is connected are, likewise, by his hand; and a number of these hymns reprinted by Orby Shipley certainly exhibit, together with many Drydenisms of manner and diction, the freedom which Dryden always exercised as a translator, together with an abundance of movement, though relatively little soaring. If they be Dryden's, they offer a further proof of the versatility of his lyric gifts; but they do not suffice to give him a place among great English writers of hymns[1].

Thus, in labours manifold and not without a disquietude of spirit from which the decline of life is rarely exempt, Dryden's days and his literary career drew nearer and nearer to their close. Advancing years, and, perhaps, other influences which it is difficult or impossible to estimate, had rendered him less consistently observant of the general habit of his youth and manhood to allow his censors and adversaries to abuse and revile him as they chose, without returning libel for libel, or lampoon for lampoon. If he could afford to contemn Milbourne, he turned upon Blackmore with almost savage energy, and attempted a *tu quoque* of very doubtful force against Jeremy Collier, in words which were not to be spoken in public till after he had himself passed away[2]. It is more pleasing to remember that, in his declining years, he had not abandoned

---

[1] The discovery that the three hymns accepted by Scott are included in *The Primer or Office of the Blessed Virgin Mary* was made independently by Orby Shipley and W. T. Burke. Twenty-three of the hymns in this *Primer* were reprinted by the former in *Annus Sanctus* (London and New York, 1884). See, for a review of the whole case, *Dryden as a Hymnodist* by the same writer (reprinted from the *Dublin Review*, 1884), and, for several of the hymns, and critical summary, appendix B. 1 in Saintsbury's edition of Scott's *Dryden*, vol. XVII; and cf. Julian, J., *A Dictionary of Hymnology* (1892), art. Dryden.

[2] Prologue and epilogue to Fletcher's *Pilgrim*.

his generous usage of encouraging the efforts of other writers—
especially of younger men such as Southern[1] and Congreve[2] and
Granville[3].   Indeed, to each of the latter pair, at different dates,
obeying a generous impulse that could not help repeating itself, he
bequeathed the laurels of which the world of letters knew him to
be the rightful wearer.   He died, after a short illness, on 1 May
1700, and, with due solemnity (though contemporary scandal
sought to distort the facts) was, less than a fortnight afterwards,
buried in Westminster abbey, in the grave of Chaucer.   Twenty
years later, by the tardy munificence of the duke of Buckingham-
shire (who did not live to see it erected) a plain monument with
an equally simple inscription was raised over his remains.

Dryden's great literary achievements and his great literary
qualities were not, and could not be, ignored by his own age,
nor have the generations which succeeded been willing or able
to belittle them.   More than any of his contemporaries, he is
entitled to be called the father of modern English prose; while,
as to English verse, the next generation might refine and, in some
respects, improve upon its model, but this model could be no other
than 'Timotheus' himself.   Congreve, to whom, in his latter years,
Dryden confidently looked to continue his literary influence, said
of him that he was equally excellent in verse and in prose, and it
would be difficult to dispute the truth of the saying.   His verse
exhibits his chosen metrical instrument, the heroic couplet, in the
fulness of its strength; but, when he returned to blank verse, as a
dramatist, he used it with notable effect; and it has been seen how
varied was his command over lyric measures, from that of the
'Pindaric' ode to those suited to the subtle madrigal or simple
hymn.   The metrical qualities of his verse will be discussed
elsewhere[4]; but its one pre-eminent quality, the infinitely varied
and always rightly judged distribution of movement in the line or
couplet or stanza, can hardly be termed a metrical quality only.   It
depends largely on sureness of tact, rapidity of insight and absolute
self-confidence in the rejection of all means not leading directly
to their end.   Whether extreme passion or profound emotion—
whether love, hatred, anger, contempt, exultant joy or poignant
grief—calls for expression within the limits of the line or couplet,
immediate room, precise place, exact emphasis is found for each

[1] *To Mr Southern, on his Comedy called 'The Wives' Excuse'* (1692).
[2] *To my dear Friend Mr Congreve, on his Comedy called 'The Double Dealer'*
(1693).
[3] *To Mr Granville, on his excellent Tragedy, called 'Heroick Love'* (1698).
[4] See *post*, chap. IX.

word or clause. And the economy is not less striking than the abundance in this feast of words. There was, in the days of Cowley, 'plenty enough, but the dishes were ill-sorted[1]'; Dryden knew how to forego, instead of sweeping in. The poetic instrument remains wholly in the service of the player's hand; and, on each occasion, it seems to give forth in perfection the music which that occasion demands.

Dryden's prose combines with an unprecedented ease of flow, and a forcible directness common to all he wrote, a lucidity of arrangement and a delicacy of *nuance* alike largely due to French example—nor can we err in regarding Corneille as having largely influenced the style of his earlier, and Montaigne that of his later, prose writings. The debt of later English prose to Dryden is inestimable; we have it on Malone's personal testimony that the style of Burke was 'originally in some measure founded on that of Dryden,' on which he had 'often heard Burke expatiate with great admiration' and whom, as Malone thought, Burke resembled more nearly than he did any other great English writer[2].

Of Dryden's contributions to a large variety of literary species, all of which he, in one way or another advanced in their development, it is unnecessary here to say more. His plays, taken as a whole, form the most notable chapter in English dramatic literature after the doors of the theatres had been once more flung open at the restoration. In his non-dramatic verse, he left scarcely any kind of poetry unattempted except the epic proper—in which, had his heart's wish been fulfilled, he would have challenged comparison with the great poet who had survived into a 'later age,' and to whom no political or religious differences ever prevented Dryden from paying an unstinted tribute of admiration. But he essayed, with marked success, a less adventurous flight in narrative poetry, and, in didactic, he created what may be termed a new form of its satirical division—political satire (with a literary subsection) in verse, in which, by means of his incomparable gallery of characters, he excelled all that sought to rival him on his own ground. His didactic poems proper are among the most successful attempts ever made to carry on the arguments of the schools in polished metrical form; but it is to their satirical element as much as to their lucidity that they owe their general freedom from tediousness. His shorter didactic and satirical pieces—largely taking the shape of prologues and epilogues—often partake, after their kind,

---

[1] *Preface to the Fables* (*Essays*, ed. Ker, vol. ii, p. 258).
[2] Malone, *u.s.* vol. i, part i, advt. p. vii.

of the *vis vivida* of his longer satires. His lyrics, in their varied
excellence, complete the roll of his poetic achievements.

And yet, although the epithet 'glorious,' which for a long time
has been attached to Dryden's name, seems appropriate to the
powers and the products of his genius, and though time cannot
change the estimate which that epithet implies, there can be little
doubt what restriction should be placed upon the tribute due to him
as a great writer and a great poet. His originality was essentially
originality of treatment. Partly, perhaps, because his temperament
was slow and reserved, and because his mind seems never to have
been thoroughly at work till he had his pen in his hand, his genius
was that which he describes[1] as 'the genius of our countrymen...
rather to improve an invention than to invent themselves.' And his
poetry—unless in isolated places where the feelings of the individual
man burst the bonds: the feeling of shame in the ode *To Anne
Killigrew*; the feeling of melancholy, mingled with a generous
altruism, in the lines to Congreve; the feeling of noble scorn for
what is base and mean in some of his satire; the feeling of the
sweetness of life and youth in a few of his lyrics—touches few
sympathetic chords in the heart. Nor does it carry the reader
out of himself and beyond himself into the regions where soul
speaks to soul. How could it have done so? This was not his
conception of his art, or of the practice of it.

The same parts and application which have made me a poet might have
raised me to any honours of the gown, which are often given to men of as
little learning and less honesty than myself[2].

Yet, even so, it were unjust as well as ungrateful to think of
Dryden as a craftsman who, by dint of taking infinite pains, learnt
the secret of simulating that which in the chosen few is inborn
What he was not, he at no time made any pretence of being.
What he did, he did with the whole strength of one of the most
vigorous intellects given to any poet ancient or modern, with
constant generosity of effort, and, at the same time, with masculine
directness and clear simplicity of purpose. And, though the work
of his life is not marble without a flaw, yet the whole structure
overtops the expanse of contemporary English literature like the
temple shining from the Sunian height over the sea.

[1] *Preface to the Fables* (*Essays*, ed. Ker, vol. II, p. 255).
[2] *Examen Poeticum* (1693) (*Essays*, ed. Ker, vol. II, p. 2).

# CHAPTER II

## SAMUEL BUTLER

SATIRE, the humorous or caustic criticism of men's faults and foibles in all their manifestations, the hotch-pot or *farrago*, as Juvenal calls it, of the vagaries of human conduct, is justly claimed by Quintilian as an entirely Latin or Italian product. So early as Ennius (b. 239 B.C.), the *lanx satura* or *olla podrida* of scraps of heterogeneous and discursive observations had been compounded; but it was not till Lucilius had seasoned it with 'Italian vinegar' that the production could be looked upon as 'satire' in the modern sense of the word. This ingredient, however, Horace declares, was, to a great extent, derived by Lucilius from the poets of the old Greek comedy. The *parabases* of Aristophanes certainly contain this element, though the concentration of their aim and object preclude the title of the discursive *satura*. Lucilius, the inventor of this kind of composition—the founder of the mocking style[1]—was also its chief exponent, and it is interesting to note that, to Lucilius, each of his three successors—Horace, Juvenal and Persius —attributes in turn his own style: Horace, his inconsequent chatter full of moral maxims and worldly wisdom; Juvenal, his fiery declamations against vice; and Persius, his homilies in praise of virtue and against hypocrisy. When Horace asserts that Lucilius had recourse to his 'faithful books' to record every mood of his impressions on all subjects, he reminds more modern readers of the practice of Montaigne, who charms us by his talk about himself and by his carefully recorded experiences on that subject.

All these tirades were conveyed in Latin hexameters, which, in Lucilius, were often of a hybrid, 'linsey-woolsey' composition, *i.e.* interlarded with Greek words. This slipshod verse became the conventional metre for satire in Latin down the ages, whether in

---

[1] Plin. *Nat. Hist.* praef. § 8 : *Lucilius primus condidit stili nasum.*

the *Anti-Claudianus* of Alain de l'Isle or in the macaronic *Baldus* of Merlin Cocai (Teofilo Folengo). In the same way, 'splayfoot' octosyllabic rimes became the medium of English satire, derived, probably, through the French, from *Le Roman de la Rose*. Satirical writing found a congenial soil in France, where the interminable *chansons de geste* required a relief. Thus were produced *Le Roman de Renart* and the *fables bestiaires*, often attributed to Ysopet, the French counterpart of Aesop. But *Le Roman de la Rose* stands out as the most important production of the kind and as exercising a widereaching influence on the literature of Europe.

From this source flowed numberless compositions, on two subjects especially, one being the *querelle des femmes*, which was taken up vigorously on both sides. Christine de Pisan leads the attack against *Le Roman de la Rose*, followed by Jean Gerson, chancellor of the university of Paris, Alain Chartier and Martin de France, author of *Le Champion des Dames* (1440—2). On the other side may be mentioned *Les XV joyes de mariage, Les arrêts d'amour*, the *Silva nuptialis* of Johannes Nevizanus and Rabelais in the third book of his *Pantagruel*: but the catalogue is a very long one. The other subject is an attack on the religious orders, especially the mendicants, the Dominicans and the Franciscans, who had been recognised by the popes in the beginning of the thirteenth century, and, from the very first, had shown extraordinary activity and influence, proving very obnoxious to the regular clergy. These two subjects can be traced in *Hudibras*, but in another and curious form : the nonconforming sects taking the place of the mendicants as butts for satire, and Hudibras and the widow respectively leading the attack and defence in the *querelle des femmes*.

Butler had also probably read Barclay's *Ship of Fools*, translated from Sebastian Brant's *Narrenschiff*. *Moriae Encomium* might well supply him with a model for his satire, while the *Adagia* of Erasmus undoubtedly furnished him with a stock of learning and literary illustration. Rabelais was thoroughly versed in all these writings, and employed them in his *Gargantua* and *Pantagruel*. Butler was a good French scholar and did not need Urquhart's translation[1], but read the French at firsthand. Zachary Grey points out in his notes several passages in *Hudibras* derived from the French satirist; but many more correspondences can be detected by a closer comparison.

[1] As to this, see vol. VII, chap. X.

Only scanty materials for an account of Samuel Butler's life survive. The son of a farmer, he was born at Strensham in Worcestershire, 8 February 1612, and died in London in the year 1680. He was educated at the cathedral school at Worcester, and, judging by his proficiency in classical literature, must have been exceedingly well grounded. Afterwards, he lived in or near Cambridge, but does not seem to have entered at any one of the colleges or to have been a member of the university. Later, he was engaged as an attendant or secretary to Elizabeth, countess of Kent, at Wrest in Bedfordshire. This was an important period of his life, for John Selden, the accomplished lawyer, passed at least three long vacations (1626—8) under the same roof, and interested himself in Butler. It may, perhaps, be fanciful to find in the lawyer's fondness for illustration and analogy in his *Table Talk* the suggestion of the similar treatment of his subjects in the droll similes and comparisons that meet us often in Butler's writings.

Some years of his early life were spent in the capacity of clerk to a succession of county magistrates; but the most important of these employments was that under Sir Samuel Luke, of Cople Hoo near Bedford, who was a fanatical puritan, one of Cromwell's colonels in the civil war, and scoutmaster for Bedfordshire and several midland counties. In this gentleman's house were frequent meetings of members of various religious and political sects, and Butler had an opportunity of noting the peculiarities and pretentions of a motley crew, which he afterwards mercilessly ridiculed in his comic epic. Here, no doubt, he composed many of his *Characters* and notes, which sometimes appear in his *Hudibras*, though some of the *Characters* were obviously written, partly, at least, after the restoration. One hundred and twenty of these *Characters* had appeared (but not till 1759) in *The Genuine Remains in Verse and Prose of Mr Samuel Butler*, edited by Robert Thyer, and, recently, sixty-eight more, together with a number of miscellaneous *Observations and Reflexions*, have been published[1]. In 1660, Butler became secretary to Richard, earl of Carbery, lord president of Wales, who appointed him steward of Ludlow castle, where many *Characters* and other compositions were written out fair for the press, as they came afterwards into the hands of his friend William Longueville.

After the restoration, Butler published the first part of his *Hudibras* in 1663, the second part in 1664, but the third part did not see the light till 1678. It was at once received with great

[1] Ed. Waller, A. R. (Cambridge English Classics), 1908.

enthusiasm, especially by Charles II, to whom it became a kind
of *vade-mecum*, and who rewarded the poet with a gratuity
of £300[1].

It is recorded that Butler contracted a marriage with a wealthy
widow, but that they lost their property by unfortunate speculations.
Another story attributes this loss to the rascality of lawyers and
accounts thus for the exceeding bitterness with which the poet
assails them.   But this is an obscure point; even the lady's name
is not known for certain.  If the question could be satisfactorily
determined, light would possibly be thrown on the relations of
Hudibras and the widow in the third part of the poem.  It seems,
however, tolerably certain that Butler passed the rest of his days
in needy circumstances and died in abject penury.  This is attested
by an epigram full of bitterness on the subject of a monument
erected to his memory in Westminster abbey in 1720 :

> While Butler, needy Wretch, was yet alive
> No Generous Patron would a Dinner give.
> See him when starv'd to death and turn'd to Dust
> Presented with a monumental Bust.
> The Poet's Fate is here in Emblem show'n;
> He asked for Bread and he receiv'd a Stone.

We have seen that he was well taught in Latin and Greek; but
we learn from one of his *Contradictions* that he gave up his Greek
studies after he had left school as ' unnecessary except to Dunces
and Schoolmasters,' and, in his *Thoughts on Learning and Knowledge*[2], he repeats that Greek is ' of little use in our times unless to
serve Pedants and mountebanks to smatter withal'; there is, however, considerable evidence that he kept up his Latin, especially in the
satirists Horace, Juvenal and Persius, from whom he derives many
thoughts and similes ; Lucan, also, he parodies in a notable passage[3].
In his prose writings (*Reflections*, etc.) he shows that he had read
Lucretius carefully ;  he employs that poet's language in illustrating
remarks aimed at the newly formed Royal Society or, as they were
styled, the 'Virtuosi of Gresham College.'   He freely showers
ridicule on Sir Paul Neale, probably the original of the astrologer
Sidrophel (perhaps a parody of ' Astrophil ') and on Lord Brounker,
president of the Society, who, in the poem entitled *The Elephant
in the Moon*, is dubbed ' Virtuoso in chief.'

---

[1] Thus, especially if the difference in the value of money be remembered, the
observation of Dennis (*Reflections on Pope's Essay on Criticism*, p. 539), 'that Butler
was starved at the same time that the king had his book in his pocket' is hardly fair
to Charles II.

[2] p. 280 (ed. 1908).          [3] i, 2, 493—502.

A knowledge of English law and legal phraseology is conspicuous in his writings, but, as might be expected, it is the technical law appertaining to the office of a justice of the peace rather than that of a constitutional lawyer, though his intercourse with Selden may have procured for him some acquaintance with that department of legal study.

The popularity of *Hudibras* caused the growth of a fungus crop of spurious imitations of Butler's prose and poetry, which were published under the title *The Posthumous Works of Mr Samuel Butler, Author of Hudibras, being a collection of Satires, Speeches and Reflections of those times.* Four or five of these productions were published afterwards in *The Genuine Remains*; but, for the most part, the collection consists of ballads, long poems and essays on various subjects relating to the times of the rebellion. A cursory examination will show them to be of distinctly inferior merit; and they are of little service in illustrating the great satire. This worthless publication reached a sixth edition in 1754; and it may have been this circumstance that induced John Clark, to whom *The Genuine Remains* came from Charles Longueville, the son of Butler's friend William Longueville, to entrust them for publication to Robert Thyer, keeper of the public library at Manchester, in November 1759. The pieces making up the collection had been written out fair in Butler's own handwriting when left to William Longueville, but had probably been composed in the rough some years earlier, many of them before *Hudibras*, seeing that they have some of the same matter in common. They consist of a volume of prose containing *Characters* and a few speeches, put in the mouths of certain politicians on stated occasions, with letters *pro* and *con.*, similarly conceived; to these are added some *Occasional thoughts.* The second volume is mainly in verse, beginning with *The Elephant in the Moon*, directed against Sir Paul Neale, a member of the Royal Society. The elephant in the moon turns out to be a fly in the telescope which had been directed to the moon for observations. Curiously enough, this subject is treated metrically twice over—in octosyllabic verse, Butler's special metre, and then in the rimed decasyllables aptly employed by Dryden and Pope. It seems as though Butler had experimented to find the most suitable vehicle for his satire. This poem is followed by nine satires, one or two of which are written in the longer metre.

The subjects of these are the absurdity of human actions and speculations; the licentious times of Charles II (long verse); gaming;

the troubles of verse and rime[1]; the foolish changes of fashion; the abuse of wine ; promiscuous marriages (long verse) ; plagiaries ; the abuse of human learning  The style and method of these satires are naturally suggestive of the influence of the Roman satirists, which may often be traced in *Hudibras*.  Inserted among these are other satirical poems, mainly on political subjects, the most notable being 'on Philip Nye's Thanksgiving Beard.' (Nye was an independent and a member of the assembly of divines, who had made himself notorious by a peculiar beard[2].)  The collection concludes with a large number of *Miscellaneous Thoughts* in epigrammatic form, many of them containing bitter reflections on the poet's illfortune in life and the undeserved success achieved by impudent self-assertion ; some are on the faults of government and the rulers of the state—a medley of melancholy pessimistic thoughts.

The *Characters* must have been suggested by the fashion brought into vogue by Casaubon's translation of Theophrastus's *Characters* in 1592, feebly imitated by bishop Hall, and superficially by Sir Thomas Overbury, and exemplified more effectively in Earle's *Microcosmographie* (1628—33)[3].  Earle was a fellow of Merton and a great friend of Lord Falkland ; Clarendon, who met Earle at Falkland's country house, Great Tew, near Oxford, and was much taken with the refined scholar, refers to *Microcosmographie* as some very 'witty and sharp discourses' which brought the author into repute.  It might, therefore, be an interesting matter for speculation as to how far Clarendon himself was indebted (for suggestions at least) to the numerous essays of this kind during the first half of the seventeenth century, in composing the wonderful delineations of character which are the chief ornaments of his *History of the Rebellion*.

Butler's *Characters* remained in manuscript for about a century and, though brought to light in 1759 in *The Genuine Remains*, they have by no means received the attention they deserve.  While, perhaps, not closely adhering to the model of Theophrastus, they are full of witty sallies and quips which bring into relief the absurdities and hypocrisy displayed by the presbyterian members of Sir Samuel Luke's *coterie*.  Butler had a special genius for noting points of comparison and making similes from small matters in

---

[1] This is translated from Boileau's second *Satire*, as was pointed out to the writer of this chapter by Mr A. A. Tilley.

[2] He is referred to in *Hudibras*, II, 2, 529—531; and in Hudibras's *Epistle* 1, 188.

[3] Cf., as to the genesis and growth of the character sketch, *ante*, vol. IV, chap. XVI, pp. 335 ff. and bibl. pp. 521—3.

common life, or from extraordinary relations of travellers or observers in fantastic science, such as Sir Kenelm Digby and Cornelius Agrippa ; his bent being essentially satirical, he had, while with Sir Samuel Luke, a rare opportunity of observing and recording the revelations made by the 'caterwauling brethren,' the self-styled saints, whose pretensions he unmasks in his *Hudibras.*

Most of his characters are merely general, but others, especially the longer, such as 'A Modern Politician,' 'An hypocritical Non-conformist,' 'A Republican,' 'A State-Convert,' 'A modern Statesman,' 'A Fifth Monarchy man,' 'A small Poet,' 'A Lawyer,' 'A Virtuoso,' 'A Justice of Peace,' 'A Fanatic,' 'An Hermetic Philosopher,' are evidently to be referred to actors on the political stage of that time, and must have supplied matter for *Hudibras* ; there are passages that have so close a resemblance to their counter-parts in the poem that one must have been derived from the other ; though there are some points in the *Characters* which show that they must have been written (at least in part) after 1664.

Of Earle's characters, about ten coincide in their subject with those of Butler, and it is interesting to compare the different style of treatment to be found in these writers. But, in every case, the method is the same. The character is drawn not in outline, but by a number of minor traits that all tell in the same direction till the portrait is fully completed. The besetting sin of the artist in this kind of description is that he often does not know when to take his hand from the picture, and goes on elaborating details till the reader is wearied.

*Hudibras* may be described as a mock-heroic poem dealing with the pretensions and hypocrisies of the presbyterians, independents and other sects which were subversive of the monarchy at the time of the great rebellion. Though it was not published till after the restoration of Charles II, Butler's sympathies were ardently royalist; but his pen, so far as we know, was engaged only fitfully in support of his convictions. His object in putting together in a considerable poem an account of the events and opinions which he had quietly recorded during the convulsive struggles of the nation must have been to ingratiate himself with the king after his return. The impelling motive may well have been poverty, together with the desire of fame.

The first known attempt at mock-heroic poetry was *Batrachomyomachia,* or the battle between frogs and mice, a burlesque on the *Iliad,* at one time absurdly attributed to Homer. Butler, of course, was acquainted with this poem, and wittily parodies title and subject in his *Cynarctomachy, or Battle between Bear and Dogs.* He was probably influenced, also, by Skelton, who, although a man of learning, attacked cardinal Wolsey and the clergy in short rimes of 'convivial coarseness and boisterous vigour'[1]. But Butler's model in style, to a very great extent, must have been Scarron, almost an exact contemporary, whose *Virgile travesti* was published in 1648—52; so Butler, who was versed in French literature, could easily adopt the salient features of this poem in *Hudibras*, which was not published till 1663. On the other side, Scarron shows acquaintance with English affairs, *e.g.* in the following couplet:

> *D'un côté vient le grand Ajax*
> *Fier comme le milord Fairfax.*
>
> Virg. trav., liv. ii.

His method is to modernise the language and actions of the ancient Vergilian heroes, and to put in their mouths the phrases of the (common) people of his own time. In the same mocking spirit, he introduces glaring anachronisms, such as the appearance of Mohammadans at the foundation of Carthage, Dido saying grace before meat, etc.

The name 'Hudibras' is derived from *The Faerie Queene* (II, 2, 17), and the setting of the poem is obviously imitated from *Don Quixote*, save that the imitation is a complete reversal of the attitude of the original. Cervantes treats the vanishing chivalry of Spain in a gentle and affectionate spirit, while showing the impossibility of its continuance in the changed conditions of life. In *Don Quixote*, every element of grandeur and nobility is attributed to the most ordinary and meanest person, building, incident or surrounding; an inn is a castle, an inn-keeper a knight, flocks of sheep are armies; a barber's basin is a golden helmet in the vivid imagination of the knight; a mess of acorns set before him prompts a discourse full of regret at the passing away of the Golden Age, when Nature herself provided simple, wholesome fare for all, without necessity for resorting to force or fraud; and justice prevails throughout. Notwithstanding the absurdity and impossibility of this revival, the reader's sympathy is ever on the side of the chivalric madman, even in his wildest extravagance. In *Hudibras*, on the contrary, the 'blasoning' or description of the knight and squire, while following the most accredited forms of chivalric romance, serves only to set forth the odious squalor of the modern surroundings. The knight's mental

---

[1] See, as to Skelton, *ante*, vol. III, chap. IV, pp. 67 ff.

qualifications are given in great detail and, after that, his bodily accomplishments—all in a vein of satirical exaggeration. Butler's purpose is to show everything in its vilest aspect. Instead of making common affairs noble in appearance, the poem reveals the boastful pretensions of the puritan knight by describing both his equipment and that of his squire squalid and beggarly, while his purpose is, not to excite pity for the poverty and wretchedness of these pitiful champions, but to provoke contempt for the disgusting condition of the wretched pair and to bring down further odium upon it. It is genre painting with a vengeance, and fully realises the account given by Pliny of the art of Piraeicus: 'He painted barbers' shops and cobblers' stalls, asses and dishes of food, and the like, thus getting the name of "painter of low life" ($\dot{\rho}\upsilon\pi\alpha\rho o$-$\gamma\rho\acute{\alpha}\phi o\varsigma$) and giving the highest pleasure by such representations.' Our own Morland and Hogarth well answer such a description, and we are fortunate in possessing illustrations of *Hudibras* designed by the latter. The sympathy between the painter and the poet must have been complete.

That Hudibras going forth 'a colonelling' is intended to represent Sir Samuel Luke is made pretty clear by the speech:

> 'Tis sung there is a valiant Mamaluke
> In foreign Land yclept————
> To whom we have been oft compar'd
> For person, parts, address and beard[1].

He is described as a 'true blue' presbyterian, ignorant, conceited, pedantic, crotchety, a pretender to linguistic, mathematical and dialectical learning, bent on a 'thorough-going reformation' by means of 'apostolic blows and knocks.' In external appearance, he was of a most droll rusticity. His beard was orange tawny (perhaps copied from Philip Nye's thanksgiving beard, or from Panurge's beard in *Pantagruel*)[2], and it was unkempt because he had vowed not to trim it till the monarchy was put down. He was hunchbacked and adorned by a protuberant paunch, stuffed with country fare of milk and butter. His doublet was buff, the colour much affected by his party, and was proof against blows from a cudgel, but not against swordcuts. His trunkhose were full of provisions; even his sword had a basket-hilt to hold broth, and was so little used that it had worn out the scabbard with rust, having been exhibited only in serving warrants. His dagger was serviceable for scraping pots and toasting cheese. His holster contained rusty pistols which proved useful in catching rats in the

---

[1] I, 1, 903—6.      [2] III, 28.

locks, snapping on them when they foraged amongst his garments for cheese. Don Quixote took no thought as to how he should obtain sustenance, while Hudibras was an itinerant larder.

All this is adapted from Cervantes or Rabelais, who themselves parodied the chivalric romances in the apparelling and blasoning of their heroes: in the same vein, Butler goes on to describe the steed and the squire. The horse was mealy-mouthed, blind of one eye, like the mare of Rabelais's Catchpole[1], and wall-eyed of the other; there are also reminiscences of Rosinante and of Gargantua's mare. It was of a grave, majestic pace, and is compared with Caesar's horse, which would stoop to take up its rider, while this one stooped to throw Hudibras. The saddle was old and worn through, and the horse's tail so long and bedraggled that it was only serviceable for swishing mire on the rider.

Ralpho the squire is an independent, with a touch of the anabaptist, despising booklore and professing to be learned for salvation by means of 'gifts' or 'new-light,' in the phraseology of those sects. Here comes in a loan from Rabelais in the account of Ralpho's mystic learning. Her Trippa in *Pantagruel*[2] is based on Henricus Cornelius Agrippa of Nettesheim, author of *De Occulta Philosophia*; these writers and Pythagorean numbers are employed in the description of the squire's accomplishments in quack astrology and almanac writing. Ralpho is a tailor and, like Aeneas and Dante, has seen 'hell'—a sartorial term of the age. meaning a receptacle for shreds and scraps.

As the pair ride forth, the true romantic method is followed, beginning with a comic invocation of the muse, who

> With ale and viler liquors
> Didst inspire Withers, Pryn and Vickars,

certain presbyterian poetasters, the last of whom is said in Butler's 'Annotations' to have 'translated *Virgils Æneids* into as horrible a Travesty in earnest as the French *Scarron* did in Burlesque.' This introduces the action, which is brought about by the discovery of a rabble intent on bear-baiting. The knight looks upon this as 'lewd and anti-Christian,' and it may be intended to represent the 'insolency of the late tumults' described in *Eikon Basilike*, which was accepted by the royalists as the composition of Charles I. The leaders of the rebellion are there styled *boutefeus*, or known incendiaries, a term here used by Butler probably in allusion to its occurrence in the tract, and explained in his 'Annotations' as a French word and, therefore, necessarily under-

---

[1] Bk. IV, chap. 12.     [2] Bk. III, chap. 25.

stood by persons of quality. Bear-baiting is quaintly derived from the constellation *Ursa Major*, which circles round the pole. The knight finds in this *Cynarctomachy* a plot to set brother against brother, so as to prevent them from offering a united front on behalf of a thorough reformation.

As, in Rabelais and *Don Quixote*, it is the conversations that bring into relief the convictions and prejudices of the interlocutors, so, in *Hudibras*, the altercations between the knight and squire, which often degenerate into recriminations, are intended to unmask the hypocritical contentions of both parties. In the very first canto, the suspicion that was rife between the presbyterian knight and the independent squire is brought out, and the warmth of religious partisanship is heightened on every subsequent occasion.

The description of the warriors on the other side, that is, the bear-baiters, is humorous in the extreme. They consist of a one-legged fiddler, Crowdero (from *crowd*, an old word for a fiddle), a bear-ward, a butcher, a tinker, Magnano (the Italian equivalent for locksmith), a virago named Trulla, a cobbler and an ostler. These have been identified by Sir Roger l'Estrange, who was a contemporary, with men who obtained posts in Cromwell's army and gained subsequent distinction. The wit and humour lavished on the description of these worthies is extraordinary, and may be exemplified in one or two cases. Talgol, the butcher, had made many orphans and widows, and, like Guy of Warwick, had slain many a dun cow; he had fought more flocks of sheep than Ajax or Don Quixote, and slain many serpents in the shape of wasps.

Cerdon, the cobbler, is compared to Hercules in the repair of wrong (in shoes):

> He raised the low and fortifi'd
> The weak against the strongest Side.

Colon, the ostler, is compared to a centaur for his riding, and

> Sturdy he was and no less able
> Than *Hercules* to cleanse a Stable;
> As great a Drover and as great
> A Critic too in Hog and Neat.

It was

> A question as to whether He
> Or's Horse were of a Family
> More worshipful;

but antiquaries gave their decision,

> And prov'd not onely Horse, but Cows,
> Nay Pigs were of the elder House:
> For Beasts, when Man was but a piece
> Of earth himself, did th' Earth possess.

Butler's peculiar trick of giving the characteristics of each person by parallels of similar accomplishments in some noted hero, but in ludicrous travesty, is, doubtless, imitated from Scarron. Rabelais delights in finding in ancient history and literature parallels to his modern instances, but does not go further, except where the general tone of the speaker dramatically requires it; but, with Butler's mocking humour, the method is reversed, and it is only for the purpose of debasing it in the application that a striking instance is found.

In order to bring Hudibras into contempt from the first, he is represented as anxious to put down bear-baiting, one of the most popular amusements of the time, and substituting for it the cult of the solemn league and covenant, which was thrust upon the English by the Scottish presbyterians. The knight feels bound, 'in conscience and commission too,' 'to keep the peace twixt dog and bear,' and dubs the whole proceeding 'pagan and idolatrous.' The squire consents to this, but, from his point of view as an independent, insists that, if there is no scriptural warrant for bear-baiting, neither is there warrant for

> Provincial, classic, national,
> Mere human creature cobwebs all.

These three words, specially applied by the presbyterians to their various synods, make Hudibras suspicious of his squire; but he puts off the argument, because it is now time for action.

The description of the battle is rendered more absurd by the high-flown epic vein in which it is set forth. The metrical devices of pauses in particular places are duly observed, as well as the repetitions of emphatic words, such as

> He Trulla loved, Trulla more bright, etc.
> And gave the Champion's Steed a thump
> That stagger'd him. The knight did stoop, etc.[1]

The bear having been badly mauled in the battle, the retreat is saved by the cobbler Cerdon and by Trulla, who leads

> The Warrior to a grassy Bed,
> As Authors write, in a cool Shade,
> Which Eglantine and Roses made,
> Close by a softly murm'ring Stream,
> Where lovers us'd to loll and dream.

---

[1] There is even an instance of aposiopesis:
> Which now thou shalt—but first our care
> Must see how Hudibras doth fare,
imitating the Vergilian *Quos ego—sed motos*, etc.

This is a ludicrous imitation of the first book of the *Aeneid*, where Venus puts Ascanius to rest in similar surroundings.

Hudibras had been victorious in the first battle and, with the help of the squire, had put Crowdero in the stocks; but, in a second encounter, after the combatants have rallied their forces, he is worsted, and, with Ralpho, takes the place of Crowdero. Even here, while Hudibras

> Cheer'd up himself with ends of Verse
> And Sayings of Philosophers,

Ralpho the independent resumes his attack on the presbyterians, and we are treated to the catch-words 'gifts,' 'illumination,' 'light,' 'synodical,' 'orders,' 'constitutions,' 'church-censures' and so forth. Challenged by the knight, he repeats his argument that synods are mystical bear-gardens, in which saints are represented by the bear and presbyters and scribes by the dogs that are set upon them. 'Synods are whelps of the inquisition,' and they have their 'triers' (or testers), whose business it is

> To cast a figure for men's *Light*;
> To find in lines of Beard and Face
> The Physiognomy of *Grace*,
> And by the sound and *twang of Nose*
> If all be sound within disclose.

The second part, which was published a year after the first, proceeds uninterruptedly with the story, taking up the case of the widow whom, in the third canto of the first part, Hudibras had after his victory wished to gain, meeting, however, with discomfiture. The widow, informed of this by *Fame* (parodied from the fourth book of the *Aeneid*), determines to visit him in the stocks, and there entices him to declare himself. Thus, we have another argument between them, in which the knight's shameless self-seeking is exposed and the superiority of the female sex is maintained. In proof of his good faith, Hudibras has to promise to submit to flagellation. The notion of whipping and the mode of carrying it out is borrowed from Don Quixote[1], where Sancho Panza is called upon to endure three thousand lashes in order to obtain the disenchantment of Dulcinea del Toboso. Hudibras solemnly swears that he will carry out this behest.

The next (the second) canto is introduced by the poet as especially full of contention, and it is here that the hypocritical casuistry of the two sects who were principally concerned in the civil war is most clearly exposed. Hudibras, after a night's

[1] Bk. II, chap. 35.

reflection, does not relish the idea of a flogging and turns to the squire for his judgment on the subject. Ralpho readily proceeds to 'enlarge upon the point.' First, it is heathenish to offer the sacrifice of whipping to idols, and it is sinful to do so in saints who are sufficiently bruised and kicked by the wicked. Moreover,

and,

> The *Saints* may claim a *Dispensation*
> To *swear* and *forswear* on occasion....

> Although your *Church* be opposite
> To ours as *Black Friers* are to *White*
> In *Rule* and *Order*; yet I grant
> You are a *Reformado Saint.*

He then, with pungent raillery, particularises breaches of faith on the part of the 'saints.' They broke the allegiance and supremacy oath, and compelled the nation to take and break the protestation in favour of the reformed religion, to swear and forswear the solemn league and covenant, to enter into and then disclaim the engagement to be true to the government without king or peers. They swore to fight for and against the king, insisting that it was in his defence, and also for and against their own general Essex. They swore to maintain law, religion and privilege in parliament, not one of which is left; having sworn to maintain the House of Lords, they turned them out as dangerous and useless.

If this be so in public life, a saint in private life can be no more bound by an oath.

> A *Saint* 's of th' heavenly Realm a *Peer*:
> And as no *Peer* is bound to *swear*,
> But on the *Gospel* of his *Honor*,
> Of which he may dispose as *Owner*;
> It follows, though the thing be *forgery*
> And false th' affirm, it is no *perjury.*

This suggests a gibe at the despised quakers, who, nevertheless, are scrupulous in this matter:

> These, thinking th' are obliged to *Troth,*
> In swearing will not take an Oath.

Hudibras agrees and insists that, like a law, an oath is of no use till it is broken. Ralpho, continuing, points out that a man may be whipped by proxy, and

> That *Sinners* may supply the place
> Of suffering *Saints* is a plain *Case.*

Hudibras jumps at this, and at once bids Ralpho be his substitute.

He refuses, and, when Hudibras becomes abusive, reminds him of the superiority of the independent party.

> Remember how in *Arms* and *Politicks*
> We still have worsted all your holy Tricks;
> *Trapann'd* your party with *Intregue*
> And took your *Grandees* down a peg;
> *New-modell'd* th' Army and *Cashier'd*
> All that to *Legion Smec* adher'd.

(*Legion Smec* is intended for the presbyterians generally, under the well known composite name 'Smectymnuus.') Hudibras retorts furiously, upbraiding his squire as an upstart sectary and a mongrel,

> Such as breed out of peccant Humors
> Of our own *Church*, like *Wens* and *Tumours*,
> And, like a *Maggot* in a *Sore*,
> Would that which gave it Life devour.

This, of course, refers to the numberless sects that sprang up at this time, holding often the strangest of views.

The champions are proceeding to blows when they are interrupted by a frightful noise caused by a woman being escorted in triumph by a rabble, for having beaten her husband. Hudibras must needs interfere, being particularly scandalised by the dishonour done to the sex that furnished the 'saints' with their first 'apostles.' He enlarges on the help women have given to the 'cause,' in language that might be a parody of Hooker[1], but the rabble sets upon them with eggs and similar projectiles, so they are glad to escape with the loss of their swords. Hudibras consoles himself, seeing a good omen in his having been pelted with dirt:

> Vespasian being dawb'd with durt
> Was destin'd to the Empire for 't.

The third canto introduces a new element. By Ralpho's advice, Hudibras entertains the notion of consulting an astrologer, Sidrophel, as to his prospects in the pursuit of the widow. The question as to the permissibility of consulting a person who is scripturally banned is decided in his favour—'saints may employ a conjurer.' The description of Sidrophel and his zany Whachum, 'an underwitch, his Caliban,' is but little inferior to the account of Hudibras and the squire at the beginning of the poem. Much of it is derived from Rabelais[2], who has collected a great number of methods of divination. Butler, however, makes considerable additions from his own store, derived from the superstitions of common

---

[1] Pref. c. III, § 13.    [2] Bk. III, chap. 25.

life. At first, Hudibras is impressed by the extraordinary knowledge displayed by the astrologer; but, afterwards, in matching his own store of learning with it, finds himself disabused, especially when Sidrophel quotes as a recent event a fictitious adventure of his own, which had appeared in a spurious continuation of the first part of *Hudibras.* This leads to the usual scuffle, in which the astrologer and Whachum are worsted, and Ralpho is despatched for a constable; while Hudibras, under the false impression that Sidrophel is dead, makes off, intending the squire to bear the charge of murder and robbery, though he himself has rummaged the astrologer's pockets.

This is the conclusion of the first and second parts of the poem, published respectively in 1663 and 1664. The third part, which takes up the story, was not published till 1678, and shows considerable difference in the treatment of the subject.

Unlike the earlier parts, it contains very few classical allusions, and these are of the most obvious kind, such as the Trojan horse and Cerberus; the style, too, is smoother and requires less explanation. This may be the result of experience and of hints received by the writer in the intervening years. But the thread of the story is taken up without interruption. The knight, having determined to abjure Ralpho, makes his way to the widow's house; but, unfortunately for him, the squire had formed the same resolution and forestalled him. When Hudibras appears, the lady is found fully informed on all points, and is able to oppose a true account to all his false claims of suffering on her behalf. The controversy for and against marriage again betrays the knight's unscrupulous selfishness, and a finishing stroke has set forth his contemptible character, when a low knocking is heard at the gate, and, flying in terror into a neighbouring room, he hides under a table. He is ignominiously drawn out and cudgelled by (as he supposes) Sidrophel's diabolical agents. Under the influence of superstitious terrors, he confesses the motives that impelled him in his suit, and answers to a catechism which divulges all his iniquities; and, that nothing may be wanting to complete his humiliation, he mistakes his squire Ralpho, who has been similarly beaten and left in the same dark room, for a more or less friendly spirit; whereupon, the pair make confession of the enormities perpetrated by the rival sects in the civil wars.

The final act of the burlesque follows in the third canto of this part, the second being a satirical account of the death of Cromwell and of the intrigues of the various parties before the restoration.

The knight, having been withdrawn from his place of torture on Ralpho's shoulders, is induced by the squire to consult a lawyer. At first, he cries down this scheme, in order to adopt it afterwards as his own. He adopts it ungraciously 'since he has no better course' and consoles himself with the, often misquoted, couplet

> He that complies against his Will
> Is of his own Opinion still.

Butler now has an opportunity of exhibiting a lawyer in what he probably considered a true light. The advice this person gives exemplifies the use that was made in the older jurisprudence of *cautelae*, or methods of getting round legal enactments, and Hudibras is instructed to ply the widow with love-letters and

> With Trains t' inveigle and surprise
> Her heedless Answers and Replies.

This counsel is followed, and we have the knight's letter and the lady's answer, in which the latter, undoubtedly, has the best of the argument.

The second canto of the third part stands quite by itself and has nothing to do with the fortunes of Hudibras. It is merely an account, more or less detailed, of the principles and politics of the presbyterians, independents and republicans during the anarchy before the restoration. Rebellion had slackened for want of plunder, and presbyterian and independent were now at logger-heads. The presbyterians were turned out, and were glad to become itinerant preachers; they were served as they had treated the cavaliers, and decried the anabaptists and fanatics as much as they had done the papists and the prelatists before. Now, the independents were prepared to pull down everything that the war had spared and to intrigue among themselves. Meantime, the royalists, true to church and crown, notwithstanding their sufferings, came together again on seeing their foes divided;

> For Loyalty is still the same,
> Whether it win or lose the Game;
> True as a Dial to the Sun,
> Although it be not shin'd upon.

'Cromwell had given up his reign, Tossed in a furious hurricane'; his feeble son had sunk under the burden of state, and now the 'saints' began their rule, but could not agree among themselves. Some were for a king, others wished to set up the fifth monarchy; some were for the Rump parliament, others for a general council of officers; some were for gospel government, others for pulling down presbyterian synods and classes; some, for opposing the papacy, putting down saints' days and demolishing churches; some, for having regular ministers, others, for soldier preachers. Some would abolish surplices and the use of the ring in the marriage service, while re-establishing the Judaic law, and putting an end to the use of the cross in baptism and to giving the names of saints to churches or streets. Others disallowed the idea of *limbus patrum,* where the souls of holy men rest till the judgment.

Meantime, the 'quacks of government,' such as Sir Anthony Ashley Cooper and John Lilburne, who saw the necessity of a restoration, were discussing matters in secret conclave. Butler gives a wonderful description of Cooper (which should be compared with Dryden's Achitophel) and of John Lilburne, who both make long speeches on present events and the way they should be met, but ultimately go off into violent recriminations as representatives of the presbyterians and the independents; till they are suddenly interrupted by a messenger who brings the news of the burning of the members of the Rump in effigy. This gives an opportunity for some rough banter on the explanation of the word rump (especially on its Hebrew equivalent *luz*), which is to be found in Butler's character entitled 'An Hermetic Philosopher'[1]. But, soon, the mob appear with the purpose of hauling out the members of this assembly and burning them. They beat an ignominious retreat, and this ends the second canto, which has been treated last, because it is disconnected with the main story of *Hudibras.*

It may be well here, in retrospect, to examine Butler's methods in the composition of his poem. The date of publication, three years after the restoration, is sufficient to suggest that it must have found an appreciative audience, at a time when the events to which it referred were fresh in men's minds, and when, as we know, a violent reaction against puritanism had set in. The learning and scientific knowledge displayed, the turns of wit, racy metaphors and quaint rimes have secured its continuance as an English classic; but, much of the legal knowledge having become obsolete, or being too technical for ordinary readers, and many of the minor historical allusions being forgotten, a continuous perusal of the book requires unusual perseverance. Moreover, the length of some of the descriptions of persons or events is trying to the patience, although the illustrations or parallels in themselves are pertinent and acute. The sparkling wit and humour displayed enlightens and relieves the discussions which make up much of the book. Humorous as are the arguments, the witty and whimsical

---

[1] *Characters,* etc., ed. Waller, A. R., p. 105.

comparisons serve as flashlights to bring into relief what might otherwise become dull by reason of its length.

Thus, the peculiarities of religious tenets are illustrated by the presbyterians, who

> Compound for sins they are inclin'd to
> By damning those they have no mind to,

and, in their cantankerousness, are

> Still so perverse and opposite,
> As if they worshipp'd God for spite;

and by the independents and anabaptists, who are dubbed 'land and water saints'; the latter are said

> To dive like wild-fowl for Salvation
> And fish to catch Regeneration.

Ralpho, who has a touch of the anabaptist, when rising from his bed, is said to 'adventure Resurrection.' A classical comparison is found in Achilles, who was

> anabaptiz'd free of wound
> . . . . . .
> All over, but the pagan heel.

The sects are ever squabbling for change of doctrine,

> As if Religion were intended
> For nothing else but to be mended.

The philosophical virtuoso, Sir Kenelm Digby, is gibed at in the description of the pouch worn by Orsin, the pugnacious bear-ward,

> Replete with strange hermetick Powder
> That Wounds nine miles point-blank would solder;

and Hudibras is represented as spurring his courser,

> Conveying sympathetic Speed
> From Heel of Knight to Heel of Steed.

Homeric and classical similes and allusions are frequent in the first two parts. We have the intervention of 'Pallas, who came in shape of Rust,' to prevent a pistol going off, and 'Mars, who still protects the stout'; a stone that strikes Ralpho is compared to that hurled by Diomed. Hudibras, in assisting Ralpho to his feet, boasts that

> Caesar himself could never say
> He got two vict'ries in a day
> As I have done, that can say, twice I
> In one day *veni, vidi, vici*.

Perhaps the comparisons from common life are more amusing; for instance, the celebrated simile :

> And like a Lobster boil'd, the Morn
> From black to red began to turn;

though this is not quite equal to its original in Rabelais, who says that lobsters are cardinalised by boiling. Very comic is the comparison of a sword that had fallen from its owner's grip to deserting rats.

> He snatched his Whiniard up, that fled
> When he was falling from his Steed,
> As Rats do from a falling House.

This is Pliny's *ruinis imminentibus musculi praemigrant*. The whole poem is a storehouse of such borrowings.

Dryden, in the dedication of his translation of Juvenal and Persius (1692), while expressing admiration of Butler for being able to put 'thought' into his verses, strongly disapproves of his choice of octosyllabic metre.

Besides, the double Rhyme (a necessary companion of Burlesque writing) is not so proper for manly Satir, for it turns Earnest too much into Jest, and gives us a boyish kind of Pleasure. It tickles awkwardly with a kind of Pain to the best sort of Readers; and we are pleased ungratefully, and if I may say so, against our liking.

But Butler knew that ridicule was his strongest weapon, and that it would please Charles II and his courtiers better than stately rhythm or fiery denunciation. Rimed decasyllabic suited Dryden's form of satire, as we see in his *Absalom and Achitophel*, and was well adapted to Pope's polished antitheses; but, for gibes and quick sallies of wit, octosyllabic metre, in competent hands, is the most fitting instrument.

As Butler died in 1680, it is impossible to say whether he contemplated a further instalment of his poem, so as to bring up the tale of his cantos to twelve, after the example of the *Aeneid*; the sixth canto, that is, the third of the second book, finishes, evidently, with a view to a continuation which is provided by the third part. But there is an incompleteness apparent in this part, suggested first by the interpolation of the second canto, which has nothing to do with the action of the poem, and which might fittingly have been introduced in a subsequent continuation, while the letter of Hudibras and the Lady's answer ought to have been incorporated in the main story rather than be left isolated. The third part is longer than the first by 590 lines and, if the two letters are added, by nearly 1340. It seems not an unfair inference that, had the satirist's life and strength permitted, an additional part of three cantos would have been added, to complete the normal number of twelve, and that the third part would not have run to so disproportionate a length.

It remains to offer a few considerations on the main purpose of Butler's satire—a frontal attack on puritanism. He probably was unaware that a change was in progress from a personal to a constitutional monarchy, disguised by a religious upheaval which might be regarded as the groundswell after the storm of the reformation. He was a fervent royalist, but kept mainly to the religious side of the question.

The publication of the *Authorised Version* of the Bible in 1611 had set men thinking of the treasure that had fallen into their hands, and very many now read persistently the one book upon which they looked as the guide to salvation. This dwelling on one authority upset the balance of mind of many whose reading was thus limited; and men learned to identify themselves with the conquering, exterminating children of Israel, and to look upon all who opposed them in politics or church doctrine as men of Belial, Moabites, Amalekites and other adversaries of Israel and of God, and as their own personal enemies, to be overthrown at any cost and by any means of force or fraud. But, as Dante says finely of another sect,

> Their meditations reach not Nazareth.

Examples may readily be found of similar perversions of Scripture; but an instance which stands out, by reason of the beauty of its language and the terrible nature of its denunciation, occurs in Milton's tract, *Of Reformation touching Church-Discipline in England,* where the reward assured to his own partisans and the punishment to be meted out to his adversaries are enunciated in startling contrast[1].

The mental exaltation arrived at by such *homines unius libri* was extraordinary, and rendered them capable of efforts in their enthusiasm which upset all calculation. So long as they were sincere in their beliefs, their conduct may have been commendable; but it is the fate of human nature, when men have attained success by these means, to become dazzled by the height of the pinnacle they have reached, and, when enthusiasm flags, to become subject to deplorable lapses. And, when the spoils of the vanquished lie at the mercy of the victors, cupidity and the baser feelings of human nature often gain the mastery over former high resolves. This was frequently the case in the period of the civil war and the commonwealth.

As an unswerving royalist, a native of a county that was

---

[1] 'Then, amidst the hymns and hallelujahs of saints,' etc.

conspicuous for its loyalty, Butler could admit the divine right of kings and allow that the king could do no wrong; but he could not allow that the opposing party could do right, especially after the confiscations and oppressions of which they had been guilty towards the royalists and the episcopalian clergy. Moreover, the Long parliament, which had included many high-minded patriots, had degenerated and dwindled into the miserable, place-loving Rump, a fit object of scorn and contempt.

Some precursors of the form and style of *Hudibras* have been mentioned; but the strange rimes which it contains, and which have helped considerably to keep it in remembrance, must not be passed by. The curious jingles of 'ecclesiastic' and 'a stick,' 'duty' and 'shoe-tie,' 'discourse' and 'whiskers,' and many more, have recalled the poem (in name at least) to many readers to whom much of the historical detail has become obsolete. In this exercise, Butler had a late rival in Calverley, whose metrical skill and delicately sensitive ear would, however, not permit him to employ any uncouth rime that his nimble fancy might suggest—every line must ring true; whereas, in Butler's jog-trot lines, a monstrous rime has the effect of relieving the monotony of the verse without being out of harmony with it.

Samuel Butler, in fine, may be looked upon as a rare but erratic genius with an extraordinary gift of satirical expression, and as a man of great learning, who might have produced a serious poem of merit, had the bent of his mind lain in that direction. Dryden expressed a belief that Butler would have excelled in any other kind of metre; and his powers in serious verse are sufficiently attested by the following extract from *Hudibras*:

> The *Moon* pull'd off her veil of Light,
> That hides her face by day from sight,
> (Mysterious Veil, of brightness made,
> That's both her lustre, and her shade)
> And in the Night as freely shon,
> As if her Rays had been her own:
> For Darkness is the proper Sphere,
> Where all false Glories use t'appear.
> The twinkling *Stars* began to muster,
> And glitter with their borrow'd luster,
> While Sleep the weary'd *World* reliev'd,
> By counterfeiting *Death* reviv'd[1].

---

[1] II, 1, 905—915. The same metaphor is employed by Milton in a magnificent passage addressed to the Deity as the author and source of light, a subject which always appealed strongly to the blind poet:

> Dark with excessive light thy skirts appear
> And dazzle heaven. (*Paradise Lost*, III, 380.)

# CHAPTER III

## POLITICAL AND ECCLESIASTICAL SATIRE

In the period following on the restoration of Charles II, satirical poetry on political subjects took permanent root in England. It is true that there had already been satires, like those of Cleiveland and the cavalier ballad-writers, written on behalf of one faction in the state against its rival, as well as lampoons upon some foreign enemy; but these had been sporadic, and have the appearance of being not so much concerted attacks as outbursts of irritation or grumblings of the governed about their rulers. Now, however, came the beginnings of an organised, continuous depreciation of each party by the other side, with a definite end in view, that is, to exclude rival politicians from power by discrediting them in public opinion. After the king's return, there became perceptible certain features of English life, political, social and literary, which specially favoured a new development of satiric literature. In politics, we have the slow integration of two parties within the constitution. Cavalier and puritan had held mutually irreconcilable views on fundamental questions, and were prepared to proceed to extremities to uphold them. It was otherwise with their successors, who were slow in becoming completely antagonistic, and were then so nearly balanced in resources and so afraid of civil war as to form the habit of toleration in fact, if not in theory. When consistent anglicans and *ci-devant* presbyterians divided between them the Long parliament of Charles II, their differences arose chiefly on matters of practical policy on which the vanquished could afford to await better times. Concerning the position of monarch and church, there was no real dispute. But there were divergences as to what measures of immediate import should be taken by the monarch and as to what extent of conformity was expedient in the church; and the actions of the restoration government were sufficiently coherent to permit of its supporters and opponents coalescing among themselves, and, in the sequel, forming the court and the country parties. A process which, at first, was very gradual, furnished forth the two combatants in a perennial duel.

At the same time, new social conditions came into being with the increased preponderance of London in the national life, and with the new and strictly urban habits which Londoners were forming. Town and country were becoming more differentiated than they had ever been before : and the townsmen, among whom we may include many members of the aristocracy who spent part of the year in London, composed an apt audience for the new kind of literary political warfare. Coffee-house and park gave an atmosphere where satire could flourish, while the increased facility of communication both altered the tastes of the country gentry by bringing them to town and maintained their allegiance to the supremacy of London by allowing the steady transmission of news-letters and pamphlets from the capital to the provinces.

Lastly, the revolution in literary ideals was peculiarly suitable for satire. Here, at least, in invective on men and things, there was ample scope for a reasoned perspicuous line, dealing with life as it was known, and for the strongly knit couplet, which simulated wit, even when not possessing it, and which was eminently well adapted for sharp, hard practicalities.

It was in the years 1666—7, when the unpopularity of Clarendon was at its height, and when the disasters of the Dutch war brought into strong relief the faults and failures of the men in power, that Sir John Denham began the series of Caroline political satires. However little merit his four *Instructions to a Painter*, dour travesties of Waller's adulation which bore the same name, might possess, they started a fresh genre. Recent events, fact or fable, were narrated in the heroic couplet with malign distortion or biting veracity. It 'made my heart ake to read,' says Pepys of the fourth satire in the series, 'it being too sharp, and so true.' Andrew Marvell, who had begun as a lyric poet, followed in Denham's wake with his *Last Instructions to a Painter* in 1667, the most powerful of these satires, and, from that date until his death in 1678, remained the ablest satirist opposed to the court[1]. *Farther Instructions to a Painter, An Historical Poem, Advice to a Painter,* and the dialogue *Britannia and Raleigh* were all from his pen ; and, before he died, imitators, such as the author of the grimly-humorous *Dream of the Cabal,* were springing up.

The common characteristic of these compositions was their journalistic nature. They were riming pamphlets professing to

[1] For a general account of Marvell's literary work see *ante*, vol. vii, pp. 180 ff.

give actual events and court secrets, in the form either of rambling narratives or of descriptions of persons taken *seriatim*. For them, art is a subordinate factor, and their rough couplets show very little of it. The ways of Charles II's court and government gave them only too much opportunity for scurrilous obscenity. Vigour, wit and humour in a high degree are to be found in them. Marvell had a real knowledge of affairs and statesmanlike insight. Not personal resentment, but a strong conviction of the evils of the day urged him on to his vituperative satire, and he stabs home with a scientific precision. In satires of this class, however, moral indignation, although it is not absent, frequently makes but a poor show, owing to the abundance of the very filth which is brought forward as justification for it. Of their contemporary influence, we can hardly doubt. So they reached their aim, which was political and not at all poetic.

A new turn was given to Charles II's reign and to English history by the panic of the Popish plot in 1678—9. The clumsy inventions spun from the prolific imagination of Oates succeeded in giving the final impulse to the completion of the inchoate parties. A definite political creed, anti-Romanism, and a definite political aim, the exclusion of the duke of York, were furnished to the country party, while passive obedience and the supremacy of the anglican church were the tenets of their opponents ; and from this contest emerge the historic whig and tory. Under these conditions of popular passion and national division, political satire could come fully into its own.

The first poet who entered the lists was John Oldham, and his special genius, the circumstances of his life and the tendencies of the day, all conspired to make him a true pioneer. In place of the journalistic writings of Marvell and his like, half platform-oratory, half 'leading-articles, he produced a satire, the merit and scope of which were of a purely literary kind. He wrote satire for satire's sake :

> Satyr's my only province and delight
> For whose dear sake alone I've vow'd to write:
> For this I seek occasions, court abuse,
> To show my parts and signalize my muse[1].

This was an innovation, but one which it was easier for Oldham to introduce than for his contemporaries. The son of a nonconformist minister, John Oldham, he was born at Shipton-Moyne, near Tetbury in Gloucestershire, on 9 August 1653. His father sub-

---

[1] *Upon a Printer.*

sequently removed to Newton in Wiltshire, from which he was ejected in 1662 ; thenceforward, he remained as a dissenting minister at Wotton-under-edge in the Cotswolds, outliving his poetic son for many years. The latter received his education at Tetbury grammar school, and was next sent to Oxford, to St Edmund's hall, in 1670. He obtained his bachelor's degree in May 1674, and then left the university to reside for about a year with his father. Neither his religious opinions at this time, we may presume, nor the independence of character which often flashes out in his verse, would incline him to take orders, with a view to a chaplaincy in some noble household and a country living as a sequel. He was evidently without means. So we find him undertaking the post of usher in Whitgift's school at Croydon until 1678, and following this by the more tolerable occupation of a private tutor, first to the grandsons of a judge, Sir Edward Thurland, and, in 1681, to the son of Sir William Hickes. This last employment brought him to the neighbourhood of London and made him acquainted with the literary men of the day, to whom his poems were already known. Rochester and one or two others had, indeed, apparently visited the young pedagogue at Croydon on the strength of his compositions then circulating in manuscript, but nothing had come of the interview. Now, however, the new earl of Kingston rescued Oldham from his scholastic thraldom, became his patron and, on occasion, his host, and offered him, we are told, the unwelcome position of his chaplain. Be this as it may, we can well imagine that the pert, satiric face which looks out of Oldham's portrait belonged to an amusing companion. The profession of a man of letters, nevertheless, in the life of the seventeenth century, could not easily be carried on except under conditions of dependence if not of servility, and Oldham's eagerness to escape from compliance to them is shown by his resolve to take up medicine for a livelihood, and by the year's study which he devoted to it. But his health was breaking down ; he is said to have been consumptive ; on 9 December 1683, he fell a victim to the smallpox at Kingston's seat, Holme-Pierrepoint near Nottingham.

This schoolmaster's life must have inclined a naturally haughty, sardonic temperament in the direction of satire. He may, also, have accustomed himself to make the most of a natural proneness to indignation, in order the more to impress his pupils. And the aloofness of his life from the capital, combined with the classical studies necessary for his occupation, was a fit environment for the first author of generalising satires, where incidental railing gives place to artistic composition without too constant a reference to immediate facts.

He does not seem, however, to have discovered his *métier* at once, for his earliest dated poem, *The Dream*, written in March 1677, was amatory, in a luscious, adolescent strain. This was composed in the heroic couplet, but he was already under the spell of Cowley and, with his usual *vis animi*, was putting all his energy into Cowleyan Pindaric odes. He was not without qualifications for the task, being both fecund in ideas and forcible in their expression. He also brought out the defects of the metre: his stanzas do not run easily; the difficulty of preserving a measure of grace in a poetical form which aspired to continual hyperbole becomes painfully obvious ; and, comparing him with Cowley, we may say that his trumpet has a brassier sound. His vice of turgidity and his often successful, but invariable, method of heaping effect on effect to reach one great towering climax, were bred under Cowley's influence. Among these exercises in a tuneless metre, some three or four stand out. The early *Dithyrambic, a Drunkard's speech in a Masque,* can claim dramatic fitness for its monotonous extravagance and has a fine rhetorical close with its reference to

> the Tomb,
> Nature's convenient dark Retiring-Room.

The ode *Upon the Works of Ben Jonson* contains just criticism, if it falls far short of the sublime, which is needlessly attempted. The *Satyr against Vertue,* however, provides a link with its author's more enduring work. Here, the Pindarique hyperbole is first used for a tirade against virtue and then to express a grandiose, if rather external, conception of vice.

> 'Tis I the bold Columbus, only I,
> Who must new Worlds in vice descry,
> And fix the pillars of unpassable iniquity.

This heavyhanded irony was taken for earnest by some of its readers, and Oldham thought it best to write later a similar high-flown recantation. But the finest of his works in this style is the ode *To the Memory of Mr Charles Morwent,* an intimate friend whose death, in 1675, probably long preceded the finished poem. In this panegyric, there is less bombast than appears in the others, and its great length makes a single movement to a climax impossible. There are happy phrases, like 'the pale Cheeks do penance in their white,' and the numerous images employed become the subject well. On the other hand, Morwent's virtues

are so universal and unlimited as to lack verisimilitude ; but this
is a fault of the Pindaric style, and not personal to Oldham.

It was in 1678 that Oldham realised his powers—by accident,
may be—in *A Satyr upon a Woman, who by her Falshood and
Scorn was the Death of my Friend.* Here, he makes use of the
heroic couplet, which was his really effective medium, to express
the uttermost of hatred. His voice seems to rise to a hoarse
scream. Railing and cursing achieve a kind of attractiveness by
reaching the acme of their power, although, perhaps, a few words
would have spoken more of the heart. In amplitude and magnificence, however, *A Satyr upon a Woman* was outdone in the
next year by his chief work, the four *Satyrs upon the Jesuits.*
The first of them was printed without Oldham's consent, in 1679 ;
and he published the whole series, with a few other poems, in
1681. They were without a dedication, a strong evidence of their
author's natural haughtiness in that age of fulsome flattery.

There does not seem to be any reason to doubt Oldham's
sincerity in his masterpiece. His nonconformist upbringing and
popular surroundings make it quite natural that he should have
shared in the frenzied panic of the Popish plot ; while his usual
extravagance of expression and of resentment, if they make us
discount his meaning, also guarantee the reality of his sentiments.
But there is also a definite artistic bias running through the poems.
Oldham enjoyed satire by his own confession, and he was a schoolmaster learned in the classics. The *Prologue* is after Persius ; the
first satire, *Garnet's Ghost,* owes its inception to the prologue by
Sylla's ghost in Ben Jonson's *Catiline* ; the third, *Loyola's Will,*
derives its 'design' from Buchanan's *Franciscanus*; the idea of the
fourth, *St Ignatius his Image,* is drawn from Horace. All these
varied debts, however, which Oldham himself owns, are thrown
into the shade by the dominating influence of Juvenal. We do
not merely find imitation of isolated passages, or even of rhetorical
artifices, like the abrupt opening of most of the satires or the
frequent employment of the climax. What is of the highest
importance is the generalising style and the habit of declamatory
highstrained invective—the love of massed and unrelieved gloom
for the sake of artistic effect. The lists of current misdeeds, the contemporary criticism or misrepresentation common in the satirist's
English predecessors, give place to fanciful general scenes, where
he tries to represent an imaginary ecstasy of wickedness.

The four satires have little intricacy of design. In the first, the
ghost of Garnet, the Jesuit instigator of the Gunpowder plot,
addresses a kind of diabolic homily to the Jesuits in conclave after

Sir Edmund Berry Godfrey's murder.  The second merely inveighs against the Society in the author's own person.  In the third, the dying Loyola gives his disciples a rule of concentrated villainy. In the fourth, his image relates the frauds supposed to be worked in Roman Catholic worship.  When we come to examine the poetic qualities of these satires in detail, we are at once struck by the harshness of the verse.  This shows itself not so much in the monotonous energy of the rhythm, although it would seem that it was this which moved contemporary criticism most, as in the extreme uncouthness of the rimes.  Oldham could rime 'enroll'd,' 'rul'd' and 'spoil'd,' together; and this is not an exception, but an instance of his regular practice.  In fact, he was unaware of the cacophony, and, when his verse was criticised, took occasion to show that he could write smoothly by the translation of two Greek pastorals, *Bion* and *The Lamentation for Adonis*.  But, in these pieces, his bad rimes recur with little less frequency, and the lack of range in his melody is brought out the more by the comparison of the refrain in *Bion*, apparently due to Rochester[1]—

> Come, all ye Muses, come, adorn the Shepherd's hearse
> With never-fading garlands, never-dying verse—

with Oldham's own refrain in *Adonis*:

> I mourn Adonis, the sad Loves bemoan,
> The comely fair Adonis dead and gone.

To proceed from questions of technique to matter, a serious defect of these satires is their continual exaggeration.  The hyperbole of Pindarics is transferred to them, and, their purpose being comminatory, the result is an atmosphere of overcharged gloom.  He accumulates horror on horror with a sole view to melodrama.  The sense of irony or ordinary humour and any faculty for dexterous mockery seem banished from his writings.  Even the satire on his peccant printer is in the grandiose style, and his stage cannon are fired off for the event.  By consequence, dramatic fitness is entirely absent from his original satires.  He places his objurgations in Jesuit mouths, making an extraordinary mixture of triumphant, conscious wickedness and bigotry.  The dying Loyola laments that 'mighty Julian mist his aims,' and that thus the Bible remained undestroyed, and declares Iscariot 'Th' example of our great Society.'  Garnet's ghost gloats over the Gunpowder plot as a rival to 'Hell's most proud exploit,' and exhorts his successors to

> have only will
> Like Fiends and me to covet and act ill.

Yet these professed villains are somehow occupied in fighting

---

[1] See Oldham's advertisement to *Poems and Translations*, edition of 1686.

'heretics' and in saving the church. The muddle is inextricable, and the sentiments are worthy of Hieronimo.

To Oldham's lack of dramatic instinct must be attributed his want of variety. His only ways of creating an effect were to lead up to a climax, to pile up the agony. In their use, indeed, he was a master. Incredible blood and thunder fill the scene ; but they, at least, make a real clamour and smell raw. There is an expansive energy and exaltation in such a passage as that on Charles IX and Bartholomew's day :

> He scorn'd like common murderers to deal
> By parcels and piecemeal; he scorn'd retail
> I' th' trade of Death: whole myriads dy'd by th' great,
> Soon as one single life; so quick their fate,
> Their very pray'rs and wishes came too late.

These lines testify to Oldham's power of finding repeatedly a vivid, impressive phrase, not merely by a verbal ingenuity, but largely through a keen realisation of the ideas which entered his narrow range of thought. He loves to obtain his effects by the jarring juxtaposition of incompatibles, in true rhetorical Latin taste. There is a fierce contempt in his 'purple rag of Majesty,' and a curious sinister dread in the reference to virtue 'with her grim, holy face.' But we should search in vain for the epigrammatic wisdom of Juvenal in his shortlived disciple. Oldham did not care enough for truth, for one thing, nor, perhaps, was his fiery temperament sufficiently philosophic. It was not through sage reflection, not through fancy or delicacy, that he gained his reputation, but by means of a savage vigour and intensity of passion which could make even his melodramatic creations live. Further, a real artistic feeling, not borrowed from his master Juvenal, is shown in the internal coherence of each satire and in the omission of trivialities, for which his tendency to generalisation was, in part, responsible. Besides, although, no doubt, he looked on the plot panic as a splendid opportunity for his peculiar talent, there is a real sincerity and magnanimity in his attitude, which disdains petty scandal and personal abuse. In this way, in his satires, he avoids both the mouthing scurrility of Marston, who had earlier attempted a satiric indignation, and, also, to an unusual degree, the characteristic obscenity of the restoration era.

The remaining works of Oldham consist of some original poems, some translations and two prose pieces. The last have little interest. One, *The Character of an Ugly Old Priest*, consists of dreary abuse of some unknown parson ; it belongs to a species of writing which had some *vogue* at the time, and, perhaps, aped, in prose, Butler's and Cleveland's fanciful railing; but it must be pronounced a failure. The other, *A Sunday-Thought in Sickness*, is an unimpressive religious composition, of which the most striking passage seems influenced by the final speech in Marlowe's *Faustus*. Nevertheless, it would not be difficult to believe that the soliloquy does, in fact, represent a personal experience; it is sufficiently natural and matter-of-fact. We know from one of his private letters that, at one time, he had led a rakish life, but that 'experience and thinking' had made him 'quit that humour.' As to his verse, only one lyric possesses any attractiveness, *The Careless Good Fellow*, a really jovial toper's song, which raises the suspicion that some other ballads ought to be ascribed to its author among the mass of contemporary anonymous work. *A Satyr concerning Poetry*, to which Spenser's ghost furnishes a clumsy *mise-en-scène*, gives a melancholy description of the lot of professional poets under Charles II; but it lacks the spirit of the attacks on the Jesuits and owes its interest to its account of Butler's latter days. Far more important is *A Satyr address'd to a Friend that is about to leave the University*, for it is the most mature of Oldham's poems and that which most reflects the man himself. He passes the possible professions of a scholar in review. There is schoolmastering—'there beat Greek and Latin for your life'—but, in brief, it is an underpaid drudgery. Then, a chaplaincy is a slavery of the most humiliating kind: 'Sir Crape' is an upper-servant who has been educated, and who must buy the benefice given him for 'seven years' thrall' by marrying the superannuated waiting-maid. Freedom at any price is to be preferred; but Oldham's aspiration, as a poet, at least, is a 'small estate,' where, in retirement, he could 'enjoy a few choice books and fewer friends.'

The translations have considerable merit. They are by no means servile, and bear obvious traces of the author's own life. *The Passion of Byblis* from Ovid has the coarse vigour of his early work. *The Thirteenth Satyr of Juvenal* is noteworthy from the characteristic way in which the note is forced. The lighter portions of the original are abbreviated, the gloomy are expanded. The guilty horrors of the sinner, impressive in the Latin, are tricked out with details of vulgar fancy and become incredible. Into Boileau's *Satire touching Nobility* are interpolated the significant and creditable lines :

> Do you apply your interest aright
> Not to oppress the poor with wrongful might?

Neither these versions nor others resembling them can be called inadequate ; but their chief importance lies in the fact that, in part, they are adaptations only. The scene is transferred to London wherever possible. Pordage takes the place of Codrus in Juvenal's *Third Satire* ; the Popish plot and its political sequels are inserted into Horace's famous description of the bore. As in so much else, so in this fashion, deliberately adopted by Oldham[1], he was the forerunner of greater men. Pope was to bring the adaptation of classic satires to contemporary circumstances to its perfection in England. And the whole department of generalising satire, in which the persons attacked, if they are real at all, are of secondary interest, and where the actual course of events and historic fact are thrust aside for the purpose of artistic unity and unadulterated gloom, finds its first worthy exponent in Oldham. Dryden, indeed, who nobly celebrated his young rival's genius, maintained his own independence, and, by transforming the narrative satire of Marvell, created a separate stream of poetry. But, if we tell over the small forgotten satires of the later seventeenth century, we find the lesser poet's influence extending over a considerable number of them. It is true that they were a ragged train.

Yet, poor stuff as these compositions might be, they exercised an undoubted influence on the events they illustrate. They were written chiefly, it would seem, for the coffee-house haunter. One Julian, a man of infamous reputation and himself a libeller, would make a stealthy round of those establishments and distribute the surreptitious sheets ; the more dangerous libels could only be dropped in the streets by porters, to be taken up by chance passers-by. Not merely was the public made intensely eager for pamphlets and squibs of all kinds in the electric political atmosphere of the last twenty years of the seventeenth century ; but, in 1679, the Licensing act, under which anti-governmental publications were restrained, expired for a time. Although a decision of the judges soon gave the crown as complete powers of suppressing unwelcome books and pamphlets as before, the previous licensing fell into disuse, and the limitation of the number

---

[1] Cf. his advertisement to *Poems and Translations* (ed. 1686) : 'This [a justification for a new translation of Horace] I soon imagined was to be effected by putting Horace into a more modern dress than hitherto he has appeared in ; that is, by making him speak as if he were living and writing now. I therefore resolved to alter the scene from Rome to London, and to make use of English names of men, places and customs, where the parallel would decently permit, which I conceived would give a kind of new air to the poem, and render it more agreeable to the relish of the present age.'

of master-printers lapsed. The consequences of even a partial unmuzzling of the press were almost immediately seen in a swarm of libels, of which a vigorous complaint was made by Mr Justice Jones in 1679 : 'There was never any Age, I think, more licentious than this, in aspersing Governors, scattering of Libels, and scandalous Speeches against those that are in authority[1].' And the judge is confirmed by a ballad, *The Licentiousness of the Times*, in the same year :

> Now each man writes what seems good in his eyes,
> And tells in bald rhymes his inventions and lies.

The Licensing act was renewed in 1685, but, apparently, without much effect. The messenger of the press could have his eyes 'dazzled,' *i.e.* could be bribed not to inform the higher authorities of a seditious publication, and it was easy to disperse copies. Thus, when the act expired for good and all, in 1695, little real change was made in the divulgation of the scandalous tracts with which we are concerned.

The output of popular satire was more vitally affected by changes in public feeling. After a prelude of compositions on the Popish plot, poems and ballads come thick and fast during the agitation for and against the Exclusion bill, which was to deprive James, duke of York, of the succession and bring in 'king Monmouth.' A series of triumphant tory productions exult over Shaftesbury and the other whig leaders in the time of the Rye-house plot and of the government's campaign against corporations. There succeeds a lull, although Monmouth's rebellion, in 1685, was the occasion of a renewed outburst ; but the second period of satiric pamphlets dates from the beginning of James II's unpopularity about the year 1687, and reaches its fever-heat in the years of revolution, after which a subsidence of satiric activity begins, until a less perfervid time draws near with the peace of Ryswick.

The satires which drew their inspiration, such as it was, from Dryden, Oldham and Marvell, were, for the most part, written in the heroic couplet, although a Hudibrastic metre appears now and again, and there are some semi-lyric exceptions hard to classify. By their nature, they were almost all published anonymously, and the veil was seldom raised later, even when the bulk of them were reprinted in such collections as the various volumes entitled *Poems*

---

[1] *The Lord Chief Justice Scroggs his Speech in the King's Bench* . . . 1679. *Occasion'd by the many Libellous Pamphlets which are publisht against Law, to the scandal of the Government, and Publick Justice*, p. 7. (Sir Thomas Jones and one or two other judges made remarks after the speech of the Chief Justice.)

*on Affairs of State.* When an author's name was affixed by the transcribers, it was, very possibly, apocryphal. Some poems written subsequently to Marvell's death were put down to him, and, on principle, Rochester was debited with the most obscene. Then, certain names are furnished by the publishers of *Poems on Affairs of State* on the title-pages of that collection. We are told that the duke of Buckingham, lord Buckhurst (later, earl of Dorset), Sir Fleetwood Sheppard, Sprat, Drake, Gould, Brady and Shadwell were responsible for some of the contents ; but the attribution of the individual pieces is rarely given ; nor do the authors' names, of inferior importance as they mostly are, give many clues in the way of style. In fact, the greater number of the regular satires might be ascribed to two authors—distinguishable from each other as writing, the one reasonably well, and the other very badly. Dryden is imitated almost invariably in the metre, Oldham frequently, and Marvell not seldom in the contents, and there is little else left by which to judge. A single type is dominant.

A better classification than that by authors is provided in these poems by their method of treatment and their themes. There were employed in them a restricted number of hackneyed forms which were often fixed by the more important poets. Cleiveland had invented the railing character of a political opponent. Denham and Marvell had brought in the *vogue* of a satiric rimed chronicle, and to Marvell is due the variation of a visionary dialogue. Oldham revived the related ghostly monologue, the satiric last will[1], and direct general invective. Dryden was the author oᴀ a kind of epic, derived from the satiric chronicle, but no longer dependent on the news of the day, and presenting its invective in the form of characters drawn with consummate ability. By the imitators of these writers, the dominant forms of satire enumerated were adopted in a more or less slavish manner together with other genres, and it is not difficult to select examples from the best defined groups.

There were written during the period over twenty *Advices to a Painter* or poems with kindred themes. For instance, one *New Advice*, written in 1679, contains a grim attack on the whigs and nonconformists after archbishop Sharp's murder. It has no mean dramatic power, and is in strong contrast to the historic and argumentative *Good Old Cause Revived* of a few monthls later. Nor did the trick tire till the close of the century. A nobler form, that of Biblical narrative, also had its misusers. Pordage, a by-word for Grub-street poverty, wrote the tame, but not abusive,

---

[1] Cf. vol. III, pp. 482 ff.

*Azaria and Hushai*, in 1682, while Settle, in his *Absalom Senior*, a mere echo of Dryden, among much nonsense has, here and there, good lines, such as:

> To what strange rage is Superstition driven,
> That Man can outdo Hell to fight for Heaven.

Brady produced an obscene *Giant's War* about the same time, and the change to a classical subject is also seen in *Tarquin and Tullia*, a bitter Jacobite attack on William III and his queen.

A most effective weapon for decrying opponents was the character, which, indeed, formed an essential part of the Biblical narrative. One of the wittiest was written by the duke of Buckingham, in his *Advice to a Painter*, against his rival Arlington; one of the loftiest is *Shaftesbury's Farewell*, a kind of inimical epitaph on the whig leader's death in Holland ('What! A republic air, and yet so quick a grave?'). Shadwell has the disgrace of unsurpassed virulence in his *Medal of John Bayes* (1682), which drew upon him a heavy punishment from the quondam friend whom he lampooned. The most cutting, perhaps, was the sham *Panegyric on King William* by the hon. J. H[oward?]. Nor should *The Man of no Honour*, where James II's subservient courtiers are assailed, be forgotten. An argumentative style is to be discerned in the description of the views of *The Impartial Trimmer*, which, in fact, is a whig manifesto of 1682, and where real knowledge and a weighty personality seem to transpire. Thus, the gap is bridged to the unadulterated argument which is to be found in the earlier tory *Poem on the Right of Succession* or in Pordage's spiritless attack on persecution, *The Medal Revers'd* (1682).

More imaginative in conception are the visions and ghosts; *Hodge's Vision* (1679) is a diatribe on the court; *The Battle Royal* (1687) is a nonconformist burlesque of papist and parson. *The Waking Vision* (1681) contains a dialogue in Oldham's undramatic manner between Shaftesbury and Monmouth. A loquacious phantom appears in most of the type. Thus, in *Sir Edmundbury Godfrey's Ghost*, written about 1679, by some whig, whose gift of sardonic wit makes us curious to know his name, the ghost is made to appear to Charles II. Humour, on the other hand, is the special talent of the tory who wrote *Tom Thynne's Ghost* in Hudibrastic metre (1682). Hell, at any rate, is under a despot, and the dead whigs have no scope for their energies,

> For none his boundless power questions,
> Or makes undutiful suggestions.

Charles II himself was called on for ghostly comment after his death. The angry tory who wrote *Caesar's Ghost* (*c.* 1637) begins quite well and impressively with the rise of the royal shade from the tomb, but tails off into the usual scurrilities, this time against the officers of James II's army at Hounslow heath. *The Ghost of King Charles II* (? *c.* 1692) also gives advice, written, possibly, by some disgusted whig, to 'the pensive prince, not given to replies.' William III.

From the ghost to the last will is a natural transition, but, whereas the ghost is almost always tragic, and with good reason, too, according to the authors, the will is sprightly and squiblike, if rather hideous, in its fun. The best, perhaps, is the attack on Shaftesbury in exile, *The Last Will and Testament of Anthony K. of Poland* (1682). The legacies, some of which are heartlessly enough invented, satirise the legatees as well as the great whig leader himself, and there is no denying the stinging wit of the whole.

Next to these sham dramatic poems we may notice the dialogues, of which Marvell's *Dialogue between two Horses* (1675) is justly celebrated. The witty humour of the piece blends well with an only too serious political indictment of Charles and his brother, and we may excuse the doggerel lilting metre as an echo of the clumsy canter of his brass and marble horses. Rochester, too, wrote a short dialogue, *The Dispute*, on the duke of York's conversion to Catholicism, which contains his accustomed rankling sting. Curiously enough, there is a satire or two, consisting of alternate recriminations between the duchess of Portsmouth and Nell Gwynn (1682), conducted much to the advantage of the English and 'protestant' mistress : but, in this species, the palm should be assigned to the octosyllabic *Dialogue* between James II and his Italian queen, which is replete with vulgar humour.

Scarcely to be distinguished from the dialogues is the ill-defined class of squibs. Their metres are varied. Some are lyric in character and form a link between compositions intended for reading and ballads intended for singing : some are in octo-syllabic lines of a Hudibrastic kind. Indeed, although they go naturally together, it is hard to give a reason for thus grouping them ; except that invective and indignation are markedly sub-ordinate in them to the wish to ridicule and scoff. 'Eminent hands,' as the booksellers would have said, were engaged in their production. Marvell made a striking success of the spirited ballad quatrains of his *Poem on the Statue in Stocks-market* (1672). Each stanza contains a separate conceit on the offering of a wealthy

Londoner to Charles II, a statue of Sobieski (of all people) being altered for the purpose to suit Charles's features. As usual with Marvell, the chief political grievances of the day are catalogued, but the prevailing tone of the indictment is one of witty pleasantry. Two of Rochester's poems also may come under this heading, *The History of Insipids* (1676), which is the least revolting among the effusions said to have led to his banishment from court. Its cold and effective malice was, at least, dangerous enough to cause some royal displeasure. Later, he displayed the same mordant wit against the whigs in the epigrammatic *Commons' Petition to the King* (1679). Still better as a work of art, and not so envenomed in substance, is the lampoon *On the Young States- men* (1680), otherwise, the 'Chits,' who were Charles II's chief advisers at the close of his reign. If not by Dryden, as the publishers claimed, the polish of this squib seems to indicate Rochester grown ripe. Two octosyllabic pieces also demand notice, one, *On the Duchess of Portsmouth's Picture* (1682), for its wrath- ful pungency, the other, a parody of *King James's Declaration* (1692), by Sir Fleetwood Sheppard, for its tolerant victorious humour. Lastly comes a group of poems in three-lined single-rimed stanzas. The metre was peculiarly suitable for sententious argument or a string of accusations, and some excellent talent went to their production. Instances of their effective employment may be seen in *The Melancholy Complaint of Dr Titus Oates*, and in *The Parliament dissolved at Oxford* (1681), a pointed, if unmetrical, production.

Along with literary satires, attempts, in this nature, of the dramatist Thomas Otway may be ranked. Their form is somewhat unusual, and, in consequence, they do not easily fall into any of the groups distinguished above. The earlier is a Pindaric ode, *The Poet's Complaint to his Muse*, written when, in 1679, the duke of York was banished, in consequence of the agitation about the Popish plot. Very long, hyperbolical, straggling and unmelodious, the *Complaint* is not an attractive piece of writing; but the name of its author and the furious attack on the potent 'Libell,' who, of course, is a whig satirist only, lend it interest. Otway's later satiric effort, the comic scenes in *Venice Preserved* (1682), where senator Antonio represents Shaftesbury, only shows to what depths of ineptitude he could descend[1]; of the power to caricature he seems devoid.

Otway, in his *Complaint*, mentions the kinds of poetry that

[1] See chap. VII, *post*.

'Libell' was proficient in, 'Painter's Advices, Letanies, Ballads. The first of these represent the would-be literary work intended for reading. The other two species, which had been, earlier, employed in mockery of the ruling puritans, were the property of the ballad-monger, and were hawked about the country to be chanted at street-corners and in taverns. Their manner is, therefore, far more popular than that of the semi-literary satires. In scurrility, indeed, there is little to choose between them. If anything, the ballads have a poorer vocabulary, and hurl a few customary epithets from Billingsgate at their opponents with a smaller amount of detailed obscenity than opportunities of the heroic couplet allow. But their strokes of criticism are mainly more coarsely done and not so strongly bitten in: their humour is more rollicking and clownish; their occasional argumentation more rough and ready; and, in it, 'the ruin of trade,' due, of course, to the wicked whigs or tories as the case might be, finds an additional prominence.

Since they were intended for popular recitation and for an immediate effect, it was necessary that they should be readily sung, and this end was attained by fitting them to tunes which were already well known and popular. This was not very difficult to achieve. A certain number of ballad-tunes were old favourites throughout the country; and the more successful operas or plays of Charles II's reign frequently left behind them some air or other which caught the general fancy and was sung everywhere. Both these sources were put under contribution by ballad-makers, and it was only rarely that a new tune had to be expressly composed for a ballad, and, being composed, was admitted into the singer's *répertoire*. The consequence was that a flavour of parody pervaded almost all the political ballads of the day. It was tempting to adopt words and phrases together with the tune; and there resulted, for instance, a whimsical contrast between 'Hail to the knight of the post,' directed against Titus Oates, and 'Hail to the myrtle shades' which began the original ballad.

Among ballad-tunes, the litany stands in the front rank. With its three riming lines and short refrain, it was, in fact, the most successful variation of the three-lined satiric verse. Its name was taken from its original refrain 'Which nobody can deny,' which was often superseded, especially when the attack was most bitter, by the litany-prayers *Libera nos, Domine, Quaesumus te, Domine,* or their English equivalents. A hortatory, and less implacable, satire, which came into *vogue* in the later days of Charles, altered the refrain again to 'This is the Time.' They were mainly, however, sung to the one tune, although *The Cavallilly Man,* a cavalier air, was occasionally used, when the lilt of the three lines and their length were suitable. The usual type may be seen by one stanza of the tory *Loyal Subject's Litany* (1680):

> From the Dark-Lanthorn Plot, and the Green-Ribbon Club;
> From brewing sedition in a sanctified Tub;
> From reforming a Prince by the model of Job,
> > *Libera nos, Domine!*

The other ballad-tunes may be conveniently divided into old and new. Of the first class, two were much more popular than their congeners. *Packington's Pound* was a lilting tune, fitted for a scheme of words not unlike parts of *The Ingoldsby Legends,* and a ready vehicle for broad and dashing fun. Its *vogue* continued unabated till the reign of queen Anne, and some of the best ballad-satires were written in it, the more easily as it admitted some small variations of structure in the verse. Almost equal to *Packington's Pound* in general favour was *Hey, boys, up go we!* or *Forty-one.* This accompanied an eight-lined stanza of vigorous movement, octosyllabic and hexasyllabic lines being alternated. The eighth line was usually the refrain, such as 'Hey, boys, up go we!' or 'The clean contrary way,' or some special one for the occasion; but it might remain undistinguished from the rest of the verse. Other old tunes only need a mention; there were used, for example, *Chevy Chase, Sir Eglamore, Eighty-eight, Cock Lawrel, Ohone, ohone, Fortune, my foe, The Jolly Beggars, I'll tell thee, Dick* and *Phillida flouts me,* all of which date from before the commonwealth.

Tom D'Urfey appears to have been the most popular ballad-composer under the restoration. Tunes of his, like *Sawney will ne'er be my love again, Now the fight's done, Hark, the thund'ring cannons roar* and *Burton Hall,* were at once made part of the ballad-monger's stock-in-trade, along with other competitors, such as *Digby's Farewell, Russell's Farewell, How unhappy is Phyllis in love, Lay by your pleading,* and a tory political tune, *Now ye Tories that glory.* All these, however, are outdone in importance by Purcell's *Lilliburlero,* which conferred an instant and extraordinary success on Thomas lord Wharton's doggerel rimes, and was, of course, employed for still poorer effusions afterwards. Here, we reach the high-water mark of the ballad's effectiveness, and, fortunately, know to whom both music and words are due[1].

---

[1] Chappell, W., *Old English Popular Music,* ed. Wooldridge, 1893, vol. II, p. 59, and Macaulay, *Hist. of England* (5th ed.), vol. II, p. 428.

With regard to most ballads, however, we are left in the dark
as to their authorship. Who was the reasoning tory humourist
who wrote the first two parts of *A Narrative of the Popish Plot*
(1679—80), or the 'lady of quality' who continued his work ? What
whig wrote the wrathful *Tories Confession* (1682), the disgusted
*Satyr on Old Rowley* (1680—1), or the scornful *Lamentable Lory*
(1684 ?) (against Laurence Hyde), or the drily humorous *Sir T.
Jenner's Speech to his Wife and Children* (1688—9)? *Nocte
premuntur.* And along with the writers of these are forgotten
their tory antagonists, the authors of the gay invective of *A New
Presbyterian Ballad* (1681), or the fiery *Dagon's Fall* (1682)
against Shaftesbury, the exulting *Tories' Triumph* (1685) or the
witty lampoon on bishop Burnet, *The Brawny Bishop's Complaint*
(*c.* 1698). Yet the names of the ballad-makers, even when known,
are rather disappointing. It was Charles Blount, the deist, who is
responsible for the clever and haughty *Sale of Esau's Birthright*
on the Buckingham election of 1679. William Wharton, a son of
Philip, fourth lord Wharton, although reputed dull, was the author
of *A New Song of the Times* (1683), one of the most brilliant of
whig squibs. Walter Pope, a physician and astronomer, wrote *The
Catholic Ballad* (1674), which displays genial pleasantry. Another
physician, Archibald Pitcairne, translated and improved the Jacobite
*De Juramento illicito* (1689). The 'protestant joiner,' Stephen
College, perpetrated some yapping pasquinades. And we find
some professionals. There was Thomas Jordan, the city poet, who
shows a fine lyrical feeling in *The Plotting Papists' Litany* (1680),
which stands quite apart in structure from the *Which nobody can
deny* series. His successor as city poet, Matthew Taubman, edited
a volume of tory compositions, of some of which he was presumably
author. Finally, the courtier, song-writer and dramatist, Tom
D'Urfey, composed several tory songs, all of them facile and tune-
ful, and one, *The Trimmer* (*c.* 1690), sardonically witty. D'Urfey
furnishes us with a sidelight on the audience of these ballads, when
he tells how he sang one, in 1682, 'with King Charles at Windsor ;
he holding one part of the paper with me.' On one side or another,
they appealed to all the nation, and their comparative popularity
was the best gauge of public opinion.

But there were good reasons for the anonymity of this political
literature, poems, ballads and tracts. If the censorship had lapsed
or was inefficient, the law of libel gave the government ample
means for punishing the publishers and authors of anything tending
to civil division. and, naturally, while the whigs had most present

reason to fear, the tories did not forget the possibility of a turn of the wheel. The last four years of Charles II saw a number of prosecutions of booksellers like Nathaniel Thompson, Richard Janeway, Benjamin Harris and others, and, although these cases do not seem to have been very efficient deterrents, they tended to make anonymity advisable as an obvious and easy precaution.

Meanwhile, a straggling and feebler race of prose satires existed under the shadow of the poems and ballads. Its comparatively scanty numbers and its weakly condition were, may be, due to the fact that prose satire could not be disentangled without difficulty from sober argument. The seventeenth century pamphleteer kept no terms with his political or ecclesiastical adversaries. His reasoning is interlarded with invective, and, if possible, with ridicule. Yet the serious content of his tract may remain obvious, and a few traits of satire are not sufficient to change its classification. In tracing the course of pure satire, therefore, we are left mostly to a series of secondrate pamphlets, the authors of which, it would seem, were distrustful of their argumentative powers and unable to employ the more popular device of rime.

One amphibious contribution, *The Rehearsal Transpros'd* (1672—3), of Andrew Marvell, deserves mention on its satiric aspect. Though that book belongs essentially to the region of serious political controversy, its author's design of discrediting his opponent by ridicule and contumely is too apparent throughout for it to be excluded from satire. As such, it possesses undeniable merits. Marvell understood the difficult art of bantering the enemy. He rakes up Parker's past history, sometimes with a subdued fun—as when he says that his victim, in his puritan youth, was wont to put more graves[1] in his porridge than the other fasting 'Grewellers'—sometimes with a more strident invective. He can rise to a fine indignation when he describes Parker's ingratitude to Milton. And there is a shrewdness in his humour which brings over the reader to his side. Yet, with all this, the wit of his book is the elder cavilling wit of the chop-logic kind. It is a succession of quips, which need a genius not possessed by Marvell to keep their savour amidst a later generation. That he had high powers in humorous comedy was shown in his parody of Charles II, *His Majesty's Most Gracious Speech to Both Houses of Parliament* (1675). Its audacious mockery and satiric grasp of a situation

---

[1] 'Graves' or 'greaves,' a fatty substance or juice. The word is clearly connected both with 'gravy' and the composition used in 'graving' a ship.

preserve its fun from evaporating, and exhibit a dramatic faculty we barely expect in the musing poet of *The Garden.*

A favourite form of prose, as of poetic, satire was the narrative. *Cabala* (1663) is a fine example. Here, we are given delightful sham minutes of meetings held by the leading nonconformists in 1662. Sardonic and malicious as it is, it includes burlesque of great talent, as when the 'well-affected' minister is described as one 'who indeed complieth with the public injunction of the Church, yet professeth they are a burthen and a grief to him.' It has a distinct affinity with a much later composition, which, however, is by a whig and directed against the Jacobites, *A true and impartial Narrative of the Dissenters' New Plot* (1690), where the extreme high church view of English history since the reformation is parodied in a brilliant, unscrupulous fashion. The gay, triumphant irony and solemn banter of the piece only set off to better advantage the serious argument which is implied and, at last, earnestly stated.

The *List of goods for sale* is a very slight thing compared to elaborate productions like the above, but it gave opportunity for skilful thrusts and lasted throughout the period. Books were the objects most frequently described, but other items appear, as in the *Advertisement of a Sale of choice Goods,* which dates from about 1670. One lot consists of 'Two rich Royal Camlet Clokes, faced with the Protestant Religion, very little the worse for wearing, valued at 4*l.* to advance half a Crown at each bidding'; which must have amused Charles II, if not his brother.

The dialogue was a favourite form for polemic in the party newspapers. It appears in *A Pleasant Battle between two Lap-dogs of the Utopian Court* (1681), where Nell Gwynn's dog, following the example of his mistress, wins the day against the duchess of Portsmouth's. So, too, there are several characters, like that written by Oldham, but none worth special notice, save that the railing style gives place to a more polished invective. Another form, the parable, was in favour under William III. It was a kind of prolonged fable, where personages of the day appear as various birds and beasts. Thus, in the nonconformist whig *Parable of the Three Jackdaws* (1696), which, perhaps, is identical with that of *The Magpies* by Bradshaw[1], the eagle stands for Charles II, the falcon for Monmouth, archbishop Sancroft is called a 'metropolitical Magpye' and the dissenters are styled 'blackbirds and nightingales.'

Along with these distinct genres there were printed some satires

---

[1] Cf. Dunton, J., *The Life and Errors of J. D.* vol. I, p. 182.

hard to classify, pretended documents, sham letters and so forth. *The Humble Address of the Atheists* (1688) to James II, a whig concoction, is superior to most of its fellows, although it has but scanty merit. Some way below it rank the mock whig *Letter from Amsterdam to a Friend in England* (1678) and *Father La Chaise's Project for the Extirpation of Heretics* (1688), in which the opponents of the two factions decorated what they imagined were the designs of whig or papist with products of a lurid fancy.

When we try to sum up the impression which these satires, in verse or prose, give us, we are struck at once by the low place which they hold as literature. Witty they often are, and with a wit which improves. We change from flouts and jeers and artificial quips to humorous sarcasm, which owes its effect to the contrast of the notions expressed, and to its ruthless precision. But even this is not a very clear advance ; the quip had, perhaps, always been a little popular form, and mere jeering continued to be the staple satire. In fact, except Oldham, who stands apart, these authors did not aim at a literary mark. They were the skirmishers of a political warfare, bandying darts all the more poisoned and deadly because it was known that most would miss their billet. Many of them were hirelings with little interest in the causes they espoused. Their virulence, which seems nowadays hideous, was mainly professional : and the lewd abuse which fills those of them which are in rime was accordingly discounted by the public. It was not a compassionate age. The very danger of the libeller's trade under the censorship made him the more unscrupulous in his choice of means. The tories, as a matter of course, harp continually on Shaftesbury's ulcer, the result of a carriage accident, and the silver tap which drained it was the source of continual nicknames and scoffs : and the whigs are equal sinners. A debauched riot reigns in most of the poetical satires, degraded into an absolute passion for the purulent and the ugly. The writers of them, it would appear, worshipped and loved animalism for its own sake, not the least when they searched through every depth of evil in order to defame their adversaries in the most brutal way possible.

# CHAPTER IV

## THE EARLY QUAKERS

THE rise of the quaker movement in England, which began with the public preaching of George Fox, just about the time of the execution of Charles I, was marked by a surprising outburst of literary activity. The new conception of religion was propagated with extraordinary zeal, and seemed likely at one time not only to change the face of English Christianity but to mould, after the quaker pattern, the religious life of the American colonies. It was essentially the rediscovery, by men and women whose whole training and environment were puritan, of the mystical element which lies close to the heart of Christianity, but which puritanism, with all its strength, had strangely missed. It was a revivified consciousness of God, bringing with it the conviction that the essence of Christ's religion is not to be found in submission to outward authority, whether of church or of Bible, but in a direct experience of God in the soul, and in a life lived in obedience to His will inwardly revealed.

The overmastering enthusiasm kindled by the new experience, due, as Fox and his followers believed, to the immediate inspiration of the Holy Spirit, impelled them to make it known by pen as well as voice. Rude countrymen from the fells of Westmorland, as well as scholars with a university training—even boys like James Parnell, who died a martyr in Colchester castle at the age of nineteen—became prolific writers as well as fervent preachers of mystical experience and practical righteousness. Books and pamphlets, broadsheets and public letters, followed one another in rapid succession, setting forth the new way of life, defending it against its adversaries, and pleading for liberty of conscience and of worship. The organisation by which they contrived to get so large a mass of writing into circulation is not yet fully understood[1]. But the fact that they found readers affords noteworthy evidence of the ferment of men's minds in that day, and of the dominance over their thoughts and lives of the religious interest.

Of all this vast output, there is not much that could possibly, by its intrinsic qualities, find any permanent place in English literature ; its chief interest now is for the curious student of religious history. Nor can it be said to have influenced in any appreciable degree the intellectual outlook of English-speaking peoples, except in so far as it was one of the unnoticed factors in the evolution of religious thought from the hard dogmatism of puritan days to a more liberal and ethical interpretation of Christianity. Most of the early quaker writings, having served their temporary purpose, were read, so far as they continued to be used at all, by the adherents of the new conception of religious life, and by few or none beside.

That is only what would naturally be expected, when we look at the forces that gave birth to these writings and at the con- ditions under which they were poured forth. The purpose of these numerous authors was not intellectual, and not (primarily at least) theological, but experimental. They felt an inward com- pulsion to make known to the world 'what God had done for them,' that they might draw others into the same experience, and into the kind of life to which it led. Moreover, the sense of direct Divine communion and guidance, in which they lived, found expression in terms that too often seemed to deny to the Christian soul any place for the artistic faculty, and even for the develop- ment of the intellectual powers. In striving to set forth what they had discovered, they used, without transcending it, the philosophical dualism of their day, which divided the world of experience into water-tight compartments, the natural and the spiritual, the human and the Divine. The terminology of the seventeenth century, even if it served well enough to set forth the 'religions of authority,' broke down when the quakers tried to use it to expound their 'religion of the Spirit.' The conception of the Divine immanence, in the light of which alone they could have found adequate expression for their experience, had been well-nigh lost. The Power which they felt working within them

---

[1] 'The history of the Quaker Press in London has yet to be written. How did the Society of Friends, who had no connection whatever with the Company of Stationers, manage to pour out so many books in defence of their principles through all this troublous period ? That has yet to be made known.' Arber, Edward, preface to the *Term Catalogues*, 1668—1709 (1903).

was set forth by them in language representing it as wholly transcendental. It was only (they believed) when 'the creature' and all his works were laid in the dust that the light of 'the Creator' could shine undimmed within their souls. In the quakers, as often in other mystics, the ascetic impulse, which a dualistic theory has usually aroused in the minds of those who take religion seriously, tended to aesthetic and intellectual poverty. Hence, it is only a few of these multitudinous works that, rising above the general level, either in thought or style, deserve attention in a history of English literature.

The most characteristic form into which the literary impulse of the mystic has thrown itself, from Augustine's *Confessions* to Madame Guyon, is that of the attempt to 'testify to the workings of God' in his soul. And in no group of mystics has that impulse found more general expression than in the early quakers. Their *Journals*, though written without pretensions to literary art, maintain a high level of sincere and often naïve self-portraiture, and the best of them contain a rich store of material for the student of the 'varieties of religious experience.' But they are seldom unhealthily introspective; they contain moving accounts of persecution and suffering, borne with unflinching fortitude, in obedience to what it was believed the will of God required; of passive resistance to injustice and oppression, recounted often with humour and rarely with bitterness; of adventures by land and sea, in which the guiding hand and providential arm of God are magnified. The quaint individuality of these men and women is seldom lost, though the stamp of their leader Fox is upon them, and their inward experiences clothe themselves in the forms of expression which he first chose, and which soon became current coin in the body which he founded. 'I was moved of the Lord' to go here and there; 'weighty exercise came upon me'; 'my mind was retired to the Lord' in the midst of outward tumult, and so forth.

George Fox's *Journal* is by far the most noteworthy of all these autobiographical efforts, and it is one which, for originality, spontaneity and unconscious power of sincere self-expression, is probably without a rival in religious literature. George Fox was a man of poor education, who read little except his Bible, and who, with pen in hand, to the last could hardly spell or construct a grammatical sentence. Yet, such was the intense reality of his experience, and such the clearness of his inward vision, that his narrative, dictated, for the most part, to willing amanuenses, burns with the flame of truth and often shines with the light of artless beauty[1]. The story of his early struggles with darkness and despair is in striking contrast with another contemporary self-portraiture, that of Bunyan in his *Grace Abounding.* Fox does not tell us of personal terrors of judgment to come; his grief is that temptations are upon him, and he cannot see light. The professors of religion to whom he turns for help are 'empty hollow casks,' in whom he cannot find reality beneath the outward show.

My troubles continued, and I was often under great temptations; I fasted much, and walked abroad in solitary places many days, and often took my Bible, and went and sat in hollow trees and lonesome places till night came on; and frequently, in the night, walked mournfully about by myself; for I was a man of sorrows in the times of the first workings of the Lord in me....

As I had forsaken the priests, so I left the separate preachers also, and those esteemed the most experienced people, for I saw that there was none among them all that could speak to my condition. When all my hopes in them and in all men were gone, so that I had nothing outwardly to help me, nor could I tell what to do; then, O! then I heard a voice which said, 'there is one, even Christ Jesus, that can speak to thy condition'; and when I heard it, my heart did leap for joy. Then the Lord let me see why there was none upon the earth that could speak to my condition, namely, that I might give him all the glory.

After telling of an inward manifestation of the powers of evil 'in the hearts and minds of wicked men,' he goes on:

I cried unto the Lord, saying, ' Why should I be thus, seeing I was never addicted to commit these evils?' and the Lord answered, ' That it was needful I should have a sense of all conditions, how else should I speak to all conditions?' and in this I saw the infinite love of God. I saw also that there was an ocean of darkness and death; but an infinite ocean of light and love, which flowed over the ocean of darkness. In that also I saw the infinite love of God, and I had great openings. . . .

Now the Lord opened to me by his invisible power, 'that every man was enlightened by the divine light of Christ'; and I saw it shine through all; and that they that believed in it came out of condemnation to the light of life, and became the children of it; but they that hated it, and did not believe in it, were condemned by it, though they made a profession of Christ. . . . These things I did not see by the help of man, nor by the letter, though they are written in the letter; but I saw them in the light of the Lord Jesus Christ, and by his immediate Spirit and power, as did the holy men of God, by whom the Holy Scriptures were written. Yet I had no slight esteem of the Holy

---

[1] The *Journal*, as hitherto printed, was edited in grammatical English by Ellwood and other Friends. The original has now been published *verbatim*, with copious notes, by the Cambridge University Press.

Scriptures, but they were very precious to me, for I was in that Spirit by which they were given forth; and what the Lord opened to me, I afterwards found was agreeable to them.

The above passages may serve to illustrate at once the simplicity and directness of Fox's style, and, also, the kernel of the new interpretation of the Christian Gospel which he and his followers proclaimed, and which brought them into constant collision with the ecclesiastics and the Bible-worshippers of their day. The *Journal* is the record, told in the same simple and often racy language, of their conflicts with 'priests' and magistrates and howling mobs; of their valiant efforts to secure justice, and to solace the oppressed in their sufferings; of troubles from the 'ranters' who joined the movement; and of the successful endeavours, made by one who was no mere fanatic, but in whose mind flowed a clear spring of more than worldly wisdom, to build up an organisation which should be proof against the anarchic tendencies of a system that recognised no ultimate authority but the Light Within.

Thomas Ellwood, son of an Oxfordshire squire, was a man of liberal education, who, though he moved in good society, was constrained in early years to throw in his lot with the despised 'people of God.' He was an intimate friend of William Penn and Isaac Penington; and, through the good offices of the latter, he was for some years engaged as reader to the poet Milton in his blindness. It was Ellwood, according to a doubtful tradition[1], who, after reading with delight the manuscript of *Paradise Lost*, suggested to Milton the theme afterwards worked out in *Paradise Regained*.

*The History of the Life of Thomas Ellwood, written by his own hand*, gives a very lively picture of his early life and home surroundings, of inward struggles, of 'passive resistance' to the monstrous tyranny of his father, and of his share in the persecutions to which all his people were subjected. His description of prisons and prison life in the seventeenth century is of great historical value. He writes in a vivid, racy style, the interest of which rarely or never flags. He hits off, in a fashion worthy of Bunyan, the characters alike of friends and persecutors; and (also like Bunyan) he intersperses his prose narrative with verses which he mistakes for poetry.

Take, for illustration, the story of John Ovey, the fellmonger magistrate 'accustomed to ride upon his pack of skins,' 'grey-

[1] Cf. *ante*, vol. VII, p. 120.

headed and elderly,' who had been a preacher among the baptists or independents and had been drawn towards Friends. Ellwood took him to a meeting at Isaac Penington's, which was unexpectedly broken up by a troop of horse[1]:

> We all sate still in our places, except my companion John Ovey, who sate next to me. But he being of a profession that approved Peter's advice to his Lord, to *save himself*, soon took the alarm, and with the nimbleness of a stripling, cutting a caper over the form that stood before him, ran quickly out at a private door (which he had before observed) which led through the parlour into the gardens, and from thence into an orchard; where he hid himself in a place so obscure, and withal so convenient for his intelligence by observation of what passed, that no one of the family could scarce have found a likelier.

Several of the party are hurried away four miles to a magistrate, but are released:

> Back then we went to Isaac Penington's. But when we came thither, O the work we had with poor John Ovey! He was so dejected in mind, so covered with shame and confusion of face for his cowardliness, that we had enough to do to pacify him towards himself.

John Gratton was another quaker of good education, brought up in the presbyterian faith in Derbyshire. Like many mystics, he was subject to deep inward exercises, frequently culminating in visions or other incursions from the deeper layers of personality; and his *Journal*, like that of George Fox, is of great interest to the student of religious psychology. He was, however, a man of sane and sober spirit, and there is no question as to his fundamental orthodoxy. He writes with ease and clearness, but lacks the crisp, pungent manner of Fox and Ellwood. Like most of his contemporaries, he is apt to be long-winded.

One of the liveliest and best written of these early autobiographies is that of Richard Davies, of Welshpool, who tells the story of his own 'convincement' and sufferings, and of the first propagation of the 'truth' in Wales.

*The Memoir of John Roberts*, of Cirencester (who died in 1683), was written by his son Daniel in 1725; yet it properly belongs to this period, since the notes from which it is compiled must have been, to a large extent, contemporary with the events described. For its brightness and unfailing humour, it well deserves a place in English literature. Oliver Wendell Holmes said of it:

---

[1] See Masson's *Milton*, vol. vi, pp. 586—8, for a lively description of the difficulties encountered by magistrates in attempting to put a forcible stop to the Friends' worship.

It is as good as gold—better than gold—every page of it. It is comforting to meet, even in a book, a man who is perfectly simple-hearted, clear-headed, and brave in all conditions. The story is admirably told too—dramatically, vividly[1].

The great mass of early quaker writings may be described as mystical, in the sense that they seek to set forth the reality of the experience of direct Divine communion, and the life of self-surrender and obedience as at once the condition and the fruit of that experience. But we may distinguish as mystical writings proper those of the works of the quakers which are not mainly autobiographical on the one hand, or controversial on the other.

William Penn, son of the admiral Penn frequently mentioned by Pepys, is the most widely known of the early quakers—chiefly as the founder and first governor of the colony of Pennsylvania. His character has been fiercely assailed by Macaulay and others; but there seems no reason to doubt that, whatever difficulties a quaker statesman may have had to encounter in putting his principles consistently into practice, he remained absolutely sincere and worthy of the respect in which he was always held by his people. Though 'convinced' of the truth of the quaker way of life at the age of 22, he does not seem to have been a mystic by temperament, but rather a clear-headed English man of action, whose principles were formed, not in the school of speculation, but in that of experience. Though possessed of rich stores of learning, and great qualities as a statesman, he can hardly be regarded as a deep thinker; and, as an author, in common with nearly all the writers of his time, he is often tedious and infelicitous in expression[2].

The best known of his early works, *No Cross No Crown*, was written at the age of 24, while he was in prison in the Tower for the 'blasphemy' of a pamphlet, *The Sandy Foundation Shaken*, in which he had assailed what were regarded as the strongholds of the Christian faith. His purpose in writing *No Cross No Crown* he describes as 'to show the nature and discipline of the holy Cross of Christ; and that the denial of self . . . is the alone way to the Rest and Kingdom of God.' This is a familiar theme with mystics; but Penn interprets the cross with the utmost puritan

---

[1] From a prefatory letter to the first complete edition, entitled *A Quaker of the Olden Time*, 1898.

[2] This criticism does not apply to *Some Fruits of Solitude* (see later), which is written in crisp and excellent English.

rigour, decrying luxury and most of the customary ways of society.
His effort is a warning against wrath to come, and only incidentally
an invitation to enjoy the crown of rest in the kingdom here and
now.

Come, Reader, hearken to me awhile; I seek thy salvation; that's my Plot;
thou wilt forgive me. A Refiner is come near thee, His Grace hath appeared
to thee; it shows thee the World's lusts, and teacheth thee to deny them.
Receive His leaven and it will change thee; His medicine and it will cure
thee. This is the Crown, but where is the Cross? Where is the bitter cup
and bloody baptism? Come, Reader, be like him; for this transcendent Joy
lift up thy head above the World; then thy Salvation will draw nigh
indeed.

To avoid giving a false impression of narrowness in Penn, it
should be added that he was a warm friend of education, and fully
alive to its importance.

'Nature,' he says (in his *Address to Protestants*), 'is an excellent book,
pleasant and profitable; but how few, alas! are learned either in the *Macro-
cosm* or their *Microcosm*! I wish this were better understood; it would be
both our honour and advantage.'

He made ample provision for education in his colony; and he was
the first statesman in power willing to run the risk of granting
absolute liberty of conscience and of worship.

More of a mystic than Penn was his friend Isaac Penington,
son of an alderman and high sheriff of London who was one of the
regicide judges. Penington was a graduate of Cambridge, as
Penn was of Oxford. The stern and gloomy Calvinism in which
he had been brought up distressed his tender spirit, and it was not
till after years of deep inward questioning and isolation, and even
of agnosticism, that he found peace at last by identifying himself
with the quakers, whose teaching he had known but had long
despised as uncouth and contrary to reason. He came to find
'the presence and power of the Most High among them,' and
declares:

I have met with my God; I have met with my Saviour; and he hath not
been present with me without his salvation; but I have felt the healings drop
upon my soul from under his wings. I have met with the true knowledge,
the knowledge of life.

Penington's writings, it has been recently said, 'are diffuse,
and on the whole unreadable.' Even the titles of his voluminous
works are forgotten now; but the purest breath of Christian
mysticism is in them for those who have the patience to find it
and the power to breathe it. Take the following passage as
typical of many others:

Know *what it is* that is to walk in the path of life, and indeed is alone capable of walking therein. It is that which groans, and which mourns; that which is begotten of God in thee. The path of life is for the seed of life. The true knowledge of the way, with the walking in the way, is reserved for God's child, for God's traveller. Therefore keep in the regeneration, keep in the birth; be no more than God hath made thee. Give over thine own willing; give over thine own running; give over thine own desiring to know or to be anything, and sink down to the seed which God sows in the heart and let that grow in thee.

Before the light dawned on Isaac Penington, he had found a kindred spirit in the youthful lady Springett (born Mary Proude), who, after the death of her husband at the siege of Arundel, married Penington, as she says herself, that she might 'be serviceable to him in his desolate condition.' 'Their love was the mature passion of pure and intense natures,' and together they suffered cheerfully the loss of worldly goods and frequent separations when Penington was thrown into prison for what he believed to be the truth. A beautiful and worthy testimony remains in the words which Mary Penington wrote, by the bedside of her sick child, when her husband had been called away from earth:

Ah me! he is gone! he that none exceeded in kindness, in tenderness, in love inexpressible to the relation as a wife. Next to the love of God in Christ Jesus to my soul, was his love precious and delightful to me. My bosom-one! that was as my guide and counsellor! my pleasant companion! my tender sympathising friend! as near to the sense of my pain, sorrow, grief, and trouble as it was possible. Yet this great help and benefit is gone; and I, a poor worm, a very little one to him, compassed about with many infirmities, through mercy let him go without an unadvised word of discontent, or inordinate grief.

There is no more pathetic figure, in the history of early quakerism, than that of the unhappy James Nayler, whose grievous lapse into sheer extravagance led him, as a sign of the coming of the living Christ, to allow a crowd of silly women to hail him as the Messiah; and who, after his case had been debated at length in the House of Commons, bore with deep contrition and exemplary patience the ferocious punishment which was meted out to him. His writings after this baptism of fire breathe the purest spirit of inward penitence and forgiving love. The following are the words of his 'last Testimony,' taken down about two hours before his death:

There is a spirit which I feel, that delights to do no evil, nor to revenge any wrong, but delights to endure all things, in hope to enjoy its own in the end. Its hope is to outlive all wrath and contention, and to weary out all exaltation and cruelty, or whatever is of a nature contrary to itself. It sees to the end of all temptations; as it bears no evil in itself, so it conceives none in thoughts to any other; if it be betrayed it bears it; for its ground and spring is in the mercies and forgiveness of God. Its crown is meekness, its life is everlasting love unfeigned; it takes its Kingdom with entreaty and not with contention, and keeps it by lowliness of mind.

Another beautiful testimony to the spirit that animated those early quakers is given by William Dewsbury who, shortly before his death, said, after a long and terrible imprisonment in Warwick castle:

This I can say, I never played the coward, but joyfully entered Prisons as Palaces, telling mine enemies to hold me there as long as they could, and in the Prison House I sung praises to my God, and esteemed the Bolts and Locks put upon me as Jewels, and in the name of the Eternal God I alway got the Victory.

The early quakers, like most Christian mystics, had no thought of setting themselves in opposition to fundamental orthodoxy as they understood it. But, inevitably, their constant appeal to the Light Within, and their consequent refusal to bow down to outward authority, brought them into fierce conflict with the religious teachers of their day, by most of whom the Bible had been erected into the final and only 'rule' of faith and practice. And so, as they were compelled to defend themselves against attacks which condemned them, with indiscriminate violence, as papists, heretics, atheists and blasphemers, the purpose of their writings became more and more directly theological. On both sides, it is to be feared, abuse counted for more than argument, and the oblivion into which these reams of printed matter have fallen cannot be said to have been undeserved.

So early as 1656, John Bunyan attacked the quakers, without explicitly naming them, in *Some Gospel Truths Opened*, and was answered by Edward Burrough and George Fox. Thomas Hicks, the baptist, roused the wrath of Ellwood by his *Dialogue between a Christian and a Quaker*; and Richard Baxter, in his *Quaker's Catechism*, complaining of their 'violent and railing language,' denounced them as 'abominable infidels,' 'Pagans' and 'a generation of the Devil.' In kindlier vein, Henry More, the Cambridge Platonist, while admitting as 'safe and reasonable' the principle of 'the light within a man,' expressed his sorrow at their 'uncouth and ridiculous' opinions, and was sorely grieved when his friend the learned and philosophical viscountess Conway (daughter of speaker Finch) joined herself to what he described as 'the most melancholy sect that ever was in the world.' To all these, and many more, the quakers issued voluminous replies[1].

Of Penn's controversial writings, *The Sandy Foundation Shaken*, which got him into the Tower; *Innocency with her Open Face*, by which he won his release; *The Christian Quaker*, and *Primitive Christianity Revived*, it is needless now to speak. A word must, however, be said concerning the prodigious *apologia* of Samuel Fisher (1666), entitled *Rusticus ad Academicos*: a work of nearly 800 quarto pages, closely printed, containing single sentences that sometimes run to a page and a half[2]. In spite of its incredible long-windedness, it is a work of great learning and sound sense. Fisher deals in a quite modern manner with the canon of Scripture, showing wide knowledge of its history, and also of the various Biblical manuscripts then accessible to scholars. He can be caustic, too, when he chooses, as when he replies to the argument of dean Owen that the Holy Spirit, while preserving somewhere the true text, has arranged variations between the MSS in order to encourage diligence in the study of Scripture—'Whence came this whiffle and whimzy within the circumference of thy figmentitious fancy?'

There is one book, out of all this welter of controversy, that can be read today with interest and profit: *An Apology for the True Christian Divinity*, by Robert Barclay, son of David Barclay, of Ury, who had served as a soldier under Gustavus Adolphus, and had afterwards joined the quakers. Robert Barclay was brought up among the strictest Calvinists in Scotland, and among Catholics during his studies in Paris; nevertheless, without any urging from his father, he, also, at the age of nineteen became a quaker.

> When I came into the silent assemblies of God's people, I felt a secret power among them, which touched my heart; and as I gave way unto it, I found the evil weakening in me, and the good raised up; and so I became thus knit and united unto them, hungering more and more after the increase of this power and life, whereby I might feel myself perfectly redeemed[3].

---

[1] In vol. i of E. Arber's *Term Catalogues*, the titles are given of 44 books written against the quakers between the years 1671 and 1680. Joseph Smith's *Bibliotheca Anti-Quakeriana* (1873), contains an alphabetical catalogue of many hundreds of these writings. George Fox's *The Great Mystery* (1659) has replies to over one hundred attacks on the quakers.

[2] The index to this extraordinary work is worth examining as a quaint example of the controversial methods of the seventeenth century. See, under the heading 'Nicknames,' the extraordinary selection of terms applied to the quakers.

[3] *Apology*, Proposition xi, § 7.

Robert Barclay is the first of the very few theologians whom the Society of Friends has produced. Possessed of remarkable natural gifts, he set himself deliberately to the study of theology, mastering Greek and Hebrew, the writings of the Fathers and the history of the Christian church. His *Apology* was written at the early age of 28, but is the work of a mature mind. It was written first in Latin, was afterwards translated into English and low Dutch and became the chief classic of the quaker faith. Learned and scholastic as it is, the style is clear and flowing, and it can be read with ease. In a series of fifteen propositions, or *Theses Theologicae,* he deals with the true foundation of knowledge, with immediate revelation, with the Scriptures, with universal and saving Light, and so forth.

The following passage will serve to illustrate at once his style and his treatment of the problem of justification:

> We understand not by this Justification by Christ, barely the good works even wrought by the Spirit of Christ; for they, as Protestants truly affirm, are rather the effect of Justification than the cause of it; but we understand the formation of Christ in us, Christ born and brought forth in us, from which good works as naturally proceed as fruit from a fruitful tree. It is this inward birth in us bringing forth righteousness and holiness in us, that doth justify us; which having removed and done away the contrary nature and spirit that did bear rule and bring condemnation, now is in dominion over all in our hearts. ... This is to be clothed with Christ, and to have put him on, whom God therefore truly accounteth righteous and just. ... By this also comes the communication of the goods of Christ into us, by which we come to be made partakers of the divine nature, as saith 2 Peter i. 4, and are made one with him, as the branches with the vine, and have a title and right to what he hath done and suffered for us; so that his obedience becomes ours, his righteousness ours, his death and sufferings ours[1].

There is very little in the writings of the early quakers that has not some directly practical or controversial aim. Among more purely literary efforts, however, mention should be made of William Penn's *Some Fruits of Solitude,* and of the rare attempts at poetry, or, rather, versification, put forth by one or two of them.

R. L. Stevenson has told of the comfort and refreshment he gained, in sickness and loneliness, from a copy of *Some Fruits of Solitude* which he picked up in the streets of San Francisco. It is a collection of aphorisms, 'fruits,' as Penn calls them, 'that may serve the reader for texts to preach to himself upon.' It has the virtue, rare, indeed, at that time and among these writers, of terseness and condensation; the maxims are expressed, without any straining after literary effect, in natural, clear and cogent

---

[1] *Apology,* Proposition VII, § 3.

English. It is lit up with a kindly humour, and its satire, while mordant at times, is never bitter or cynical. The first part was written between 1690 and 1693, when Penn was living in seclusion in London under suspicion of treachery, owing to his former friendship with James II. Twice he was arrested and brought to trial on a charge of disloyalty, but, on both occasions, was discharged. This explains why the book was published anonymously, but its authorship has now been conclusively proved[1]. The second part, *More Fruits of Solitude*, dates from just after the accession of queen Anne.

The following will serve as evidence of the pungent brevity with which Penn could express himself when he chose:

> Truth often suffers more by the heat of its defenders than from the arguments of its opposers.
> Let the People think they govern, and they will be governed.
> The Humble, Meek, Merciful, Just, Pious, and Devout souls, are everywhere of one religion; and when death has taken off the mask they will know one another, though the diverse liveries they wear here makes them strangers.
> Speak properly, and in as few words as you can, but always plainly; for the end of speech is not ostentation, but to be understood.
> This is the comfort of friends, that, though they may be said to die, yet their friendship and society are, in the best sense, ever present, because immortal.

Of poetry, in the writings of the early quakers, there is nothing that deserves the name. Such versification as we find is, for the most part, prosaic disquisition on moral and spiritual themes, marked by piety without inspiration, and facility without imagination. Thomas Ellwood, in addition to the 'poems' which are scattered through his autobiography, issued *A Collection of Poems on Various Subjects*, from which we extract the following:

> He's a *true* lover, not who can subdue
> Monsters and giants for his mistress' sake,
> And sighs perhaps, and weeps, with much ado
> For fear she should some other happy make;
> But who so far her happiness prefers
> Before his own, that he can be content
> To sacrifice his own to purchase hers,
> Though with the price of his own banishment.

The quakers, as is well known, gave to women an equal place with men in the ministries of the spiritual life; and perhaps the only approach to poetry in their literary output, before the days of Barton and Whittier, is to be found in a little volume of letters

---

[1] See *A Quaker Post Bag*, 1910, p. 27.

and poems entitled *Fruits of Retirement,* by Mary Mollineux (born Southworth), published shortly after her death in 1695. It includes the following *Meditations in Trouble*:

> O Whither is he gone? Or where
> Shall I go mourn, till he appear,
>   Who is my life, my love?
>   Alas, how shall I move
> Him to return, that's secretly retired
>   Like unto one displeased,
>   Who, till he be appeased,
>   My heart cannot be eased?
> He is one lovely, and to be admired!

It might have been expected that the deep inward experiences of these quaker mystics would have found spontaneous expression in lyrical verse, but so it was not to be. Very early, their spiritual life became confined in bonds, and freedom and spontaneity were largely lost in a rigour of thought and life that left little scope for originality of inspired expression. With the eighteenth century, the glow of the first experience faded, and the third generation of the quakers, while retaining much of the purity and unworldliness and spirituality of their predecessors, became, for the most part, the children of a tradition. Quietism settled down upon them, a quietism which, while it produced noble fruit in a John Woolman and an Elizabeth Fry, left the majority more concerned to maintain the discipline of a 'peculiar people' than to make known a spiritual Gospel to the world.

# CHAPTER V

## THE RESTORATION DRAMA

### I

WITH the ordinance of 2 September 1642, commanding the closing of the theatres and the total suppression of stage plays, the long and brilliant chapter of the drama that had known the triumphs of the days of Elizabeth and her two successors came to an abrupt and dismal end. Although declared rogues by a later act and threatened with the whipping-post for pursuing their calling, the actors did not at once obey these stringent laws[1]. We hear of performances 'three or four miles, or more, out of town,' and of plays acted at the Cockpit, for example in 1648, when 'a party of soldiers beset the house and carried the actors away in their habits to Hatton House, then a prison.' During the commonwealth, occasional performances were connived at, 'sometimes in noblemen's houses... where the nobility and gentry met, but in no great numbers'; at others, in seasons of festivals such as Christmas or Bartholomew fair, even at the old playhouses, among them the Red Bull. But, even with bribes to the guard at Whitehall, immunity against arrest and safety from rough handling for auditor and actor were not to be assured. It is not wonderful that, during the rebellion, the players declared themselves, almost to a man, on the side of the king. Several of them served with distinction on the royalist side; but the end of the war found most of them in exile with their betters or reduced to poverty[2].

---

[1] For the texts of the most important of these laws, see Hazlitt, W. C., *The English Drama and Stage*, 1543—1664, Roxburghe Library, 1869, pp. 63—70.

[2] On this topic, see Wright's *Historia Histrionica*, first published in 1699, reprinted in Dodsley, vol. xv.

Amusements of the dramatic kind being now under the ban, various devices were employed to evade the letter of the law[1]. Interesting among these were the 'drolls' or 'droll-humours,' as they were called—farces or humorous scenes adapted from current plays and staged, for the most part, on extemporised scaffolds, at taverns and fairs, and sometimes, even, at regular theatres[2]. Thus, a 'droll,' entitled *Merry Conceits of Bottom the Weaver*, was printed as early as 1646, and a dozen or so by Robert Cox, notable for his performance in them. A large collection entitled *The Wits, or Sport upon Sport*, collected by Francis Kirkman the bookseller, appeared in the early seventies, when the acting of these things had been superseded by the revival of the more regular drama. It may be remarked, in passing, that the application of the term 'droll' to stage recitals in commonwealth days is alike distinguishable from its earlier employment to signify a puppet or a puppet-show and from the use of the word 'drollery' which was applied to any piece of humour or ribaldry in verse[3]. Among 'drolls' derived from well known plays may be named *The Grave Diggers' Colloquy* from *Hamlet*; *Falstaff, The Bouncing Knight* from *Henry IV*; and *The Buckbasket Mishap* from *The Merry Wives*. Other scenes, like Cox's *Humours of Simpleton the Smith* and *John Swabber* were inventions of the actors. All were contrived to please the vulgar and appeal to the least refined.

Towards the close of Cromwell's rule, the laws against dramatic entertainments appear to have been somewhat relaxed, and Sir William D'Avenant, who had been governor of the king and queen's company of players, acting at the Cockpit, and had held a patent, dated 1639, empowering him to erect a new playhouse, was obviously the man first to provide for a returning interest in plays. D'Avenant's earlier plays and masques[4] have already been mentioned in a previous volume of this work. The son of an Oxford tavern keeper, and, if the story be authentic, Shakespeare's godson, D'Avenant had been taken up by the court; he had staged plays in the manner of Fletcher as early as 1630; had succeeded Ben Jonson as poet laureate in 1638, and, later, had served the royal

---

[1] Such was the masque of the Inner Temple, November 1651, Gardiner, *History of the Commonwealth and the Protectorate*, vol. II, pp. 11, 12.

[2] Ward, *History of English Dramatic Literature*, vol. III, p. 280.

[3] J. W. Ebsworth's reprint of *Westminster Drolleries*, 1672, is a collection of humorous verse and non-dramatic. His introduction, sometimes cited in this connection, little concerns the dramatic 'droll.' Halliwell-Phillipps reprinted several Shakespearean 'drolls' in 1859.

[4] See *ante*, vol. VI, p. 240.

party through many vicissitudes afield and in intrigue abroad and at home, suffering imprisonment for several years and narrowly escaping the gallows. In the later years of the commonwealth, he had lived more quietly in London and, at length, chiefly through the influence of the lord-keeper, Sir Bulstrode Whitelocke, obtained authority for the production of a species of quasi-dramatic entertainment which, though given at private houses, was public in so far as money was taken for entrance. D'Avenant's earliest venture in this kind was entitled *The First Day's Entertainment at Rutland House*, 'by declamation and music, after the manner of the ancients,' printed in 1657, and staged 21 May of the previous year. By some, this venture has been called 'an opera'; and, strangely enough, D'Avenant refers to it by this title in his prologue and elsewhere. *The First Day's Entertainment* is really made up of two pairs of speeches, the first by Diogenes and Aristophanes successively 'against and for, public entertainment, by moral presentation,' the second, in lighter vein, between a Parisian and a Londoner on the respective merits of the two cities. The whole was diversified with music by Coleman, Lawes (composer of the music of *Comus*) and other musicians of repute in their day. D'Avenant had made provision for four hundred auditors, but only a hundred and fifty appeared. Emboldened, however, by this qualified success, he projected a more ambitious entertainment. This was the celebrated *Siege of Rhodes*, 'made a representation by the art of prospective in scenes and the story sung in recitative music,' presented in August 1656. In an address 'To the Reader,' which appears in the first edition of that year, but was not afterwards reprinted, D'Avenant points out that

the story as represented ... is heroical, and notwithstanding the continual hurry and busy agitations of a hot siege, is (I hope) intelligibly conveyed to advance the characters of virtue in the shapes of valour and conjugal love.

The author was too close to triumphant puritanisn not to feel it necessary to justify the moral aspects of his art. Of the recitative music, an 'unpracticed' novelty in England, the author tells us that it was 'composed and exercised by the most transcendent of England in that art'; and it is clear that the cast was chosen with reference to this important operatic feature. As to the five changes of scene, he regrets that 'all is confined to eleven foot in height and about fifteen in depth including the places of passage reserved for the music': a 'narrow allowance,' he continues, 'for the fleet of Solyman the Magnificent, his army, the Island of Rhodes and the varieties attending the siege of the city.' *The*

*Siege of Rhodes*, on the dramatic side, is an amplified situation, laying no claim to plot, characterisation or variety save such as arises from change of scene, appropriate costume and attendant music. *The Rehearsal*[1] ridicules a battle 'performed in recitative music by seven persons only'; and it must be confessed that this 'first English opera' is dramatically as absurd as its species has continued, with certain exceptions, ever since. *The Siege of Rhodes* is often described as the first English play to employ scenery and the first in which an actress appeared on the English stage. Neither of these statements is correct. Changes of scenery and even 'perspective in scene' were in *vogue*, if not common, long before 1656[2]. As to women on the stage, not to mention some earlier examples, Mrs Coleman, who 'played' the part of Ianthe in *The Siege*, had already sung in *The First Day's Entertainment* and was chosen, doubtless, in both instances for her voice rather than for her acting[3]. In 1658, D'Avenant opened the Cockpit theatre in Drury lane, producing there two similar operas, *The Cruelty of the Spaniards in Peru* and *The History of Sir Francis Drake*[4]. Their 'historical' intent and scenic novelty may well have disarmed puritan suspicion, though Richard Cromwell is said to have ordered an enquiry into the performance at the Cockpit, of which, however, nothing came.

Affairs were now moving rapidly towards the restoration of king Charles. General Monck arrived in London in the first days of February 1659/60, and one John Rhodes, a bookseller and sometime keeper of the wardrobe of the king's company at Blackfriars, obtained a licence from the existing authorities for the formation of a dramatic company. A second company gathered at the Red Bull, a third at Salisbury court in Whitefriars, and Sir Henry Herbert, master of the revels, awoke to the duties (and prospective emoluments) of an office for long years held by him in hope and abeyance. Upon his restoration, king Charles issued a patent to Thomas Killigrew and Sir William D'Avenant,

---

[1] Act v, sc. 1.

[2] In the performance of Cartwright's *Royall Slave* at Oxford, in August 1636, the scene was changed eight times. See the quarto of this play of 1639. Jonson alluded to 'a piece of perspective' in 1600, *Cynthia's Revels*, induction, Gifford-Cunningham's *Jonson*, vol. II, p. 210.

[3] French actresses appeared in London as early as 1629 and were very unfavourably received; in masques and like entertainments ladies had long taken prominent part. On this topic, see Lawrence, W. J., 'Early French Players in England,' *Anglia*, vol. XXXII, p. 61.

[4] Incorporated in *The Playhouse to be Let*, printed in the folio of 1673.

empowering them to 'erect' two companies of players[1]. This raised a storm of protest, especially from Herbert, who immediately petitioned the king and council and brought action in the courts, singling out D'Avenant as his peculiar foe and describing him as one who had 'obtained leave of Oliver and Richard Cromwell to vent his operas at a time when your petitioner owned not their authority[2].' In the first instance, combination, and then a second division, of the two companies followed; but, before long, the claims of Herbert were adjusted and the two royal patentees were upheld. Their troupes soon became known, Killigrew's as the king's, and D'Avenant's as the duke of York's, company of players. In 1661, the latter company removed to a new playhouse built for them in Lincoln's inn fields, Portugal row, and, later, in 1673, after the death of D'Avenant, to the sumptuous theatre in Salisbury court, Fleet street, a site previously known as Dorset garden. D'Avenant's house was commonly called 'the opera' from the performance of musical plays there. But D'Avenant by no means gave an undivided attention to such productions. The king's company (Killigrew's), variously housed before 1663, removed in that year to the Theatre Royal in Drury lane, Covent garden.

Thomas Killigrew, a member of a loyal Cornish family, had been reared a page in the court of Charles I, and continued a favourite companion of that monarch's son and successor. As groom of his majesty's bedchamber, Killigrew remained a privileged servant in the royal household and was reputed, from his ready colloquial wit, the king's jester. His earlier plays were written abroad and acted before the closing of the theatres. Among them are *The Prisoners, Claracilla* and *The Princess,* tragicomedies of approved adventurous romantic type. They mark, in their extravagance of adventure, exaggerated character and inflated rhetoric, a step from the immediate imitators of Fletcher to the restoration heroic play, and group naturally with the like efforts of Sir William Lower and Lodowick Carlell. A later tragicomedy by Killigrew, *Cecilia and Clorinda,* borrowed its subject, in part, from *Le Grand Cyrus,* a sufficient indication, perhaps, of the general nature of the poet's sources for serious plays. Among several comedies that appear in the collected

---

[1] This patent bears date 21 August 1660, and is issued to the two patentees jointly. It is printed entire by Malone in the prolegomena to his edition of Shakespeare, 1821, vol. III, pp. 249—251.

[2] See the same, p. 247, where the petition of Sir Henry Herbert and other papers in this controversy are reprinted.

edition of Killigrew's works, 1664, *The Parson's Wedding*, likewise a pre-restoration play, is the most conspicuous. This is a comedy of almost unexampled coarseness, a quality which the author had not found in his source, Calderon's *Dama Duende*. Many of Killigrew's plays were acted after the reopening of the theatres and *The Parson's Wedding* enjoyed unusual popularity. Two other Killigrews, brothers of Thomas, brought their contributions to the stage[1]. Sir William Killigrew published, in 1664, three plays, *Selindra*, *Pandora* and *Ormasdes, or Love and Friendship*. The last was subsequently rewritten under the influence of the new heroic drama. A fourth dramatic work of this author, *The Siege of Urbin*, has been with justice described as 'a capable and sympathetic play.' Not all of these were acted. Henry Killigrew, a younger brother, wrote but one play, so far as is known. It was published first in 1638 under the title *The Conspiracy*, and, rewritten, in 1653, as *Pallantus and Eudora*. Thomas Killigrew the younger, also a writer of plays, belongs to a later generation.

The works of Sir William D'Avenant, posthumously collected, bear date 1683. D'Avenant staged most of his plays and some of them were not undeservedly successful. Several of his rewritten plays, such as *Love and Honour*, *The Wits* and *The Platonick Lovers*, long remained popular favourites; but his work subsequent to the restoration is made up largely of older dramas refashioned to meet new conditions. Thus, we hear of *Macbeth*, staged with 'alterations, amendments, additions and new songs' besides a *divertissement*, and of Beatrice and Benedick thrust into *Measure for Measure* and the result renamed *The Law Against Lovers*. *Romeo and Juliet* was transformed into a comedy and acted alternately with the Shakespearean version[2].

The *répertoire* of the first years of the restoration exhibits an active revival of the masterpieces of the earlier drama. Between the opening of the new theatres and April 1663, Pepys saw *Othello*, *Henry IV*, *A Midsummer Night's Dream*, Jonson's *Silent Woman*

---

[1] See bibliography.

[2] As to James Howard's *Romeo and Juliet*, see *ante*, p. 20 note 3. As to D'Avenant and Dryden's version of *The Tempest*, and Shadwell's alterations see *ante*, p. 28 and note 2. Other like adaptations are Shadwell's *Timon of Athens*, Ravenscroft's *Titus Andronicus*, Tate's *King Lear*, and Betterton's *Henry IV*. D'Avenant rewrote *The Two Noble Kinsmen* as *The Rivals*, Waller transmuted *The Maides Tragedy* into a comedy by a new fifth act, Betterton adapted *The Prophetesse*, Vanbrugh *The Pilgrim*, D'Urfey *The Sea Voyage*, Tate *The Island Princesse*, all of them originally Fletcher's. Farquhar's *Inconstant* is an adaptation of *The Wild-Goose Chase*.

and *Bartholomew Fayre*, Fletcher's *Tamer Tamed*, *The Beggars Bush* and Beaumont's *Knight of the Burning Pestle*, Middleton's *Changeling*, Shirley's *Cardinall*, Massinger's *Bond-Man* and several more[1]. *Hamlet* was among the first plays revived, and it furnished one of Betterton's most signal triumphs. A taste for the heroic in drama, a heritage from Fletcher and his imitators in the previous age, is noticeable in D'Avenant's own *Siege of Rhodes* and, more especially, in his really fine tragicomedy, *Love and Honour*. How this was to spring into full flower in the heroic plays of Dryden, Orrery and others, has been already shown in an earlier chapter[2]. The beginnings of opera, also, may be postponed for the moment.

A distinctive feature of the earlier drama of the restoration is its reflection of the current political reaction. The playwrights, to a man, extolled absolute monarchy and branded as disloyal any- one who failed obsequiously to observe and follow the lead and the wishes of the king. As to the puritan, while he was in power, few had dared openly to lampoon him; but, with the swing of popular loyalty back to the monarchy, the church and the old established order of things, the puritan became fair game for the satire of his foes. General Monck was still in the north, and Lambert, sent to oppose him, had been but recently deserted by his troops, when John Tatham staged his satirical piece of dramatic journalism, *The Rump*. Tatham had been a contriver of pageants for the city and had written a pastoral, *Love Crowns the End*, so far back as 1632, a tragedy of no great merit, ominously called *The Distracted State*, and a piece of bitter satire against the Scots, whom the author appears especially to have hated, entitled *The Scotch Figgaries*. In *The Rump, or the Mirrour of the Late Times*, Tatham boldly lampoons Lambert, Fleetwood, Hewson and other notabilities of the moment, representing the widow of Crom- well as an undignified scold and lady Lambert as preposterously and irrationally eager to thrust her husband into the succession to the protectorate, so that she may be addressed 'your highness.' Several scenes of this comedy are not without a certain comic effectiveness; and the final reduction of these lofty personages to street vendors, peddling their wares, displays the popular humour and temper of the moment. Another typical comedy of the type is Sir Robert Howard's *The Committee*, produced in 1665 and long

---

[1] A list of the plays of Rhodes's company is made up largely of works of Fletcher. See Genest, vol. I, p. 31.

[2] See *ante*, chap. I.

popular[1]. It tells directly and not without force the story of a hypocritical puritan committee of sequestration, made up of such personages as Nehemiah Catch, Jonathan Headstrong and Ezekiel Scrape, and how they and a dishonest guardian were outwitted by two clever maidens and their cavalier lovers. A better written comedy, though it was less successful in its day, is Cowley's *Cutter of Coleman Street*, brought out by D'Avenant among his earliest ventures[2]. While such characters as 'merry, sharking' Cutter, who turns puritan for his worldly welfare and has visions of the downfall of Babylon, are amusing, and the dialogue abounds in clever thrusts at the cant and weaknesses of fallen puritanism, Cowley's comedy cannot be pronounced a dramatic success. Nevertheless, the truthfulness of his portraiture of colonel Jolly, the drunken cavalier, reeling on the edge of dishonesty, and driven in his need to composition with 'the saints,' brought down on the poet's head the displeasure of some who know no vices excepting those that flourish among their enemies. Comedies satirising the puritans continued popular throughout the reign of Charles II, as is seen from such productions as Lacy's *The Old Troop* (before 1665), Crowne's *City Politics*, 1673, and Mrs Behn's *The Round-heads*, 1682, a shameless appropriation of Tatham's *The Rump*.

Turning now to individual playwrights of the restoration not incidentally treated in the paragraphs above, we find some that preserved untouched the older traditions of English comedy. Foremost among them was John Wilson, a native of Plymouth, and a student of the law, called to the bar in 1646. Through the good offices of the duke of York, whose secretary he had been in Ireland, Wilson became recorder of Londonderry and, throwing himself into the Jacobite cause, remained in Dublin after the accession of king William. He died in London in 1696. Wilson is the author of four plays, the earliest of which, *The Cheats*, was written in 1662 and enjoyed an extraordinary popularity on the stage. It is a prose comedy frankly following the manner of Jonson. Mopus, the quack astrologer, the sharking bravoes, Bilboe and Titere Tu, the nonconformist minister Scruple who finds the light that leads to conformity on £300 a year, but is steadied in protest against the wiles of Babylon by an offer of 400—all are pure Jonson, but rung to new changes that defy the suggestions of plagiarism. Not less Jonsonian is Wilson's second comedy, *The*

---

[1] Cf. *ante*, chap. I, p. 20 note 3.

[2] Cowley's play was originally called *The Guardian*. It was acted at Cambridge in 1641, and published under this earlier title in 1650. Cf. *ante*, vol. VII, p. 62.

*Projectors,* 1664. Here, a group of these sharks (a favourite subject for ridicule with Jonson himself) are represented, busy with their victim, Sir Gudgeon Credulous, and the long line of usurers on the stage is bettered in Suckdry and his servant and foil, Lean-chops[1]. Wilson's comedy is vigorous, full of effective and good-humoured caricature, and successfully imitative of the better features of his master's art. Besides these excellent comedies, Wilson is the author of a tragedy, *Andronicus Comnenius,* of admirable conduct and vigour, and written in blank verse of a freedom compacted with firmness that recalls the better work of the previous age. The actual story of Andronicus Comnenus, hypocritical, treacherous and pitiless in his murderous path of devastation to a throne, strangely parallels the story of the hunch-back Richard of historical and dramatic fable. Such, however, seems to have been the author's literary conscience that, save for one scene, which closely resembles the courtship of lady Anne by Richard, he has treated his theme originally and with inventive variety[2]. The date of *Andronicus Comnenius* is noticeable; for, in 1664, the stage was ringing with Dryden's *Rival-Ladies,* and his and Sir Robert Howard's *Indian Queen.* Wilson's fourth play, *Belphegor, or the Marriage of the Devil,* printed in 1691, is less interesting, though elaborated with much detail. The story, referable to Machiavelli's well known *novella,* had been treated before in English drama and may have been suggested to Wilson by Jonson's unsuccessful play of similar theme, *The Divell is an Asse*[3].

Among other names which occur in the dramatic annals of the years immediately following the return of king Charles is that of Sir Robert Stapylton, the author of a comedy, *The Slighted Maid,* described by Genest as 'a pretty good comedy' and as 'not acted for the first time in 1663[4].' Stapylton's tragicomedy, *The Stepmother,* followed in the same year. He is the author, too, of a tragedy on Hero and Leander. Stapylton was a translator from French and the classics, and of some repute in his day. His post as gentleman-usher to king Charles doubtless disposed him, like other royal servants, to an interest in the drama. Whether the trivial but witty comedy, *Mr Anthony,* printed in 1690, be the

---

[1] This play was likewise influenced by the *Aulularia* of Plautus.

[2] Compare *Richard III,* act I, sc. 2, and *Andronicus Comnenius,* act IV, sc. 3. Wilson nvariably writes Comnenius for Comnenus.

[3] Compare Haughton's *The Devil and his Dame,* mentioned in Henslowe's diary, and especially Dekker's *If It Be Not Good, the Divel is in it.*

[4] Genest, *Some Account of the English Stage,* vol. I, p. 46.

work of Roger Boyle, earl of Orrery, or not, its clear following
of the models of earlier comedy is sufficient to place it here[1].
Orrery is memorable for his heroic dramas, which have been already
noted[2]. The duke of Newcastle, too, and his clever duchess had
both long been dabblers in the drama. But, neither the tutorship
of Ben Jonson, nor that of Shirley later, contrived to produce in
either of the pair results deserving serious attention from the
student of literature. Two comedies by the duke—*The Humorous
Lovers* and *The Triumphant Widow*—were acted 'after the restoration' and printed in 1673. Twenty-one plays by the duchess
were published in a folio volume of 1662. They have been described
as 'fertile in invention and as tending to extravaganza and an
excess of unrefined fun[3].' Thus, in the midst of a steady revival
of the plays of the old drama, extending, in accordance with the
gross taste of the court, to comedies of Middleton and Brome, the
first years of the restoration passed by.

But comedy, on the revival of the stage, was not to be confined
to the satire of contemporary allusion and a following of the
humours of Jonson. In a striking passage of his *Life of Dryden*,
Sir Walter Scott declares that the English audience of the restoration

had not the patience for the regular comedy depending upon delicate turns
of expression and nicer delineations of character. The Spanish comedy,
with its bustle, machinery, disguise and complicated intrigue, was much more
agreeable to their taste[4].

And this is true, although French models were drawn upon far
more frequently than Spanish, in whatever degree the finer lines
of the former were, at times, obscured in the process. The degree
and character of the influence of Spanish literature on the drama
of England has been much misunderstood. The position taken by
Ward, many years ago, to the effect that the connection between
the Spanish and the English drama is far from intimate and that
'among the elements peculiar to the Spanish drama none can be
shown to have been taken over by our own and assimilated to its
growth,' may be declared to be a position substantially correct[5].
The earliest English play directly traceable to a Spanish source is

---

[1] Genest, *Some Account of the English Stage*, vol. I, p. 129, dates the acting of this
play, 1671—72. Pepys described another comedy of Orrery, *Guzman*, as 'as mean
a thing...as hath been upon the stage a great while.' *Pepys's Diary*, ed. Wheatley,
vol. VIII, p. 296.

[2] See *ante*, p. 21 note 1.          [3] Ward, vol. III, p. 335.

[4] *Dryden*, ed. Scott-Saintsbury, vol. I, p. 62.

[5] Ward, vol. III, p. 267.

*Calisto and Melebea,* an adaptation to the stage of the dramatic novel, *Celestina,* the work, chiefly if not wholly, of Fernando de Rojas, and published about 1530. This work has already been described, together with the violent didactic conclusion with which the unknown English adapter made amends for his choice of so romantic a story[1]. As is well known, the Spanish scholar, Juan Luis Vives, friend of Sir Thomas More, visited England on the invitation of Henry VIII, who placed him as a reader on rhetoric at Corpus Christi college, Oxford. It has been thought that the English dramatic version of *Celestina* may have had some relation to Vives and his visit, although he anathematised the Spanish production as a work of infamy in his treatise *De Institutione Christianae Feminae.* It is somewhat strange that *Calisto and Melebea* had no successor. However, it played its part in relieving the old moral drama of abstractions by the substitution of living human figures in a story of actual life. It was to Italy, not to Spain, that the predecessors of Shakespeare, as well as most of his contemporaries, turned instinctively for romantic material. Spain was an enemy and, as such, was maligned and misunderstood[2]. Yet the figure of Philip, once a sovereign of England, was represented in at least one chronicle history with dignity; and a number of dramas, strictly Elizabethan, laid their scene in the peninsula and affected to follow annals of Spain[3]. Kyd's *Spanish Tragedie* and its imitation or burlesque, *The First Part of Jeronimo,* remain of undiscovered source; and Greene's *Alphonsus King of Arragon* is a composite of the biography of more than one sovereign of that name, as his queen Eleanor of *Edward I* is an outrageous distortion of one of the most estimable and charitable women that ever sat on the throne of England. The same playwright's *Battell of Alcazar* and the anonymous *Captain Stukeley,* which deals in part with the same topic, drew on material more nearly approaching the historical. Yet neither of these, nor *Lusts Dominion* (although details of the death of the king in that piece have been thought to have been suggested by the death of Philip II), can be traced to any definite Spanish source, much less to anything bearing the title of Spanish literature. Nor need we surmise that such lost

[1] See *ante,* vol. v, pp. 99, 100.
[2] On the mutual repugnance of the two nations in the sixteenth and seventeenth centuries, see some excellent paragraphs by Schevill, R., in *Romanische Forschungen,* xx, 1907, pp. 626—634.
[3] Philip II appears as a character in Thomas Heywood's *If you know not me, You know no bodie.* A *Philip of Spain,* now lost, is mentioned by Henslowe in 1602.

productions as Wadeson's *Humorous Earle of Gloster with his Conquest of Portingall* (1600), *The Conqueste of Spayne by John a Gaunt*, in which Day, Hathway and Haughton conspired, or Chettle and Dekker's *Kinge Sebastiane of Portingalle* (these last two in 1601), were any more closely associated with actual literature of the peninsula, however this last may have touched on a topic of some contemporary historical interest. Indeed, the number of English dramas up to the death of Elizabeth which can be traced even remotely to a source ultimately Spanish is surprisingly small. Marlowe's *Tamburlaine* was partially drawn from Pedro Mexia's *Silva de varia lección*; but this last had been translated into Italian, French and English (by Thomas Fortescue in his *Foreste or Collection of Histories*) long before Marlowe came to write. And, in Shakespeare's *Two Gentlemen of Verona*, the story of Julia and Proteus was suggested by that of Felix and Felismena in the second book of the *Diana* of the Portuguese-Spaniard Montemayor. But the probable intervention of the now lost play, *The History of Felix and Philiomena*, acted 3 January 1585, should dispose of any theory of a direct Shakespearean contact with this much-exploited Spanish source. Other Shakespearean examples of 'Spanish influence' have been affirmed. Such are the correspondences between *Twelfth Night* and the *Comedia de los Engaños* of Lope de Rueda; but both could have found a common source in Bandello or, possibly, in 'a dramatised version by an academy at Siena called *Gl' Ingannati*'; and such, too, is the notion that Shakespeare drew on *Conde Lucanor* for his *Taming of the Shrew*, a comedy obviously recast from the earlier anonymous *Taming of a Shrew*, combined with a plot of Italian extraction, immediately derived from Gascoigne's comedy, *Supposes*. A more interesting suggestion is that which traces the sources of *The Tempest* to the fourth chapter of 'a collection of mediocre tales,' entitled *Noches de Invierno*, the work of one Antonio de Eslava and first published at Pamplona in 1609[1]. Fitzmaurice-Kelly has given the weight of his authority to a respectful treatment of this source, adding:

This *provenance* may be thought to lend colour to the tradition that Shakespeare dramatised an episode from *Don Quixote*—a book that he might

---

[1] For this and much else in these paragraphs, the writer is indebted to Fitzmaurice-Kelly's most valuable paper, *The Relations between Spanish and English Literature*, 1910. See, also, two notes by Perott, J. de, on this topic and a Spanish parallel to *Love's Labour's Lost* in the *Shakespeare-Jahrbuch*, vol. XLV, 1908, pp. 151—4; and the valuable paper by Schevill, R., 'On the Influence of Spanish Literature on English in the Early Seventeenth Century' in *Romanische Forschungen*, *u.s.*

easily have read in Shelton's translation published in 1612, or, perhaps, even in the manuscript which Shelton had kept by him for some four or five years. At any rate, the following entry occurs under the date 1633 in the register of the Stationers' company:—'*The History of Cardenio* by Mr. Fletcher and Shakespeare, 20s.'[1]

As to Spanish personages interspersed through Elizabethan drama, it has been well said: 'They were either arrogant, boastful, pompously affected or cruel,' sheer caricatures, in a word, drawn with an unfriendly pen[2]. Middleton's Lazarillo in *Blurt Master-Constable* (a sad perversion of that delightful rascal, his namesake of Tormes), and Jonson's ridiculous caricature in the pretended Don Diego of *The Alchemist* are sufficient illustrations of this[3]. As to the boasters and bullies of the playwrights, Bobadill, Captain Tucca, Ancient Pistol and the rest, there was no need to bespeak them in Spain. For such traits of the kind as were not derived from observation can show a clear literary descent from the *Miles Gloriosus* of Plautus. That Shakespeare contrived to keep his Don Armado human, as well as absurdly lofty and vainglorious, is partly due to the fact that Armado is the portrait of an actual mad Spaniard, known as 'fantastical Monarcho,' who haunted the London of his day. And Armado, too, had had his immediate literary model in Lyly's contribution, Sir Thopas in *Endimion*, to the Plautine line of descent just mentioned.

Towards the end of the reign of king James I, Spanish literature became better known in England, and we naturally look for the effect of this on English drama. But this relation was still general and established largely through French and Italian translation; and it is easy to make too much of it. The plays of Beaumont and Fletcher have been alleged to disclose more especially that contact between the dramas of the two nations which some scholars have striven anxiously to establish; and this, notwithstanding the accurate statement of Dryden as to dramatic plots that 'Beaumont and Fletcher had most of theirs from Spanish novels[4].' Some seventeen of the fifty-two plays commonly attributed to Beaumont and Fletcher have been traced, in a greater or less measure of indebtedness, to Spanish literature.

---

[1] *U.s.* pp. 21, 22.

[2] Underhill, J. G., *Spanish Literature in the England of the Tudors*, 1899, p. 357.

[3] Middleton might have had his Lazarillo in English, long since translated by David Rowland and printed in 1576. There is no reason for assuming that Ben Jonson knew Spanish; his few allusions to *Don Quixote* and the Spanish phrases of *The Alchemist* to the contrary notwithstanding. See Schevill, R., *u.s.* pp. 612, 613.

[4] Preface to *An Evening's Love, Works of Dryden*, ed. Scott-Saintsbury, vol. III, p. 252.

Eighteen others remain unidentified as to source, and some of these disclose a content and a manner not unlike the ruling traits of the drama of Spain. If, then, we consider the almost incredible mass of the writings of Lope de Vega (to mention him only), unread by English and even by Spanish scholars, and further keep in mind that those conversant with Spanish drama are not always conversant with English and *vice versa*, it would be rash to affirm that the last word has been said on a topic as yet not seriously opened. Our present information, however, may be set forth as follows, although, with regard to the plays on Spanish subjects attributed to Beaumont and Fletcher, it should be premised that most of them were composed at a date precluding the possibility that Beaumont had a hand in them[1]. Cervantes was Fletcher's favourite Spanish author; and he seems to have been acquainted solely with his prose. From the *Novelas Exemplares*, the English poet drew the major plots of *The Chances, The Queene of Corinth, The Faire Maide of the Inne* and *Loves Pilgrimage*, with the underplot of *Rule a Wife And have a Wife* as well. *The Custome of the Countrey* is derived from the romance of *Persiles y Sigismunda*, the last work to come from the great Spaniard's hand. As to *Don Quixote*, apart from possible suggestions for certain episodes of Beaumont's *Knight of the Burning Pestle*[2], the plot of *The Coxcombe*, an episode of *The Double Marriage* and a personage of *The Prophetesse* have been traced by various critics to the same immortal romance[3]. Besides Cervantes, Fletcher drew on Lope de Vega for his *Pilgrim*, on Juan de Flores for *Women pleas'd* and on Gonzalo de Cespedes for *The Spanish Curate* and *The Maid in the Mill*; and not one of these originals is a play, nor need Fletcher have read a word of Spanish to have become acquainted with them; for all had been translated into French or English and were readily accessible to his hand[4]. About two only of the Fletcherian plays has any question on these points arisen. *Loves Cure*, first printed in the folio of 1647, but commonly dated back to the early years of king James, has been referred to a comedy by Guillen de Castro, written at

---

[1] Cf. *ante*, appendix to vol. VI, chap. V.

[2] On this topic, see the sane words of Schevill, *u.s.* pp. 617—624; and the introduction, by Murch, H. S., in his ed. of this play, *Yale Studies in English*, 1908.

[3] See, on this topic, Fitzmaurice-Kelly, preface to Shelton's *Don Quixote*, Koeppel, 'Quellenstudien,' *Münchener Beiträge*, 1895, and Rapp, *Studien über das englische Theater*, 1892.

[4] See the *résumé* of this subject in the present writer's *Elizabethan Drama*, vol. II, p. 215.

so late a date as to make it quite impossible that Fletcher could have seen it[1]. Again, Fletcher's *Island Princesse* has been referred to a source in the writings of the younger Argensola, not translated out of Spanish at such a date that Fletcher could have seen it[2]. But these matters are still under discussion, and, on this particular subject, we may take refuge in the judgment of Fitzmaurice-Kelly who writes: 'Suffice it to say that, at the present stage, the balance of probabilities is against the view that Fletcher knew Spanish[3].'

If we turn to other dramatists, we find an occasional contemporary of Fletcher following in his footsteps. *The Spanish Gipsie*, a tragicomedy by Middleton and William Rowley, is made up of an effective combination of two stories of Cervantes, *La Fuerza de la Sangre* and *La Gitanilla*. Rowley collaborated, too, with Fletcher in *The Maid in the Mill*, a comedy based on a story of Gonzalo de Cespedes, translated by Leonard Digges and called *Gerardo, the Unfortunate Spaniard*. Rowley's own powerful tragedy *Alls Lost by Lust*, draws on Spanish story, though his precise source remains problematic[4]. Once more, *A Very Woman*, by Massinger, is derived from a story of the *Novelas Exemplares*. The same dramatist's *Renegado* is said to be based on Cervantes's *Los Baños de Argel*, and similarities have been traced between the same two authors in *The Fatall Dowry* and the interlude, *El Viejo celoso*. Moreover, it is said that neither of these Spanish pieces was translated in Massinger's lifetime, although this is not to be considered certain. We may not feel sure that a Spanish play has actually influenced an English play by direct borrowing, until we reach Shirley, who, on credible authority, is reported to have utilised *El Castigo del Pensèque* of Tirso de Molina in *The Opportunitie* and Lope de Vega's *Don Lope de Cardona* in *The Young Admirall*. Fitzmaurice-Kelly sceptically observes, even as to these examples: 'a minute demonstration of the extent of Shirley's borrowings would be still more satisfactory[5].'

The last two volumes of *Dodsley's Old Plays* contain several dramas of the restoration which are Spanish in scene. Of these, *The Rebellion* by Thomas Rawlins seems wholly fanciful with its hero disguised as a tailor and its crowded and improbable in-

---

[1] Stiefel in *Herrig's Archiv*, vol. xcix, p. 271.

[2] See the same in vol. ciii, pp. 277 ff.

[3] *The Relations between Spanish and English Literature*, pp. 22, 23.

[4] On the topic, see the edition of the play by Stork, C. W., *Publications of the University of Pennsylvania*, 1910, vol. xiii, p. 70.

[5] *The Relations*, as above, p. 23.

cident. *The Marriage Night*, printed in 1664, by Henry viscount Falkland is an abler drama, reproducing, however, in more than one forcible passage, personages and situations of the earlier Elizabethan drama. Both of these were written before the closing of the theatres, but it is doubtful if the latter was ever acted. Other pre-restoration dramas of Spanish plot are *The Parson's Wedding*, which Killigrew had of Calderon's *Dama Duende*, and Fanshawe's translation of two comedies of Antonio de Mendoza[1]. With Tuke's *Adventures of Five Hours* (written in 1662) and Digby's *Elvira, or The Worst Not always True* (printed in 1667), we reach unquestionable examples of the immediate adaptation of Spanish dramas to the English stage. This is not the place in which to dilate on the glories of the Spanish stage, the moral purpose of Alarcon, the brilliancy and wit of Tirso de Molina, the happy fertility of Lope de Vega, the clarity of thought and lofty sentiment of Calderon, greatest of the Spanish dramatists. Both the comedies just mentioned are favourable specimens of the popular *comedias de capa y espada*, invented by Lope de Vega. Two ladies, a gallant and his friend, their lovers, a jealous brother or a difficult father, with the attendant servants of all parties; mistake, accident, intrigue and involvement, honour touched and honour righted—such is the universal recipe of the comedy of cloak and sword. As to these adapters of the species to England, George Digby, earl of Bristol, had played no unimportant part as ambassador of king James I at Madrid, where he translated two other comedies of Calderon besides *No Siempre lo Peor es Cierto*, the original of *Elvira*. Sir Samuel Tuke had served at Marston moor and followed the prince into exile. He was much favoured by Charles, who is said to have suggested *Los Empeños de Seis Horas* (now assigned to Antonio Coello and not, as formerly, to Calderon) as 'an excellent design' for an English play[2]. *Elvira* is little more than a translation, stiff, formal and, while by no means wanting in action, protracted if not chargeable with repetitions. It was not printed until 1667, and we have no record of the performance of it. Tuke's *Adventures of Five Hours* is a better play and, as rewritten, was sufficiently adapted to the conditions of the English stage to gain a deserved success. Into the relations of Tuke's play to the coming heroic drama of Dryden, we cannot here enter. Its importance, despite its Castilian gravity and some rimed couplets, seems, in this respect, likely to be exag-

---

[1] *Fiestas de Aranjuez* and *Querer por solo querer*, printed in 1670 and 1671.
[2] Fitzmaurice-Kelly, J., *Littérature Espagnole*, traduction Davray, 1904, p. 345.

gerated[1]. So, too, although important as the earliest play of
Spanish plot acted after the restoration, it is too much to claim for
*The Adventures* the 'reintroduction' of a type of the drama of
intrigue 'which, from that day to this, has never left the English
stage[2].' Dryden attacked *The Adventures*, but Pepys declared :
'when all is done, [it] is the best play that ever I read in my
life[3].'

The coffers of Spanish drama, thus opened, continued to afford
English playwrights their treasures. Dryden's *Rival-Ladies* and
*An Evening's Love or the Mock Astrologer* have been referred
to Spanish sources : the last is Calderon by way of Corneille.
Dryden's earliest dramatic effort, *The Wild Gallant*, has also been
thought to be of Spanish origin. But this is an error, referable
to a misreading of the prologue ; the source is certainly English
and, doubtless, Dryden's own invention[4]. With Sir Thomas St
Serfe's *Taruzo's Wiles, or the Coffee House*, founded on Moreto's
*No puede ser*, the earl of Orrery's *Guzman* and Mrs Behn's *Dutch
Lover* and *The Rover*, we complete the list of dramas in the earlier
years of the restoration which have been alleged to be of Spanish
plot[5]. Crowne's *Sir Courtly Nice* is a later comedy, said, likewise, to have been suggested by the taste of king Charles and
derived from Moreto's *No puede ser*, and 'the most amusing
scenes' of Wycherley's comedy, *The Gentleman Dancing-master*,
have been assigned to a source in Calderon's *El Maestro de
Danzar*. More commonly, however, Spanish influences filtered
into England through the drama of France. It may be doubted
whether any 'Spanish plot' of Dryden exhibits more than an
indirect origin of this nature. In later decades, this was almost
invariably the case. Thus, Steele's *Lying Lover, The Perplexed*

---

[1] See Child, C. G., in *Modern Language Notes*, vol. xix, 1904, p. 166, and the
unpublished thesis of Gaw, A., on this play, 1908, in the library of the University of
Pennsylvania. Cf. *ante*, p. 16 note 2.

[2] Hume, M., *Spanish Influence on English Literature*, 1905, p. 291.

[3] *Pepys's Diary*, ed. Wheatley, H. B., vol. v, p. 403.

[4] Dryden's words, 'It is your author's lot To be endangered by a Spanish plot,'
not 'with a Spanish plot' as often quoted, refer to his rivalry with Tuke's *Adventures*,
not to the source of his own play. Just below, he affirms, 'This play is English and
the growth your own.' This point is made by Gaw in his thesis, referred to in a note
above.

[5] *The Dutch Lover* is referred by Langbaine to a Spanish story ; *The Rover* is
an adaptation of Killigrew's *Thomaso*. For both of these, see below, p. 141 of this
volume. *The False Count*, 1682, is another play by Mrs Behn of Spanish type.
Langbaine finds 'a hint' in it, however, 'borrowed from Molière's *Les Précieuses
Ridicules*.'

*Lover* of Mrs Centlivre and Colley Cibber's *She Would and She Would Not* are derivative plays and only remotely Spanish.

We may summarise what has been said on a subject of considerable difficulty as follows. Spanish literary influences on the drama in Tudor times were slight and confined, almost entirely, to an occasional plot, derived, as a rule, through some foreign intermediary. In the reign of James I, Beaumont and Fletcher, Massinger and William Rowley, alone among dramatists of note, drew on Spanish sources for their plays; and, though the question cannot be regarded as definitely settled, it seems likely that their sources lay wholly in fiction, translated into other and, to them, more familiar languages of the continent or into English. It was in the reign of king Charles I, that Spanish drama for the first time came into a closer touch with the English stage. That touch was closest at the restoration, when the cavalier returned with his foreign luggage and the taste of the king conspired with the experiences of his courtiers to foster many experiments. But Spanish influence was soon eclipsed by that of France, aided by the strong national spirit that prolonged the influence of Jonson and his contemporaries for generations after their decease.

In turning to a consideration of the influences of French literature on the drama of the restoration, it is customary to give unusual weight to the example of the *romans de longue haleine*, those extraordinary expressions in protracted hyperbole of ideal conduct, sentiment and conversation, with which the finer spirits of the days of Louis XIV sought to elevate and ennoble social life[1]. But, as a matter of fact, much of this influence was already in full flood far back in the reign of king Charles I, as the cult of Platonic love, about 1633, and the ideals of love and honour which it fostered are alone sufficient to attest[2]. To what extent the ideals of this one time fashionable cult may be surmised to have persisted to affect appreciably the conduct of the returning exiles is a question for the historian of social conditions. On the drama, such ideals had a marked, if superficial, effect. The life of the court of king Charles II, was, at best, a coarse replica of that of Versailles; and the heroic drama, the roots of which lie deeper than in the supersoil of romance, reproduced mostly externals, grandiloquence of language, loftiness of sentiment, incredible

[1] For a list of restoration plays referred to the influences of the romances of the Scudérys and other like writers, see Ward, vol. III, p. 309 note.

[2] See, as to this, especially D'Avenant's apotheosis of Platonic love in his grand masque, *The Temple of Love*, his *Love and Honour*, both 1634, and his *Platonick Lovers*, 1635.

valour, with courtesy and honour drawn and twisted into an impossible code. More immediate in its effects was the contemporary French stage, in which much of the literature of exaggerated sentiment was reproduced by forgotten authors, who live now only in the satire which their extravagance inspired in the commonsense of Boileau. But the subject of this influence, and of that of the classicism of Corneille and Racine in particular, as well as the use of the rimed couplet in the English drama, and its relations to the heroic play are treated elsewhere ; our concern here is with comedy[1].

It was in 1653 that Molière, after his long apprenticeship in the provinces, brought out his *L'Étourdi* in Paris; and, from that date onward to his death, just twenty years later, he remained the master and the example of the most brilliant comedy of modern times. Molière's earlier work thus corresponds, in point of time, with the latest years of exile, when many Englishmen of rank were amusing themselves in Paris, and peculiarly open to lighter impressions from the idleness of their lives. No one foreign author has been so plundered by English playwrights as Molière ; and his humane spirit, his naturalness, adaptability and dramatic aptitude stood the borrowers in good stead, in recalling them from the intricacies of Spanish intrigue and the wearisome repetition at second hand of the 'humours' of Ben Jonson. That the finer qualities of Molière, his verve, his buoyancy, ease and success of plot, and sure characterisation, escaped his English imitators is not to be denied ; for, apart from the circumstance that few of them were men of more than mediocre parts, the genius of Molière towers above the imitation of any age. A list of the borrowings of restoration comedy from the drama of Molière and his contemporaries would unduly burden this page. D'Avenant, Dryden, Sedley, Wycherley, Vanbrugh, Crowne and Shadwell all owe debts of plot, character, design and dialogue to French comedy ; and, even where the debt may not be specifically ascertainable, the

---

[1] Cf. *ante*, pp. 14 f. and 18 ff. and *post*, chap. vii. As to these influences, it is well to remember that translation and adaptation from the French by no means set in, for the first time, with the restoration. Apart from the early direct influence of the Senecan Garnier on Kyd, Greville, Alexander and others, and the plays drawn from French sources by Fletcher and his group, which it is not pertinent here to recount, Sir William Lower had translated the *Polyeucte* of Corneille in 1655 and *Horace* the year after ; Carlell, his *Héraclius*, about the same date, and 'several persons of honour,' Waller, Sedley, Godolphin and the earl of Dorset, were busy with a translation of his *Pompée*, afterwards completed by Mrs Katherine Philips, 'the Matchless Orinda,' encouraged by lord Orrery, and produced at Dublin in *February* 1663. (She also translated four acts of *Horace*.)

tone of the play, the method of its conduct and the conception of its personages declare the dominant influence of France. To mention only some examples, Molière supplied scenes, personages or suggestions to D'Avenant's *Playhouse to be Let*, Dryden's *An Evening's Love, Amphitryon* and *Sir Martin Mar-All*, to Sedley's *Mulberry Garden*, Wycherley's *Country Wife, The Plain Dealer*, Shadwell's *Sullen Lovers* and *The Miser* and Crowne's *The Country Wit* and *The English Frier*; while Corneille, Racine, Quinault were levied on by the playwrights just named and by others besides.

The influence of French ópera on the like productions in England is a matter of less certainty. The attribution of D'Avenant's experiments in musical drama to direct influences, either from Italy or from France, seems dubious, if not fanciful, if his previous experience as a writer of masques for the court of king Charles I is taken into account. Although Italian opera had been introduced into France so far back as 1645 and 'the first French opera,' 'a pastoral,' had been performed some fourteen years later, this by-product of the drama was not thrust into general acceptance and popularity until the days of the celebrated partnership between Lulli, the king's musician, and the librettist Quinault, the first opera of whose joint effort, *Cadmus and Hermione*, was acted in 1673[1]. Meanwhile, however, Cambert, composer of 'the first French opera,' had written his *Pomone*, the earliest opera heard by the Parisian public; and, when his rivalry with Lulli for the control and management of the opera in Paris ended in the latter's triumph, Cambert came over to London and, as leader of one of king Charles's companies of musicians, took his part in the introduction of French opera into England[2]. Cambert's associate in his operatic labours was the abbé Pierre Perrin, who had supplied the words for 'the pastoral' as well as for *Pomone*. Another product of this partnership was *Ariane, ou Le Mariage de Bacchus*; and an opera of that title was sung in French at the Theatre Royal in Drury lane in January 1674[3]. An English version of this opera, published simultaneously with the French version at the period of production, reads *Ariadne, or The Marriage of Bacchus*, 'an Opera

[1] On these subjects, see Parry, Sir C. H. R., *The Oxford History of Music*, vol. III, p. 225, and Lavoix, H., *La Musique Française*, pp. 90, 100. *Les Fêtes de l'Amour et de Bacchus*, with which Lulli opened his 'Opera' in the rue Vaugirard in the previous November, is described as little more than a ballet, a species of entertainment long familiar in France.

[2] *The Oxford History of Music*, vol. III, p. 295.

[3] See *Evelyn's Diary*, under 5 January 1673/4.

or a Vocal Representation, first composed by Monsieur P[ierre] P[errin]. Now put into Musick by Monsieur Grabut, Master of his Majesty's Musick.' And it is further said that Cambert super-intended the production[1]. Whatever the solution of this tangle, English musicians now took up the writing of opera, Matthew Locke staging his *Psyche* in 1675 and Purcell, *Dido and Aeneas,* his first opera, in 1680. Dryden's imitations of French opera, of which *Albion and Albanius,* 1685, is a typical example, came later; and so did the tasteless adaptations of earlier plays to operatic treatment, Shakespeare's *Tempest* and Fletcher's *Pro-phetesse,* for example, done to music, often of much beauty and effectiveness, by the famous musician of his day, Henry Purcell. The opera, according to Dryden, is 'a poetical tale, or fiction, represented by vocal and instrumental music, adorned with scenes, machines, and dances'; and he adds, somewhat to our surprise, 'the supposed persons of this musical drama are generally super-natural[2].' Unquestionably, the opera lent itself, like the heroic play, to sumptuous costume and ingenious devices in setting and stage scenery; and it is not to be denied that, then as now, its devotees set their greatest store on the music and on the fame of individual singers[3].

'I am no great admirer,' says Saint-Évremond, 'of comedies in music such as nowadays are in request. I confess I am not displeased with their magnificence; the machines have something that is surprising, the music in some places is charming; the whole together seems wonderful. But it... is very tedious, for where the mind has so little to do, there the senses must of necessity languish[4].'

A discussion of the history of Italian opera in England would be out of place here, since it came first into England with the new century. That men of the taste and judgment of Dryden and Purcell in their respective arts should have lent their talents to the composition of these 'odd medleys of poetry and music' only proves the strength of contemporary fashions in art.

---

[1] Lawrence, W. J., 'Early French Players in England,' *Anglia,* vol. XXXII, pp. 81 82, and Nuitter et Thonan, *Les Origines de l'Opéra Français,* pp. 303 ff.

[2] Preface to *Albion and Albanius, Works of Dryden,* ed. Scott-Saintsbury, vol. VII, p. 228. Compare, also, the definition of Saint-Évremond: 'An odd medley of poetry and music wherein the poet and the musician, equally confined one by the other, take a world of pain to compose a wretched performance.' *Upon Operas, Works of Saint-Évremond,* translation ed. 1714, vol. II, p. 87.

[3] 'Our thoughts run more upon the musician than the hero in the opera : Luigi, Cavallo, and Cesti are still present to our imagination ... Baptist is a hundred times more thought of than Theseus or Cadmus.' *Ibid.* pp. 86, 87.

[4] *Ibid.* p. 85.

But it was well that, before these general French influences had made themselves felt, a new dramatist, also schooled in France, began in his productions to give expression to the contemporary ideal of polite society and to adapt to the changed conditions of the moment the most persistent form of drama, the comedy of manners. Of the earlier life of Sir George Etherege, we know next to nothing. It has been inferred from an allusion by Dryden, that Etherege was born in 1634 and, by means of other inferences, that he came of an old Oxfordshire family[1]. It seems unlikely that Etherege was ever a student at either university; but his easy conversancy with French and the ways of the French capital point to a long sojourn in Paris. The first work of Etherege was *The Comical Revenge, or Love in a Tub*. It was published in 1664 and may have been produced for the first time late in the previous year. This comedy was an immediate success and Etherege found himself, in a night, famous. Thus introduced to the wits and the fops of the town, Etherege took his place in the select and dissolute circle of Rochester, Dorset and Sedley. On one occasion, at Epsom, after tossing in a blanket certain fiddlers who refused to play, Rochester, Etherege and other boon companions so 'skirmished the watch' that they left one of their number thrust through with a pike and were fain to abscond. Etherege married a fortune, it is not certain when, and, apparently for no better reason, was knighted. On the death of Rochester, he was, for some time, the 'protector' of the beautiful and talented actress, Mrs Barry[2]. Ever indolent and procrastinating, Etherege allowed four years to elapse before his next venture into comedy. *She Would if She Could*, 1668, is a better play than *The Comical Revenge*, and such was the popular expectation of it, when produced, that, as Pepys tells us, though he and his wife were 'there by two o'clock, there were one thousand people put back that could not have room in the pit.' Unhappily, success was partially defeated, because, adds Pepys, 'the actors...were out of humour and had not their parts perfect[3].' Etherege now doubled his former period of indolence and silence, and, eight years later, in 1676, doubtless stung by a deserved rebuke in Rochester's *Session of the Poets*, produced his last and best comedy, *The Man of Mode, or Sir Fopling Flutter*. Of the later years of Etherege,

---

[1] *Dryden to Etheredge, The Works of Sir George Etheredge*, ed. Verity, 1888. p. 403.

[2] The particulars of these passages in the life of Etherege will be found in Meindl's study of the poet, *Wiener Beiträge*, vol. xiv, 1901, pp. 66—73.

[3] *Pepys's Diary*, ed. Wheatley, vol. vii, p. 307.

we know much, owing to the existence of one of his *Letterbooks*, kept by his secretary at Ratisbon, where he was English resident from 1685 to a time early in 1689. From certain allusions, Etherege has been supposed to have held similar posts else-where, in Sweden and, possibly, in Turkey. But, of this, there is no proof. The particulars of his life in an uncongenial diplomatic exile need not concern us. His correspondence, which included letters to and from Dryden, is full of life and gossip about the wits of his time, all of it expressed with the gaiety, candour and foppish wit of which Etherege, in his plays, is the acknowledged master. Etherege is supposed to have died, about 1690, at Paris. Handsome, witty, brave, profligate though he was, and, perhaps, as has been charitably suggested, having but a weak head for wine, the story that 'Sir George Etheredge died by falling down stairs in a drunken fit,' rests solely ' on the authority of a friend of the family,' repeated by Oldys[1].

Different opinions have been broached as to the place of Etherege in the history of restoration drama, although no two much at variance can be held by those familiar with the spirit, gaiety and brilliancy of the prose dialogue of his comedies. The discovery of more than one copy of an edition of *The Comical Revenge*, dating 1664, has brought Etherege's claim to the intro-duction of rimed couplets as a regular dramatic metre on the restoration stage into direct competition with that of Orrery[2]. Although Etherege abandoned this innovation in his other two comedies, wisely writing them in prose, in which he is at his best, this fashion of distinguishing more serious and elevated scenes and passages of a comedy by couching them in heroic couplets was continued by certain of his fellows[3]. But the authority of the writer who has urged the above-mentioned claim on behalf of Etherege, further invites us to assume that he 'loitered long enough in Paris' after the first rush of the royalists homewards 'for Molière to be revealed to him,' and that, with a new idea thus formed ' of what comedy ought to be,' he returned to England and ' founded English comedy as it was successively understood by Congreve, Goldsmith and Sheridan[4].' Now, indubitably, Etherege had none of his happy, conscienceless art from Jonson. With the making up

---

[1] *Works of Etheredge*, ed. Verity, A., introduction, p. xxvii.

[2] See Gosse, E., 'Sir George Etheredge,' in *Seventeenth Century Studies*, ed. 1897, p. 265, where the relations of Etherege, in this respect, to Dryden's *The Rival-Ladies* and D'Avenant's *Siege of Rhodes* are discussed. As to Orrery's claim, see *ante*, chap. I, p. 18 and note 2.

[3] Note, more especially, Sedley's *Mulberry Garden*.     [4] Gosse, *u.s.* pp. 266, 267.

of his personages out of changes on a single humour, strained and contorted, Etherege discarded any pretensions to the knitting together of a plot. He also discarded literary as well as dramatic constructiveness, and it is not impossible that Molière pointed him the way to a freedom from rule which Etherege pressed to licence. But the merit of Etherege seems to lie less in his eschewing the moribund fashion of Jonson's humours, than in a certain natural genius whereby he was able to put upon the stage a picture, very little heightened, of the roistering, reckless idleness and licentiousness that actually characterised the brilliant, graceless fops whose society he frequented. 'The man of quality, who can fight at need with spirit and verve, but whose customary occupation is the pursuit of pleasure without dignity and without reflection'—this is Etherege's theme; it is his very self, recurring in Sir Frederick Frollicke, in Courtall and Freedom, 'two honest gentlemen of the town,' in *She Would if She Could* and in the masterly circle of fops—Dorimant, Medley, Bellair and Sir Fopling Flutter—each one of them equally 'the man of mode.' 'Nature, you know,' says Etherege of himself, 'intended me for an idle fellow, and gave me passion and qualities fit for that blessed calling; but fortune has made a changeling of me and necessity forces me to set up for a fop of business[1].' As to the women of Etherege, they are fashionable, extravagant, witty as the men and as bold in their intrigues and amours; there is no maiden's blush among them. They are such, in a word, as the restoration rakes and *roués* knew them.

Attention has been called to Etherege's graphic touches of scene, costume and place in the gay little west-end that knew him. He is at home in Mulberry garden, a place of public resort and entertainment, with bordered alleys and adjacent arbours in which to eat syllabub and to carry on 'hazardous flirtations' like those of Mistress Ariana and Mistress Gatty, two naughty runaways from chaperonage; or, again, in the shop of Mrs Trinket in the New Exchange, a species of Arcade, whither ladies go a-shopping for 'a few fashionable toys to keep 'em in countenance at a play or in the Park,' and where gallants 'scent their eyebrows and periwigs with a little essence of oranges or jessamine,' as did Courtall while waiting for lady Cockwood. But the superlative quality of Etherege as a writer of comedy is the ease and naturalness of his prose dialogue, which, almost uniformly witty and, at

---

[1] *Letterbook* under date 8 March 1688, quoted by Gosse, *Seventeenth Century Studies*, ed. 1897, p. 296.

times, really brilliant, is seldom overdone and unsuited to his personages, as is not infrequently the case with Congreve. The very frivolity of Etherege disarms criticism. Who would break a butterfly on the wheel? For the time, English men and women in good society had lapsed into an excess of gallantry, enjoying their orgy with incorrigible frankness and *abandon*, and avowing their enjoyment with incorrigible flippancy and shamelessness. In Etherege, comedy, for the moment, touched nature once more, for such was nature in the society of the restoration. Congreve is remote and studied in comparison, for he wrote of these things when in actual life they had come to be mitigated by a measurable return of public manners to healthier conditions; while, as to Sheridan, equally a disciple of Etherege, his comedies in fact only perpetuated a picture of life that had long since ceased to be much more than a brilliant tradition of the stage.

The closest immediate follower of Etherege in comedy is Sir Charles Sedley, whose earliest comedy, *The Mulberry Garden*, 1668, is based, in part, on Molière's *L'École des Maris* and is written in that mixture of prose and heroic couplets which Etherege introduced in his *Comical Revenge*. An intimate in the chosen circle of the king, Sedley was as famous for his wit as he was notorious for the profligacy of his life. Nevertheless, he appears to have been a capable man of affairs and, as a writer, gained a deserved reputation alike for the clearness and ease of his prose and for a certain poetic gift, more appreciable in his occasional lyrics than in the serious parts of his dramas. *The Mulberry Garden*, no bad comedy in its lighter scenes, is bettered in *Bellamira, or the Mistress*, 1687, which, though founded on the *Eunuchus* of Terence, presents a lively, if coarsely realistic, picture of the reckless pursuit of pleasure of Sedley's day. *The Grumbler*, printed in 1702, is little more than an adaptation of *Le Grondeur* of Brueys and Palaprat. Sedley's tragedies call for no more than the barest mention. His *Antony and Cleopatra*, 1667, reprinted as *Beauty the Conqueror*, is among the feeblest as it is the latest, of heroic plays written in couplets. His *Tyrant King of Crete*, 1702, is merely a revision of Henry Killigrew's *Pallantus and Eudora*, little amended in the process[1].

With examples such as these among writers who pretended to gentle manners and birth, and with Dryden descending to the dramatic stews, it is not surprising to find lesser writers and

---

[1] On this topic, see Genest, *u.s.* vol. x, p. 158, and Lissner, M., in *Anglia*, vol. xxviii, pp. 180—3.

stage hacks throwing decency to the winds and substituting sheer scurrility for wit, and brutality for force of passion. John Lacy (who died in 1681) is a familiar example of the popular actor turned playwright. Out of a couple of the comedies of Molière, butchered in the process, he compounded *The Dumb Lady, or The Furrier made Physician*, 1669 ; in *Sawny the Scot, or The Taming of the Shrew*, 1667, Grumio is raised to the chief part in that much abused comedy of Shakespeare ; while, in *Sir Hercules Buffoon*, 1684, a more original effort, even the braggart and the fool, immemorial stock figures of comedy, suffer degradation. The best comedy of Lacy is *The Old Troop* (before 1665), in which he tells, with rude and broad native humour, experiences of his own when soldiering in the royalist army in civil war times, and, incidentally, maligns and abuses fallen puritanism. Even more popular in his day was Edward Ravenscroft, the author of a dozen plays extending over a career of nearly twenty-five years. Ravenscroft pillaged the previous drama at large and Molière in particular, taking his earliest comedy and greatest success, *Mamamouchi, or the Citizen Turned Gentleman*, 1671, from *Le Bourgeois Gentilhomme* and *Monsieur de Pourceaugnac*. In his palmy days, Ravenscroft dared to measure his wit with Dryden[1]. But his one conspicuous quality was his success in boisterous farce. It was this and its scandalous satirical nature that secured to his *London Cuckolds*, first acted in 1682, an annual revival on the stage on lord mayor's day for nearly a century[2]. His other plays, among them an alteration of *Titus Andronicus*, call for no mention here[3].

It is assuredly a matter for comment that the first woman to write professionally for the English stage should have begun her career at a moment when the morality of English drama was at its lowest ebb. Aphra or Aphara Behn was born at Wye in 1640, the daughter of John Johnson, a barber. With a relative, whom she called her father, who had been nominated lieutenant-governor of Surinam, she went to reside there ; and, on his death, remained with his family, marrying a Dutch merchant named Behn about 1658. With her husband, she returned to London and, apparently, lived in some wealth and position until 1666, in which year her husband died. Having made the acquaintance of the king

---

[1] See the original prologues to *Mamamouchi*, and *The Careless Lovers*, and, likewise, the prologues to Dryden's *Marriage-à-la-Mode* and *The Assignation*.

[2] See *The Tatler*, no. 8.

[3] For a list of comedies by minor writers, printed within the first two decades following the restoration, see the bibliography to this chapter.

in the time of her prosperity, she was sent to Antwerp as a spy ; but, finding her services unrecognised and unpaid, she turned, about 1670, to letters for a livelihood. Mrs Behn's novels, in which she is a true forerunner of Defoe, do not concern us here nor her interesting anticipation of some of the ideas of Rousseau in the most famous of her stories, *Oronooko*. Between 1671 and 1689, the year of her death, Mrs Behn wrote assiduously for the stage, turning out no less than fifteen dramas. Though she observed the nice laws of mine and thine with little more punctiliousness than did her male contemporaries, it is not to be denied that Mrs Behn is inventive in situations if not in whole plots, ingenious in keeping her figures in almost incessant action and in maintaining an interminable flow of vivacious dialogue[1]. Her most popular play was *The Rover, or The Banished Cavaliers*, which took the fancy of the town in 1677, and to which she wrote a second part in 1681. In both of these plays, the central figure is a swashbuckling sea captain ashore, the victim of every pretty face and the hero of a string of questionable adventures. The scene of the first part, Naples in carnival time, must have lent itself to brilliant and varied stage setting. *The Rover* is taken entire from two unacted comedies of Thomas Killigrew, entitled *Thomaso the Wanderer*, which, it may be suspected, contain not a little matter autobiographical, though, otherwise, as frankly 'borrowed' from English playwrights of the past as Mrs Behn herself 'borrowed' from Killigrew[2]. Mrs Behn's next comedy, *The Dutch Lover*, 1673, is a favourable specimen of the conventional comedy of cloak and sword, the scene, as in the second part of *The Rover*, being Madrid. *The Dutch Lover* is said to be 'founded on a Spanish romance written by the ingenious Don Francisco de las Coveras styled *Don Fenise*[3].' Another class of Mrs Behn's comedies are those of her own contemporary town life, most of them lifted bodily from earlier English plays and made coarse in the process. For example, *The Debauchee*, 1677, is based on *A Madd Couple well*

---

[1] Siegel puts it that Mrs Behn began with serious, romantic dramas, such as *The Young King* and *The Forced Marriage*, and her one (?) tragedy, *The Moor's Revenge*, but went over to comedy in *The Rover*, first acted anonymously, in deference to the loose tastes of the time. See 'Aphra Behn's Gedichte und Prosawerke,' in *Anglia*, vol. xxv, pp. 98—101.

[2] See Baker, D. E., *Biographia Dramatica*, ed. 1812, vol. iii, p. 232, where some of these 'borrowed decorations' of Killigrew are referred to their originals in Carew, Fletcher and Jonson. Both of Killigrew's plays are said to have been written in Madrid.

[3] Langbaine, 1691, p. 19 ; and see Hazlitt, *Collections and Notes*, 1867—76, p. 104. There is, of course, no such Spanish author as 'Coveras.'

*matcht* by Richard Brome ; *The Town Fop*, of the same date, on
Wilkins's *Miseries of Inforst Mariage*. The most characteristic comedy of this group is *The City Heiress*, 1682, in which
Mrs Behn has broadened even the humour of Middleton's *A Mad
World, My Masters*, unquestionably her source, and combined it
with suggestions from *The Guardian* of Massinger. Nothing
could be more unfortunate than the criticism that finds for
Aphra Behn a model in Jonson[1]. That lady's art was predatory,
and she took any author's property as her own, painting with
realistic, if conventional, brush the fops, the *roués*, the maids and
misses of Etherege and Sedley in their eternal embroilment
of questionable amorous intrigue. In *The Roundheads*, 1682,
Mrs Behn conveyed Tatham's plot of *The Rump* entire to her
comedy and thickened the whole with the addition of one of her
favourite situations[2]. In one of her latest plays, *The Widow
Ranter*, not published until 1690, after her death, Mrs Behn
treated a historical event of recent occurrence in the colony of
Virginia—the rebellion, as it was called, of Nathaniel Bacon—
and produced a result, with all its absurdities, of no small
originality. Mrs Behn was a very gifted woman, compelled to
write for bread in an age in which literature, and especially
comedy, catered habitually to the lowest and most depraved of
human inclinations. Her success depended on her ability to write
like a man. On the score of morality, she is again and again more
daring and *risquée* than any of her male competitors in the art
of playmaking, and she is as frivolous and as abandoned in
speech as the worst of them all. But, as has been well said, it
remains difficult for us to believe that a woman whose literary
talents commended her to the friendship and association of Dryden
could have been degraded in her personal life.

William Wycherley was born in 1640 of a substantial Shropshire family. He was educated, at first, in France, where he
frequented good society ; but, with the coming back of the king,
entered at Queen's college, Oxford, which, however, he left without a degree[3]. Later, at the Inner Temple, Wycherley led the
gay and frivolous life of a man about town and made those
observations of the conversation and manners of his time that

[1] Gosse in the *Dictionary of National Biography*, vol. IV, p. 130.
[2] Siegel, *u.s.* p. 104, finds three of Mrs Behn's comedies especially written
'in service of the royal cause.' These are *The City Heiress*, in which a puritan-
minded usurer is ridiculed, *The Rump* and *The False Count*. All these plays
appeared in 1682. This was the time of the Popish plot; and Dryden's *Absalom and
Achitophel* had been published in November 1681.
[3] 'He was much noticed by the celebrated Duchess of Montausier (Julia de Ram-
bouillet),' Ward, vol. III, p. 461 note.

he, later, reproduced successfully in his plays. When a very old man, Wycherley told Pope that he had written his first comedy, *Love in a Wood*, when he was but nineteen, that is, in 1659—60. This seems an error, as all the evidence points to the first performance of this play in 1671, and to its inspiration in the earlier work of Etherege and Sedley. Indeed, the dramatic activity of Wycherley was comprised within a period of less than five years, as *The Plain Dealer*, the fourth and last of his comedies, was on the stage not later than the spring of 1674. It was the success of *Love in a Wood*, added to a handsome person, that brought Wycherley to the notice and favour of the king's mistress, the duchess of Cleveland. To her, he dedicated his comedy on its publication, and, by her, he was drawn into the shameless circle which she ruled. But neither wealth nor honours accrued to Wycherley from this intimacy. And, some years later, meeting lady Drogheda, a young widow of fortune, Wycherley married her, losing thereby the favour of the king and a post of tutor to one of the royal children. His wife proved imperious, jealous and ill-tempered and, when she died, years later, left the unfortunate poet very little besides an expensive lawsuit. It was not until James had come to the throne that the author of *The Plain Dealer* was remembered, his debts paid and a pension of £200 a year settled upon him. Wycherley outlived all the companions of his youth and middle age, dying in December 1715. His strange literary friendship with Pope, who was nearly fifty years his junior, and his later halting and abortive verses, may be passed by here. It is not to be denied that Wycherley was much esteemed by his friends, among whom, it must be remembered, were Dryden, Pope and Dennis. The old *roué* was credited with fairness of spirit and an outspoken contempt of deceit, qualities of his own 'plain dealer,' as well as with a 'tenderness of temper' and a tendency to do justice to others for which we should not be altogether disposed to look in his own Manly.

*Love in a Wood, or St James's Park*, Wycherley's earliest venture in comedy, was suggested in subject, as in title, by the recent success of Sedley's *Mulberry Garden*, which it parallels in its scenes in the park, as *The Mulberry Garden* parallels Etherege's earlier *The Comical Revenge*. To draw up serious indictments of plagiarism in cases such as these is a sheer waste of ingenuity[1]. The novelty of a locality admirably fitted for

[1] See, however, the treatment of this topic by Klette, J., *William Wycherley's Leben und dramatische Werke*, Münster, 1883.

the masquing and intrigue that delighted the age was a sufficient inspiration for all three comedies. The construction of *Love in a Wood* is somewhat better than that of Etherege's plays ; it is, however, not nearly so well written as any one of them, although the dialogue is direct, witty and idiomatic and, doubtless, closer to the colloquial speech of the day than Etherege's brilliant repartees. The characters, while presenting nothing beyond the usual 'young gentlemen of the town,' the coxcomb, the usurer, the matchmaker, the affected widow, are well defined and drawn with strokes as vigorous and, at times, as coarse as are their actions and their language. *The Gentleman Dancing-master* was first staged towards the close of the year 1671, and we are surprised to hear that 'it was not much liked, and was acted only six times[1].' This really diverting comedy presents a marked improvement in the way of simplicity and unity on Wycherley's previous effort. The Frenchified gull, the Englishman turned Spaniard, and the device of a foolish suitor employed by a clever maiden to further her flirtation with his rival—all are time honoured properties of the earlier stage. The incident, too, on which the whole plot turns, that of a lover forced, under fear of discovery, to pretend himself a dancing-master, is borrowed from Calderon's comedy, *El Maestro de Danzar*, which, in turn, goes back to Lope de Vega. But there remains much that is inventive and original in the English comedy, and the dialogue has developed in wit, and especially in a certain quality of daring and suggestive innuendo and double meaning of which this dramatist is peculiarly master.

*The Country Wife* was, doubtless, on the stage before the end of the year 1673. It is one of the coarsest plays in the English language, nor can it be said that this quality is referable to either of the comedies of Molière, *L'École des Femmes* and *L'École des Maris*, which furnished hints to the English playwright. And yet, despite the idea on which the whole action turns, *The Country Wife* is not only skilfully planned and exceedingly well written, but it is not devoid of the gravity of true satire. Indeed, it is in this play, the *dramatis personae* of which include not a single truly virtuous personage, that we perceive Wycherley to have passed beyond the careless art of Etherege, which contents itself with merely picturing the age in its wantonness and folly, and to have entered the more sombre regions of satire, in which these things are referred for contrast and reprobation (even if unconsciously) to the normal standards of men of decent life.

[1] Genest, vol. I, p. 137.

But, not until we reach *The Plain Dealer*, Wycherley's last and best comedy, do we recognise that this savage blasphemer in the halls of beauty and of art is, after all, at heart a moralist, indignantly flagellating vice as well as gloating over her deformities. *The Plain Dealer* was first acted, with acclamation and success, in 1674, and printed three years later. While certain scenes of it were suggested by Molière's famous *Le Misanthrope*, Wycherley's masterpiece cannot but be regarded as an admirably bold, effective and original piece of dramatic satire. Here, the satirist is no less plainspoken than in *The Country Wife*, but, in the faithful Fidelia (perilous reincarnation of the Viola of a cleaner age), in the clearsighted running commentary of Eliza and in the integrity of Freeman, the author has set before us his own rough but honest standard of life and conduct, by means of which we may judge the justice and effect of his satiric strokes. Manly, 'the plain dealer,' is a brute; but it is the wickedness and hypocrisy of the age that has made him such. An infatuation for straightforward conduct and plain dealing has made him blind to the real qualities of men and women; and, while he sees through superficial pretence and affectation, he is like a child in the hands of those who humour his whims. *The Plain Dealer* seems unpleasantly true to life. But for the normal restoration taint it might have approached tragedy in the completeness of Fidelia's passionate devotion and in the gravity of Manly's disillusionment. As it is, *The Plain Dealer* is a notable work, compactly written, carefully planned and effectively executed, and, in its honest purpose to castigate vice, not unworthy of the ideals of Ben Jonson himself. The man who thus mercilessly exposed the vice, social chicanery and hypocrisy of his age, who thus laughed to scorn its follies and petty subterfuges, was no mere wanton. In the tonic of Wycherley's *Plain Dealer*, English comedy recovered momentarily a sense of the actual relations of contemporary social conditions to better standards. But it was easier to follow Etherege than Wycherley. The frivolous always shun the ferule of the moralist; and, hence, 'the artificial comedy' continued its primrose path, until called to account by the trumpeted warnings of Jeremy Collier and the honest endeavours of Steele to redeem the fallen stage, which had now, like a broken but unrepentant profligate, been brought to a reckoning with the past.

# CHAPTER VI

## THE RESTORATION DRAMA

### II

#### CONGREVE, VANBRUGH, FARQUHAR, ETC.

WILLIAM CONGREVE, a spoilt child of life and literature, was
born in 1670 at Bardsey, near Leeds. He came of an ancient
family, long settled in Staffordshire; and it was due to the accident
of his father's commanding the garrison at Youghal that he sat
upon the same bench with Swift at Kilkenny school and finished
his studies at Trinity college, Dublin. In 1691, he was admitted to
the Middle Temple, deserted law for literature, like many another,
composed a story called *Incognita, or Love and Duty Reconciled*,
in which Aurelian, the son of a Florentine nobleman, plays an
austere part, and of which Dr Johnson rightly said that 'he would
rather praise than read it,' and then, in 1693, came upon the town
with *The Old Bachelor*.

It was Congreve's signal good fortune to appear at the right
moment. The theatre then enjoyed a larger licence and a loftier
repute than ever before. The town asked no other favour of its
comic writers than to be amused, and the interpreters of comedy
rose to the full height of their opportunity. 'No stage,' said
Cibber with perfect truth, 'at any one period, could show thirteen
actors, standing all in equal light of excellence, in their profession'; and it was these actors who came loyally to Congreve's aid.
The incomparable Betterton, the acclaimed master of them all,
and the enchanting Mrs Bracegirdle portrayed the two chief
characters. The poet's colleagues endorsed the approval of the
pit. Dryden, then in the plenitude of his power, generously
hailed the rising star. He declared that he had never seen such
a first play, and gave the young author the practical benefit of
his advice. Congreve, after his wont, set no great value upon his
achievement. 'When I wrote it,' said he, in his reply to Collier,

'I had little thoughts of the stage; but did it, to amuse myself, in a slow recovery from a fit of sickness.' If it amused its author, it amused, also, its spectators. Its success was triumphant, and the fortunate Congreve became famous in a day.

In his preface to the published play, Congreve pleaded in extenuation an ignorance of the town and stage. No plea was necessary; and, if his ignorance of the town were confessed, the stage had left him no lessons to learn. With him, indeed, the craft of the stage was instinctive. From the very first he translated whatever he saw and heard in terms of the theatre. The comedy, which beguiled 'a slow recovery,' displays all the technical adroitness of an old hand. The dialogue is polished to an even surface; the play of wit flashes like sunlight upon water; of the writing no more need be said than that it is Congreve's own. For the rest, *The Old Bachelor* wears upon it every sign of youth and inexperience. Neither of the two stories which are interlaced, none too closely, in its plot is fresh or original. Though none of Congreve's contemporaries could have written the play, any one of them might have devised its fable. In other words, Congreve is playing supremely well the tune of the time. Heartfree and Silvia are but counters of artificial comedy. The marriage of the lady in the mask, which unties the knot of the play, is no better than an accepted convention of the stage. Bluffe, Sharper, and Wittol, who conduct the underplot, are stock characters of a still older fashion. They might have stepped out from Ben Jonson's comedy of humours. When Bluffe says: 'Sir, I honour you; I understand you love fighting, I reverence a man that loves fighting, sir, I kiss your hilts,' you recognise the authentic accent of Bobadill. Even Fondlewife, that 'kind of mongrel zealot' owes less to life than to Zeal-of-the-land Busy. In the scene where Lucy, Silvia's maid, altercates with Setter, the pimp, the language is marked by all the bombast of youth, which Congreve presently laid aside. Says Setter: 'Thou art some forsaken Abigail we have dallied with heretofore, and art come to tickle thy imagination with remembrance of iniquity past.' And Lucy replies: 'No, thou pitiful flatterer of thy master's imperfections! thou maukin, made up of the shreds and parings of his superfluous fopperies!' This is the language neither of life nor of comedy, and it was doubtless acceptable to the audience by its mere expectedness.

But if we put aside the youthful extravagance of some passages and the too frequent reliance upon familiar types, we may discern in *The Old Bachelor* the true germs of Congreve's comedy. Not merely is the style already his own; his purpose and sense of character are evident on every page. Belinda, an affected lady, who 'never speaks well of Bellmour herself, nor suffers anybody else to rail at him,' might be a first, rough outline of Millamant. And Bellmour sketches, in a single speech, the whole philosophy of the poet: 'Come, come,' says he, 'leave business to idlers, and wisdom to fools: they have need of 'em: wit be my faculty, and pleasure my occupation, and let father Time shake his glass.' Henceforth, wit was Congreve's faculty, pleasure his occupation; and he succeeded so well that time still shakes his glass at him in vain.

In the same year (1693), *The Double-Dealer* was played at Drury lane, and Congreve's reputation, great already, was vastly enhanced. In character, style and construction, *The Double-Dealer* is far above its predecessor. The one fault commonly imputed to it is that it has too grave a motive for a comedy of manners. Lady Touchwood is in love with Millefont, to whom Cynthia is promised. Maskwell, lady Touchwood's gallant, knows her secret, and attempts to use it for Millefont's discomfiture and his own conquest of Cynthia. Such is the simple story, told with a simplicity of purpose in which Congreve himself took a proper pride.

'The mechanical part of it,' said he, in the dedication addressed to Charles Montague, 'is regular.... I designed the moral first, and to that moral I invented the fable, and do not know that I have borrowed one part of it anywhere. I made the plot as strong as I could, because it is single, because I would avoid confusion, and was resolved to preserve the three unities of the drama.'

That he succeeded in his design none will deny. *The Double-Dealer* is sternly classical in construction, and moves, from the rise of the curtain in the first act to the fall of the curtain in the fifth, to a settled end and with a settled purpose. The machinery of the play is still conventional. A wrong letter given to Sir Paul by lady Plyant, the villain surprised from behind a screen —these are the keys which unlock the plot. We might forget their simple artifice, were it not for the conscious villainy of Maskwell. That surpasses pretence and belief. Maskwell, indeed, is the familiar villain of melodrama. He is the ancestor in a direct line of Blifil and Joseph Surface, 'a sedate, a thinking villain,' as lady Touchwood calls him, 'whose black blood runs temperately bad.' The violence of his scenes with this lady exceeds the proper limit of comedy, and his discovery by lord Touchwood verges upon the tragic:

'Astonishment,' he exclaims, 'binds up my rage! Villainy upon villainy! Heavens what a long track of dark deceit has this discovered! I am confounded when I look back, and want a clue to guide me through the various mazes of unheard-of treachery. My wife! damnation! my hell!'

But there is no anticlimax. Congreve, with characteristic restraint, permits Maskwell after his unmasking to say no word.

Indeed, were it not for Maskwell's inveterate habit of soliloquy, he might trick us almost as easily as he tricks Millefont.

'Why let me see,' he murmurs, 'I have the same force, the same words and accents, when I speak what I do think, and when I speak what I do not think —the very same—and dear dissimulation is the only art not to be known from nature.'

And, again, 'I will deceive 'em all and yet secure myself: 'twas a lucky thought! Well, this double-dealing is a jewel.' Here Congreve resolutely parts company with nature, and relies upon an artifice of the stage, an artifice which he defends with considerable ingenuity. 'A man in a soliloquy,' he argues, 'is only thinking, and thinking such matter as were inexcusable folly in him to speak.' In other words,

because we are concealed spectators of the plot in agitation, and the poet finds it necessary to let us know the whole mystery of his contrivance, he is willing to inform us of this person's thoughts; and to that end is forced to make use of the expedient of speech, no other better way yet being invented for the communication of thought.

That is as good a defence of soliloquy as may be made, and, employed by Congreve, soliloquy had this advantage: it gave the author an opportunity, which he was quick to seize, of Sophoclean irony. None of the personages of the drama, except lady Touchwood, knows what is evident to the audience, that Maskwell is a villain. When Millefont says, 'Maskwell, welcome! thy presence is a view of land appearing to my ship-wrecked hopes,' the sense of irony is complete, and Congreve plays upon this note with the highest skill.

But it is not for its fable or for its Sophoclean irony that *The Double-Dealer* is chiefly admirable. Rather, we wonder today, as the town wondered then, at its well drawn characters and its scenes of brilliant comedy. Lord and lady Froth, who might have been inspired by the duke and duchess of Newcastle, are masterpieces of witty invention. The scene is never dull when her ladyship, a true *précieuse*, counters the gallantry and *bel air* of Mr Brisk, the most highly finished of coxcombs, with her coquettish pedantry. And is not Sir Paul Plyant, a kind of Fondlewife in a

higher sphere, an excellent creature? And is not the vanity of
his lady touched with a light and vivid hand? When she accepts
Millefont's addresses to Cynthia as an assault upon her own
honour, bidding him 'not to hope, and not to despair neither,'
the true spirit of comedy breathes upon us. That the play was
illreceived, until it won the approval of the queen, is surprising.
Dryden, the omnipotent dispenser of reputations, had no doubt of
its merit. He wrote such a set of commendatory verses as might
have put a seal upon the highest fame. He pictured himself as
worn with cares and age, 'unprofitably kept at Heaven's expense,'
and living 'a rent-charge on his providence.' He implored Congreve to be kind to his remains, to defend his departed friend,
and 'to shade those laurels, which descend to him.' Meanwhile,
he lavished the most generous praises upon him whom he looked
upon as his inevitable successor:

> In easy dialogue is Fletcher's praise;
> He moved the mind, but had not power to raise.
> Great Jonson did by strength of judgment please;
> Yet doubling Fletcher's force, he wants his ease.
> In differing talents both adorned their age;
> One for the study, t'other for the stage.
> But both to Congreve justly shall submit,
> One matched in judgment, both o'ermatched in wit.
> . . . . . . . . . .
> This is your portion, this your native store;
> Heaven, that but once was prodigal before,
> To Shakespeare gave as much; she could not give him more.

This, of course, is the hyperbole of friendship. Congreve was
supreme in his own realm; it was not for him to match his
prowess against greater monarchs.

With all good faith, Dryden adjured Congreve to maintain
his post: 'that's all the fame you need.' In *Love for Love*,
his next comedy, Congreve did far more than maintain his post.
He travelled one stage further towards the final triumph of *The
Way of the World*. In 1695, Betterton and the best of his
colleagues, having a just quarrel with the patentees of Drury
lane, and being empowered by the king's licence to act in a
separate theatre for themselves, opened the famous house in
Lincoln's inn fields with *Love for Love*. The success of the play
was without precedent and well merited. At each step, Congreve
approached nearer to life as to the summit of his art. It is true
that the pure comedy of *Love for Love* is intricated with a farce,
in which Prue and Young Ben play their parts. It is true, also,
that the hoyden's nurse had been a convention upon the stage ever

since the performance of *Romeo and Juliet*.  But she affords a
relief to the brilliant flash of Congreve's wit, and, as for the sailor,
if he be not 'accounted very natural,' he is 'very pleasant,' as
Dr Johnson observed long ago.  For the rest, it may be said that
at last Congreve has entered into his kingdom.  In every scene, he
shows himself a perfect master of his craft.  The exposition of the
plot is perfect.  Jeremy, although he speaks with Congreve's voice,
is the best servant in the whole range of comedy.  You will search
in vain for a truer picture of a curmudgeon than Sir Sampson
Legend, compact of humour and ill nature, whose 'blunt vivacity,'
as Cibber calls it, was marvellously portrayed by Underhill.
Foresight, that 'peevish and positive' old fellow, with an absurd
pretence to understand palmistry, astrology, physiognomy, dreams
and omens, was familiar to all frequenters of the theatre in those
days of occult and half understood superstitions.  When the two
meet to discuss the marriage of Ben and Angelica, they vaunt
their excellence in alternate strains.

'But I tell you,' brags Foresight, 'I have travelled, and travelled in the
celestial spheres, know the signs and the planets, and their houses ... know
whether life shall be long or short, happy or unhappy, whether diseases are
curable or incurable.  If journeys shall be prosperous, undertakings successful; or goods stolen recovered, I know—'

Sir Sampson's *riposte* is magnificent :

'I know,' thus he interrupts, 'the length of the Emperor of China's foot;
have kissed the great Mogul's slipper, and rid a hunting upon an elephant
with the Cham of Tartary.—Body o' me, I have made a cuckold of a king,
and the present Majesty of Bantam is the issue of these loins,'

a valiant boast, the repartee to which,—'thou modern Mandeville!
Ferdinand Mendez Pinto was but a type of thee, thou liar of the
first magnitude!'—seems singularly ineffective.

But it was upon Valentine, the lover of Angelica, that Congreve
lavished all the resources of his art.  There is a nobility of phrase
and thought in Valentine's encounters with his father, Sir Sampson,
which may be called Shakespearean in no mere spirit of adulation.
In these passages, Congreve rises to a height of eloquent argument,
which gives a tragic force to his work.

'Why, sirrah,' asks Sir Sampson, 'mayn't I do what I please? are you not
my slave? did I not beget you? and might not I have chosen whether I
would have begot you or not? 'Oons, who are you? whence come you? ...
Come, uncase, strip, and go naked out of the world, as you came into 't.' 'My
clothes are soon put off,' replies Valentine; 'but you must also divest me of
reason, thought, passions, inclinations, affections, appetites, senses, and the
huge train of attendants that you begot along with me.'

Still better, as diction or invention, are the speeches of the mad Valentine, who speaks with the very voice of Hamlet.

> Alas, poor man! his eyes are shrunk, and his hands shrivelled; his legs dwindled, and his back bowed, pray, pray for a metamorphosis. Change thy shape, and shake off age; get thee Medea's kittle and be boiled anew; come forth with labouring callous hands, a chine of steel, and Atlas shoulders.

But all is not on this high plane. Ben and Prue, Tattle and Scandal carry us away to the lower slopes of farce, and when Mrs Frail meets her sister, Mrs Foresight, it is a contest always of gaiety. No scene in Congreve's plays is touched with a lighter hand than that in which Mrs Foresight asks Mrs Frail where she lost her gold bodkin: 'O Sister, Sister!' And Mrs Frail demands in answer, 'if you go to that where did you find this bodkin? O Sister, Sister! Sister every way.'

After the triumph of *Love for Love* at the theatre in Lincoln's inn fields, Congreve agreed to give the managers a new play every year, if his health permitted, in exchange for a 'full share.' In 1697, he produced, not another comedy, but *The Mourning Bride*, a rash experiment in the later Elizabethan drama. To a modern ear *The Mourning Bride* is sad fustian. The action, such as it is, is enwrapped in impenetrable gloom. Prisons and burial-vaults are its sombre background. The artifice—disguise—upon which its plot turns is borrowed from comedy, with the simple difference that the wrong man is not married but murdered. In other words, Manuel, king of Granada, personates Alphonso for jealousy of Zara:

> There with his bombast, and his robe arrayed,
> And laid along as he now lies supine,
> I shall convict her to her face of falsehood.

Were it not that Manuel is decapitated by his favourite, we might be assisting at captain Bluffe's marriage with the masked Lucy. But the taste of the time hailed it as a masterpiece. It was heard with enthusiasm, and held the stage for many years. Stranger still is it that Dr Johnson pronounced the description of the temple in the second act 'the finest poetical passage he had ever read.' It is idle to discuss the vagaries of criticism, though few will be found now to mistake the pompous platitude of Congreve for poetry. For the rest, the play opens with one of the oftenest quoted lines in English—'Music hath charms to soothe a savage breast'; its third act concludes on a famous tag, the sense of which is borrowed from Cibber:

Heaven has no rage, like love to hatred turned,
Nor hell a fury, like a woman scorned;

and its production was but an interlude in the career of Congreve.

Three years later, in 1700, Congreve's masterpiece, *The Way of the World*, was played at the theatre in Lincoln's inn fields. That it was a failure on the stage is not remarkable. It was written to please its author's fastidious taste not to chime with the humour of the age. It was, in brief, a new invention in English literature. It is deformed neither by realism nor by farce. The comic spirit breathes freely through its ample spaces. 'That it succeeded on the stage,' says Congreve, 'was almost beyond my expectation.' There is no hint of grossness in the characters. They are not of the common sort, 'rather objects of charity than contempt,' which were then popular on the stage. In brief, it was Congreve's purpose

to design some characters, which should appear ridiculous, not so much through a natural folly (which is incorrigible, and therefore not proper to the stage) as through an affected wit, a wit, which at the same time that it is affected is also false.

And so, he set upon the boards a set of men and women of quick brains and cynical humours, who talked with the brilliance and rapidity wherewith the finished swordsman fences. They are not at the pains to do much. What Congreve calls the fable is of small account. It is difficult to put faith in the document which unravels the tangle and counteracts the villainy of Fainall. The trick played upon lady Wishfort, that most desperate of all creatures, a lady fighting an unequal battle with time, does no more than interrupt the raillery, which, with a vivid characterisation, is the play's excuse. The cabal nights, on which they come together, and sit like a coroner's inquest on the murdered reputations of the week, and of which Sheridan's imitation fell far below the original, demonstrate at once what manner of men and women are the persons of the drama. Witwoud, indeed, is the very triumph of coxcombry, with Petulant for his engaging foil. He never opens his lips without an epigram, and in his extravagant chatter climbs to the topmost height of folly. 'Fainall,' says he, 'how's your lady... I beg pardon that I should ask a man of pleasure and the town, a question at once so foreign and domestic.' And again: 'A wit should be no more sincere than a woman constant; one argues a decay of parts, as t'other of beauty.' How light, and cynical, and wellbred it all is, in spite of its purposed affectation!

And the other characters, Mrs Marwood and the Fainalls, though the deeper seriousness of intrigue inspires them, are drawn with a perfect surety of skill and knowledge.

But Mrs Millamant and Mirabell overtop them all. The warfare of their wits and hearts is the very essence of the drama. George Meredith has said with justice that the play might be called 'The Conquest of a Town Coquette'; and, when the enchanting Millamant and her lover are on the stage, our interest in the others fades to nothingness. By a happy stroke, Millamant does not appear until the second scene of the second act, but Mirabell has discoursed of her qualities, and you are all expectancy. And nobly does the love-sick Mirabell hail her approach. 'Here she comes, i'faith, full sail, with her fan spread and her streamers out, and a shoal of fools for tenders; ha, no, I cry her mercy!' It is impossible to think of anything save the apparition of Dalila, in *Samson Agonistes,*

> That so bedeckt, ornate, and gay,
> Comes this way sailing
> Like a stately Ship
> Of Tarsus, bound for th'Isles
> Of Javan or Gadier
> With all her bravery on and tackle trim,
> Sails fill'd, and streamers waving.

And Mrs Millamant reveals herself at once as a woman of fashion, sated with life. Instantly she strikes the note of nonchalance in her famous comment upon letters. 'Nobody knows how to write letters and yet one has 'em, one does not know why. They serve one to pin up one's hair.' Then, she and Mirabell fall bravely to the encounter. 'Nay, 'tis true,' says he, 'you are no longer handsome when you've lost your lover; your beauty dies upon the instant; for beauty is the lover's gift.' 'Lord, what is a lover, that it can give,' asks Millamant. 'Why, one makes lovers as fast as one pleases, and they live as long as one pleases, and they die as soon as one pleases; and then, if one pleases, one makes more.' Whenever Millamant is upon the stage, Congreve is at his best. The speeches which he puts in her mouth are all delicately turned and finely edged. She is a personage by and of herself. She comes before you visibly and audibly. She is no profile, painted upon paper, and fitted with tags. Her creator has made her in three dimensions; and, as she always differs from those about her, so she is always consistent with herself. Mirabell knows her when he says that 'her true vanity is in her power of pleasing.' She is, indeed, a kind of Beatrice, who strives with a

willing Benedick. But, though she loves her Mirabell, yet will she
not submit. When he, lacking humour as a lover would in the
circumstances, complains that 'a man may as soon make a friend
by his wit, or a fortune by his honesty, as win a woman by plain-
dealing and sincerity,' how deftly she turns his gravity aside!
'Sententious Mirabell!' And it is to Mrs Fainall, not to her lover,
that at last she acknowledges, 'well, if Mirabell should not make
a good husband, I am a lost thing—for I find I love him
violently.'

But, before the end, there is many a battle to be fought. In
her contest with Mrs Marwood, the spurned beauty, she hides her
passion behind a veil of malicious merriment. 'I detest him, hate
him, madam,' declares Mrs Marwood. 'O madam, why so do I,'
answers the defiant Millamant, 'and yet the creature loves me,
ha! ha! ha! how can one forbear laughing to think of it.' Nor
will she dwindle into marriage without an exaction at every step.
She'll be solicited to the very last, nay, and afterwards. It is not
for her to endure 'the saucy looks of an assured man.' And so she
makes terms with Mirabell, and he, in turn, offers conditions of
matrimony, in a scene which for phrase and diction Congreve
himself has never surpassed. Even at the last, she will yield only
with an impertinence. 'Why does not the man take me? would you
have me give myself to you over and over again?' And Mirabell
replies, 'Ay, and over and over again.' Thus, they share the
victory; and, as you lay down the play, in which incense has been
offered to the muse of comedy, you feel that *The Way of the
World*, for all its malice, all its irony, all its merriment, is as
austere as tragedy, as rarefied as thought itself.

Congreve, then, carried to its highest perfection what is known
as the artificial comedy or comedy of manners. He regarded
himself as the legitimate heir of Terence and Menander, and
claimed with perfect justice to paint the world in which he lived.
Something, of course, he owed to his predecessors, and to the noble
traditions of the English stage. Shakespeare, as has been hinted,
was ever an example to him, and at the beginning of his career he
worked under the domination of Ben Jonson. Of those nearer to
his own time, he was most deeply indebted to the lighthearted
Etherege. But, being himself a true master of comedy, he took
for his material the life about him, a life which still reflected the
gaiety of king Charles's court. The thirty years which had passed
since the restoration, when Congreve began to write, had not
availed to darken 'the gala day of wit and pleasure.' A passage,

in which he describes the composition of *The Way of the World*, reveals in a flash his aim and ambition.

'If it has happened,' he writes in a dedication addressed to Ralph earl Montague, 'in any part of this comedy, that I have gained a turn of style or expression more correct, or at least more corrigible, than in those that I have formerly written, I must with equal pride and gratitude ascribe it to the honour of your Lordship's admitting me into your conversation, and that of a society where everybody else was so well worthy of you, in your retirement last summer from the town.'

When due allowance is made for the terms of a dedication, in which accuracy is asked of no man, it is easy to believe that, in lord Montague's country house, he found that wit and sparkle of life which he transferred to his scene, 'as upon a canvas of Watteau'— a Watteau, whose gaiety and elegance are tempered by malice.

But the life which he painted was not the life of common day. It was a life of pleasure and gallantry, which had a code and speech of its own. No man ever selected from the vast world of experience what served his purpose more rigorously than Congreve. He never cared for seeing things that forced him to entertain low thoughts of his nature. 'I don't know how it is with others,' said he, 'but I confess freely to you, I could never look long upon a monkey, without mortifying reflections.' Nor was he one who saw life whole. His sympathy was for 'persons of quality,' and he lived in a world situate on the confines of cynicism and merriment. Had he ever descended to realism his comedies might have been open to reproach. But the scene, in which his Plyants and Froths, his Mirabells and Millefonts, his Millamants and Angelicas, his Brisks and Tattles, play their parts, is, like their names, fantastic enough half to justify the famous paradox of Charles Lamb. Even while we admit that Congreve painted what he chose to see, we may yet acknowledge that the persons of his drama 'have got out of Christendom into the land of—what shall I call it?—of cuckoldry —the Utopia of gallantry, whose pleasure is duty, and the manners perfect freedom[1].'

It is in the interpretation of this gallantry that Congreve displayed his true genius. He was, above and before all, a man of letters. It was not enough for him, as for most of his contemporaries, to devise an ingenious situation or to excite the laughter of the pit by the voice of boisterous fun. He had a natural love and respect for the English tongue. He cared supremely for the making of his sentences. His nice scholarship

---

[1] See Lamb's essay *On the Artificial Comedy of the Last Century*.

had taught him the burden of association which time had laid
upon this word or that. He used the language of his own day like
a master, because he was anchored securely to a knowledge of the
past. In point and concision, his style is still unmatched in the
literature of England. There is never in his writing a word too
much, or an epithet that is superfluous. He disdains the stale
artifices wherewith the journeyman ties his poor sentences
together. As a stern castigator of prose, he goes far beyond the
example of his master, Molière. And this sternly chastened prose,
with its haunting memories of Shakespeare and Jonson, its flashing
irony, and its quick allusiveness, is a clear mirror of Congreve's
mind. The poet's phrase is penetrated and informed by the wit
and raillery of the poet's thought.

In nothing does Congreve prove his art more abundantly
than in the rhythm and cadence of his speech. His language
appeals always to the ear rather than to the eye. So fine a
master of comic diction was he, that, in every line he wrote, you
may mark the rise and fall of the actor's voice. His words, in
brief, were written to be spoken; he sternly excludes whatever
is harsh or tasteless; and we in our studies may still charm our
ears with the exquisite poise of his lines, because the accent still
falls where he meant that it should fall, the stage effect may still be
recovered in the printed page. He arranges his vowels with the
same care which a musician gives to the arrangement of his notes.
He avoids the clashing of uncongenial consonants, as a maker of
harmonies refrains from discord. Open *Love for Love* or *The Way
of the World*, where you will, and you will find passages which, by
the precision wherewith they fit the voice, would give you pleasure,
were they deprived of meaning.

Congreve was thirty when he gave *The Way of the World*
to the theatre. He wrote no more for the stage[1]. The history of
letters shows no other instance of defection so great as this.
Several reasons for his sudden abandonment of letters have been
suggested—the cold reception of *The Way of the World*, or the
blundering attack of Jeremy Collier. The reasons are insufficient.
The natural aristocracy of Congreve's mind makes light of such

---

[1] We cannot reckon in his work the share he had in *Squire Trelooby*. Here
for the sake of completeness is his account of the matter, given in a letter to Joseph
Keatly on 20 May 1704: 'The translation you speak of is not altogether mine; for
Vanbrugh and Walsh had a part in it. Each did an act of a French farce. Mine, and
I believe theirs, was done in two mornings; so there can be no great matter in it. It
was a compliment made to the people of quality at their subscription music, without
any design to have it acted or printed further.'

rebuffs as these.   A better reason is not far to seek.   In depicting
society Congreve had fallen in love with it.   He turned willingly
from art to life, for which his character and his studies alike fitted
him.   He was by temperament what himself would have called a
man of quality.   He might have sat for the portrait of Valentine
or Mirabell.   He lavished in talk his incomparable gifts as an
intellectual gladiator, choosing only a quieter field for their display.   The generosity of his friends placed him above and beyond
the irking of want or debt.   Soon after the production of *Love
for Love* he was appointed commissioner for the licensing for
hackney coaches, an office which he held until 1707.   Commissioner of wine licences from 1705 to 1714, secretary for
Jamaica from 1714 onwards, he enjoyed also a place in the Paper
office, and lived in comfortable affluence upon £1200 a year.
Taking but a modest interest in politics, he kept aloof from the
strife of parties, and neither side was urgent to strip him of his
emoluments.   When—in 1711—he feared to be deprived of his
commissionership of wine licences, Swift waited upon 'my Lord-
Treasurer,' successfully pleaded the cause of Congreve, and was
able to reassure his friend.   'So I have made a worthy man easy,'
he writes, 'and that is a good day's work.'   Few of his contemporaries had more or more closely attached friends.   Halifax
accepted his dedication and guarded his interests.   Of Dryden's
generous sympathy towards him something has already been said.
It was to him that Steele dedicated his *Miscellanies*, and that
Pope addressed the famous epilogue of his *Iliad*, which does equal
honour to himself and to Congreve.

Such were some of Congreve's intimates, nor did his wealth of
friendship proceed from mere complacency.   He was not every
man's friend because he was no man's enemy.   The social graces
were active in him.   His talk must have been an easy echo of his
comedies.   Swift, the sternest of judges, 'dined with him and
Estcourt' on one occasion, 'and laughed till six.'   Though long
before his death he was acclaimed the greatest man of letters in
his time, though he lived in an atmosphere of grandeur, his kindly
services were always at the disposition of others.   'On another
visit he gave me a Tatler,' says Swift, 'as blind as he is, for
little Harrison.'   The courage and gaiety of his heart were undiminished by gout or by that fiercest scourge of a scholar, the
loss of his eyesight.   As the passage of the years separated him
further from the triumphs of the stage, the writer was lost in the
man of the world.   'He is so far from being puff'd up with vanity,'

wrote Giles Jacob, 'that he abounds with humility and good nature. He does not show so much the poet as the gentleman.' It was this worldly front, which he showed to Voltaire in 1726, and which shocked the French philosopher, avid of literary fame. Congreve, in conversation, dismissed his masterpieces as trifles, and received Voltaire on the foot of a gentleman, who lived very plainly. Voltaire replied that, had Congreve had the misfortune to be a mere gentleman, he would not have visited him. Both men spoke justly. But Voltaire did not sufficiently appreciate the natural reticence of the Englishman, who, without the slightest vanity, was still unwilling to discuss the masterpieces, which lay a quarter of a century behind him.

Thus, he lived a discreet, well ordered life, visiting the country houses of his friends, gossiping at Will's, seeking such solace as Bath or Tunbridge Wells might afford him. Of Mrs Bracegirdle, the enchantress, whose genius embellished his plays, he remained unto the end the friend and neighbour. To the duchess of Marlborough, the wife of Francis Godolphin, he was bound in the bonds of a close attachment. When he died in 1729 he left £200 to the actress, and to the duchess £10,000, a sum which might, as Johnson says, 'have given great assistance to the ancient family, from which he was descended.' For this disposal of his wealth Congreve has been rated by Macaulay in his best Orbilian manner. At this distance of time and with our imperfect knowledge of his motives, it seems rash to condemn the poet, whose generosity was rewarded after her own guise by the duchess of Marlborough. Davies tells us that she had

an automaton, or small statue of ivory, made exactly to resemble him, which every day was brought to table. A glass was put in the hand of this statue, which was supposed to bow to her Grace, and to nod in approbation of what she spoke to it.

This is the mere frippery of fame. Posterity, content, like Voltaire, to forget the gentleman, remembers the poet, who used the English tongue with perfect mastery, and who, alone of his race and time, was fit to tread a measure in wit and raillery with Molière himself.

It would be difficult to find a more obvious contrast to Congreve than Sir John Vanbrugh. In the sense that Congreve was a man of letters Vanbrugh was not a man of letters at all. He was wholly unconscious of the diction, which for Congreve was a chief end of comedy. Cibber spoke the truth when he said that the best scenes of Vanbrugh's plays 'seem'd to be no more than his common conversation committed to paper.' In other words, Vanbrugh wrote as he talked, without reflection and with great good humour. But, if the gift of artistic expression were denied him, he lacked not compensations. He was a man of a bluff temper and vigorous understanding, who easily communicated to his works the energy and humour of his mind. Like many another of foreign descent, he was more English than the English, he engrossed in his own temperament the good and evil qualities of John Bull. Thus it was that he delighted in farce, not of situation but of character, and he separated himself from the other writers of comedy by a vivid talent of caricature. He overcharged the eccentricity of his personages with so bold a hand as to anticipate the excesses of Gillray in another art. In brief, he was a highly competent gentleman, who found no enterprise too difficult for his courage and intelligence. He was a man of affairs, a soldier, a herald, an architect; and, no doubt, following the fashion, he sat himself down to write a comedy with the same easy carelessness wherewith he undertook to build a palace. Few men known to history were more of a piece than he. In his life, as in his works, he was a simple, sturdy, natural Englishman, devoid alike of affectation and concealment. Pope ranked him among the three 'most honesthearted real good men' of the Kitcat club, and his dignity wrung from Swift, not apt for apology, a public regret that he had once satirised 'a man of wit and humour.'

His grandfather, a merchant of Ghent, had found an asylum in London from the persecutions of the duke of Alva, had followed his craft with success, and had left two sons, the younger of whom, Giles, was the father of the dramatist. Nothing is known of Sir John's youth and training. In 1691, when he was twenty-seven years of age, he was clapt up in the Bastille as a suspected spy, meditated a comedy within its comfortable walls, and, as Voltaire owns with surprise, was never guilty of 'a single satirical stroke against the country, in which he had been so injuriously treated.' Six years later, in 1697, he produced *The Relapse or Virtue in Danger*, and instantly established his reputation. This broad and lively farce, which at once caught the popular favour, owed its inspiration to Cibber's *Love's Last Shift*. The character of Sir Novelty Fashion in that play made an instant appeal to Vanbrugh's fancy; he raised the beau to the peerage, with the title of lord Foppington, and converted Cibber's puppet into a brilliant caricature. It is easy to find fault with the fable of *The Relapse*. It is less a play than two plays spliced into one. Loveless, 'resolved this once to launch into temptation,' and Berinthia, willing to abet him, cannot engage our interest. The farce exists for the proper display of lord Foppington, Sir Tunbelly Clumsey and Miss Hoyden. Here, indeed, are three caricatures after Vanbrugh's own heart. What they do matters not. It is what they say that reveals their eccentricities. Lord Foppington is the true fop of the period, with all his qualities exaggerated. His title gives him unfeigned delight. 'Strike me dumb—my Lord—your lordship—... Sure whilst I was a knight, I was a very nauseous fellow. Well 'tis ten thousand pawnd well given—stap my vitals.' He has the idle elegance of his kind. When the tailor tells him that if his pocket had been an inch lower down, it would not have held his pocket-handkerchief, 'Rat my pocket-handkerchief!' he exclaims, 'Have I not a page to carry it?' So he finds his life a perpetual 'raund of delights,' and believes himself acceptable to all. When Amanda strikes him in her defence, 'God's curse, madam,' he cries, 'I am a peer of the realm!' No better foil could be found for him than Sir Tunbelly, the ancestor in a direct line of squire Western. That he bears a close resemblance to nature need not be admitted. That he is an excellent piece of fooling cannot be denied. He holds siege in his country house, asks at the approach of a stranger whether the blunderbuss is primed, and, when he and his servants at last appear on the scene, they come armed with 'guns, clubs, pitchforks, and scythes.' Miss Hoyden is first cousin to Prue, and shows you in a phrase her true character. 'It's well I have a husband a coming, or i'cod, I'd marry the baker, I would so.' While these immortal three are on the stage, they excite our whole-hearted mirth. Their fate cannot touch us, for in ridicule they transcend the scale of human kind.

*The Provok'd Wife*, produced in 1697, is, in all respects, a better play. Sir John Brute is Vanbrugh's masterpiece. Caricature though he be, there are many touches of nature about him. He is the beau inverted, the man of fashion crossed with the churl. And he is fully conscious of his dignity. 'Who do you call a drunken fellow, you slut you?' he asks his wife. 'I'm a man of quality; the King has made me a knight.' He would not give a fig for a song that is not 'full of sin and impudence.' His cry is 'Liberty, and property, and old England, Huzza!' He stands out in high relief by the side of lady Brute and Belinda, who speak with the accent of everyday, and who are far nearer to common life than are the fine ladies of Congreve. His servants rival their masters in impudence; and Rasor and Mademoiselle are worthy all the praise which Hazlitt[1] has bestowed upon them.

It has been Sir John Vanbrugh's fate to prove an inspiration to our English novelists. Sir John Brute has long been a commonplace of fiction, and made a last appearance as Sir Pitt Crawley in *Vanity Fair*. Still more vivid as a painting of life than *The Provok'd Wife* is the fragment, *A Journey to London*, left unfinished at Vanbrugh's death. There is very little that is dramatic in this masterly sketch. It is but a picture of manners, of the impact of the country upon the town. How well are the characters drawn! Sir Francis Headpiece, a softened Sir Tunbelly; John Moody, his servant, who 'stumps about the streets in his dirty boots, and asks every man he meets, if he can tell him where he may have a good lodging for a parliament man'; young Squire Humphrey, the unlicked cub of the country side—are painted in colours fresh to the drama. They have taken their place, one and all, in English fiction, and it is easy to measure the debt which Fielding and Smollett owed to Vanbrugh's happy fragment.

Like many others of his contemporaries, Vanbrugh did a vast deal of journeywork. He botched a comedy of Fletcher's; he translated plays from Boursault, from d'Ancourt, from Molière, and, through Le Sage, from the Spanish. None of his versions is memorable, save *The Confederacy* (1705), englished from d'Ancourt's *Les Bourgeoises à la Mode*, and completely transformed in the process. As mere sleight of hand, *The Confederacy* claims our admiration. Closely as it follows the original, it is racy of our soil. As you read it, you think, not of the French original, but of Middleton and Dekker. It is as though Vanbrugh had breathed an English soul into a French body. Though he added but three scenes, though he never strays far, even in word, from the prose of d'Ancourt, he has handled his material with so deft a hand that he has made another man's play his own and his country's. Dick Amlet and Brass are of the true breed; Mrs Amlet would not have disgraced the earlier age of comedy; and the quickness of the dialogue, the speed of the action carried the play for many a year down the current of success.

The last years of Vanbrugh's life were devoted to architecture, and to its consequent disputes. His first experiment in the art —Castle Howard—was finished under happy auspices. The theatre, which he built in the Haymarket, the single failure of a fortunate life, involved him in disaster, because he forgot that the

---

[1] See Hazlitt's lectures on *The English Comic Writers*.

chief end of a theatre is to transmit what was spoken on the stage to the audience, and because he did not foresee that the Haymarket would prove inaccessible to the quality. Blenheim, interrupted though it was by the meanness and temper of the implacable duchess, was one of the triumphs of his career. Confused in construction, like *The Relapse*, it is as vividly effective as the most brilliant of the author's comedies. A finished artist in neither medium, he was lifted high above such difficulties as perplex smaller men, by his courage and good temper. He suffered the fate of the great Perrault, with whom he may fittingly be compared, from the wits of his time. But detraction never checked the buoyancy of his spirit, and he died, still untouched by the years, in 1726.

Twenty-eight years before the death of Vanbrugh—in 1698—Jeremy Collier[1] had startled the town with his *Short View of the Immorality and Profaneness of the English Stage*, and as Congreve and Vanbrugh are arraigned therein with especial bitterness, something must here be said of this unforgotten, acrid controversy. The attack upon literature was not new. Evelyn had already deplored the license of the stage. In his preface to *Prince Arthur*, Sir Richard Blackmore had complained that the poets used 'all their wit in opposition to religion, and to the destruction of virtue and good manners in the world.' The old question of art and morals had been debated with rare intelligence by Robert Wolseley in 1685, by way of preface to *Valentinian*, and Joseph Wright, in his *Country Conversations* (1694) had protested against the attacks made by the stage upon virtue and the clergy. Jeremy Collier, then, addressed a public inured to his argument, which he pressed with a ferocity beyond the reach of his immediate predecessors. A clergyman and non-juror, Collier was indicted for absolving Friend and Parkyns at Tyburn, and, refusing to give himself up, was outlawed. As a critic, if critic he may be called, Collier was a patient pupil of Thomas Rymer, whose style, method and paraded erudition he most faithfully mimicked. He did but apply the 'good sense,' wherewith Rymer demolished Shakespeare, to the comedies of his time. Indeed, it is not too much to say that had the *Short View of Tragedy* not been written, we never should have seen the *Short View of the Immorality and Profaneness of the English Stage*. When Rymer says: 'Should the Poet have provided such a husband for an only daughter of any noble Peer in England, the Blackamoor must have changed

[1] As to Jeremy Collier's general activity as a historian and essayist, see *post*, vol. IX.

his skin to look our house of Lords in the face,' and roundly declares 'that there is not a monkey that understands nature better, not a pig in Barbary that has not a truer taste of things' than Othello, you see the cupboard from which Jeremy Collier filched his good things.

Relying upon Rymer, Collier went boldly to the attack. The playwrights, he asserted, were immodest, profane, and encouragers of immorality. He made an appeal to universal history, that he might prove the baser wickedness of Englishmen. As little a respecter of persons as Rymer, he lets his cudgel fall indiscriminately upon the backs of great and small. 'Aristophanes his own plays,' says he, 'are sufficient to ruin his authority. For he discovers himself a downright atheist.' He shares his master's contempt of Shakespeare, who, says he, 'is too guilty to make an evidence: but I think he gains not much by his misbehaviour; he has commonly Plautus' fate, when there is most smut there is least sense.' His comment on Ophelia matches Rymer's demolition of Desdemona. Having extolled Euripides for seeing to it that Phaedra's 'frenzy is not lewd,' he proceeds:

Had Shakespeare secur'd this point for his young virgin Ophelia, the play had been better contriv'd. Since he was resolved to drown the lady like a kitten, he should have set her swimming a little sooner.

There we have the key to his 'criticism.' Again, he will not permit the smallest reference to the Bible in a comedy. When Sir Sampson in *Love for Love* says, 'your Sampsons were strong dogs from the beginning,' Collier's comment is characteristic: 'Here you have the sacred history burlesqu'd, and Sampson once more brought into the House of Dagon to make sport for the Philistines.' He is indignant that lord Foppington should confess that 'Sunday is a vile day,' though the statement is perfectly consonant with the part. That Valentine, in *Love for Love*, should murmur 'I am truth,' fills the non-juror with fury. 'Now a poet,' says he, 'that had not been smitten with blasphemy would never have furnished frenzy with inspiration.' The thought of *The Relapse* drives him to the verge of madness: 'I almost wonder,' says he, 'the smoke of it has not darkened the sun, and turned the air to plague and poison.'

The worst offence of all committed by the dramatists is, in his eyes, the abuse of the clergy. 'They play upon the character and endeavour not only the men but the business.' If he had his way, he would forbid the introduction of any priest, heathen or Christian, into literature. 'The author of *Don Sebastian*,' says he, 'strikes at the bishops through the sides of the Mufti, and borrows the name of the Turk to make the Christian ridiculous.' Then, with a tedious circumstance, he discusses the priesthood in all climes and ages, approves Racine, who brings a high priest into *Athalie*, but 'does him justice in his station,' and awards the true palm to Corneille and Molière, who set no priest upon the stage. 'This is certainly the right method, and best secures the outworks of piety.' And, after a priest, he best loves a man of quality. Plautus wins his approval because his boldest 'sallies are generally made by slaves and pandars.' He asks indignantly what quarter the stage gives to quality, and finds it extremely free and familiar. That Manly in Wycherley's play should call a duke a rascal he confesses is very much *plain dealing*. 'What necessity is there,' he demands, 'to kick the coronets about the stage, and to make a man a lord, only in order to make him a coxcomb?' Plainly there is no necessity; but the fact that Collier should put the question is the best measure of his irrelevance.

It was Collier's supreme error to confuse art with life. He had but one touchstone for the drama, and that was the habit of his kind. He laid it down for an axiom that nothing must be discussed upon the stage which was contrary to the experience of his own blameless fireside. He assumed that the poet was an advocate for all the sins which he depicted; that, if he brought upon the stage a thief or an adulterer, he proudly glorified theft and adultery. Never once did he attempt to understand the artist's motive or point of view, to estimate the beauty and value of words, to make allowance for the changing manners of changed times. His mind was not subtle enough to perceive that, in Congreve's words, 'it is the business of the comic poet to paint the vices and follies of human kind.' As he could see no difference between art and life, so he could not separate satire from the thing satirised. That lord Foppington is held up to ridicule did not hinder his condemnation. His famous comment upon Juvenal convicts him of absurdity. 'He teaches those vices he would correct, and writes more like a pimp than a poet....Such nauseous stuff is almost enough to debauch the alphabet, and make the language scandalous.' And he does not understand that, if Juvenal be not justified, then he himself is guilty of the crimes which he imputes to Congreve and Vanbrugh.

So the worthy non-juror laid about him, fathering vice upon blameless words, and clipping wiser, better men than himself to fit his bed of Procrustes. And even if we allowed that there was no difference between deed and speech, that a writer who mentioned a crime had already committed it, that, in fact, every theatre should be supplied with a gallows, and a judge and jury sit permanently in the Green Room, it would still be easy to convict Collier of injustice, especially towards Congreve. Nothing can be said in a critic's favour who detects profaneness and immodesty in *The Mourning Bride*, who condemns the mere use of the words 'martyr' and 'inspiration,' who finds a depth of blasphemy in the sentence 'my Jehu was a hackney-coachman.' There can be no doubt, however, that Collier's pamphlet enjoyed all the success which scandal could bring it. For a while the town talked and thought of nothing else. The king issued a solemn proclamation against vice and profaneness. Congreve and D'Urfey were prosecuted by the Middlesex magistrates. Fines were imposed upon Betterton and Mrs Bracegirdle. Then, alarmed at the publicity of the pamphlet, the poets began to write in their defence. More wisely guided, they would have held their tongues. The encounter could not be closely engaged. Jeremy, having said little to their purpose, should have been ignored. To demolish his principles might have been worth while. To oppose him in detail was merely to incur another violent onslaught.

As they used other weapons, and fought another battle than Collier, neither Congreve nor Vanbrugh emerged with credit from the encounter. 'Congreve,' said Cibber, 'seemed too much hurt to be able to defend himself, and Vanbrugh felt Collier so little that his wit only laughed at his lashes.' Vanbrugh, indeed, had put forth an admirable defence in anticipation, and with an evident reference to Rabelais.

'As for your saints,' he wrote in a preface to *The Relapse* '(your thorough-pac'd ones, I mean, with skrew'd faces and wry mouths) I despair of them; for they are friends to nobody: They love nothing but their altars and themselves; they have too much zeal to have any charity; they make debauches in piety, as sinners do in wine; and are as quarrelsome in their religion, as other people are in their drink: so I hope nobody will mind what they say.'

That is in the right vein. But it was Farquhar, who, in an ingenious little work, *The Adventures of Covent Garden*, justly ascribed to him by Leigh Hunt, made the wisest comment of all, to the effect

that the best way of answering Mr Collier was not to have replied at all; for there was so much fire in his book, had not his adversaries thrown in fuel, it would have fed upon itself, and so gone out in a blaze.

The others flung themselves into the controversy with what spirit they might. Dryden, worn with the battle of life and letters,

looked wearily on the fray. He owned that in many things Collier
had 'taxed him justly,' and added 'if he be my enemy, let him
triumph.' But he did not plead guilty, as is generally supposed,
without extenuating circumstances and without the stern condemnation of his adversary.

'It were not difficult to prove,' said he, 'that in many places he has
perverted my meaning by his glosses; and interpreted my words into
blasphemy and bawdry, of which they are not guilty. Besides that he is too
much given to horseplay in his raillery; and comes to battel, like a dictator
from the plough. I will not say, *the Zeal of God's House has eaten him
up*; but I am sure it has devoured some part of his good manners and civility.'

D'Urfey rushed into the field with a preface to *The Campaigners*,
like the light horseman that he was, and with a song of *The New
Reformation* dismissed the non-juror from his mind:

> But let State Revolvers
> And Treason Absolvers
> Excuse if I sing:
> The Scoundrel that chooses
> To cry down the Muses,
> Would cry down the King.

With far greater solemnity did Dennis, who himself was not
attacked by Collier, defend the *Usefulness of the Stage, to the
Happiness of Mankind, to Government, and to Religion.* Collier
replied to Congreve with superfluous violence, to Vanbrugh and
Dennis with what seemed to him, no doubt, an amiable restraint.
For years the warfare was carried on in pamphlet and prologue,
and echoes of it may be heard to-day. The high respect in which
Collier has been held remains a puzzle of criticism. Macaulay, for
instance, finds him 'a singularly fair controversialist,' and at the
same time regards Rymer as the worst critic that ever lived, not
perceiving that their method is one and the same; that, if Collier
is in the right of it, so is Rymer. No doubt, the hand of tradition
is strong, but to forget all that has been said in the non-juror's
favour, and to return to his text, is to awaken rudely from a dream.
There seems to the present writer nothing of worth in Collier's
pamphlet, save the forcible handling of the vernacular, which he
owed, as has been said, to Rymer. Not even is his sincerity
obvious. He strains his sarcasm as he strains his argument. 'His
object was to abolish not to reform the stage, and he should have
begun, not ended, with his *Dissuasive from the Playhouse* (1703).
And if the respect lavished upon him is surprising, still stranger
is the conviction which prevails of his influence. Scott and Macaulay, Leigh Hunt and Lecky speak with one voice. Yet a brief

examination of the facts proves that Collier's success was a success
of scandal and no more[1]. The poets bowed their knee not an inch
in obedience to Collier. They replied to him, they abused him,
and they went their way. Congreve's true answer was not his
*Amendments* but *The Way of the World.* Vanbrugh showed in
*The Confederacy* how lightly he had taken his scolding. Farquhar
made his first flight in December, 1698, and nobody can assert that
he clipped the wings of his fancy with Collier's shears. Meanwhile,
the old repertory remained unchanged in the theatres. The pages
of Genest, a much surer guide than tradition or desire, make evident the complete failure of Collier's attack. Dryden, Shadwell,
Aphra Behn and D'Urfey, Ravenscroft and Wycherley were still
triumphant. In the very year of Collier's supposed triumph, *The
Mourning Bride*, the peculiar object of his attack, 'brought the
greatest audience they have this winter.' Congreve, the most
bitterly maligned of all, seized the highest popularity. *Love for
Love* flourished in the nineteenth century. *Don Quixote*, which
Collier thought he had left dead on the field, was still played
a quarter of a century after the fray, and *The Country Wife* long
outlived it. Nor were the alterations, said to have been introduced
into the plays, of a feather's weight. To change Valentine's 'I am
truth' into 'I am honest' was to spoil a fine passage, not to recast
the stage; and Vanbrugh's transformation of the drunken clergyman, in whose robes Sir John Brute disguised himself, into a
drunken woman, was not made until 1725. The new plays were
of no other fashion than the old. Cibber's *Careless Husband*
(1704), Charles Shadwell's *Fair Quaker of Deal* (1710), Gay's
*Three Hours after Marriage* (1717), the comedies of Mrs Centlivre
and Fielding afford no evidence of a chastened spirit. Sir Richard
Blackmore, who had anticipated Collier, did not conceal his disappointment.

'The stage has become impregnable,' he wrote in 1716, 'where loose poets,
supported by numbers, power, and interest, in defiance of all rules of decency
and virtue still provide new snares and new temptations to seduce the people,
and corrupt their manners.'

The reformation, in brief, was, as Tom Brown called it, 'a drowsie
reformation,' and when it came in fact, it came not from the
admonitions of Jeremy Collier who was remembered only as a

[1] Oldmixon, in his *History*, accurately estimated the effect of Collier's attack.
'Neither the actors nor the poets,' he wrote, 'much regarded it. There was a little
awe upon them at first, but it wore off, and this attempt to reform them was the sport
of what wit they had in their plays, prologues, and epilogues.'

cat-o'-nine-tails of the stage, or as a proper jest for an epilogue, but from a change in the manners of the people.

George Farquhar appeared too late to feel the parson's whip. He began his career as Congreve was closing his, and he could look upon the fierce dispute with an eye of contemptuous impartiality. That Collier would have spared him there is no reason to believe, for though in temperament as in art he differed from his contemporaries, he claimed the full licence of his time. A man in whom there was no disguise, he unpacked his heart upon paper. Whatever he knew and saw, all the manifold experiments of his life, he put unrestrainedly into his comedies. Ireland, the recruiting officer, the disbanded soldier, love, the bottle, and the road—these he handled with the freedom and joyousness of one who knew them well. In a word, he broke the bonds of tradition, and declared, when he was truly himself, that gallantry was merely one aim of mankind. Of Congreve it is impossible to deduce anything from his plays. Like all great artists, he is enwrapped in a cloak of aristocratic impersonality. Farquhar, living and breathing without the shackles of art, reveals himself to us in every scene of his plays. Humour and high spirits were always his. He was lighthearted whatever befel him, and, having a natural propensity to ease, knowing, moreover, that he had very little estate, 'but what lay under the circumference of his hat,' he expected misfortune and faced it without a murmur.

His love of ease made him impatient of study, and this impatience is discernible in his works. He knew not how to polish his dialogue. If it advanced the action of his piece or gave an additional touch to character he was content. Though he manifestly owed something to Thomas Heywood in his sense of the open air and his treatment of the countryside; though, like the rest of his age, he had read Molière, and could borrow a scene of *Le Bourgeois Gentilhomme* for his *Love and a Bottle*, it is not by his literary preferences that you judge him. Few comic poets who keep a place in the history of the stage were less truly men of letters than he. For the rules of his craft he cared not a jot. He used, without shame, all the threadbare expedients of the theatre. There is not one of his plays whose plot is not unravelled by disguise. Leanthe, Oriana, and Silvia all masquerade as men. Clincher and Tom Errand in *The Constant Couple* exchange their clothes. Even the blameless Angelica, in *Sir Harry Wildair*, not content with being a ghost, must don the finery of Beau Banter.

But we let him trick us as he will. We know that he looks upon the world with honest eyes, and sees that therein which escaped the others. And, as for the critics, says he, they may go hang. He spurns the unities, roundly declaring that 'the rules of English comedy don't lie in the compass of Aristotle or his followers, but in the Pit, Box, and Galleries.'

If you would understand his plays, you must perforce know something of his life. Born at Londonderry in 1677, he went, in 1694, to Trinity college, Dublin, composed a Pindarick ode at 14, and, though intended for the church, found his way easily to the stage. To be an actor was his earliest ambition, and he appeared at the Smock Alley Theatre in the part of Othello. The discomfiture caused him by stage-fright was greatly enhanced by an accidental wound which he inflicted on a fellow-player, and he gladly took the advice of Robert Wilks, who remained his lifelong friend, and who played the chief part in all his plays save one, to write a comedy. So it was that, in 1698, he came to London with *Love and a Bottle* in his pocket, and made an instant conquest of the theatre. The comedy, which has little to commend it save a vivid sense of life and movement, is, doubtless, autobiographical. Farquhar himself must have sat for Roebuck, the young Irishman freshly arrived in town, and it is easy to believe that the artifice wherewith Lyrick, the dishevelled poet, escaped his creditors, was part of Farquhar's own experience. The dramatist, in brief, whose youth would excuse grosser absurdities than are here exhibited, displays more energy than skill. His comedy is crude and filled with crudities, but a bluff sincerity shines through it all, and it is not surprising that an audience, accustomed to disguises as the traditional trappings of the stage, should have received it with favour.

A year later followed *The Constant Couple, or a Trip to the Jubilee*, which owed something of its plot to an imitation of Scarron's *City Romance*, entitled *The Adventures of Covent Garden*, justly ascribed to Farquhar, as has been said, by Leigh Hunt. This comedy, a clear advance in workmanship, was hailed as a masterpiece with acclamation. Though it is not free from artifice, it is far better constructed than *Love and a Bottle*, and its hero, Sir Harry Wildair, appeared a beau of a new breed to a generation sated with Foppingtons. He has honour and courage, he has lived abroad, and he does not bound his horizon, like Sir Novelty Fashion, with the creations of his tailor. And Clincher, the false beau, the discreet Colonel Standard, and lady Lurewell herself, though not quite unknown to comedy, have something in them of the blood and bone of human kind. In 1701 Sir Harry Wildair appeared in another play, of which he is the eponymous hero, and renewed his career of wit and cynicism. Truly 'the gentleman from France,' as Farquhar called his Wildair, enjoyed the freedom of the British stage, and brought fame if not wealth to the author of his being.

Thereafter came two failures, and then, in 1705, a piece of good fortune sent Farquhar on military duty to Shrewsbury. His recruits, as he tells us, were reviewed by his general and his colonel, and could not fail to pass muster. More than that, he brought back with him a comedy, *The Recruiting Officer*, which he dedicated 'to all friends round the Wrekin,' and which, for him, was the beginning of a new drama. Henceforth he has done with the town and its gallants for ever. The example of Congreve and Vanbrugh compels him no more. He takes for his material the episodes of a broader life, and helps to bridge the chasm which lies between the comedy of manners and the English novel, upon whose beginnings he had a profound influence. He has done what he could to make an end of disguise, though Silvia must perforce put on the breeches. The most of his characters are natural men and women, not above nor below the stature of mankind. His soldiers, as has been pointed out, are no longer *milites gloriosi*, pale reflections of Bobadill, but such as himself, whom he paints as Captain Plume, and his comrades. Costar Pearmain and Thomas Appletree are true men of the soil. Even Silvia is far remote from the fine ladies who for twenty years had railed and bantered on the stage. 'The common jealousy of her sex,' as Plume says, 'which is nothing but their avarice of pleasure, she despises.' In brief, Farquhar had at last found his way. He had put a new set of characters in a new scene. He had added something fresh to the material of comedy.

A year later was played *The Beaux' Stratagem*[1], in construction as character the masterpiece of its author. Full of the gaiety and bustle of the road, it depicts the life of taverns and the highway. Here are travellers burdened with trunks and bandboxes. There is Boniface to fleece them, with his gag and his cunning, and Gibbet to take what Boniface has left. The whole comedy moves

---

[1] In 1704 he had produced, with the aid of Peter Motteux, a farce in three acts called *The Stage-Coach*. It was adapted from *Les Carrosses d'Orléans*, by Jean de la Chapelle, and its chief interest is that it seems a rough sketch for *The Beaux' Stratagem*.

in an atmosphere of boisterous merriment. Aimwell and Archer
are beaux drawn from the life, not taken from a comedy, generous,
gallant, and light-hearted. And Cherry and her catechism; is
there not humour there? Throughout the play, Farquhar criticises
life in a humaner fashion than any dramatist since the author
of *The English Traveller*. He does not possess the artistry of
Congreve; he was, perhaps, a beginning of the sentimental comedy,
of that passion to be both merry and wise which has been the
ruin of our stage; but he looked upon life with the eye not of
Will's coffee-house but of a man, and the result is that *The Beaux'
Stratagem* is not indelibly marked with the date of its birth[1].

His muse was happier than his life. An ill-provided pocket
could not keep pace with the joyousness of his heart. A lack of
pence interrupted the course of his harmless pleasures. He took
delight always in fresh scenes and quick impressions; the pictures
of Holland, which he drew in his letters, prove how well he
understood the art of travelling; and, held fast in the bonds of
penury, he was seldom able to escape from Covent Garden. If
misfortune was abroad, it was certain to fall on him. A noble
patron persuaded him to pay his debts by the sale of his commission, promising him another: that other never came. In 1703
he married a lady who pretended to be a fortune, and who, for love
of Farquhar, had concealed her poverty. Here was a plot which
might have served him for a comedy, and which, with him cast for
the chief *rôle*, could have had only a tragic ending. Being Farquhar,
he harboured no resentment for the trick that had been put upon
him, but 'behaved to her with all the delicacy and tenderness of
an indulgent husband.' Nothing could daunt the brave serenity
of his spirit. If he clung to the gaiety of the beau, he never knew
the beau's cynicism. He has sketched himself in a page which you
may well believe is without flattery, and he confesses himself so
great an epicure that he 'hates all pleasure that's purchas'd by
excess of pain.' He, at any rate, did not accept Sir Harry Wildair's
theory of life.

'I would have my passion,' he writes in a passage of evident sincerity, 'if
not led, at least waited on by my reason; and the greatest proof of my
affection that a lady must expect is this: I would run any hazard to make us
both happy, but would not for any transitory pleasure make either of us
miserable.'

It was not within his compass to make them both happy. His
friend Wilks, missing him at the theatre, discovered him lodged in

[1] For Lessing's debt to Farquhar consult an excellent article by J. G. Robertson in
*The Modern Language Review*, vol. II (1907).

a back garret in St Martin's Lane. He advised him to write a play which should be instantly put upon the stage. 'Write!' says Farquhar, 'it is impossible that a man can write common sense who is heartless, and has not a shilling in his pocket.' Wilks gave him twenty guineas, and, in six weeks, *The Beaux' Stratagem*, that marvel of merriment and good-humour, was finished. It hints by no sign that the author wrote it with 'a settled sickness upon him,' nor 'that before he finished the second act he perceived the approaches of death.' It was produced on 8 March 1707, and Farquhar lived just long enough to hear of its triumphant success. A last note to the friend of his brief life, Wilks, was found among his papers:

> Dear Bob, I have not anything to leave thee to perpetuate my memory, but two helpless girls; look upon them sometimes, and think on him who was to the last moment of his life thine, G. Farquhar.

An epilogue fittingly spoken by a gallant man whose life was in dire conflict with his theory of living, and whose courage, in suffering, sustained him to the end.

Whenever this or that battle of literature is engaged, the leaders are attended by a vast mob of camp-followers, who without natural talent or obvious ingenuity, hope to share the spoils of victory. Thus it was that the masters of comedy saw their works mimicked and the repute of their craft not enhanced by eager, industrious journeymen. The most of these preserve their names and no more in the annals of the stage. Now and again they emerge, for some quality of wit or good nature, from the rest and, with their half-forgotten works, prompt the curiosity of the historian. Thomas Shadwell[1], poet laureate, for instance, enjoyed a popularity in his own day which is not easily explicable in ours. Literary skill was not among the gifts of his mind. He had a trick of invention, and was determined to turn the best models to account. But when he had invented (or adapted) his puppets, he handled them so carelessly, that they long since lost their interest for us. The sense of style, the mastery of language, which might have tempered their extravagance, were lacking to him, and he resembled the facile playwrights of to-day in refusing to look upon the drama as a branch of literature. In his preface to *The Sullen Lovers* he proudly professed himself a pupil of Ben Jonson, whose variety of 'humours' he attempted to reproduce, and whom, he

[1] See above, Chapter I.

thought, 'all dramatic poets ought to imitate.' His debt to Ben Jonson was infinitely less than his debt to Molière. *The Sullen Lovers* is based upon *Les Fâcheux*; *Bury Fair*, his masterpiece, owes its fantastic characters to *Les Précieuses Ridicules*; and *The Miser* is no more than a perversion of *L'Avare.* Yet so good a conceit of himself had Shadwell, that he thought he did his masters no discredit. '' Tis not barrenness of wit or invention that makes me borrow from the French,' he boasted, 'but laziness.' To be lazy is a greater sin, in the realm of art, than to be barren. He patronised Shakespeare as amiably as he patronised Molière. When he had mangled *Timon of Athens*, 'I can truly say,' he wrote, 'that I have made it a play.' Yet with all his shortcomings he held the stage for a quarter of a century. His *Epsom Wells* was praised by Saint-Evremond. He had the wit to make Don Juan the hero of *The Libertine*, and with *The Squire of Alsatia* he scaled the topmost height of his popularity. This last play has many faults. Its story is incredible. The cant used by the rufflers of Whitefriars is handled with so little tact, that it seems an excrescence upon the dialogue rather than a part of it. Yet how much excellent material it contains was revealed by Sir Walter Scott, who made a free use of it in *The Fortunes of Nigel.* Briefly, the vices and virtues of hasty Shadwell have been well summed up by Rochester in four lines:

> 'Shadwell's unfinished Works do yet impart
> Great Proofs of force of Nature, none of Art,
> With just bold Strokes he dashes here and there,
> Showing great Mastery with little Care.'

It is this judgment which, together with Dryden's satire, has preserved the name and fame of Shadwell from oblivion.

Another camp-follower was Thomas D'Urfey, a French Huguenot by descent and a habitant of Grub Street by profession, who turned his hand to prose or verse, composed songs, elegies, and panegyrics, wrote tales, tragical and comical, contrived operas and pantomimes, satirised ministers, cultivated the friendship of kings, changed his politics as he changed his coat, and left behind him a vast number of boisterous farces and bombastic melodramas. A scurrilous fellow in his life and speech, he was the familiar friend of all, was called 'Tom' by high and low, and for nearly half a century played a part in the life of his time. Addison remembered 'King Charles the Second leaning on his shoulder more than once, and humming over a song with him.'

He was important enough to incur Buckingham's disfavour, and lives undeservedly in the distich:

> And sing-song D'Urfey, placed beneath abuses,
> Lives by his impudence, and not the Muses.

His more serious plays, mere burlesques of tragedy, are in 'Ercles' vein.' *The Siege of Memphis* and *The Famous History of the Rise and Fall of Massaniello* may scarcely be matched, for sheer fustian, in English literature. Thus it is that Genovino, the Jesuit, apostrophises the friends of Massaniello:

> Shout on, ye sons of clamour, louder still,
> And fright the Grandees with obstreperous noise,
> Whilst I secure in Darling Policies
> Am pleased with the success of my Designs
> Against this vile ungrateful City Naples.

For two parts, of five acts each, D'Urfey sustains his rant at this high level, interrupting it, characteristically, with songs. The fourth act opens with a fisherman's rousing chorus, and the serious business of the fifth act is pleasantly beguiled by an encounter, in amœbean strains, between two fish-fags. Thus, the method and temperament of D'Urfey are sufficiently displayed, and a mere glance at *Massaniello* will explain why his friends vastly preferred his songs to his tragedies.

The plays which he dignifies by the name of comedy are, one and all, the broadest of broad farces. There is no trick of the time which he does not employ. The thinnest disguises are sufficient to deceive his simple heroes. His country squires are guilty of wilder antics than any devised by Vanbrugh. As he borrowed from his contemporaries, so his poor treasury of wit was rifled by his successors. Madam Fickle, in the comedy of that name, gave Farquhar a hint for the lady Lurewell of *The Constant Couple*, and the well-deserved misfortunes of Beau Clincher and Old Smuggler owe something to the disaster which overtakes Beauford and Brainworm in *The Virtuous Wife*. Many years later, in 1709, D'Urfey astonished the town with a play of a wholly new pattern. It was called *The Modern Prophets*, and was described by Steele as 'a most unanswerable satire against the late spirit of enthusiasm.' The writer

'had by long experience observed,' wrote *The Tatler*, 'that, in company, very grave discourses had been followed by bawdry; and therefore has turned the humour that way with great success, and taken from his audience all manner of superstition, by the agitations of pretty Mrs Bignell, whom he has with great subtlety, made a lay-sister, as well as a prophetess.'

Of the virtues which should grace a comic poet D'Urfey had none. He showed not even a passing interest in human character; he knew no other wit than horseplay.  In brief, save in the writing of songs, he was a man of very slender talent, and it is a high tribute to his amiable qualities that his memory has been so long and so clearly preserved.

Colley Cibber was what D'Urfey was not, a born man of the theatre.  An actor by temperament, a comic poet by accident, he took a perfect measure of the public taste, and he knew his colleagues as he knew the pit and boxes.  He could fit himself and them with parts nicely suited to the talent of each.  The result is that his plays are no more than delicately poised machines, which run easily enough upon the stage, but creak horribly in the study.  Congreve's criticism of Cibber's first play, *Love's Last Shift*, the justice of which Cibber in his candid way publicly acknowledged, would serve as a criticism for them all.  'It has only in it,' said Congreve, 'a great many things that were like wit, that in reality were not wit.'  Even when he declared that he drew from life, he succeeded in making the portrait lifeless as stone.  Lady Betty Modish, in *The Careless Husband*, is said to have owed not a little to Mrs Oldfield's manner of converse.

'There are many sentiments in this character,' the author confesses, 'that I may almost say, were originally her own, or only dress'd with a little more care, than when they negligently fell from her lively humour.'

Yet Lady Betty is essentially a puppet of the stage.  As you listen to her wit, when it encounters the wit of Sir Charles Easy or Lord Foppington, your mind never flits for a moment to the talk of human beings.  You are reminded, at every page, of that phrase-book of ironic genius, Swift's *Polite Conversation*[1].

However, Cibber, being a man of the theatre, cared as little for human character as for literature.  It was for him to fill the pit and boxes, and he filled them for two generations.  In the making of plays he was an expert, and he cared not whose work it was that he adapted.  He improved Shakespeare with as light a heart as he improved Mrs Centlivre.  His most important service to the stage of his time was the invention of a new kind of beau in Sir Novelty Fashion, who was accepted by Vanbrugh as a type, and held the stage until he was reincarnated as Lord Dundreary. Services such as this hardly outlast the author who does them, and

---

[1] As to the relation of Cibber's later plays to sentimental comedy, see the retrospect *infra* in vol. **x**.

Colley Cibber has a claim upon our regard, which all his journey-work would not merit. He left us in his *Apology for his Life* an incomparable record (published in 1740). It is to his talent of observation, to his good-humour, and to his sense of justice that we owe the best set of theatrical portraits that ever came down to us. As much as words can tell, he has told us of Mrs Bracegirdle and Betterton, of Leigh and Nokes, of Estcourt and Powell, of all the brilliant actors, who in our golden age of comedy made the representation of that comedy possible. And he has done this with never a jealous word, with never a hinted dislike at a prosperous rival. Above all, he has drawn an imperishable portrait of himself, a man protected against insult by a triple brass of confidence, whose vanity smiled untouched at the fierce assaults of desperate enemies. That presently he was chosen by Pope to succeed Theobald on the throne of folly gave him a strange pleasure, and he discovered, I think, the real reason of Pope's choice. 'Right or wrong,' said he, 'a lick at the laureat will always be a sure bait, *ad captandum vulgus*, to catch him little readers.' It was, in effect, the laureate unworthy of his wreath that the great poet attacked, and the poet's shaft should have been directed against the court which put Cibber in a false position. His laureate odes, sunk in the waters of oblivion, no longer trouble us. We may even forget the skilful maker of stage-plays. The historian of the theatre, the apologist, who has left behind him the best commentary that we have upon the comedy of manners, will still be entitled to the world's gratitude, though he wears the bays no longer on his brow.

# CHAPTER VII

## THE RESTORATION DRAMA

### III

#### TRAGIC POETS

THE lesser tragic writers of this period, uninspired as most of their work seems when judged on its own merits, fall inevitably to a still lower level by comparison with the amazing literary powers of their great leader, Dryden. They have all his faults and only a small and occasional admixture of his strength and resource. In tragedy, as in other departments of literature, the genius of Dryden overtops, on a general estimate, the productions of his lesser contemporaries, and how closely his lead in the drama was followed may be correctly estimated from the fact that, in 1678, on his abandoning the use of rimed verse in the drama, his followers also dropped this impossible form, wisely reflecting, no doubt, that when Dryden was not satisfied as to its success, they might be sure of its failure. The productions of the lesser tragedians, however, in which a desire to catch the humour of the public and to flatter the mood of the hour is the most frequently recurring characteristic, remain most valuable as helping to furnish a clear idea of the state of the drama and the prevailing standard of taste.

The drama on the re-opening of the theatres was subjected to a flood of new influences. Paramount among these was the influence of the court, to which dramatists and actors alike hastened to pay the homage of servile flattery. This lack of independence on the part of the dramatists of the day, coupled with the general relaxation of morals consequent on the restoration, account, in a large measure, for the degradation into which tragedy in England sank. While comedy retained, in its brightest manifestations at all events, some redeeming wit and humour, tragedy fell to a level of dulness and lubricity never surpassed before or since. It should not be overlooked that, in this period, attendance at the theatre became a constant social habit, and the theatre itself a great

social force ; and in this way alone can be explained the success
on the stage of much portentous rubbish.  People went to the
theatre not because they were interested in the drama but because, to the exclusion of almost all other interests, they were
interested in one another.  This is strikingly brought out by
Crowne in the epilogue to *Sir Courtly Nice*, where he says of the
audience :

> They came not to see plays, but act their own,
> And had throng'd audiences when we had none.

It must also be remembered that this was an age which bred a
succession of great actors and actresses, who occupied an unpre-
cedentedly large share of the public attention.  As Colley Cibber
said, speaking of Lee's *Alexander the Great* :

> When these flowing Numbers came from the Mouth of a *Betterton* the
> Multitude no more desired Sense to them than our musical *Connoisseurs*
> think it essential in the celebrate Airs of an *Italian* Opera[1].

The same must have been even more true of such a woman as
Mrs Barry.   Lee, Crowne and a host of others were perfectly
capable of writing plays, with a French polish, to suit these new
conditions ; but they are unreadable to-day.   The crowd of
lesser restoration dramatists perfectly understood what would
be effective on the stage, and for the rest they relied on incredible bombast and threadbare stage devices.   It has been seen
how, notwithstanding all the changes which had taken place in
the literary and social conditions of the times, and in those of
the performance of plays, the theatres were reopened in 1660
with favourite old plays ; but now, side by side with the surviving
traditions, new influences were at work[2].   Among these influences,
the operatic element, which owed its first introduction to
D'Avenant, became specially powerful in tragedy, and helped
to bring about its degradation.   Another important factor in the
development of tragedy, viz. the influence, direct and indirect,
of French romance and drama, produced its first important
result in the heroic play, which has been discussed in treating of
the works of its chief representative and unapproached master,
Dryden[3].

The heroic play was not, however, an entirely new growth.
For the most part, it was French, but the influence of the Elizabethan dramatists may also be traced in it ; and though, at first

---

[1] *An Apology for his Life*, ed. Lowe, R. W., 1889, vol. I, 106.
[2] Cf. *ante*, chap. v, pp. 121 sq., 127 sqq., 132 sqq.
[3] Cf. note, chap. I, pp. 20 sqq.

sight, it may appear to represent a departure from previous
methods and ideals, and to be a distinct breaking-away from the
established traditions of tragedy in England, yet a more careful
examination shows that, in the main, it was the natural successor of
the late Elizabethan drama, modified according to prevailing tastes,
and confined within the pseudo-classical limits which were the
order of the day.   Under these conditions, it is not surprising that
the heroic play did not take deep root in English soil.   By 1680,
tragedies in verse were going out of fashion, and the English tragic
manner, as opposed to the French, began to re-assert itself in the
work of contemporary dramatists.

The works of the great French dramatists had, also, a considerable direct influence on English tragedy during the restoration
period; and this is particularly true of Pierre Corneille.   A version
of the *Cid* by Joseph Rutter had been acted before 1637 'before
their Majesties at Court and on the Cockpitt Stage in Drury Lane'
—it is said under the special patronage of queen Henrietta Maria.
This, the first translation of Corneille into English, was followed, in 1655 and 1656, by two very poor blank-verse versions of
*Polyeucte* and *Horace* respectively, executed by Sir William Lower.
Neither piece seems to have been acted.   The masterpieces of
French drama were, therefore, not unfamiliar in translation, and,
shortly after the restoration, Corneille found a worthy translator
in the person of Mrs Katherine Philips—'the Matchless Orinda.'
Her version of *Pompée*, in rimed verse, was produced in Dublin early
in 1663 with great *éclat*, and increased her already high reputation.
It was also successfully produced in London, and published there,
in the same year.   In 1664, another version of *Pompée* 'by certain
Persons of Honour'—Waller and lord Buckhurst were the moving
spirits—was successfully produced ; and, in the same year, *Hera-
clius* was reproduced by Lodowick Carlell.   This last met with great
success, though it does not attain the respectable level of others in
the same batch of translations.   Mrs Philips, meanwhile, encouraged
by the success of *Pompey*, began to translate *Horace*; but she died
before completing more than the first four acts.   Her version,
completed by Sir John Denham, was published in 1669 together
with her other works; but, in later issues, a conclusion by Charles
Cotton was printed.   Charles Cotton had himself printed a translation of the whole play in 1671; his version, however, was never
acted.   In the same year, 1671, John Dancer's translation of
*Nicomède* was acted at the Theatre Royal in Dublin.   While
Corneille thus became known and appreciated in England, his

contemporary Racine had to wait for anything like general acceptation until the next century, though signs are not wanting that he was being studied in England during the last quarter of the seventeenth century. The industrious Crowne put forth, in 1675, an utterly inadequate version of *Andromaque*, which did not meet with any favour, no hint being given of the extraordinary coming success of Ambrose Philips's adaptation of the same piece in 1712. Otway's *Titus and Berenice*, though a careful and scholarly version, and abounding in the pathetic touch which was his secret, met with but moderate success on the stage[1]. The same was the case with two other versions of plays by Racine—*Achilles, or Iphigenia in Aulis* by Abel Boyer (1700); and *Phaedra and Hippolitus* (1706) by Edmund Smith (who, a few years later, supplied Rowe with material for his *Lady Jane Gray*), when the tragedy was first produced. Public taste, no doubt, was being educated, for, in 1712, *The Distrest Mother*, Ambrose Philips's skilful adaptation of *Andromaque*, met with immediate and lasting popularity, and Smith's *Phaedra and Hippolitus* was revived many times, with marked success, from 1723 onwards.

On the whole, French influence on English tragedy, at this time, has been exaggerated; such as it was, it affected rather the outward form than the inward spirit. Much was written to prove that the French mode, which was a reversion to classic rules, was the right mode, and most of the earlier plays of the period bear marks of the influence of these discussions. But, for the last quarter of the century, the drama in the hands of Otway, Southerne and Rowe was essentially a descendant of earlier English work. The result of the controversy is admirably summed up by Thorndike: 'The laws of the pseudo-classicists,' he says, 'were held to be measureably good, but Shakespeare without those laws had been undeniably great[2].'

After Dryden, the foremost place among the dramatists of the restoration age is, undoubtedly, held by Thomas Otway. Born in 1652, at Trotton in Sussex, he was educated at Winchester and Christ Church, Oxford, but he left the university without taking a degree. After an unsuccessful appearance in Mrs Aphra Behn's *Forc'd Marriage* (1671), he devoted himself to writing for the stage. His first play, *Alcibiades*, a tragedy in rimed verse, was

---

[1] And this was probably due to his having tacked on to it Molière's *Fourberies de Scapin*.

[2] Thorndike, A. H., *Tragedy*, p. 249.

acted in 1675 at the new theatre in Dorset garden by the duke of York's company, including the Bettertons and Mrs Barry. It is a dreary and stilted piece, and, though the heroic play was then at the height of its vogue, *Alcibiades* met with but little success. In his next play, *Don Carlos* (1676), Otway was more happy. Though still hampered by bombast and rimed verse, the scenes are handled with some vigour, and the play seems to have been effective on the stage, and very popular. It ran for ten nights and was frequently revived. The plot is taken from the Abbé de Saint-Réal's historical romance of *Don Carlos* (1673), of which a translation into English had appeared in 1674. The same source, at a later period, supplied Schiller with the plot of a tragedy bearing the same title as Otway's ; but, though the English poet was not unknown in Germany, there is no evidence to show that Schiller made use of his work. The part of Philip II was played by Betterton, who produced all Otway's subsequent plays—a remarkable proof of their attractiveness from an actor's point of view.

Two capable versions of French plays followed (1677)—*Titus and Berenice* from Racine's *Bérénice* and *The Cheats of Scapin* from Molière's *Fourberies de Scapin*. The latter held the stage for more than a hundred years.

While Otway was away in Holland on military service, his first comedy, *Friendship in Fashion,* was produced (1678). His genius, however, most assuredly did not lie in the direction of comedy. On his return to London, Otway produced (1680) *The History and Fall of Caius Marius*[1], half of which tragedy, as he frankly admits in the prologue, is taken bodily from *Romeo and Juliet*. In the same year (1680) appeared *The Orphan*, a tragedy in blank verse, and the earlier of the two plays upon which Otway's reputation rests. The plot is supposed to have been suggested by Robert Tailor's comedy *The Hogge hath lost his Pearle* (1614), which it resembles, or, more probably, by a work entitled *English Adventures. By a Person of Honour* (attributed to Roger Boyle, earl of Orrery), published in 1676, which narrates the escapades of Charles Brandon, duke of Suffolk. With this play, Otway stepped out of the rank and file of restoration dramatists into his own particular place among great English tragedians. He abandoned the artificial emotions of heroic personages in favour of the joys and sorrows of ordinary human life. *The Orphan* is, for the

---

[1] It is probable that this tragedy was produced before *The Orphan*, for it occurs in the *Term Catalogue* (ed. Arber, 1903) for Michaelmas term 1679, while *The Orphan* occurs *ibid.*, for Easter term 1680, six months later.

period, a singularly domestic play. Two brothers, Castalio and
Polydore, are in love with Monimia, their father's ward. Castalio
secretly contracts himself to her in marriage; but Polydore, over-
hearing their plans for meeting, and unaware of the nature of
the tie which unites them, contrives to supplant his brother on
the wedding night. Castalio, seeking admittance to the bridal
chamber, is supposed to be Polydore and rudely repulsed; and
he spends the night cursing all womankind. With the morrow
come explanations, and the misery of the situation becomes clear.
Whether the plot makes too large demands on the reader's credulity,
or whether it shocks his sense of decorum, the pathetic irony of the
situation in which the characters find themselves is indisputably
brought home with great tragic force.

A comedy called *The Souldier's Fortune* followed (1681)[1], in
which the poet drew upon his military experiences. Langbaine
discovered in this piece numerous borrowings—notably from
Boccaccio and Scarron; but the episodes are so common to plays
of intrigue that it is difficult to say whence Otway derived them.
There is, however, more than a suggestion of Molière's *L'École
des Maris*.

Otway's next play, *Venice Preserv'd, or a Plot Discover'd*, a
tragedy in blank verse, was first acted in February 1682. The story
of this tragedy is taken from an anecdotal history entitled *La
Conjuration des Espagnols contre la république de Venise en* 1618,
published in 1674 by the Abbé de Saint-Réal. An English translation had appeared in 1675. The finest character in the play,
Belvidera, is, however, purely the creation of the poet's genius;
and the scenes between her and Jaffier, the weak, but at heart
noble, conspirator who is persuaded by his wife to reveal the plot
to the senate, are beyond praise. Jaffier, torn between his
passionate affection for Belvidera and his almost equal devotion
to his friends and their cause, presents a signally true picture
of the human soul seeking vainly to reconcile contending ideals.
His remorse and shame under the stinging reproaches of his dear
friend and fellow-conspirator Pierre, his inability to free himself
from the clinging love and fascination with which Belvidera has
enmeshed him, his agony of grief on the senate's breach of its
promise to spare the lives of all the conspirators as the reward
of his treachery—all these successive phases through which his
sensitive, but weak and vacillating, spirit has to pass are depicted
with consummate skill and true tragic power.

---

[1] This may have been acted earlier, on Otway's return from Holland.

Otway's political leaning reveals itself in the secondary title, with its obvious reference to the popish plot, and, still more clearly, in the prologue and epilogue; and the play is further disfigured by some scandalous 'comic' scenes, written to ridicule Anthony, earl of Shaftesbury, in the character of Antonio, a lascivious old senator.

In *Venice Preserv'd* and, to a less extent, in *The Orphan*, Otway produced plays which, for intensity of feeling and for the display of elemental emotions, are worthy to rank with the later masterpieces of the Elizabethan age, and with some of Fletcher's plays in particular. The language of their finest passages is of a notable simplicity, admirably conveying the poet's conception of his characters. Unfortunately, passages of noble poetry are, at times, intermixed with lines of almost ludicrous ineptitude. More pathetic and convincing pictures of women overwhelmed by grief, confusion and hopelessness cannot be imagined than those drawn by Otway in his Monimia—'the trembling, tender, kind, deceived Monimia'—and the still finer Belvidera—a masterpiece of insight into the human heart. Both characters were originally performed by Mrs Barry, the celebrated actress who appeared in Otway's first play, *Alcibiades*, and for whom the poet had conceived a hopeless passion. Some of his letters to her have been preserved, and prove how deeply he had fallen under her influence. His unrequited passion for this fascinating woman had a manifest share in the uplifting of his genius from the dusty commonplaces of lesser restoration drama to the heights of characterisation and expression which he reached in his two great tragedies.

*The Orphan* and *Venice Preserv'd* were extremely popular, and were played with some frequency down to the middle of the nineteenth century. Both plays are full of opportunities for effective acting, and the principal characters in them continued to be among the greatest triumphs, not only, when first produced, of the Bettertons and Mrs Barry, but, also, of their most distinguished successors. Mrs Siddons and Miss O'Neill were famous Belvideras and Monimias; Pierre was one of John Kemble's most signal successes; and Garrick many times played Pierre, Jaffier and Chamont[1].

*The Atheist, or The Second Part of The Souldier's Fortune*

---

[1] *Venice Preserv'd* was revived at Sadler's Wells, in 1845, with Phelps as Jaffier and Mrs Warner as Belvidera, and, as recently as 1904, the play was acted in London by the Otway Society.

completes the list of Otway's plays. It was produced in 1684 and is as unsatisfactory as his previous efforts in comedy. In addition to the plays mentioned above, Otway wrote some poems and translations of no great importance. The most ambitious of the poems are *The Poet's Complaint of his Muse* (1680), which is full of curious autobiographical touches ; and *Windsor Castle*, published posthumously in 1685, a panegyric on Charles II. He also wrote, according to the fashion of the day, a few prologues and epilogues for his fellow-dramatists. He died, in 1685, in the utmost want and misery—one account says of actual starvation.

Though Otway failed as an actor, he possessed a strong sense of dramatic possibilities ; and it is the combination of this sense with an original and individual genius, that will preserve his two chief efforts from oblivion[1].

Nathaniel Lee, son of a clergyman, was born about 1653, and educated at Westminster and Trinity college, Cambridge, where he graduated B.A. in 1668. His early experiences bear a strong resemblance to those of Otway. Like him, Lee began his life in London in reliance upon some of the fitful patrons of letters in whom the age abounded, and, also like Otway, he, in the same year at the same theatre, failed utterly as an actor. The first plays—and there is not much to choose between them—of the two dramatists alike appeared in 1675. Between that date and 1681, Lee produced in rapid succession eight tragedies and a tragi-comedy, all with quasi-historical settings. His first play, *Nero, Emperour of Rome* (1675) was succeeded, in 1676, by *Sophonisba, or Hannibal's Overthrow*; which seems to have been inspired by Orrery's *Parthenissa*. To 1676, also, belongs *Gloriana, or The Court of Augustus Caesar*. These three are heroic plays, for the most part in rimed verse, and thoroughly typical of the period. In 1677, Lee, following Dryden's lead, produced the blank verse play entitled *The Rival Queens, or The Death of Alexander the Great*, which proved an immediate and lasting success. It is founded on *Cassandre*, a romance by La Calprenède, upon whose *Cléopâtre* Lee had already drawn for some of the incidents in his *Gloriana*. There followed, in 1678, *Mithridates, King of Pontus*,

---

[1] For Hazlitt's criticism of these two plays see his Lectures on the Dramatic Literature of the Age of Elizabeth, L. viii (*Collected Works*, edd. Waller, A. R. and Glover, A., vol. v, pp. 354—5). In his first lecture (*ib.* p. 181) Hazlitt declares that 'with the exception of a single writer, Otway, and of a single play of his (*Venice Preserv'd*) there is nobody in tragedy and dramatic poetry...to be compared to the great men of the age of Shakespear and immediately after.'

another blank verse play; and, in 1679, Dryden and Lee co-operated in the composition of *Œdipus, King of Thebes*. *Theodosius, or the Force of Love*, one of Lee's most successful plays, was produced in 1680, and was acted very frequently throughout the eighteenth century. *Caesar Borgia, Son of Pope Alexander the Sixth* (1680), *Lucius Junius Brutus, Father of His Country* (1681), and *The Princess of Cleve*, acted in 1681, but not printed until 1689, are all more or less reminiscent of French romances of the Scudéry type. (*La Princesse de Clèves*, by the countess de La Fayette, was a late masterpiece of this school of fiction.) In 1682 Dryden and Lee again joined hands in *The Duke of Guise*. Most of this play was Lee's work, and was drawn from a piece called *The Massacre of Paris*, which, though written some years previously, had not then been produced. In 1684 appeared *Constantine the Great*, his last play, if we except the aforesaid *Massacre of Paris* (1690). Lee went out of his mind in 1684 and was confined to Bedlam until 1689, when he was released. He had been given to drink all his life; and, in 1692, an excess of this kind brought about his death.

Lee's plays are not without a certain imposing picturesqueness and broad effectiveness; but he entirely lacked the sense of measure and proportion, with that of humour. Neither delicacy of perception, nor the power of characterisation—in short, none of the finer qualities of the dramatist—are to be found in him. His personages talk at the top of their voices on all occasions—happy or the reverse—while rant and confusion, blood and dust, ghosts and portents and hysterics, effectually conceal from all but the most persevering student the occasional nobler features of Lee's imagination. It is hardly fair, perhaps, to judge his plays by reading them in cold blood. They were intended for acting; and, as acting plays, they have abundantly justified themselves. *The Rival Queens* and *Theodosius* supplied favourite parts to many of the most gifted tragic actors not only of their own day, but, also, in the next century. Alexander, in *The Rival Queens*, was one of Betterton's most popular *rôles*, and he played leading parts in all Lee's later productions; while Hart and Mohun acquired fame in his earlier pieces. At a later date, Charles Kemble and Mrs Powell and Edmund Keen and Mrs Glover revived *The Rival Queens* with marked success. And it is easy to understand how thrilling, in their hands, must have been the scenes of white-hot elemental passion in which Lee abounds. He was consistently a candidate for immediate popular favour. He gave the court what it liked—heroic plays on French lines, with a strong appeal to the senses, and characters capable of being played with immense effect and *abandon* by gifted actors and actresses. It may be accounted a significant, though hardly a surprising, fact that, at a time when almost everything—good, bad and indifferent —has been reprinted, no publisher has been found courageous enough to undertake an edition of Lee. No analysis of his extra-vagance can give so distinct an impression of it as an example, and the following description in *Lucius Junius Brutus*, of a young boy's grief, is typical of many similar absurdities scattered up and down his plays:

> His pretty eyes, ruddy and wet with tears,
> Like two burst Cherries rolling in a storm[1].

On the other hand, the lines frequently quoted :

> Thou coward! yet
> Art living? Canst not, wilt not, find the road
> To the great palace of magnificent Death,
> Though thousand ways lead to his thousand doors
> Which day and night are still unbarred for all[2]?

may be taken as an instance of Lee at his best. Now and again, a stray verse or metaphor reminds us of the Elizabethan heights from which the restoration dramatists had fallen so far. But these beauties are few and far between, and it must be frankly confessed that, to-day, Lee is almost unreadable.

The birthday and parentage of John Crowne, one of the most prolific of the crowd of restoration dramatists, are alike unknown. From recent researches it appears probable that he was the son of William Crowne, who emigrated to Nova Scotia, and that he was born about 1640. He was certainly in London in 1665, for his first work appeared in that year, the romance entitled *Pandion and Amphi-genia*. In 1671 was acted and published his tragicomedy *Juliana, or the Princess of Poland*—the first of a long series of dull and half-forgotten tragedies. It was succeeded by *The History of Charles the Eighth of France* (1672), in rimed couplets, and *Andromache* (1675), in prose. The last seems to have been a mere adaptation of a translation, chiefly in verse, by another hand, of Racine's *Andromaque*. In 1675 also appeared the masque *Calisto, or the Chast Nymph*, acted at court by members of the royal family and household. It is without charm, and owes whatever interest it

---

[1] Act v, sc. 2.    [2] *Oedipus*, act v, sc. 1.

may retain to the personalities of the performers, and to the fact that, on the occasion for which it was written, Dryden, the poet laureate, was passed over in favour of Crowne through the interest of Rochester.

Crowne's first comedy, *The Country Wit*, was acted in 1675. It is founded on Molière's *Le Sicilien, ou l'Amour Peintre* (1667), and, in Sir Mannerly Shallow, contains a sort of first sketch of the type—that of the pompous gull—which Crowne afterwards developed with marked success into the Podestà (in *City Politiques*), Sir Courtly Nice (in the play of that name), and Lord Stately (in *The English Frier*).

Then followed three tragedies of absolute dulness, *The Destruction of Jerusalem* (1677); *The Ambitious Statesman* (1679), of which the theme and sources are alike French; and *Thyestes*, taken from Seneca (1681). The concentrated horror of the last-mentioned piece has led to its receiving more notice from Crowne's critics than his other tragic productions[1]; but there is not any nobility in his treatment of the awful story. Shortly before the appearance of this tragedy, Crowne, in 1680, produced a hash of Shakespeare's *Henry VI, Part II*, which he called *The Misery of Civil-War*, and followed this, in 1681, with *Henry the Sixth, the First Part. With the Murder of Humphrey, Duke of Glocester*.

His best comedies came next: *City Politiques* (1683), and *Sir Courtly Nice, or It cannot be* (1685). The date of the former of these pieces, long a subject of debate[2], is now established. In its elaborate and very amusing satire on the whigs, despite Crowne's perfunctory professions to the contrary, the originals from which some of the portraits were drawn may be detected without difficulty. Titus Oates masquerades as Dr Panchy, and Stephen Colledge is introduced in the guise of a bricklayer; while frequent hits are made at Shaftesbury in the person of the Podestà of the very un-Neapolitan 'Naples' where the action is supposed to take place.

[1] Lamb thought it worth while to include scenes from this as well as from other plays by Crowne in his *Extracts from the Garrick plays*.

[2] *Biographia Dramatica* gives the date of production as 1675; while several other authorities, including Genest, state that it did not appear until 1688. The earlier of these dates is, from internal evidence, impossible; for Dryden's *Medal*, published in 1682, is referred to by name, and the play is full of satire about plots and counterplots, burning the city and letting in the French. It seems probable that this comedy was confused with *The Country Wit*, which actually appeared in 1675; in any case, the publication of the *Term Catalogues* establishes beyond further question the fact that *City Politiques* was first published in 1683. It was re-issued in 1688.

*Sir Courtly Nice* is by far the best of Crowne's plays, and has in it something of the true spirit of comedy which, in this age, reached its height in the group of comic dramatists headed by Congreve[1]. It is founded on Moreto's play *No puede ser guardar una mujer* (No holding a Woman), which is itself an imitation of Lope de Vega's *Mayor Imposibile* (The greatest of impossibilities). An English version of Moreto's comedy, by Sir Thomas St Serfe, had been produced without success in 1668, under the title *Tarugo's Wiles, or the Coffee-House* ; but Crowne does not seem to have been aware of its existence. In any case, the principal characters in Crowne's play are new. Sir Courtly himself, with Hothead and Testimony—an admirably contrasted pair, representing, in a most diverting manner, the extreme factions of the age—and Surly are all due to Crowne's invention[2].

The tragedies of *Darius* (1688), *Regulus* (1692) and *Caligula* (1698) call for no more than a passing mention. Crowne's last two comedies are, however, more interesting. *The English Frier* (1690) is a mordant satire on the personal lives and characters of the Catholic priests who had been high in favour at the court of James II. Father Petre has been suggested as the original of Father Finical; and the satire is certainly on much the same lines as that of several scandalous narratives of 'the Martin's' life[3]. The piece owes much to Molière's *Tartuffe* (printed 1669), well known in England by this time.

The story of *The Curious Impertinent* in *Don Quixote*, which had been used ten years previously by Southerne in *The Disappointment, or the Mother in Fashion*, furnished Crowne with a central idea for his last comedy *The Married Beau* (1694). It is less witty and coarser than his other comedies[4]. Crowne seems to have been alive in 1701.

Lee has been called an inferior Otway, and Crowne, so far as

[1] See, *ante* chap. VI.
[2] Hothead is charged with not often attending church—'What then, I'm for the church.' Timothy wants to know whether we can't be saved unless we go to Oxford. Sir Courtly, though he has bestowed 'some garniture on plays, as a song or a prologue,' holds to the principle that 'Men of quality are above wit.' The play is full of allusions to the politics of the day, and an entirely new verb 'to Godfrey' is introduced, in obvious allusion to the murder of Sir Edmund Berry Godfrey in 1678. Mountfort was unequalled in the part of Sir Courtly Nice, which he performed at its original production at the Theatre Royal, though Colley Cibber made a great success of the part in the eighteenth century, when it was frequently revived.
[3] Cf. *ante*, chap. I, p. 48.
[4] According to Downes's *Roscius Anglicanus* (facsimile reprint, 1886, p. 45) Crowne produced a further comedy, *Justice Busy*; but it 'prov'd not a living play' and was never printed.

his tragedies are concerned, might be called a second-rate Lee. His plays have all Lee's turgidity, with none of that author's redeeming though crazy picturesqueness. They preserve a dead level of mediocrity, and it seems almost incredible that such a piece as *The Destruction of Jerusalem* could ever have gained the marked success which it undoubtedly secured. Nothing but mounting elaborate enough to impress an uncritical audience could have saved such plays as these from immediate and final damnation. Such originality and talent as Crowne possessed found vent in his comedies; and it may be pointed out that, of all the tragic dramatists of the time who wrote comedies, he alone produced any that have a claim to be remembered. His *Sir Courtly Nice* is a genuinely comic and living personage, and, though he has found numerous imitators, the creation of the type belongs to Crowne.

Thomas Southerne (or Southern, as his name is spelt in the first editions of all his plays), was of Irish parentage; but he spent his life in London, where his career was in striking contrast to those of most contemporary dramatists, as to both its length and its conduct. He produced two highly successful plays exactly calculated to hit the public taste, and by no means without intrinsic merit. Southerne seems to have possessed considerable personal charm and was a valued friend of several of the most distinguished men of his day. He enjoyed the intimate friendship of Dryden, who wrote prologues and epilogues for several of his plays and who, in 1692, entrusted him with the task of completing the last act of his *Cleomenes* and revising the whole. Printed at the end of his *Works* (1774) is a delightful letter addressed to him by Lord Orrery, dated 1733, beginning 'My dear Old Man,' which breathes throughout a spirit of the warmest friendship and regard. Southerne's dedications sufficiently show that these were no isolated instances. Not only was his literary work successful in obtaining for him admiration and regard, but he also reaped from it substantial pecuniary profit[1].

In his first play, *The Loyal Brother* (1682), Southerne discloses strong tory sympathies, and the character of Ismael is supposed to convey the inevitable attack on Shaftesbury. The play is taken from a novel called *Tachmas, Prince of Persia*, translated from the French by P. Porter in 1676.

---

[1] For the copyright of *The Spartan Dame* (by no means his best play), Chetwood the bookseller paid one hundred and twenty pounds, and Southerne is stated to have made altogether five hundred pounds profit out of this rather commonplace production.

This was followed by four comedies, for the most part in prose. *The Disappointment, or the Mother in Fashion* (1684) is (once more) founded on the story of *The Curious Impertinent* in *Don Quixote*. *Sir Anthony Love, or The Rambling Lady* (1691) was 'acted with extraordinary applause,' the part of Sir Anthony being 'most masterly played' by Mrs Mountfort. *The Wives Excuse, or Cuckolds make themselves* (1692) was not so successful, and seems to have given offence in some quarters by its too faithful delineation of polite life. *The Maids' Last Prayer, or Any, rather than Fail* (1693) is chiefly notable as containing a song said to have been the earliest acknowledged piece of Congreve's writing. However, Southerne's strength[?] did not lie in comedy, though his comic productions are, in general, considerably less gross, and decidedly more witty, than those of most of his contemporaries; and it was not until 1694 that, in *The Fatal Marriage, or the Innocent Adultery*, he achieved a play worthy of his talent. This popular drama was founded on Mrs Aphra Behn's novel *The Nun, or The Perjur'd Beauty*. Its success was immediate[1]. *The Fatal Marriage* was frequently acted during the eighteenth century, Garrick, in particular, reviving it, in an abridged version, in 1757[2].

In 1696 appeared Southerne's other great success, *Oroonoko, or the Royal Slave*, like its predecessor a mixture of blank verse and prose. Mrs Behn again supplied the plot in her novel of the same name, and the piece, as adapted by Hawkesworth, had an even longer life than *The Fatal Marriage*. It is not, however, intrinsically so effective; though the novelty of its story and setting (a slave plantation in the West Indies), and the acting of Verbruggen, as the noble-minded, if somewhat tedious, negro, the hero of the piece, gave it a high place in public favour.

In none of his last three plays did Southerne reach so high a level. *The Fate of Capua* (1700) was a failure; nor can *The Spartan Dame* (1719), founded on Plutarch's *Life of Agis*, in spite of its stage success, be pronounced a good play. *Money the Mistress* (1726), Southerne's last production, was quite unsuccessful; its plot is taken from the countess D'Aulnoy's *Travels into Spain*. When at his best, Southerne reminds us of Otway in his power of

---

[1] Mrs Barry played Isabella, which remained one of her most telling parts. Betterton played Villeroy, Isabella's second husband.

[2] On this occasion, Mrs Cibber played Isabella to Garrick's Biron. Later, Mrs Siddons played the same part with immense effect, and it remained her most popular part outside Shakespeare.

pathos and his perception of stage effect. The character of Isabella is well conceived and worked out with great sympathy. Her gradual yielding to the importunate advances of Villeroy, her second husband, and her grief and horror at the discovery that Biron, her first husband, is alive, and has returned to her, are depicted with considerable power, and are not unworthy to be compared with passages of Fletcher. The introduction of Isabella's and Biron's child is a stroke of dramatic genius, and must have materially strengthened the play, as the same device has strengthened many a popular drama since. Indeed, *The Fatal Marriage* and *Oroonoko* may be regarded as the prototypes of a host of popular melodramas. Yet, though, on occasion, a master of stage effect, Southerne never rises, and did not aspire to rise, above supplying the dramatic needs of his day. In another age, he might, perhaps, have done better things; for, though he pandered to the vicious tastes of his audiences, he seems fully to have realised how far it was necessary to sink in order to gratify those tastes; and he half apologised—not without reason—for the 'comic' scenes in his best two plays.

Elkanah Settle and Thomas Shadwell were described by Dryden as

> Two fools that crutch their feeble sense on verse;
> Who, by my muse, to all succeeding times
> Shall live, in spite of their own doggrel rhymes[1];

and, in Settle's case, at all events, the prophecy has come true. Of the numerous publications which remain to show the fruits of his busy pen, scarce one is read to-day. He made a bid for success in almost every department of literature; but he is only remembered as Doeg, the victim of some of the most scathing lines in English satirical poetry.

Settle began his career as a dramatist with the tragedy *Cambyses, King of Persia*, produced, according to Downes[2], by Betterton in 1666, when it met with considerable success. It was not printed till 1671, and was followed by *The Empress of Morocco* (1673). For a brief period, the latter play carried all before it; and the applause bestowed on it, together with the absurd comparisons of Settle to Dryden, to the detriment of the latter, which it evoked, seem to have more or less turned Settle's head. As a matter of fact, *The Empress of Morocco* owed its success

---

[1] *Absalom and Achitophel*, Part II.
[2] *Roscius Anglicanus* (facsimile reprint (1886)), p. 27.

mainly to the good offices of Rochester, who patronised Settle to annoy Dryden. It displays considerable ingenuity and knowledge of stage effect, always Settle's strong point[1]. The success of the play, and the pompous manner of its publication, drew forth some abusive *Notes and Observations*, said, by Dennis, to have been the joint work of Crowne, Dryden and Shadwell, to which Settle replied; and, though Crowne claimed the lion's share of the attack, a paper war arose between Settle and Dryden.

*The Empress of Morocco* was succeeded by *Love and Revenge* (1675); and *Ibrahim, the Illustrious Bassa* (1677), founded on Madeleine de Scudéry's romance, turned by her brother Georges into a play of the same name. From that time until 1718, Settle produced a large number of plays, mostly bombastic tragedies of the poorest sort, the very names of which are now unfamiliar. About 1680, he made the first of his several changes of political tenets and opened fire on the adherents of the court and catholic party, his earliest patrons. The disgraceful play, *The Female Prelate*, marks this stage in his career. In 1683, he was a tory once more, and involved himself in an acrimonious controversy concerning the popish plot. In 1691, he was appointed city poet, and, in that capacity, produced the annual pageant on lord mayor's day, of which the official printed record for several years is extant. In the duties of this office, Settle must have found himself at home, for the fertility of his scenic invention is undoubted. It was not, however, sufficiently lucrative to keep him from want, nor did he turn his coat cleverly enough to profit greatly by these successive changes. He sank lower and lower, and, at last, was obliged to write drolls for Bartholomew fair, and even, according to a tradition maliciously repeated by Pope, to act in them himself. In 1718, the forlorn hack found a haven in the Charterhouse, where he died early in 1724.

Before considering Nicholas Rowe, whose principal plays belong to the earlier years of the eighteenth century, we may mention the names of a few tragic dramatists of even slighter calibre than Elkanah Settle's.

John Dennis, the butt of many of Pope's most savage sarcasms, but well equipped as a literary critic[2], was the father of a very

---

[1] The principal interest which, at the present day, attaches to this declamatory performance is due to the engravings which were published with the play in 1673, and which give a very good idea of the magnificence of the Dorset garden theatre, both without and within.

[2] His *Three Letters on the Genius and Writings of Shakespeare* (1711) were written

numerous literary progeny, the dramatic section of which included tragedies, comedies and a masque. But, though he borrowed with equal freedom from Euripides, Tasso, and Shakespeare, his efforts were almost uniformly unsuccessful. In the closing years of the seventeenth century, he produced the comedy *A Plot and No Plot* (1697), a satire on the Jacobites; and *Rinaldo and Armida*, a tragedy founded on Tasso, played in 1699.

Of the seven plays written by John Banks, the most successful were *The Unhappy Favourite, or the Earl of Essex* (1682) and *Vertue Betray'd, or Anna Bullen*, also acted in 1682. He seems to have been an admirer of Lee, and faithfully reproduced that author's worst characteristics. Like Lee, he plundered the French romances, and, in 1696, brought out a play taken from *Le Grand Cyrus*. His *forte*, however, was melodrama based on English history, and, in this field, he enjoyed a great popular success.

John Hughes belongs, in point of time, to the next period, but his manner is emphatically that of the restoration. Besides the operas *Calypso and Telemachus* (1712) and *Apollo and Daphne* (1716), he wrote a piece called *The Siege of Damascus*, which was produced on the day of the author's death (17 February 1720), and was received with much approval. It owes much to D'Avenant's *The Siege* (printed 1673); and its success, as well as that of Hughes's other dramatic efforts, depends largely on the opportunities for spectacular display which it affords. His plays, nevertheless, show considerable power of construction, and are often forcibly and picturesquely written.

George Granville, lord Lansdowne, besides a disastrous adaptation of *The Merchant of Venice*, produced, in 1696, the comedy entitled *The She-Gallants*, and, in 1698, *Heroick Love*, a tragedy sufficiently described by its composite title. Both these pieces seem to have been successful. His last effort, an opera entitled *The British Enchanters*, was produced by Betterton in 1706 and well received[1].

Edward Ravenscroft, though chiefly a writer of comedy, produced a tragicomedy called *King Edgar and Alfreda* (1677); and a tragedy, *The Italian Husband*, acted 1697, and full of horrors. It was probably suggested by a tale in Thomas Wright's *The Glory of God's Revenge against Murther and Adultery* (1685).

in reply to Rymer, and are creditable to Dennis's perception of the greatness of Shakespeare's tragic genius; his earlier critical works likewise deserve notice. His disputes with Collier, Addison and Pope belong to the literary biographies of those writers.

[1] Cf. *ante*, p. 53 note.

Mrs Aphra Behn, though principally known through the medium of
her comedies and novels, wrote several tragedies, the first of
which, *Abdelazer, or the Moor's Revenge* (1677), was altered from
Marlowe's *Lust's Dominion*[1].  Mrs Manley, who achieved an unenviable reputation as a novelist, also produced several lurid
tragedies, of which the first, *The Royal Mischief*, appeared in 1696.
Thomas Rymer, author of *The Tragedies of the Last Age* (1678)
and of other critical work, in which he attacked the Elizabethan
tragic poets, chiefly on account of their failure to observe the
unities[2], published, in 1678, one of the last rimed tragedies in
*Edgar, or the English Monarch*, which strictly observes the
classic rules.

Nicholas Rowe holds a unique position as forming a link between the late restoration dramatists and those of the Augustan
age.  For, though all his plays were produced in the early years of
the eighteenth century, his work is thoroughly typical of the drama
at the close of the restoration period, and he is more at home with
Banks and Southerne than with the writers of the age of Pope.

Born in 1674, in comfortable circumstances, Rowe, in due
course, was called to the bar, but soon abandoned law in order to
devote himself wholly to literature.  His first play, *The Ambitious
Step-Mother*, was produced, in 1700, at Lincoln's Inn fields by
Betterton, and was well received.  It is one of the large group of
plays in which the scene is laid in conventionally 'eastern' surroundings.  This was followed by *Tamerlane* (1702), which,
as a drama, is ineffective; it has, however, a certain historic
interest, for Louis XIV, the author tells us, was satirised under
the name of Bajazet—the villain of the piece, while the high-
minded hero, a sort of Admirable Crichton among princes, and
much given to improving the occasion—was intended to personify
William III.  It was revived yearly on 5 November, the anniversary of the landing of William of Orange, until 1815.

Rowe's next piece, *The Fair Penitent* (1703), proved one of
the most popular plays of its time.  It is borrowed, as to plot,
from Massinger and Field's *The Fatal Dowry* (1632); but Rowe
greatly reduced the older play, omitted its force and flavour, and
deluged his version with a moral tone which is all his own.  This

---

[1] As to her comedies, see *ante*, pp. 140—2.

[2] *A Short View of Tragedy* appeared in 1693.  Rymer was appointed historiographer-
royal in 1692, and published 15 volumes of his *Foedera* between 1704 and his death in
1713.  Cf. *post*, vol. IX.

simple domestic drama, written, like Rowe's other tragedies, in
rather fluent blank-verse, met with extraordinary success and was
constantly before the public till 1825, or thereabouts. The author
promises in the prologue that 'you shall meet with sorrows like
your own.' The public found that Rowe kept his word; and, to
this fact, and to the rather cheap appeal of the last act, with
its accumulated furniture of the charnel-house and the grave,
rather than to any depth of tragic power in the play, the longevity of the piece must be attributed. The 'haughty, gallant,
gay Lothario' of this tragedy has become a familiar synonym
for a heartless libertine, and was the model for Lovelace in
Richardson's *Clarissa Harlowe*. No play was more popular in
the eighteenth century[1].

Rowe's solitary comedy, *The Biter*, produced in 1705, was a
failure. According to Johnson, the author's applause was the
only sound of approval heard in the theatre at its production.
It was succeeded by the tragedy *Ulysses* (1706), a tedious and
ineffective drama which lacks Rowe's usual strong appeal to the
pity of his audience. Neither this play nor *The Royal Convert*
(1707)—very dull, with a background of mythical British history—
calls for special comment. Rowe's last two plays bear a strong
likeness to one another. *The Tragedy of Jane Shore* 'in imitation of Shakespeare's style,' produced in 1714, has been said to bear
no closer resemblance to Shakespeare than is to be found in the
fact that like some of his plays it is based upon an episode in the
history of England. It is, however, a good acting play, which,
even now, has not entirely disappeared from the stage. It afforded Mrs Siddons one of her most tremendous opportunities for
realistic acting. As Jane Shore, drifting half-starved about the
streets of London, eye-witnesses report that the audience 'absolutely thought her the creature perishing through want'—and
'could not avoid turning from the suffering object.'

In the following year (1715), Rowe succeeded Tate as poet
laureate and produced his last play, *The Tragedy of the Lady
Jane Gray*. This play, as well as its predecessor, and, to some
extent, Rowe's other dramatic works, display a certain nobility of
outlook and purity of purpose, in marked and refreshing contrast

---

[1] Among the most interesting revivals were those by Garrick in 1743 and 1746,
when he played Lothario, and those of 1782 and subsequent years when Mrs Siddons,
as Calista, electrified her audiences, particularly in the scene with Horatio in the third
act, where he accuses her of being false to her husband and his friend, Altamont. In
1803, a revival of the play took place, when the cast included Mrs Siddons and both
the Kemble brothers.

to the pruriency in which the English drama had for half a century been steeped. The unexceptionably moral and patriotic tone of Rowe's last play, as well as its protestant spirit, affords a very striking proof of the change that had come over the English stage since the revolution and the publication of Jeremy Collier's *Short View*.

Like Otway, Rowe attempted to move his audiences to pity and terror; but, with few exceptions, his dramas leave us cold and unmoved. He contrives situations with considerable skill, but he generally fails to make his characters rise to them; nor do they give vent to their feelings in language which is always either touching in itself, or suitable to the surrounding circumstances. His plays are the calm and finished performances of an author who felt but faintly the emotions which he sought to portray, and who, by the introduction of what he very aptly calls 'the pomp of horror,' hoped to find his way to the feelings of his readers. Criticism and the public taste, in fact, have alike moved far since Johnson wrote of Rowe's *The Fair Penitent*, 'There is scarcely any work of any poet at once so interesting by the fable, and so delightful by the language.' He has, however, other claims to the respect of posterity. Of the significance of his edition of Shakespeare's works (1709), something has been said in an earlier volume[1]; while his translation of Lucan's *Pharsalia*, which was first published as a whole in 1718 (shortly after his death), and of which at least nine editions appeared between that date and 1822, is, probably, at the present day, his least forgotten work. He also translated in verse Boileau's *Lutrin* (1708). Rowe was an accomplished modern, as well as classical, scholar, and his personality is one of dignity, as well as of interest, in the history of English literature.

---

[1] See vol. v, chap. xi, pp. 267—8.

# CHAPTER VIII

## THE COURT POETS

THE career of the Court Poets is an episode not merely in the history of literature but in the history of manners. In their lives as in their art, they were an outspoken protest against the domination of the puritans. Whatever their predecessors in their stern morality had disdained, they pursued with a rare fervency of spirit. The chief end of their ambition was to catch pleasure on the wing, and they gave to pleasure a liberal interpretation. Gallantry was not enough for them. No courtier could hope to win the approval of his sovereign who had not given proof of his 'wit,' who had not publicly burned incense before the muse of frivolity. So it came about that, in Sedley's phrase, 'every fop wrote songs,' that few refrained from libelling their friends in satire, and that a freedom in written, as in spoken, speech matched the prevailing freedom of thought and conduct.

The court, in brief, cherished an ideal hitherto strange to English austerity. It no longer took a keen interest in rival policies. The bitter conflict of the civil war, followed by the domination of Oliver, had obscured the spark of patriotism which burned only in a few loyal hearts. The king and his courtiers were determined to amuse themselves. They had learned in Paris how to temper their magnificence with wit and *politesse*, and, in the glamour of beauty and courage, they forgot the long, dark days when all the decorative arts of life had been banished, when even the smile of irony was deemed a disgrace. Charles II, a monarch to whom most things were easy save wisdom, led the band of revellers, preferred the ribaldry of Buckhurst and Sedley to the grave advice of Arlington, sauntered away his days in the society of his mistresses, and delighted in satire, even though it was directed against himself. It was a golden age, truly, in which life seemed desirable for its own sake, and in which nobody thought of its drearier purpose. *Les plus honnêtes gens du monde*, says

Saint-Évremond, *ce sont les Français qui pensent, et les Anglais qui parlent.* And at Whitehall, which he graced by his presence for many years, he might have encountered them both.

Such is one side of the medal. The reverse is less attractive. If it were frivolity whose muse reigned in Whitehall, it was a pompous frivolity. There was very little spontaneous gaiety in the court of the returned king. The intention to be gay was so loudly expressed that it seemed to come from the head rather than from the heart. The sense of relief, the determination to be happy at all costs, suggest that a spice of malice flavoured the joyousness of the courtiers. In what they said and did there was no trace of the golden mean. Their merriment was too often the merriment of constraint. Rochester declares in one of his letters that it wasn't safe for a man to leave the court, if he didn't want to be hanged. The exploits set forth in the *Mémoires de Gramont*, are, so to say, conscious of reaction. Their persistent monotony fatigues us who read of them, as perchance they fatigued the courtiers who are their heroes. The king and his friends were too flagrantly industrious in the pursuit of pleasure. Gramont himself was not content to rely upon his own graces for success. He wooed his goddesses with 'gloves, pocket looking-glasses, elegant boxes, apricot paste, essences, and other small wares of love.' To be jealous without being in love, to play for stakes so high that they could not be paid without distress, to indulge in practical jokes which had no better excuse than physical infirmity—these are not the marks of happiness. They were the misfortunes of everyone who came within the circle of Whitehall. The manners of the time thus proved the best material for satire and comedy. There was, perhaps, more joy in their contemplation than in their exercise. Pepys, who lived on the fringe of the Court, was gay, because he carried his indomitable gaiety into the simplest affairs of his life. We can believe that there was a flash of genuine gaiety at Epsom, when Nell Gwynn and Buckhurst 'kept mery house' there. But the pleasure of Charles II's court was marred by the inverse of puritanism. It was austere even in its love-making.

At times, the courtiers broke through all the bonds of restraint. They thought it no shame to commit acts of violence in the streets. Once upon a time, Buckhurst and his friends killed a tanner at Stoke Newington whom they suspected of theft, and whose pockets they emptied, as of stolen goods. A far worse scandal was caused by Sir Charles Sedley's amazing apparition at Oxford Kate's in Bow street. He came in open day, as Pepys tells us, into the Balconie and showed his nakedness ... and abusing of scripture and as it were from thence preaching a mountebank sermon from the pulpit, saying that there he had to sell such a powder as should make all the women run after him, 1,000 people standing underneath to see and hear him, and that being done he took a glass of wine, and drank it off, and then took another and drank the King's health.

It is not surprising that the unbridled conduct of Sir Charles Sedley and of Buckhurst, who was of the company, came near to causing a riot, brought the offenders before the court, and received from the lord chief justice 'a most high reproof.' The news of these pranks, moreover, went abroad, and lost nothing, we may be sure, in the telling. The voice of scandal was noisy and unscrupulous, then as now ; and, though it is evident that the 'wits' were not innocent of brutality, it is unfair to judge all their lives by one or two episodes. Hasty generalisation is ever the foe of truth, and charges are more lightly made than refuted. No man, for instance, was ever so careless of his reputation as Rochester, and even he protests in a letter addressed to Savile against an unfounded indictment. Accused of the same folly as that of which Sedley and Buckhurst were guilty, he was eager in excuse.

'For the hideous deportment,' he writes, 'which you have heard of, concerning running naked, so much is true, that we went into the river somewhat late in the year, and had a frisk for forty yards in a meadow, to dry ourselves.'

The trivial adventure was instantly turned to his disgrace, and so deeply sensible was he of the public contempt that he confessed himself 'extremely revived at the receipt of a kind letter from an old friend.' 'I ever thought you an extraordinary man,' says he, 'and must now think you such a friend, who, being a courtier, as you are, can love a man, whom it is the great mode to hate.'

Nor was exaggeration the only foe of the wits. Many there were, without a spark of talent, who imitated the vices of Rochester and Sedley, and who, by their senseless extravagance, brought their betters into contempt. When wit became a fashion, the fools could ape it, and the poets have been compelled ever since to bear a weight of unmerited odium. Pepys once strayed into the society of these pretenders, and their talk made even his hard heart ache. 'But, Lord! what cursed loose company was this,' says he, 'that I was in to-night, though full of wit; and worth a man's being in once to know the nature of it, and their manner of talk, and lives.' Pepys's curiosity no doubt got the better of his judgment, and the wit of these men, who called themselves the 'Ballers,' was probably as false as their pretence. They are memorable only because they did the poets an injustice—an injustice which no less a man than

Dryden has removed. None knew better than he their talents and their lives, and he treated them as true Augustans, praising their *eruditam voluptatem.*

'We have,' said he, like the poets of the Horatian age, 'our genial nights, when our discourse is neither too serious nor too light, but always pleasant, and for the most part instructive; the raillery neither too sharp upon the present, nor too censorious on the absent, and the cups only such as will raise the conversation of the night, without disturbing the business of the morrow.'

As in duty bound, he who had been admitted to these banquets of wit and sense defended them against the detraction of pedants. The wits, said he, were insulted by those who knew them not.

'As we draw giants and anthropophagi'—to cite his words—'in those vacancies of our maps, where we have not travelled to discover better, so those wretches paint lewdness, atheism, folly, ill-reasoning, and all manner of extravagances amongst us, for want of knowing what we are.'

It was not difficult to rebut precise charges. The wits, described by the ignorant, were the fops whom Dryden and his friends banished. As for blasphemy and atheism, even if they were not ill manners, they were worn threadbare. In other words, the true wits are blamed for the excesses of those who had never tasted the waters of Helicon.

If the court poets needed a defence, they could not have found a wiser, juster defence than Dryden's. But even when they have been relieved of the crimes of which others were guilty, there is another misunderstanding which should be dispelled. The brutalities of Rochester, Buckhurst and Sedley were the brutalities of a fierce, unscrupulous youth, and mere incidents in long and honourable careers. To pretend that these courtiers carried their pranks into a ripe old age is to endow them with perpetual strength and high spirits. Rochester, it is true, died on the very threshold of middle life. The rest grew sober with the years. Buckhurst was presently transformed into a grave and taciturn man, well versed in affairs, and entrusted, in William III's absence, with the regency of the kingdom. Sedley, too, turned politician, was guilty of 'reflections on our late proceedings' and delivered speeches upon ways and means. In brief, the court poets were like those who, in other times, shared their talent and temperament. They seized life with both hands, and wrung from it at each stage whatever of varying ease and pleasure it held.

And they were men of action as well as men of letters. There was scarcely one of them that had not taken arms in the service of their country. They proved their gallantry on the field of battle as on the field of love. In later years, a charge of cowardice was brought against Rochester. The bravery of his youth is beyond dispute. He was but seventeen when he went to sea with Lord Sandwich, and, on board *The Revenge*, took part in the famous attack upon Bergen, where the Dutch ships had taken refuge. Of this action he left a spirited account in a letter addressed to his mother. A year later he was in the great sea fight, serving under Sir Edward Spragge, and there gave a signal proof of his courage.

'During the action,' says Burnet, 'Sir Edward Spragge, not being satisfied with the behaviour of one of the Captains, could not easily find a Person, that would cheerfully venture through so much danger, to carry his commands to that captain. This Lord offered himself to the service, and went in a little boat through all the shot, and delivered his message, and returned back to Sir Edward: which was much commended by all that saw it.'

Buckhurst was not a whit behind Rochester in courage; he was present, a volunteer, on the duke of York's ship in the battle of 3 June 1665, when the Dutch admiral's ship was blown up with all hands. But it was Mulgrave who saw more active service than any of them. At the age of seventeen, he was on board the ship which prince Rupert and Albemarle jointly commanded against the Dutch, and, when the war was brought to a close, he was given a troop of horse to guard Dover. At the next outbreak of war, he was again at sea with his kinsman, the earl of Ossory, on board *The Victory*, when he chose, as Dryden says in a passage of unconscious humour, 'to abandon those delights, to which his youth and fortune did invite him, to undergo the hazards, and, which was worse, the company of common seamen.' And so bravely did he bear himself that he was given the command of *The Katharine*, 'the best of all the second rates.' Nor was this the end of his military career. He was presently colonel of the regiment of foot which his own energy had raised, served for the sake of experience under Schomberg and Turenne, and, finally, in 1680, went to the relief of Tangier with two thousand men, and was triumphantly successful.

There is thus a strong uniformity in the lives of the wits; and poetry was even a closer bond between them than the service of their king. They essayed the same tasks, they sang the same tunes, each in accord with his own talent. They composed prologues for their friends; they laid sacrilegious hands upon the works of Shakespeare and Fletcher, which they changed to suit the humour of the 'quality.' They wrote songs in honour of Corinna and Phyllis, Chloris and Olinda. They delighted in an insipidity of phrase which kept their passion harnessed to 'good

sense.' Only in satire did they give a free rein to their eager
antipathies and generous impulses. They played with the counters
of an outworn classicism, and attempted to pass off 'Cupid,'
'Bacchus' and the rest as the current coins of poetry. They
bowed the knee to the same masters, and believed that originality
consisted in the imitation of Horace and Boileau. Yet, for all
their study, they were, for the most part, amateurs. 'Wit is a good
diversion but base trade,' said Sedley, and, with the exception of
Rochester, a born man of letters, not one of them had the power
of castigating his verses into perfection. It was not for these
happy triflers to con their manuscripts by day and night, to guard
them for ten years from the eager eye of the public. They threw
them off in their hours of ease, and did not make them proof
against the attack of time. They were precisians without being
precise. They followed those whom they considered the best
models. The Stagyrite is ever on their tongues, and if they could
they would have obeyed his laws. Their highest ambition was
to equal Horace. But they could not be at the pains to use his
file. It is the true mark of the amateur to begin a work as a
poet and to end it as a versifier. They had happy thoughts these
court poets; they hit upon ingenious images; an elegance of
phrase was not beyond their reach. What they found almost
impossible was to sustain the level of their inspiration. When
Sedley begins a song with the lines,

> Love still has something of the sea,
> From whence his mother rose,

you are reminded of the Greek anthology, and think you are in the
presence of a little masterpiece. But the poet soon loses interest
in his work, and relies upon the common words and familiar
metaphors of his day. Even at the third line, 'No time his slaves
from doubt can free,' the illusion is dispelled. And it is this carelessness, characteristic of them all, which makes it difficult to
distinguish the works of one from another, and explains the many
false inscriptions, which perplex the reader. 'Lord Dorset and
Lord Rochester,' says Pope, 'should be considered as holiday-
writers, as gentlemen that diverted themselves now and then with
poetry, rather than as poets.' From this condemnation, Rochester
must be excluded. His energy and concentration entitled him to
be judged by the highest standard. The others cannot resent a
wise and just sentence.

This union of poetry with the court had one evil result. It
involved literature in an atmosphere of coxcombry. Social

eminence appeared the very inspiration of Apollo. To deserve
the bays nothing was necessary save to be a person of honour.
All the resources of eloquent flattery were exhausted in the praise
of noblemen who condescended to poetry. Criticism was thus
poisoned at its source. A poet should be judged by his poetry
and by nothing else. The accidents of his life should not be
permitted to cloud our judgment. To find a peculiar virtue in a
courtier's verses is no better and no worse than to hail a farmer's
boy as a man of genius merely because he follows the plough.
And it is difficult to read the contemporary eulogies of Buckhurst,
Mulgrave and the rest with patience. Of course, the utmost
latitude may be granted to dedications. No writer is upon oath
when he addresses a dedicatory epistle to friend or patron, and if
only he content himself with making a panegyric of his patron's
character or person no harm is done, while a pleasant tradition is
observed. When, for instance, Sir Francis Fane assures Rochester
that, after his charming and most instructive conversation, he
'finds himself, not only a better poet, a better philosopher, but,
much more than these, a better Christian,' you smile, as, no doubt,
Rochester smiled at Sir Francis Fane's temerity and lack of
humour. You cannot smile when Dryden, who should have been
a king among them all, stoops to the very servitude of praise,
acclaiming in the language of extravagance not their graces, not
their gallantry, not their wit flung lightly across the table, but
their poetry. In thus honouring Buckhurst and Mulgrave, he dis-
honours the craft of which he was a faithful follower, and his
offence is less against humour than against truth. To confess at
the outset, as Dryden confesses, that 'the Court is the best and
surest judge of writing,' is a mere hyperbole, which may be
excused. His praise of Rochester, vague though it be, displays
all the vice of a false judgment.

' Wit,' he writes, ' seems to have lodged itself more nobly in this age, than
in any of the former, and the people of my mean condition are only writers
because some of the nobility, and your Lordship in the first place, are above
the narrow praises which poesy could give you.'

The statement is abject in humility, yet still without pretence to
criticism. He goes furthest astray when he speaks of Buckhurst.
It is Buckhurst the poet, not Buckhurst the courtier, that he extols,
and thus, upon every line that he devotes to his friend, he lays
the foundation of error. He congratulates himself that he was
inspired to foretell Buckhurst to mankind, 'as the restorer of
poetry, the greatest genius, the truest judge, and the best patron.'

Never for a moment does he hesitate to compare him with the greatest  He declares that Buckhurst forgives

the many failings of those, who, in their wretched art, cannot arrive to those heights, that he possesses from a happy, abundant, and native genius: which are as inborn to him, as they were to Shakespeare, or for aught I know, to Homer.

So he sets him high above all living poets.  'Your Lordship,' says he, 'excels all others in all the several parts of poetry, which you have undertaken to adorn.'  And, again: 'the most vain, and the most ambitious of our age have...yielded the first place without dispute.'  As his lyric poems are 'the delight and wonder of this age,' so they will prove 'the envy of the next.'  And it is of satire that he is 'the most perfect model.'  'If I have not written better, confesses Dryden, 'it is because you have not written more.'  Finally, in a comparison of ancient and modern, he divides the wreath of glory between Shakespeare and Buckhurst.  'This age and the last,' he declares, 'especially in England, have excelled the ancients in both these kinds, and I would instance in Shakespeare of the former, in your Lordship of the latter sort.'  What boots it, after this eulogy, to call Buckhurst the king of poets?  It would have been less mischievous to call him the king of men.

With the same recklessness of adulation, Dryden praises Mulgrave's *Essay of Poetry*.  He read it, he says, with much delight, as much instruction and not without some envy.  He assures his patron that the anonymity of the work was 'not altogether so fair, give me leave to say, as it was politic.'  The motive was clear enough.

'By concealing your quality,' writes Dryden, 'you might clearly understand how your work succeeded, and that the general approbation was given to your merit, not your title.  Thus, like Apelles, you stood unseen behind your own Venus, and received the praises of the passing multitude; the work was commended, not the author; and I doubt not, this was one of the most pleasing adventures of your life.'

It was not like Mulgrave to remain long in the dark, and the adventure, if pleasing, was soon over.  As for Dryden, he could sink lower (or rise higher) even than this in the scale of adulation.  A couplet upon Mulgrave remains, his masterpiece of bathos:

How will sweet Ovid's ghost be pleased to hear
His fame augmented by an English peer!

The poets themselves, being men of the world, knew what value to put upon Dryden's panegyrics.  The best of them, Rochester and Buckhurst, treated their own poems with a lighthearted disdain.

They left others to gather up the flowers which they scattered with
a prodigal hand. If they are to be accounted artists, let it be
in life not in verse. Poetry was but an episode in their multi-
coloured careers; and, though we may wisely neglect the lives of
greater poets, with them, criticism inevitably becomes biography.
John Wilmot, earl of Rochester, the one man of undisputed genius
among them, will ever be memorable for the waywardness and
complexity of his character, for the vigour and energy of his verse.
Few poets have suffered more acutely than he from the flattery of
friends or the disdain of enemies. The lofty adulation offered at
his youthful shrine was soon turned to a violent malignity, and, in
the clash of opinions it is not easy to disengage the truth. He was
born in 1647 at Ditchley near Woodstock, the son of the pleasure-
loving, wary, ambitious Henry Wilmot who fought for his king,
and who, after Worcester, shared the wanderings and hardships
of Charles II. Educated 'in grammar learning' at Burford, in
Oxfordshire, he entered Wadham college in 1659, was created a
master of arts in 1661, 'at which time he, and none else, was admitted very affectionately into the fraternity, by a kiss on the left
cheek from the Chancellor of the University (Clarendon), who then
sate in the supreme chair to honour that Assembly.' A veritable
child of the muses 'he lisped in numbers.' At the age of twelve, he
addressed a respectable copy of verses 'to his Sacred Majesty on
his Restoration,' and mourned in English and Latin the death of
Mary, princess of Orange. Having taken his degree, he travelled
in France and Italy, and, at eighteen, returned to England and
the court, a finished scholar and an accomplished gentleman.
None of the courtiers who thronged Whitehall made so brilliant
an appearance as Rochester. All the gifts of nature were his.

'He was a graceful, well-shaped person,' says Burnet, 'tall and well made.
He was exactly well-bred, and what by a modest behaviour natural to him,
what by a civility become almost as natural, his conversation was easy and
obliging.'

He had a talent of intimacy and persuasiveness, which none could
resist. Even when his words lacked sincerity, they won the hearts
of his hearers.

*Il entre dans vos goûts*, said a woman, who was not in love with him, *dans
tous vos sentiments ; et tandis qu'il ne dit pas un seul mot de ce qu'il pense,
il vous fait croire tout ce qu'il dit.*

He gained an easy ascendancy over the court and assumed all the
freedoms of a chartered libertine. Once upon a time, as Pepys

tells us, he had a difference with Tom Killigrew, whose ear he boxed in the presence of the king. This barbarous conduct, says the diary,

do give such offence to the people here at court, to see how cheap the king makes himself, and the more, for that the king hath not only passed by the thing, and pardoned it to Rochester already, but this very morning the king did publicly walk up and down, and Rochester I saw with him as free as ever to the king's everlasting shame, to have so idle a rogue his companion.

Not even the people at court could for long harbour a feeling of resentment against the insolence of Rochester. Charles himself was ever ready with a pardon. Though he banished Rochester many times from his presence, he as often recalled him. The truth is that, in Burnet's words, 'the King loved his company for the diversion it afforded him.' Little as Charles appreciated the bitter satires upon 'Old Rowley,' he could not but forgive the satirist. Though Rochester professed a hatred of the court, it was the only place in which his talents found a proper freedom, and he always returned thither, so long as his health lasted. Nor was it only the licence of his speech that involved him in disgrace. At nineteen, to repair the sole deficiency of his lot, he had seized upon Mrs Mallett, a great beauty and a great fortune, 'by horse and foot men,' put her 'into a coach with six horses, and two women provided to receive her,' and carried her away. The king, who had tried in vain to advance the match, was 'mighty angry,' and sent Rochester to the Tower. But the *triste héritière*, as Gramont calls her, did not long withstand the fierce suit of her lover, and Rochester, as his letters show, made a reasonably fond husband. Indeed, though after the adventure what most strongly attracted him was the lady's fortune, he honourably repented of his greed, and presently tells her that her money 'shall always be employed for the use of herself and those dependent on her... so long as he can get bread without it.'

Adventure, in truth, was the passion of his life. When he could not seek it in the field of battle, he must find it perforce in the tamer atmosphere of the court. He had a perfect genius for disguise, and delighted to assume the likeness now of a porter now of a beggar. Like the true histrion that he was, he neglected no part of his craft, and entered into the very skin of the character he chose to impersonate.

'Sometimes to follow some mean amours,' says Burnet, 'which for the vanity of them he affected, at other times merely for diversion, he would go about in odd shapes, in which he acted his part so naturally, that even those who were in the secret and saw him in these shapes could perceive nothing by which he might be discovered.'

In one of his banishments, he and the duke of Buckingham, also in disgrace, found an inn to let on the Newmarket road. Entering into the joyous spirit of masquerade, they took the inn, and each in turn played the part of landlord. Less with the purpose of selling their ale than to get what sport they might out of the ramble, they invited the whole countryside to frequent feasts, and with the help of their neighbours, enacted a veritable comedy. At last Rochester became enamoured of a wood-nymph, compared with whom 'Salmacis was not more charming,' and whom he visited in the garb of an old gentlewoman, thus giving the court the matter of not a little gossip, before the king, passing by that road to Newmarket, took him into favour again. But his greatest exploit in this kind was to set himself up in Tower street for a German (or Italian) astrologer, who declared that he had discovered the profoundest secrets of nature and promised infallible remedies for every disease. His success in the city was immediate, and his fame so quickly spread to the other end of the town that the courtiers flocked to hear his eloquence and to profit by his wisdom. So well contrived was his disguise, that his nearest friends did not know him; and, as Hamilton tells us, but for an accident he would have numbered Miss Jennings and Miss Price among his patients. None knew better than he how to beat the drum and to urge the passers-by into his booth. As Alexander Bendo, he put himself high above 'the bastard-race of quacks and cheats.' He was ready to cure the spleen and all the other ills of mankind. Above all, he declared that he had learned in a long sojourn abroad how art assists nature in the preservation of Beauty. Under his treatment women of forty should bear the same countenance as girls of fifteen. There was no miracle of embellishment that he would not undertake. 'I will also preserve and cleanse your teeth,' he boasted, 'white and round as pearls, fastening them that are loose.' And he did not underrate the benefits which he was ready to confer.

'Now should Galen himself look out of his grave,' said he, 'and tell me these are baubles below the profession of a physician, I would boldly answer him, that I take more glory in preserving God's image in its unblemished beauty upon one good face, than I should do in patching up all the decay'd carcases in the world.'

That is in the proper key of extravagance, and it is not wonderful that courtiers and citizens alike sought out Alexander Bendo at his lodgings in Tower street, next door to the sign of the Black Swan.

Thus it was that he spent the interludes of enforced exclusion from court. Nothing could tame the ardent gaiety of his spirits, or check his boisterous love of life and pleasure. His tireless wit came to the aid of his inclination, and his deep knowledge of literature made him welcome even among the serious. Like Gramont, he sought joy everywhere, and carried it with him into every company. His unwearied curiosity sustained him in the most hazardous adventures and taught him how to make light of the worst misfortunes. Burnet declares that he had conquered his love of drink while upon his travels, and that, falling once more into a society that practised every sort of excess, he was brought back to it again. It is probable that no vast persuasion was necessary. His constant disposition was toward gaiety and mirth, and

'the natural bent of his fancy,' to quote Burnet's words, 'made him so extravagantly pleasant, that many to be more diverted by that humor, studied to engage him deeper and deeper in intemperance, which at length did so entirely subdue him, that, as he told me, for five years together he was continually drunk.'

When Burnet wrote these words, he desired, no doubt, to make the worst of Rochester. The greater the sin was, the greater the conversion. And thus it was that Rochester's vices became legendary, that Rochester himself was chosen as an awful example of demoniacal passion, a kind of bogey to frighten children withal.

Yet far worse than his manifold intemperance, in the eyes of his contemporaries, were his principles of morality and religion. Evelyn found him 'a very profane wit,' and, doubtless, he took a peculiar pleasure in shocking that amiable philosopher. Worse than all, he was 'a perfect Hobbist,' and, upon his Hobbism, his glaring vices seemed but evanescent spots. He freely owned to Burnet, with a smile, let us hope, that

though he talked of morality as a fine thing, yet this was only because he thought it a decent way of speaking, and that as they went always in clothes though in their frolics they would have chosen sometimes to have gone naked, if they had not feared the people, so though some of them found it necessary for human life to talk of morality, yet he confessed they cared not for it.

As in prose, so in verse, Rochester delighted to outrage his critics. Dryden charged him with self-sufficiency, and out of his mouth he might have convicted him. Thus writes Rochester in *An Epistolary Essay*:

> Born to myself, I like myself alone;
> And must conclude my Judgment good, or none:
> For cou'd my Sense be nought, how shou'd I know
> Whether another Man's were good or no.

If then I'm happy, what does it advance
Whether to Merit due, or Arrogance?
Oh, but the World will take Offence thereby!
Why then the World shall suffer for't, not I.

But it was not the world which suffered. It was Rochester. Like all men who set out to astonish the citizen, to put the worst possible construction upon his own words and acts, he saw his self-denunciation accepted for simple truth. Even Dr Johnson did not rise superior to the prejudice of Rochester's own contemporaries. He, too, thought that Rochester's intervals of study were 'yet more criminal' than his 'course of drunken gaiety and gross sensuality,' and thus proved how long endures the effect of mystification.

As has been said, it is difficult in the clash of opinions to disengage the character of Rochester. *Fort impie, fort ordurier dans ses propos et ses écrits*—such is Hamilton's judgment.

There has not liv'd in many Ages (if ever) so extraordinary, and I think I may add so useful a Person, as most Englishmen know my Lord to have been, whether we consider the constant good Sense, and the agreeable Mirth of his ordinary Conversation, or the vast Reach and Compass of his Invention

—so says Wolseley, his loyal panegyrist. Somewhere between these two extremes the truth will be found. Rochester was as little 'useful' as he was *fort impie, fort ordurier*. He was a man, not a monster, a man of genius, moreover, and, in his hours, a man of rare simplicity and candour. A good friend, a kind, if fickle, lover, he has left behind in his letters a better proof of his character than either obloquy or eulogy affords. His correspondence with Henry Savile does equal credit to them both. Rochester's letters are touched with the sadness which underlay his mirth, yet, what spirit is in them, what courage, even when he confesses himself 'almost blind, utterly lame, and scarce within the reasonable Hope of ever seeing London again'! As sickness overtakes him, he leans the more heavily on Savile's friendship.

'Harry,' he writes, "'tis not the least of my Happiness, that I think you love me; but the first of my pretensions is to make it appear, that I faithfully endeavour to deserve it. If there be a real good upon earth, 'tis in the name of *Friend*, without which all others are fantastical. How few of us are fit stuff to make that thing, we have daily the melancholy experience.'

His letters to his wife, moreover, exhibit us a Rochester that has hitherto been obscured from view. Whimsical, humorous, ironic, he appears in them also, but something else than the cynical hunter after pleasure. He shows himself curious concerning the details of household management. He discusses oats and coal, deplores the want of ready cash, which is hard to come by, and hopes his wife excuses him sending no money, 'for till I am well enough,' thus he writes, 'to fetch it myself, they will not give me a farthing, and if I had not pawn'd my plate I believe I must have starv'd in my sickness.' Here, indeed, is an unfamiliar Rochester, in dire straits of poverty, pawning his plate to keep his restless soul within its case, and nearer to the truth, perhaps, than the monster painted in their blackest colours by anxious divines.

Two episodes in Rochester's career have involved him in charges of dishonour, from one of which he cannot emerge with credit. In both, Mulgrave was engaged, and it is easy to believe that the antipathy which separated the two men was innate and profound. When neither of them was of age, Mulgrave, being informed that Rochester had said something malicious of him, sent colonel Aston to call him to account. Rochester proved, even to Mulgrave's satisfaction, that he had not used the words, but Mulgrave thought himself compelled by the mere rumour to prosecute the quarrel. He owned his persistence foolish, and Rochester, as it was his part to choose, elected to fight on horseback. They met at Knightsbridge, and Rochester brought with him not his expected second, but 'an errant life-guards-man, whom nobody knew.' Aston objected to the second as an unsuitable adversary, 'especially considering how well he was mounted.' And, in the end, they agreed to fight on foot. Whereon, Rochester declared that 'he had at first chosen to fight on horseback, because he was so weak with a certain distemper, that he found himself unfit to fight at all any way, much less on foot.' Accordingly, no fight took place, and Mulgrave's second lost no time in spreading a report injurious to Rochester, upon whom henceforth was fostered a reputation for cowardice. The charge is not fully sustained. Rochester, it seems, was too weak to fight a-foot, Mulgrave objected to fight on horseback, being worse mounted. A little ingenuity might have turned the blame on either side, and Mulgrave, by his own confession, was persisting in a quarrel which had no justification. But Rochester, with his customary cynicism, shrugged his shoulders, and replied to the charge of cowardice with a famous couplet:

> Merely for safety, after Fame they thirst,
> For all men would be Cowards if they durst.

The origin of his quarrel with Dryden is by no means creditable to his honour or his generosity.

'He had a particular pique to him,' says Saint-Évremond, 'after his mighty success in the Town, either because he was sensible, that he deserved not that applause for his Tragedies, which the mad, unthinking audience gave him,... or out of indignation of having any rival in reputation.'

Whatever might be the cause of Rochester's malice, its effect was to set up Crowne in opposition to Dryden, a piece of impudence which nothing but Rochester's influence at court could have carried off. And no sooner had Crowne enjoyed his unwarranted success than Rochester withdrew his favour, 'as if he would still be in contradiction with the Town, and in that,' says Saint-Évremond with uncontested truth, 'he was generally in the right, for of all Audiences in polite Nations, perhaps there is not one which judges so very falsely of the drama.' With this piece of injustice Rochester was not content. If he had been, *An Essay on Satire* soon gave him, as he thought, another ground of anger. That he should have attributed this piece of weak and violent spite to Dryden speaks ill of his criticism. He might have discerned the hand of Mulgrave in every line. Perhaps he believed them accomplices. At any rate, as Dryden was going home one night from Will's to his lodging, he was waylaid by a pack of ruffians and soundly beaten. There is no doubt that Rochester was guilty of the outrage. His guilt stands confessed in a letter to Savile. 'You write me word,' says he, 'that I am out of favour with a certain poet.... If he fall on me at the Blunt, which is his very good Weapon in Wit, I will forgive if you please, and leave the Repartee to Black Will, with a Cudgel.' The punishment he meted out to Mulgrave was better deserved, and delivered in verse. As for Dryden, whose genius, as whose age, should have protected him, he passed by Rochester with a single reference. 'An author of your own quality, whose ashes I will not disturb,' he wrote to Buckhurst, with a magnanimity which, even at this distance of time, it is hard to condone.

At the age of thirty-three, Rochester died, his wild oats sown, and his mind turned to ampler purposes. Though his cynical temper was still unconquered, his wit began 'to frame and fashion itself to public business.' As one of his friends tells us, he was 'informing himself of the Wisdom of our Laws and the excellent Constitution of the English Government, and spoke in the House of Peers with general Approbation.' That he would ever have grown into a statesman is unlikely. The scandal of his life had destroyed his authority. Besides, he was a poet, to whom politics

would ever have seemed a base trade. What he did for the solace of
his reputation was to make an edifying end, and to prove a chance
of exhortation to two divines. That these worthy men made him
out rather worse than he was is probable. Burnet, at any rate,
told us something of him by the way and set forth his views with
impartiality. So much may not be said of the Rev. Robert
Parsons, who merely handed him over, as an inverted hero, to the
authors of the chapbooks.

Such was the life and death of one who set forth his character
in his writings with the utmost candour. Though he was never
at the pains to gather together his flying sheets, though he is said
on his deathbed, one hopes falsely, to have desired the destruction
of his poems, it is his poems which still give us the true measure
of his genius. Yet, even here, misunderstanding has pursued him.
The worst that he wrote has been acclaimed to be the best.
Johnson declares that the strongest effort of his muse is his poem
entitled *Nothing*[1], a piece of ingenuity, unworthy his talent. Still
more foolish has been the common assumption that Rochester's
poems are unfit to be read. In some few, he reached a height of
outspoken cynicism rarely scaled by an English poet. But the
most of his works may be studied without fear, and judged upon
their very high merits. Tonson's collection contains more than 200
pages, and amply justifies the claim, made for it by Rymer, that it
consists 'of such pieces only as may be received in a virtuous court,
and not unbecome the Cabinet of the severest Matron.'

It was in satire above all that Rochester excelled. For this
kind, he was richly endowed by nature and art. He had studied
the ancient models with constancy and understanding. The
quenchless vigour of his mind found its best expression in castigating the vices and foibles of humankind, which he knew so
well. His daring and malice equalled his vigour, and he attacked
Charles II, the Royal Angler, or Nelly, the reigning favourite, with as
light a heart as he brought to the demolition of Sir Car Scroop, the
purblind knight. He wrote the heroic couplet with a life and
freedom that few have excelled, and the most that can be said in his
dispraise is that, like the rest of the courtiers, he knew not the use
of the file. 'Rochester,' said Andrew Marvell, with the voice not
of flattery but of criticism, 'is the only man in England who has

---

[1] *Nothing* as a theme was long a commonplace. Johnson compares with Rochester's
verses Passerat's Latin poem *Nihil* (1567). Two years before Passerat, Sir Edward
Dyer had written a tract in prose, *The Prayer of Nothing*, which had suggested a popular
broadside, with the same title, printed in J. P. Collier's *Book of Roxburghe Ballads* (1847).

the true vein of Satire,' and Marvell, in speaking of satire, spoke
of an art which he himself had practised with success. And that
Rochester looked upon satire as an art is evident from the answer,
which he gave to Burnet, who objected that revenge and falsehood were its blemishes.

'A man,' said he, 'could not write with life, unless he were heated with
Revenge, for to make a Satire without Resentments, upon the cold Notions of
Philosophy, was as if a man would in cold blood cut men's throats, who had
never offended him. And he said, the lyes in these Libels came often in as
ornaments that could not be spared without spoiling the beauty of the Poem.'

His masterpiece, without doubt, is *A Satire against Mankind*.
Imitated from Boileau, it bears in every line the impress of
Rochester's mind. The energy of its thought and style separates
it sharply from its original, and, if you compare the two works, you
may find a clue to the difference between French and English.
The one is marked by order, moderation, and good sense. The
other moves impetuous like a torrent, and sweeps out of its way
the prejudices of all time. In cynical, closely argued contempt
of man this satire is unmatched; in expression, it surpasses the
most vivid of Rochester's works. The denunciation of reason,

> an *ignis fatuus* of the mind,
> Which leaves the light of Nature, Sense, behind,

is a purple passage of English poetry, in which the optimist can
take no delight. Its conclusion is the very quintessence of hopelessness.

> The misguided follower climbs with pain
> Mountains of Whimsies heaped in his own brain;
> .    .    .    .    .    .    .    .
> Then old Age, and Experience, hand in hand,
> Lead him to Death, and make him understand,
> After a Search so painful, and so long,
> That all his life he has been in the wrong.

Like many of his contemporaries, Rochester followed Horace
in making verse a vehicle of criticism. His 'Allusion to the Tenth
Satire of the First Book' may be said to contain his literary
preferences. With candour and sound judgment, he characterises
the most eminent of his contemporaries. He declines to be
'blindly partial' to Dryden, defends Jonson and Shakespeare
against detraction, ridicules the 'tedious scenes' of Crowne,
whom he had used as the instrument of his jealousy, and detects
a sheer original in Etherege, who returned the compliment by
painting him as Dorimant. He finds the right epithets for 'hasty
Shadwell' and 'slow Wycherley,' chooses Buckhurst for pointed

satire, and extols the 'gentle prevailing art' of Sir Charles Sedley.
For the uncritical populace, he expresses his frank contempt.
'I loathe the rabble,' says he, ''tis enough for me'

> If Sedley, Shadwell, Sheppard, Wycherley,
> Godolphin, Butler, Buckhurst, Buckingham
> Approve my Sense, I count their Censure Fame.

It is Rochester's added distinction that, almost alone in his
age, he wrote lyrics touched with feeling, even with passion.
Though, at times, he makes sport of his own inconstancy, though,
like the rest, he rimes 'kisses' with 'blisses' and 'heart' with
'smart,' he could yet write

> An Age in her Embraces past,
> Would seem a Winter's Day;

or, still better, those lines to his mistress, which begin, 'Why dost
thou shade thy lovely face,' and which none of his fellows approached.
Here, the metre is as far beyond their reach as the emotion:

> Thou art my Way: I wander if thou fly.
> Thou art my Light: if hid, how blind am I.
> Thou art my Life: if thou withdraw'st, I die[1].

Nor should ever be forgotten that masterpiece of heroic irony
*The Maim'd Debauchee*, who, like a brave admiral, crawling to
the top of an adjacent hill, beholds the battle maintained, 'when
fleets of glasses sail around the board.' You can but say of it, as
of much else, that it bears the stamp of Rochester's vigour and
sincerity in every line, and that he alone could have written it.

Sir Charles Sedley, if he lacked Rochester's genius, was more
prosperously endowed. He was rich as well as accomplished, and
outlived his outrageous youth, to become the friend and champion
of William III. Born in 1639, he preceded Rochester at Wadham
college, and came upon the town as poet and profligate at the
restoration. Concerning his wit, there is no doubt. Pepys pays
it a compliment, which cannot be gainsaid. He went to the
theatre to hear *The Maides Tragedy*, and lost it all, listening to
Sedley's discourse with a masked lady 'and a more pleasant
rencontre I never heard,' and his exceptions 'against both words
and pronouncing very pretty.' Dryden describes Sedley as 'a more
elegant Tibullus,' whose eulogy by Horace he applies to him:

> *Non tu corpus eras sine pectore: Dii tibi formam,*
> *Dii tibi divitias dederant, artemque fruendi.*

He applauds above all the candour of his opinions, his dislike
of censoriousness, his good sense and good nature, and proclaims
the accusations brought against him as 'a fine which fortune

---

[1] See appendix to second impression.

sets upon all extraordinary persons.'  It is certain that, with
the years, his gravity increased, and the quip which he made
to explain his hostility to James II, who had taken his daughter
for his mistress, and made her countess of Dorchester, was but an
echo of his lost youth.  'I hate ingratitude,' said he, 'the King
has made my daughter a countess; I can do no less than try to
make his daughter a Queen.'

As a poet, he followed obediently the fashion of the time.
He wrote *The Mulberry Garden*, which failed to please Pepys
or to provoke a smile from the king, and *The Tyrant King of
Crete*.  He perverted *Antony and Cleopatra* into rime, and permits
the Egyptian queen to speak these last words:

> Good asp bite deep and deadly in my breast,
> And give me sudden and eternal rest.    [*She dies.*

He translated Vergil's *Fourth Georgic* as well as the *Eclogues*,
and composed a poem on matrimony called *The Happy Pair*,
which was long ago forgotten.  Such reputation as he has guarded
depends wholly upon his songs.  What Burnet said of him might
be applied to them with equal truth: 'he had a sudden and
copious wit, but it was not so correct as lord Dorset's, nor so
sparkling as lord Rochester's.'  He had far less faculty than
either Rochester or Dorset of castigating his idly written lines.
He was content with the common images of his day, with the
fancy of *Gradus ad Parnassum*.  The maids and shepherds of
his songs like their 'balmy ease' on 'flowery carpets' under 'the
sun's genial ray.'  Their only weapons are 'darts and flames.'
In the combination of these jejune words there can be no feeling
and no surprise.  But Sedley had his happy moments, in which
he discarded the poor artifices of his muse, and wrote like a free
and untrammelled poet.  *Phyllis is my only Joy*, apart from its
metrical ingenuity, has a lyrical sincerity which has kept it fresh
unto this day.  Written to be sung, it is the work not of a fop
but of a poet.  A near rival is 'Not Celia that I juster am,'
memorable for its epigrammatic conclusion,

> When Change itself can give no more,
> 'Tis easy to be true.

When he condescends to lyrical patriotism, Sedley is seen at his
worst.  Not even his hatred of James II can palliate such doggerel as

> Behold the happy day again,
>   Distinguish'd by the joy in every face;
> This day great William's life began
>   Soul of our war and guardian of our peace.

For the rest, Rochester's criticism of Sedley is not without truth. He praised the gentle Art,

> That can with a resistless Power impart
> The loosest wishes to the chastest Heart.

Sedley's early ambition could not be more justly or delicately expressed.

The reputation of Charles Sackville, Lord Buckhurst and then earl of Dorset, is a puzzle of literary history. An age lavish of panegyric exhausted in his praise all its powers of flattery. In no other poet will you find so vast a disproportion between his works and the eulogies they evoked. Some specimens of Dryden's adulation have already been quoted. And Dryden did not stand alone. Prior was his friendly rival in exaggeration.

'The manner in which he wrote,' said he of Buckhurst, 'will hardly ever be equalled.... Every one of his pieces is an ingot of gold, intrinsically and solidly valuable; such as wrought or beaten thinner, would shine thro' a whole book of any author.'

For every virtue of his friend's writings Prior found a happy image. 'There is a lustre in his verses,' he wrote, 'like that of the sun in Claude Lorraine's landskips; it looks natural, and is inimitable.' And when we turn from the encomiasts to the poet's own works, we find them to be no more than what Johnson called them, 'the effusions of a man of wit, gay, vigorous, and airy.'

Buckhurst was, above all, a satirist. He had the mordant humour, the keen eye, the perfect concision of phrase, essential to one who lashes the follies of his age. He knew not how to spare the objects of his contempt. He left upon his enemies not the flicker of irony, but the indelible mark of his scorn. Rochester, in a line of praise, not of ill-nature, as Dryden took it, called him 'the best good man with the worst natur'd Muse,' a line which Buckhurst's addresses *To Mr Edward Howard* seem to justify. Of their skill and energy, there can be no doubt. Their victim, assuredly, found them deficient in good taste. 'The gentleman,' says Prior, 'had always so much the better of the satirist, that the persons touched did not know where to fix their resentments, and were forced to appear rather ashamed than angry.' It was more anger than shame, I imagine, that attacked Edward Howard, when he read Buckhurst's ferocious lines upon his plays.

The best known of all his works is the celebrated song, *To all you Ladies now at Land,* a true ballad in form and rhythm, touched in every line with the inborn wit and sentiment of its author, who sees the sea with the eye of a landsman and courtier, and who sends his tears a speedier way than the post: 'The tide shall bring them twice a day.' Tradition has persuaded the world to believe that they were 'written at sea, in the first Dutch war, 1665, the night before an engagement.' As Johnson says, 'seldom any splendid story is wholly true,' and this splendid story must be abandoned. The hereditary intelligence of the earl of Orrery made Johnson suspicious, and today we have surer intelligence even than lord Orrery.

'By coach to my Lord Brunker's,' wrote Pepys on 2 January 1665, 'by appointment, in the Piazza in Covent-Guarding; where I occasioned much mirth with a ballet I brought with me, made from the seamen at sea to their ladies in town.'

Though Pepys says that Sir W. Pen, Sir G. Ascue and Sir J. Lawson 'made them,' it is evident that it is Buckhurst's 'ballet' that is in his mind, and as Pepys knew it six months before the battle, clearly Buckhurst did not write it at sea, with the expectation of an engagement upon him. The time and place of its writing, however, do not lessen the admirable quality of the ballad, which keeps its place in our anthologies by its own shining merits.

Nevertheless, not his ballad, not his satires, not his songs, quick as they are with epigram and wit, justify the praises which have been generously bestowed upon their author. It may be that we have but a fragment of his work; that, as Prior suggests, he cared not what became of his verses when the writing of them had amused his leisure. Many of his happiest efforts may have been preserved only by memory, like the sayings of the ancient Druids. If that be so, they have perished as utterly as the Druids and their wisdom. The mere rumour of them cannot affect our judgment, and we are driven to conclude that it was Buckhurst the man, not Buckhurst the poet, who won the universal esteem. The follies of his youth were easily forgiven, or, rather, the excellences of his maturer years showed the brighter with his follies for a background. His character was as amiable as his pen was acrid. Rochester, never lavish of compliments, paid him the highest that ingenuity could devise. 'He did not know how it was,' said he, 'but my Lord Dorset might do anything, yet was never to blame.' His skill in diplomacy, his tact in affairs, are acknowledged by all, and he was evidently one of those who, without effort, claim and keep the respect and affection of their fellows. Prior's eulogy of his virtues is as sincere as it is eloquent, and if we estimate his poetry more modestly than his contemporaries, we may still echo their praises of his character and person.

It would be difficult to find a greater contrast to Buckhurst than John Sheffield, earl of Mulgrave, and duke of Buckinghamshire, who was as little able to hold the sympathy of his age as to preserve the reputation of poet which once was his. Not even the tongues of flatterers can defend him successfully against the assault of truth.

'He is a nobleman of learning,' wrote Macky, 'and good natural parts, but of no principles. Violent for the High Church, yet seldom goes to it. Very proud, insolent, and covetous, and takes all advantages. In paying his debts unwilling; and is neither esteemed, nor beloved: for notwithstanding his great interest at court, it is certain he has none in either House of Parliament, or in the country.'

The conduct of his quarrel with Rochester, and whatever else is known of him, justify this harsh opinion. As a writer of verses, he is fluent and undistinguished. His *Temple of Death* has no better claim to be remembered than his *Ode on Love*. In *The Vision*, which was written during a voyage to Tangier, we come with surprise upon a line, 'odd antic shapes of wild unheard of things,' which is not made up of current phrases, and echoes the true sentiment of romance. His *Essay on Satire*, which cost Dryden an encounter with Black Will, belies the principles which he himself has set forth: the accent of the scold is heard in every line. The work by which he is best known is *An Essay upon Poetry*, a piece of rimed criticism, then fashionable. It is neither profound nor original. Even as a chapter in the history of criticism it is not valuable, because whatever of wisdom it contains is borrowed from Boileau. It is full of commonplaces, his own and others. 'Nature's chief masterpiece,' says he, 'is writing well.' Number and rime he finds 'but vulgar arts,' and employed in vain without genius, 'for that's the soul.' He discourses, without illumination, of satires, songs, odes and epics. As for dialogue, he finds that 'Shakespeare and Fletcher are the wonders now,' pays a lofty tribute to Homer—'Read Homer once, and you can read no more,' and in the second edition, published nine years after the first, in 1691, puts Milton on the topmost pinnacle of fame, above even Tasso and Spenser. This is the highest feat of his intelligence, and he would have deserved still greater credit for it, had not Roscommon anticipated him. In general, he leans to the school of 'good sense'; he accepts Dryden's definition of wit, 'exact propriety of word and thought,' and would judge poetry by a rigid standard of life. In condemning 'such nauseous songs as the late Convert made,' he voided his spleen against his old enemy, Rochester, and suggested his dislike of the sheer wit of restoration comedy. His condemnation inspired

Robert Wolseley, in his preface to *Valentinian* (1685), valiantly to defend the memory of his friend Rochester, and to strike a blow for the freedom of poetry.

'It never yet came into any man's Head, who pretended to be a Critick,' says Wolseley, 'except this Essayer's that the Wit of a Poet was to be measured by the worth of his Subject, and that when this was bad, that must be so too; the manner of treating the subject has hitherto been thought the true test, for as an ill Poet will depresse and disgrace the highest, so a good one will raise and dignifie the lowest.'

Poetry, it may be assumed, was but an interlude in the life of Mulgrave. Politics were always his chief employment, from which he retired only while William III was on the throne. The favourite of queen Anne, he held high office during her reign, opposed the duke of Marlborough, ill requited the queen's amiability by inviting the princess Sophia to England, and built the palace in the park, which, more than his works, keeps green his name. Wentworth Dillon, earl of Roscommon, on the other hand, meddled in the affairs of the court as little as he practised its vices. Born in Ireland during the reign of Strafford, his kinsman, he was given the name of that statesman, who presently sent him to his own estate in Yorkshire to be educated. He showed an aptitude for learning, and, as his biographer says, 'attain'd to write in Latin with classical elegance and propriety.' When the blow fell upon Strafford, Roscommon was sent to Caen to complete his education, and spent the years of civil war in learning the life and language of foreign countries, 'applying himself particularly to the knowledge of medals, which he gained in perfection.' He returned to England at the restoration, a scholar, an honest man, and something of a prig. He had but one vice, the unamiable vice of gambling, with which he diminished his resources, and which once, in Dublin, went near to cause his death. A friend of Dryden, he engaged that great man's sympathy for his favourite project, the founding of a British Academy which should 'refine and fix the standard of our language.' And the academic bent of his mind is seen in his verses. His *Essay on Translated Verse* might well have been an exercise presented to an academy of letters. It is tame, frigid and uninspired. Johnson says he is 'the only correct writer of verse before Addison,' a judgment which sets a strange meaning upon correctness. The poets to whom Roscommon owes the greatest debt are Horace, whom he says he has served more than twenty years, and Boileau, whose apologue of the quack he introduces into his poem without pertinence. The style of the

*Essay* never rises above a prosaic commonplace. It is only by courtesy that we call such couplets as these poetry:

> Provok'd too far, we resolutely must
> To the few virtues that we have be just,

or

> From hence our gen'rous Emulation came,
> We undertook, and we perform'd the same.

The few precepts which he gives us would not prove of the smallest use to the translator. They are little else than the platitudes generally beloved by moral guides. Polonius himself might have composed this specimen:

> The first great work (a Task perform'd by few)
> Is that yourself should to yourself be true.

He was as resolute a champion of 'good sense' as Rymer himself, and he treats Homer with the same scant courtesy which the author of *A Short View* meted out to Shakespeare:

> For who, without a qualm, hath ever lookt
> On holy garbage, tho' by Homer Cookt,
> Whose rayling hero's, and whose wounded gods
> Make some suspect, He snores as well as nods.

In the controversy between morality and art, he is strongly ranged on the side of morality. 'Want of decency is want of sense,' says he in a line that Mulgrave pilfered. He shines most brilliantly in aphorisms, but he cannot sustain his wisdom; and what most surprises us in *An Essay on Translated Verse* is its reception. In Granville's eyes, he, with Mulgrave's aid, had entirely eclipsed 'the Stagyrite and Horace.' Henceforth, said this too flattering critic, 'we need no foreign guide.' But let it not be forgotten that Roscommon, before Mulgrave, discerned the genius of Milton and the splendour of blank verse. His theory was better than his precept. In his version of *Ars Poetica*, he proved that, however deep might be his admiration of Milton, he could not emulate the noble dignity of his style. Nevertheless, the merit of one who, in 1684, dared to write blank verse, is not that he uses it well, but that he uses it at all. Perturbed by the religious strife which followed James II's accession to the throne, Roscommon took the prudent resolution, says his biographer, 'to pass the remainder of his life at Rome, telling his friends it would be better to sit next to the chimney when the chamber smok'd.' He did not effect his purpose. Overtaken by the gout, he died suddenly, reciting as he died two lines of his own:

> My God, my father, and my friend,
> Do not forsake me at my End.

# CHAPTER IX

## THE PROSODY OF THE SEVENTEENTH CENTURY

In the last summary of prosodic progress given in this work[1], we saw how, with Spenser, something like a new era of English versification was reached; how that versification was again adjusted to the demands at once of metrical form and of the ear; how, by Spenser himself, and by his contemporaries, 'poetic diction' of the best sort was once more constructed; and how, in short, something like the Chaucerian position was once more attained, but with the metrical forms immensely varied, and with these forms adjusted to a condition of the language which has proved relatively permanent.

Spenser died in the penultimate year of the sixteenth century, Dryden in the last year of the seventeenth, and the period between the two deaths witnessed large and definite prosodic progress: not always in the limited and flattering acceptation of the word, but always progress in the true historical sense. Many of the examples and evidences of this—the dramatic blank verse of Shakespeare and his elder and younger craft-fellows; the remarkable array of later Elizabethan, Jacobean and Caroline lyric; the practical creation of non-dramatic blank verse by Milton; the rival forms of stopped and overflowing couplet—have been separately considered under the heads of the greater and lesser poets who exemplified them. These particular considerations will only be summarised here to the extent necessary for a general view of the whole tendencies and results of the prosodic period. But an attempt will be made to map this out clearly; for, historically, if we consider, there is hardly a more important field of English versification in existence.

The point to start with, and to keep in mind as steadily as possible, is that the effort to drag English prosody out of its fifteenth century Slough of Despond—the effort begun by Wyatt and Surrey, continued by Sackville and his contemporaries and completed by Spenser—resulted, almost inevitably, in somewhat

[1] See *ante*, vol. III, chap. XIII.

too great insistence on strict and nearly syllabic regularity of metre. The elasticity and variety of English verse which had been the most precious heritage from the union of Teutonic and Romance qualities had been a little lost sight of, even to the extent of the strange delusion—formulated as theory by Gascoigne in the face of facts, and evidently entertained by much greater and later poets in practice—that English possessed a foot of two syllables, iambically arranged, and that foot only.

Had this delusion not been counterworked, the loss would have been immense; but, fortunately, the counterworking went on in two—in fact in three—important directions. In the first place, the abundant composition of songs for music necessitated now the admixture, now the constant observance, of 'triple time.' In the second, metrical composition in this triple time, with no idea of music, was popular; and, though not much affected by the greater poets, it was sporadically cultivated by the lesser, from Tusser onwards. But the great instrument, pattern and storehouse (to regard it from different points of view) in the recovery—slowly though this recovery was effected—was blank verse.

It is one of the paradoxes frequent in prosodic as in other history that this verse, in its origin and for some considerable time, might seem to have been chosen as the very sanctum of the foot of two syllables only. In Surrey, you will not find a trisyllabic foot; except, and then rarely, by giving value to a syllable (such as one or other of those in 'spïrït') which was probably, if not certainly, meant by the poet to be slurred—though it may improve the verse to unslur it. So, in the rare fragments (such as Gascoigne's *Steele Glas*) of other non-dramatic sixteenth century work; and so, almost more, when the drama seized on blank verse, or blank verse on the drama. The tramp of *Gorboduc* is as unbroken as the ticking of a clock, as the 'rub-dub'—not yet 'rub-*a*-dub'—of the drum to which it was early compared.

But it was impossible for a true dramatist who was also a true poet to remain content with the single-moulded, middle-paused, strictly iambic 'decasyllabon.' Although this forms the staple verse of Peele and Greene and Marlowe, occasional escapes of passion break through the restraints in all directions, though the trisyllabic foot is still very uncommon with them. But Shakespeare, in a manner dealt with more in detail in the proper place, gradually dispenses with all restraints not absolutely necessary to the retention of the general rhythm of the line. Only, perhaps, by reading successively—with attention to the scansion—say, a passage of

*Gorboduc* and one of the famous *Hamlet* soliloquies; and by following up this pair with another—say, one of Turbervile's poems and a song from *Much Ado about Nothing*, *As You Like It*, or *The Tempest*—can anyone who has not deliberately studied prosody appreciate the recovery of liberty in its process and in its fulfilment. There will not be found any real 'irregularity'—lines of intended similarity will never be observed to vary in 'accent' or 'foot division'—whichever arrangement may be preferred. The blank verse will sometimes extend itself to alexandrines, perhaps, in a few cases, to fourteeners, and sometimes contract itself to fragments (*i.e.* lesser multiples of the unit than five), which may end with half, as well as whole, feet. The lyrics may—generally will—present arrangements of different multiples. But these multiples, in the lyric case, will be adjusted to a definite stanza-symphony, and, in both cases, the individual correspondent lines, though they may present syllabic difference, will be found to be essentially equivalent—trisyllabic, occasionally monosyllabic, feet (or accent groups) being substituted for dissyllabic[1].

---

[1] The actual opening lines of *Gorboduc* will do perfectly well, with the observation that the rime of ' shame ' and ' blame ' is a mere accident, though rather an interesting one, as showing that it was still difficult to avoid ' dropping into ' this ornament of poetry.

> The si|lent night | that brings | the qui|et pause,
> From pain|ful tra|vails of | the wea|ry day,
> Prolongs | my care|ful thoughts | and makes | me blame
> The slow | Aurore | that so | for love | or shame
> Doth long | delay | to show | her blush|ing face,
> And now | the day | renews | my grief|ful plaint.

Here, every foot is dissyllabic and dissyllabic only: while there is hardly one, even ' Aurore ' or ' -vails of,' which is not, according to ordinary English pronunciation, a pure iamb. And every line has five, and five only, of such feet without an eleventh syllable, and even without a prosodic overrun, though there may be no stop in punctuation, and even a connection in sense, at ' blame ' and ' shame,' with the next verse.

Now take a *Hamlet* piece, observing that rearrangement of the lines, though in some cases possible, will not affect the argument. For you will never get them into exact decasyllabons. Neither will allowance of, or insistence on, slur help to bridge the difference, for there is nothing in the *Gorboduc* passage like ' gen'ral ' or ' ign'rant.'

> For He|cuba !
> What's He|cuba | to him | or he | to He|cuba?
> That he | should weep | for her? | What should | he **do,**
> Had he | the mo|tive and | the cure | for pass|ion
> That I | have? He | would drown | the stage | with tears,
> And cleave | the gen|ĕrăl ear | with hor|rid speech,
> Make mad | the guil|ty and | appal | the free—
> Confound | the ig|nŏrănt ănd | amaze | indeed
> The ve|ry fa|culties | of eyes | and ears.
> Yet I |

and so forth. Here, you have a mode of procedure as different as possible. Even if anyone objects to the alexandrine in ' What's Hecuba,' he will have to allow redundance

This instinctive carrying out, however, of the principles which have been shown in previous chapters as at work since the thirteenth century, at least, was not thoroughly understood by any poet except Shakespeare. His contemporaries and successors in lyric, with a few exceptions, though they fully comprehend line variety in length and the stanza symphony produced thereby, did not venture on any large proportion of equivalence in individual feet. And there was not any harm in this, for the construction of their stanzas, with alternation of long and short lines, was so intricate and varied that it almost produced the effect of foot-substitution. But, in blank verse, the result of insufficient understanding was more disastrous. They saw the

to the extravagant extent of three syllables; even if, as pointed out above, he denies the trisyllabic feet '-neral ear,' '-norant and,' preferring 'th' ignō|rant' or 'the ign'|rant' or some other monstrosity or cacophony, the racked or erased syllables will still confront him. There is redundance which cannot be explained away in 'pass|ion'; there is overrunning not merely of sense or grammar but in the whole rhetorical prosodic cadence and complexion of the passage. And the fragmentary lines 'For Hecuba' and 'Yet I,' if this last be taken separately (and, if it be not, as in the folio, it will make another alexandrine or another trisyllabic redundance), are perfectly regular —two feet in the one case, one in the other.

Now to lyric. This piece of Turbervile

> The green | that you | did wish | me wear
> Aye for | your love
> And on | my helm | a branch | to bear
> Not to | remove—
> Was ev|er you | to have | in mind
> Whom Cu|pid hath | my fere | assigned

is pretty enough; but, if its grammar is rather poetically free, its metre is as prosodically strict and limited as possible. Once more, nothing but dissyllabic feet and, once more, all those feet evidently intended for iambs—any doubt about '*Aye* for' and '*Not* to' being removed by comparison with the other stanzas. Compare Ariel:

> Where | the : bee | sucks : there | suck I
> In | a : cow|slip's : bell | I : lie
> There | I : couch | when : Owls | do cry
> On | the : bat's | back : do | I : fly
> Af|ter : sum|mer : merrily—
> Mer|rily : mer|rily : shall | I live : now
> Un|der the : blos|som that : hangs | on the : bough.

Here, there are two possible ways of scansion indicated by the straight and dotted lines respectively—the one representing iambic-anapaestic with anacrusis, the other trochaic dactylic, but both far from the straight and direct iambic run. And so Amiens, in actually corresponding lines:

> Who doth | ambi|tion shun|,

strict iambs; but

> And loves | to lie | *i' the sun* |

with anapaest substituted in one place.

It is only necessary to add that an objection sometimes made, 'Oh! but these are different *tunes*,' is quite beside the mark. The tunes may have been instrumental in suggesting prosodic arrangements; but the difference of the arrangements themselves remains.

writing everywhere on the wall, 'Be bold!': they omitted to notice the single warning, 'Be not too bold!'

The first excess of audacity was in the direction of the redundant syllable. This, the occasional virtue of which had been understood even by the Marlowe group, and was perfectly utilised by Shakespeare, was carried, even by him, in his latest plays, dangerously near, though never quite over, the limit. Whether the similar exaggeration by Beaumont and Fletcher was original or imitated—whether it preceded or followed *Cymbeline, The Winter's Tale* and *The Tempest*—is a controversial point, and, therefore, not to be treated at length or positively pronounced on as matter of fact here. The opinion of the present writer is in favour of imitation and following on the part of 'the twins.'

But the added exaggeration of redundance, though it pleases different people differently when largely used, can hardly be regarded as inconsistent with the retention of a sound standard of blank verse in at least the dramatic variety. It is otherwise with careless and exaggerated handling of the other means of varying the measure—alteration of line length, shift or neglect of pause and substitution of syllable groups. By neglecting to keep the normal standard at least present in the background, so far as these alterations are concerned, blank verse, already deprived of the guard of rime, simply tumbles to pieces. It actually does so in the work of D'Avenant, of Suckling and of not a few lesser men, in the last fifteen or twenty years before the closing of the theatres. No wonder that, after the restoration, we find it for a time losing hold of the drama itself; and stigmatised as 'too mean for a copy of verses' outside drama. The real wonder is at the magnificent audacity of Milton in experimenting with it for dramatic or semi-dramatic purposes so early as the date of *Comus* (actually after D'Avenant's *Albovine*, if before Suckling's *Aglaura*) and in choosing it (exactly how much later is unknown) for the vehicle of *Paradise Lost*. But this is to anticipate. There is much to be said of early seventeenth century prosody before Milton and in the days when he was writing but little verse. Especially, we have to deal with the resurgence and (after some vicissitudes) establishment of the decasyllabic couplet.

This couplet, it has been said, had been comparatively little practised in the fifteenth and the greater part of the sixteenth century. Except Dunbar, or whoever was the actual author of *The Freiris of Berwik*, no one had got a real grip of it before Spenser in *Mother Hubberd's Tale*. But Drayton practised it early in a form like Chaucer's own, neither definitely 'stopped' nor definitely 'enjambed'; and a phrase of his in prose, 'the attraction of the gemell' [twin] or 'geminell' (as he elsewhere calls it), combines with Jonson's exaltation of it (transmitted to us by Drummond) as an important tell-tale. The effect of the closing couplets of Fairfax's *Tasso* is also attested in prose by Dryden on the direct authority of Waller. But, earlier than Fairfax, Marlowe, in *Hero and Leander*, had set the example, in extraordinarily attractive form and matter, of the overlapped kind; and, on the whole, this was preferred in the first half of the century. The chief practitioners of it in the first quarter were Browne, Wither and, perhaps, the enigmatic Chalkhill; in the second, Shakerley Marmion and William Chamberlayne.

This variety has many attractions, evident even in these early examples, and fully developed later by Keats and William Morris. So far as the subject goes, its superiority for narrative hardly requires demonstration. The narrator acquires almost the full liberty of prose in regard to the shortening and lengthening of his sentences and to their adjustment in convenient paragraphs. He need neither 'pad' in order to spread the sense into a couplet, nor break the sense up in order not to exceed the two lines. His rime is not intrusive or insistent; it neither teases nor interrupts. On the other hand, the form provides him with all the additional enticements of poetry, rhythm, rime itself as an agreeable accompaniment, the advantage of a more coloured and abundant diction, the added ornament of simile and other poetic figure.

Unfortunately, as in the case of the freer blank verse, these very advantages involve great temptations and great dangers, of which some fuller account will be found in the chapter on the lesser Caroline poets[1]. The absence of restraint on sentence construction leads to confused and inconsecutive writing, which, in its turn, does almost more harm to the story than the power of varying sentence length and of jointing sentences together does good. But this is not all: the verse itself suffers, as verse. The rime, if it escapes the danger of excessive prominence, incurs that of being simply merged in the flow of overlapping lines. This means that it also loses the power of fulfilling its function as 'time-beater,' and that the individual line becomes flaccid and imperfect in *ictus*. In fact, a general slovenliness comes over it; and, whether by accident or definite causation, no chapter of English poetry is more remarkable than this for ugly contractions,

---

[1] See vol. VII, chap. IV.

not to be saved by the most liberal allowance of trisyllabic feet, for libertine accentuation and for other *laches* of the kind.

On the other hand, the stopped form which had existed separately in Chaucer himself, which was not unfrequent in Spenser and Drayton and which, when the octave became popular, almost obtruded itself as a constant *coda*, presented a combination, beyond all question unrivalled in English poetry, of strength, neatness and regular music. The encomiastic exemplification of Sir John Beaumont[1] shows us, with perfect clearness, and in effective terms, what its admirers and practitioners found and liked in it. The sweetness of the stanza, itself regular enough but 'long drawn out,' had palled on them; the new overlapped paragraphs were not regular and were more long drawn out still; while a third variety of couplet, which the satirists and, especially, Donne were attempting[2], revolted them, not without reason, by its roughness. It may, perhaps, be questioned whether those to whom obvious and unmistakable regularity is the chief charm of verse have attained to the full understanding of it; but it is certain that, for a very large number of persons, perhaps even a considerable majority, regularity does provide this charm. They found it in the stopped decasyllabic couplet, combined with the further charm of exact and emphatic rimes, as well as with that (which seems, also, to have appealed very strongly to popular favour) of limitation of sense to a manageable modicum of metre.

The history of this 'battle of the couplets,' as it has been termed, turns on the names and work of the poets mentioned and of others. It must not be supposed—and, indeed, will hardly be supposed by any one conversant with literary history—that any one of them was a positive and exclusive propagandist of either kind. Waller, who obtained his traditional title 'reformer of our numbers' from his practice in the stopped kind, wrote some of his latest, and some of his best, work in the other. Cowley, too, affected both; though there is no doubt that his

---

[1]
  The relish of the Muse consists in rhyme:
  One verse must meet another like a chime.
  Our Saxon shortness hath peculiar grace
  In choice of words fit for the ending-place,
  Which leave impression in the mind as well
  As closing sounds of some delightful bell.

This passage, which is much longer, occurs in his verses addressed to king James concerning the true form of English poetry.

[2] The theory sometimes maintained that this roughness, especially in Donne's own case, was a deliberate revolt from Spenserian smoothness, if not a deliberate attempt at a new stress prosody, does not commend itself to the present writer.

*Davideis*, with its deliberate introduction of the alexandrine to vary, weight and extend the stopped form, was of great moment. On the other hand, as has been observed, Chamberlayne, the author of *Pharonnida*, the longest and the best of the enjambed couplet poems, employs the stopped form in his *England's Jubile*. But, little by little, this form triumphed; and its superior adaptation to the styles of poetry most popular after the restoration—satire, didactics, epistles and the like—must have won the day for it, even if the faults of its rival[1] had been less gross. Nothing can be wisely regretted which gave us first Dryden and then Pope. But, even if these great masters had not found in the stopped couplet a metre exactly suited to their respective powers, its *regulative* quality—the way in which it once more drove doggerel out of English verse—would amply validate its claim to respect.

In miscellaneous metric, the performance of the first third of the century is, also, very noteworthy, though in no single respect of equal importance to that of the progress of blank verse and the rivalry of the two couplets. Among endless experiments in lyric, a peculiar form or phase of the old ballad or common measure (8 6 8 6 *a b a b*) was developed by Jonson, Donne and others, the most famous example of which is Jonson's cento from the Greek of Philostratus, 'Drink to me only with thine eyes.' In this, by judicious fingering of the vowel sounds, and of the run of the metre, a cadence arises which is almost peculiar to the period and which is of extraordinary beauty. By Jonson, again, and by his disciples Herbert and Sandys (the latter important, also, in the decasyllabic couplet), the peculiar inclusive arrangement of rime in 'long' measure (8 8 8 8 *a b b a*) which is now associated (probably for all time) with Tennyson's adoption of it in *In Memoriam*, was hit upon, though not largely used or thoroughly perfected. And the same lyrical genius which, in Jonson, was happily united to other gifts and characteristics not often found in its company, enabled him to practise what are sometimes called 'epode' arrangements—alternations of shorter and longer lines in couplet— with singular felicity. Nor would it be possible to summarise in any general terms of value the remarkable combinations of lines, from the monosyllabic to the fourteener, with which his contemporaries and successors experimented, from Campion to Herrick in point of time, and from Milton to John Hall in point of importance.

This admirable practice in lyric was itself of great value in

[1] See, again, vol. vii, chap. iv.

that regulative process which has been pointed out as one of the chief duties incumbent on prosody during the century for counter-balancing the tendency of blank verse in its decadence and that of the enjambed couplet. But one of the names mentioned at the close of the last paragraph indicates by itself at once this process of regularisation and one of sanctioning and arranging liberty. The progress of Milton's metrical development and practice, and the way in which he ranks with Chaucer, Spenser and Shakespeare as one of the four chief pillars of English prosody, have been explained in the chapter specially devoted to him[1]. It may, however, be summarised here, in a slight variation of the words used above, as the ordering of freedom. His verse paragraphs, the use of the pause which helps powerfully to constitute them, the majestic adaptation of his diction to his metre, his cunning management of word sound and word colour—all these things must fill a great place in the estimate of him as poet and prosodist. In the general history of the latter subject, they become not insignificant but of minor importance, compared with the iambic and trochaic equivalence of his octosyllabic couplets in *L'Allegro*, *Il Penseroso*, *Arcades* and *Comus*, and of still less importance when compared with the so-called 'irregularity' (call it what you will and explain it on what theory you choose) of the blank verse of *Paradise Lost*. The first of these inspires Dyer in the early eighteenth century and Blake in the later with measures almost miraculously alterative of the prevalent tunes; the second, though it produces, at least up to Cowper's latest work, nothing equally beautiful as imitation, works in a fashion less delightful, perhaps, but more beneficial still. For these Miltonic anomalies—call them trochaic and anapaestic substitution, elision, slur, irregularity of stress, wrenched accent or, once more, what you will—insist, in any case, on receiving attention. They will not let you alone : and you cannot let them alone. It is admitted, with unimportant exceptions, throughout the eighteenth century that Milton is a very great poet ; and yet he is constantly out of apparent harmony, at least with the accepted rules of poetry. Even if you edit or alter him out of his own character, as did Bentley and Pemberton ; if you elide him into cacophony like most people of that time ; if you scold him for licentious conduct like Bysshe and Scott of Amwell and Vicesimus Knox and even Johnson, the 'shameless stones' of his actual verse architecture remain unaltered, massive, resplendent. At any moment, some

[1] See vol. vii, chap. v.

one may come who will read their lesson aright ; at all moments, they keep that lesson ready. Unless you cut Shakespeare and Milton out of the book of English literature, the secret of English prosody remains and will remain open.

With one important development of prosody during his time, however, Milton had little to do, though the experiments of *Samson* show that he may have thought of it latterly[1]. This was the employment of the anapaest—not in occasional substitution for the iamb, but as the principal base-foot of metre[2]. It has been pointed out repeatedly that such use, between the time of doggerel and the mid-seventeenth century, is rare in literature though authentically established by Tusser, Humfrey Gifford, Campion and others. But folk-song kept it ; and, in such pieces as *Mary Ambree*, which, perhaps, is as early as 1584, there is no mistake about it. Yet literary poets are still shy of it, and it is curious how rare it is in the work of a man like Herrick, which would seem imperatively to demand it, and which actually gets a pseudo-trisyllabic effect out of strictly dissyllabic bases. In spite of the pressing invitation of music, closely connected as it is with the lyric of this period, there hangs about the triple time a suggestion of frivolity and vulgarity which is formulated preceptively at the beginning of the next century by Bysshe. Long before that, however, it had forced itself upon book-poetry. Ere 1650 had been reached, Cleiveland in his *Mark Antony* and *Square-Cap*, Waller in his *Saraband*—both popular and widely read versifiers— had employed it. But Cleiveland's handling is very uncertain ; and this uncertainty as to whether the authors meant iambic and trochaic movement with trisyllabic substitution, or a mainly trisyllabic measure with similarly occasional dissyllabic equivalence, persists as late as some examples of Dryden.

This last named poet, however, brought his great metrical skill, and his almost unchallenged authority, to the support of trisyllabic measures, alike in many songs and lyrics scattered about his plays, and in others not attached to any drama, but published in his *Miscellanies*. The other numerous collections of the middle and late seventeenth and the early eighteenth centuries, from the *Musarum Deliciae* of Mennes [Minnes] and

---

[1]      Drunk | with idol|atry drunk | with wine
is possible, though, in the immediate context, not necessary.

[2] The term anapaest is used because the present writer is convinced that almost all mainly trisyllabic measures in English reduce themselves to that foot. But it is probable that in many, if not most, cases, and certain that in some, the writers thought of their movement as dactylic.

Smith to the *Pills to Purge Melancholy* of Tom D'Urfey, testify at once to the popularity of the movement and to the increasing skill of poets in it. The form which it most ordinarily takes is the four-footed anapaestic quatrain, rimed in couplets and well illustrated by *Mary Ambree* itself. Some years before the close of the seventeenth century, this form was taken up and perfected by a poet who could not be pooh-poohed as unlettered, Matthew Prior. It continued, indeed, for the best part of the eighteenth century to be regarded as a 'light' measure, in more than the character of its movement; in fact, the approach to more serious uses was made earlier by the three-, than by the four-footed variety. But the point of importance is the making good of a place of vantage and security for a metre very different in character from that which was to hold the actual domination of English prosody for more than a hundred years.

Another, and somewhat similar, 'place of arms' was established somewhat earlier, in the form of the octosyllabic couplet, by Butler, and further fortified, not merely by Prior himself, but by Swift, who was not unimportant, likewise, in regard to the anapaest. This form was by no means the same as the Miltonic; and was also, for a long time, more or less identified with satiric and other semi-serious verse. It did not, as a rule, permit itself to 'fail in a syllable,' as Chaucer quaintly and apologetically puts the *rationale* of the other kind; and so it commended itself to the strong and growing contemporary love for order. Butler marked its time unmistakably; and, while avoiding singsong, he thus avoided, at the same time, the colourless fluency which syllabic exactitude had too often invited or allowed (for instance, in Gower). But he indemnified himself for exactitude within the line by large extension at the end into double and even triple rime; and his manipulation of the rime generally, even without this extension, was marked by a pungency which, of itself, would have given character to the verse. Prior, and Swift when he did not aim at special burlesque effect (as, of course, Butler had almost always done), reduced what has been called the 'acrobatism' of the measure, but made it into something much more than an 'easy jingle'—a narrative and 'occasional' medium of unsurpassed capacity, providing an invaluable easement, if not a definite correction, to the larger couplet.

But the way in which the course of events and the genius of Dryden 'settled the succession of the state' of prosody for some century and a half to come in favour of that couplet itself is the point of importance for the rest of this chapter. And, in order to

exhibit it to advantage, a short recapitulation of the actual state
itself, at about the year 1660, should be given.

By this time—as the reader of these chapters will have perceived, if he has taken the trouble to read them consecutively—
almost the whole province of English prosody had been consciously
or unconsciously explored, though no ordnance map of it had been
even attempted, and very large districts had not been brought under
regular cultivation.  Its life, to change the metaphor, had passed
from the stage of infancy in the twelfth, thirteenth and fourteenth
centuries to an almost premature state of accomplished growth at
the close of the last named, but had gone through a serious fit of
disease in the fifteenth.  It had recovered magnificently during
the later sixteenth and earlier seventeenth, and, within this time,
had practically, though not theoretically[1], completed the pioneer
exploration above referred to.  But certain dangerous symptoms
had recurred in the breakdown of blank verse, in the roughness of
the satirists, in the flaccidity of the heroic enjambed couplet;
while the great tonic work of Milton, unlike that of Chaucer, was
not at once appreciated, though, perhaps for that very reason,
it had a deeper and more lasting effect.  The immense increase of
range which had been given by the practice of the various stanzas,
of lyric, of octosyllable and decasyllable, of one other curious
development yet to be noticed and, above all, of blank verse,
had seemed, sometimes, to overpower the explorers' sense of
rhythm and metrical proportion—to afflict them with a sort of
prosodic vertigo.  Either Milton or Shakespeare would have been
a hazardous specific for this, inasmuch as neither—and, more
especially, not Shakespeare—used a technically rigid versification.
Nothing has ever been devised—probably nothing ever could be
devised—so efficacious for medical purposes in this condition of
things as the stopped heroic couplet.

The development excepted above has been reserved for this
place because it went on side by side with that of this couplet
itself, and occupied, as it were, the position of privileged ally.
This was the so-called 'Pindaric' of Cowley and his followers.
More or less irregular strophes of great beauty and very considerable length had been achieved by Spenser; and Ben Jonson had
attempted regular strophic correspondence, as, in fact, did Cowley
himself.  But the Pindaric which he principally practised and
personally made popular, which Dryden raised to a really great

[1] The few theorists between the death of Spenser and that of Dryden will be dealt
with at the end of this chapter.

poetic medium, in which 'cousin Swift' made notoriously un-successful attempts and which, in the late seventeenth and early eighteenth century, burdened the English *corpus poeticum* with masses of intolerable verse, had no regular correspondence in the line composition of strophe and antistrophe, and no regular division of strophe, antistrophe and epode. It was merely a fortuitous string of stanzas, of unequal but considerable length, individually composed of lines also unequal in length, but arranged and rimed entirely at the poet's discretion. The verse was, ordinarily, iambic and adhered to this measure with tolerable strictness—passages in triple time being only inserted in pieces (like Dryden's *Alexander's Feast*, but not his *Anne Killigrew* ode) intended for musical perform-ance. It, therefore, did not act, like the anapaestic, and the octo-syllabic, as an escapement from the heroic in the way of equivalent substitution ; though, to some extent, it did so act in the less important matters of line-length, pause and strictly coupled rime. In later times—first, as regularised by Gray and, since the romantic movement, in both regular and irregular forms—it has pro-duced much magnificent poetry. But few of its practitioners, except Dryden, between 1650 and 1750, made of it anything but a row of formless agglomerations of line and rime—now hopelessly flat, now absurdly bombastic—often, if not usually, a mere mess of prose, rhythmed with the least possible effect of harmony and spooned or chopped into linefuls, after a fashion as little grateful or graceful as might be. It is, on the whole, during this period, a distinctly curious phenomenon ; but, in more ways than one, it adds evidence of the fact that period and metre were only well married in the heroic couplet itself.

To say that this couplet could not have received its actual firm establishment without Dryden would, perhaps, be less philosophical than to say that the necessity of its establishment in its turn necessitated the arising of a poet like Dryden. If Pope and he had changed places, it is pretty certain that the domination of the form would have been much shorter than it actually was. For Dryden had by no means Pope's attachment to the couplet, the pure couplet and nothing but the couplet; and his own form of it was much affected by precedent poetry, thereby, as it were, gearing the new vehicle on to the old. He took from Fairfax and Waller the sententious tramp of the stopped measure ; he took from Cowley the alex-andrine licence with its powers of amplification and variation ; he took—perhaps from nobody in particular—the triplet with its similar reinforcement. He early adopted the use of the same word, emphatically repeated in different places of consecutive or neighbouring lines so as to give relief to the unvarying smoothness and the clockwork balance of the strict Wallerian type. Above all, after he wrote his first batch of couplet poems near the time of the restoration itself, and before he wrote his great satiric and didactic pieces in the same measure twenty years later, he had an enormous amount of practice in it through his heroic plays. The actual poetic value of them does not here matter at all. A man of Dryden's metrical gift could not have written even ten or twenty thousand nonsense verses without becoming a thorough master of the metrical capacities of his instrument. But, as a matter of fact, little as the couplet may be suited to the necessities of the stage, those necessities themselves force it to display capacities which it would not otherwise show. People may laugh at (without, as a rule, reading) *The Indian Queen* and *Tyrannic Love, The Conquest of Granada* and *Aureng-Zebe*. But it is as certain as any such thing can be that, without his practice in these plays, Dryden's couplet would never have attained the astonishing and unique combination of ease and force, of regularity and variety, which it displays in *Absalom and Achitophel* and *Mac Flecknoe*, in *Religio Laici* and *The Hind and the Panther*. Nor was it merely in the couplet itself that Dryden maintained that unceasing and unstereotyped variety of practice, which made his last examples of this particular metre in the *Fables* perhaps the capital instances of their particular kind. He took good care never to allow himself the sterilising indulgence of the single string. Reference has been made to the excellence of his smaller lyrics (far too often not so much undervalued as ignored) and of his larger; the stately dignity of his decasyllabic quatrains in *Annus Mirabilis*, though somewhat stiffer than it would have been if written at a later date, is admirable in itself; he shows himself, rarely as he tried them, a master of easy octosyllables; and his blank verse, when he returned to it in *All For Love*, is of really splendid kind pro- sodically, and has seemed to some almost the last English example of the form (except certain still more splendid but much rarer and briefer flashes of Lee) which really unites poetical and dramatic quality.

All this practice, with its variety and its excellence, is reflected in, and, probably, to no small extent contributed to, the peculiar quality of what, after all, is Dryden's main poetic instrument—the couplet. This couplet is not, like Pope's, 'bred in and in' and severely trained and exercised to a typical but somewhat limited perfection. It is full-blooded, exuberant, multiform, showing, sometimes, almost the rush of the anapaest, though it seldom—perhaps never intentionally—admits the foot itself, and sometimes almost the mass of the blank verse paragraph, though its pairs or occasional triplets are usually complete in themselves. Dryden attains his effects in it not merely by the special devices already noted—alexandrine, triplet, repetition of emphasised word in different place—but by an omnipresent and peculiar distribution of the weight which, almost self-contradictorily destitute of heaviness, characterises his verse. He poises and wields and flourishes it like a quarterstaff with shifting load inside it. In doing this, he necessarily often neglects the middle pause, and, not unfrequently, breaks his line into sections brought about by pauses and half pauses, which are superadded to, and, in a way, independent of, the strict metrical division. Thus, a line partly quoted already

> To set|tle the | succes|sion of | the state

is perfectly normal—five-footed or five-accented—to all but those who deny the possibility of length or accent to 'the' and 'of,' while even they can manage the fivefold subdivision in other ways. But, in addition to this, Dryden has communicated to it a threefold rhetorico-prosodic arrangement

> To settle—the succession—of the state,

which, as do other things like it in other lines, entirely frees the general context from the objection of mechanical jointing into merely equal lengths. He has also a great tendency to 'bear up' the ends of his lines and his couplets with important words—especially when he uses middle pause—as in

> They got a villain, and we lost a—fool,

or

> Had more of lion in her than to fear.

But all this variation was strictly subjected, in Dryden's case, to what he and his contemporaries, with almost everybody up to the early part of the nineteenth century, and not a few people since, called 'smoothness' or 'sweetness'—the origination of which they were wont to attribute to 'Mr Waller.' That is to say, you could never mistake the distinct iambic—and five-spaced iambic—distribution of the line. Monotony was avoided; but confusion of the base of the versification was avoided still more definitely and peremptorily. It is to this double avoidance that the *differentia* of the Drydenian couplet is due, and to it the

astonishing hold which that couplet, in—but not exclusively in—
the permutations which it underwent, maintained for nearly five
generations after Dryden began, and for more than three after he
had brought it to full perfection.

It was natural that the somewhat tyrannous way in which its
supremacy was exercised—the way in which, as may be seen later,
measures of more strictly poetical quality than itself were ostra-
cised or pooh-poohed—should make the revolt violent when that
revolt came.  It is natural that, even to the present day, vindication of its merits should seem like treason to these measures, in
the eyes of wellmeaning, but somewhat uncatholic, lovers of poetry
itself.  But no one who holds the balance true can share these
feelings.  The couplet of Dryden and its follower, to which we
have not yet come, the couplet of Pope, together with other still
later varieties, blends of the two, are not the be-all and end-all
of English prosody : they leave out much and even forbid something that is greater than they.  But the varieties constitute a
very great metrical group in themselves.  Fresh varieties of the
stopped form—not much practised in the nineteenth century or in
the twentieth, as yet—have been foreshadowed by Keats, in *Lamia*,
and by Tennyson, in a brief but extraordinarily fine passage of
*The Vision of Sin.*  But, whatever has been and whatever may
come, and whatever sins of omission and exclusion be on its head,
it established in the English ear a firm sense of rhythm that is
really rhythmical, and a notion—which may easily be carried too
far, but which is eminently salutary in itself—that combinations of
verse and arrangement of sense should obey some common law.
It is no treason, it is only reason, to combine with enthusiasm for
the prosody of Shakespeare and Milton and Shelley, admiration
for the prosody of Jonson, of Pope and (above both) of Dryden.

This chapter would be incomplete without a few remarks on
the preceptive prosody of the seventeenth century, although, in
amount of definite utterance, it is singularly meagre.  Some
*obiter dicta* of Drayton and others have been noted above.  But
the classical metre quarrel, which furnishes much matter for
the middle and late sixteenth century, had died down with the
duel of Campion and Daniel ; the serious attention of the first
two generations of the century was directed to other things than
prosody, and the revival of general criticism in the third did not
take prosodic form, while the very multiformity and diversity of prosodic practice, during the earlier period, may have had something

to do with the absence of theory. There is a very curious and interesting preface by an unidentified 'J. D.' (who cannot have been John Donne and is unlikely to have been John Dryden) to the posthumous *English Parnassus* of Joshua Poole (1656—7), containing some rather acute criticism on the prevailing faults of its transition date. There are, also, the interesting remarks of Samuel Woodford[1] as to Milton's versification. Milton himself, in his scornful denunciation of rime before *Paradise Lost*, has touched the subject, though he has hardly done so in the preface to *Samson Agonistes*. But the main interest under this particular head is an interest of a somewhat Hibernian kind, for it regards two things that are not in existence, though we have assurance, if not evidence, of the strongest kind that they formerly were.

Jonson and Dryden, who were both, in a way, literary dictators, the one for the first, the other for the last, third of the century, were also men from whom prosodic discussion might naturally have been expected, and from whom it ought to have been exceptionally valuable. Not only were both possessed of exceptional and unusually varied practical command of metre, but both had a strong inclination to criticism; a sound acquaintance, in Jonson's case more specially with ancient, in Dryden's with modern, literature; and a vigorous argumentative faculty. Moreover, we know, on their own authority, that both did treat, or, at least, intended to treat, the subject thoroughly. But, in neither case does any full treatment exist, and—which is more provoking—though we may guess, we cannot, if (as, indeed, is not very commonly done) we control our guesswork by positive evidence, be at all certain what the general purport of either would have been.

The facts as to Jonson are these. He glances at prosody in his incompleted *English Grammar*, distinguishes English from classical quantity, but quits the subject with promise of treatment 'in the heel of the book'—which heel was either never reached, or perished in the burning of his study. In *Discoveries*, there is little or nothing prosodic. In the more dubious, but probably, in the main, trustworthy, *Conversations with Drummond*, however, there are prosodic touches of great but tantalising interest. When a man thinks Abraham Fraunce 'a fool' for writing quantitative hexameters and John Donne worthy of 'hanging for not keeping accent,' the opinions are noteworthy enough; but, as it happens, they might be connected and systematised in quite different ways.

---

[1] See vol. VII, chap. V.

Spenser's metre, it is said, did not please Jonson ; but there are several ways in which it may have displeased him. The central statement—most definite in one part and most ambiguous in another part—is that he not merely intended 'to perfect an Epic Poem... all in couplets, for he detested all other rimes,' but had

actually written a Discourse of Poesy both against Campion and Daniel, especially this last, where he proves couplets to be the bravest sort of verses especially when they are broken like hexameters, and that cross-rhymes and stanzas... were all forced.

Now, except as to the growing dislike of the stanza, where we have the above mentioned corroboration of Drayton, and the preference of the couplet, where we have the corroboration of the whole history just surveyed, this gives us very little positive information. Indeed, the phrase 'broken like hexameters' is almost hopelessly susceptible of various and even opposite interpretations. Those who like to take separate phrases, place their own interpretations upon them and then infer and deduce away merrily, may reconstruct Ben Jonson's *Discourse of Poesy*. The present writer declines the task, though he feels tolerably certain as to the probable drift of some passages.

The situation repeats itself, with a curious general similarity, at the other end with Dryden. In his copious critical work, passages of definite prosodic bearing are extraordinarily few, and mostly slight and vague. There is, indeed, one exception, in the *Dedication of the Aeneis*[1]. This contains a disclaimer of hiatus caused by 'the want of a *caesura*' (as he oddly calls elision), which disclaimer is extended into a valuable general rule that 'no vowel can be cut off before another when we cannot sink the pronunciation[2]; some curious comparisons of English with French and Italian prosody; a commendation of the occasional alexandrine (warranted by Jonson and Cowley); and one or two other things. But the most important sentence is, again, a 'pain of Tantalus.' 'I have long had by me the materials of an English *Prosodia* containing all the mechanical rules of versification, wherein I have treated, with some exactness, of the feet, the quantities and the pauses.' Alas! either these materials were never worked up (though 'I have treated' looks positive enough) or else both they and the working up were lost. It may, indeed, be observed in passing, that the absence of any 'remains' or

---

[1] *Essays*, vol. ii, p. 217, ed. Ker, W. P.

[2] It should be observed that this rule is far reaching ; and that, in particular, it cuts at those systems of Miltonic and other prosody which would dissociate pronunciation from metrical value.

posthumous publication of any kind in the case of a writer so prolific and industrious as Dryden is remarkable.

But, however this may be, the English *Prosodia,* apparently, is in limbo with *A Discourse of Poesy*; and, in this case, as in the other, we can only conjecture what the contents would have been. By an odd sequence, however, which was probably not a coincidence merely, Dryden had been but a few months in his grave when the first book deserving the name of 'an English *Prosodia*' appeared. The work of Bysshe does not belong to this chapter; but it is evidently deduced—imperfectly, pedantically and one-sidedly enough—from the practice of the period of Dryden himself, though it excludes or depreciates, and sometimes explicitly condemns, many of the saving graces and enfranchising easements which characterise Dryden's work. But its faults look forward rather than backward and, therefore, we must not say any more of it for the present.

It is, however, worth while to point out that even Dryden, with his remarkable acuteness and catholicity of appreciation, would have been hard put to it to devise a *Prosodia* which should do equal justice to the verse of the generation before him and that of his own youth, as well as to his own and that of his contemporaries. The changes were not only too great but too intricate and too gradual to be discriminatingly allowed for by anyone without larger assistance from what one of his own admirable phrases calls 'the firm perspective of the past.' That assistance has been utilised here as much as possible ; and it is hoped that the result may at least help some readers to do something like the justice which even Dryden could hardly have done to the verse of the whole period covered in the present chapter.

# CHAPTER X

## MEMOIR AND LETTER WRITERS

### I. EVELYN AND PEPYS

DIARIES are usually written for the writer's own private in
formation, and their production has been common in most ages.
They have sometimes been made use of as the foundation for
subsequently published reminiscences; but very few have been
printed as they were originally written. The two great exceptions
to this general rule are the diaries of John Evelyn and Samuel
Pepys, and these may be ranked as distinguished illustrations of
two distinct classes of diary. The one is a record of occurrences
in the life of the writer, and the other a relation of a mixture of
incidents and confessions.

The latter must be the rarer of the two, and Pepys's work is
supreme in its class. Of the former class, two examples covering
somewhat the same period as that occupied by Evelyn and Pepys
are known. The *Diurnall* of Thomas Rugge, which covers the
years 1659 to 1672, still remains unprinted; but Narcissus Luttrell's
*Brief Historical Relation of State Affairs* (1678—1714) was published in 1857[1]. It ends abruptly, with an unfinished sentence, on
1 April 1714. As Luttrell lived more than eighteen years after this
date, dying on 27 June 1732, it is possible that some volumes of
the diary have been lost. He was well known as a collector of
books, broadsides and manuscripts; but Thomas Hearne, in his
diary, gives a very unflattering portrait of the man. Luttrell's
diary contains passages of interest concerning Evelyn, Pepys,
Dryden and many of their contemporaries. These two books are
of historical value, but they are largely compiled from the news-
letters of the time and are not of any literary value. The diaries

---

[1] Luttrell's original MS (in 17 vols. 8vo), which was bequeathed (towards the end of
the eighteenth century) to All Souls college, Oxford, by Luttrell Wynne, is preserved in
the college library.

of Evelyn and Pepys, besides being of great historical interest as contemporary records, also hold a high position among literary works.

In face of the fact that both Evelyn and Pepys were men of mark, it seems strange that these valuable historical documents, although known to be in existence, were allowed to remain in manuscript until the first quarter of the nineteenth century. If, for one moment, we consider what the history of the restoration era would be if all we have learned from these two writers were blotted out, we shall see at once how greatly their writings have added to our knowledge of that period. It will be remembered, how Macaulay once dreamt that a niece of his had forged Pepys's diary, and that the news, as well it might, plunged him into 'the greatest dismay[1].'

It was primarily due to the intelligence of William Upcott, bibliographer and devoted lover of autographs, that Evelyn's diary first saw the light. On Upcott's being employed by lady Evelyn, the owner of Wotton, to inspect her collection of manuscripts, his attention was particularly attracted to the original manuscript of the diary. When, by his advice, its publication was decided upon, it was thought expedient to obtain the services of the Surrey antiquary and topographer William Bray as editor. Bray, who was an elderly man when he undertook the task, did not do very much towards the illustration of the book; but Upcott continued his interest in the work and was an able assistant to him. The diary and correspondence was published in 1818, and received by the public with great satisfaction; a second edition appeared in the following year, and the diary has continued to be reprinted as a standard work in a large number of different forms.

The two volumes issued in 1818 contain several references to Samuel Pepys, and these seem to have directed the practical attention of the master of Magdalene college, Cambridge (George Grenville), to the somewhat mysterious six volumes written in shorthand which were carefully preserved in the Pepysian library. He took the opportunity of a visit by his distinguished kinsman lord Grenville, who, as secretary of state for foreign affairs, was well acquainted with secret characters, to bring the MS under his notice. Lord Grenville, puzzling over its pages, left a translation of a few of these, an alphabet and a list of arbitrary signs for the use of the decipherer that was to be. These aids to his work were handed to John Smith, then an undergraduate of

---

[1] Trevelyan, Sir G. O., *Life and Letters of Lord Macaulay*, 1878, vol. **II**, p. 428.

St John's college (afterwards rector of Baldock, Herts), who undertook to decipher the whole. He began his labours in the spring of
1819 and completed them in April 1822, having thus worked for
nearly three years, usually for twelve or fourteen hours a day.
This was a great and difficult undertaking, carried out with
complete success. The decipherer, writing on 23 March 1858,
gave the following particulars as to his work:

> The MS. extended to 3012 quarto pages of shorthand, which furnished
> 9325 quarto pages in longhand and embraced 314 different shorthand charac-
> ters, comprising 391 words and letters, which all had to be kept continually
> in mind, whilst the head, the eye and hand of the decipherer were all engaged
> on the MS.

Smith says that the eminent shorthand writer William Brodie
Gurney assured him that neither he nor any other man would ever
be able to decipher it, and two other professors of the art confirmed
his opinion[1]. The shorthand used by Pepys was the system of
Thomas Shelton, author of *Tachygraphy*, 1641, although Lord
Braybrooke was under the impression that it resembled Rich's
system. This opinion put some persons on a wrong scent, and it is
affirmed that two friends in America, who usually practised two
modern and briefer systems, corresponded with each other in
Rich's, which they had mastered out of interest in Pepys.

Evelyn and Pepys were lifelong friends, and they had many
business relations in connection with the navy which were carried
on in a spirit of mutual esteem. There was a certain likeness
between the two men in public spirit and literary tastes; but
there was, perhaps, still more divergence in their characters, as
shown by their respective diaries. Both were of gentle birth, but
Evelyn belonged to the class of 'men of quality,' and was a
frequenter of courts, while Pepys had to make his own way in the
world by his tenacity of purpose and great abilities. Although the
two diaries are closely united in popular esteem, they differ greatly
in the length of the periods which they cover as well as in the
character of their contents. Evelyn's work practically deals with
the whole of his life, having been begun at a comparatively early
age and continued until a short time before his death, while Pepys's
(although of considerably greater length) only occupies a little
over nine years of his busy career.

The figure of John Evelyn stands out in our history as a representative of the model English country gentleman—a man of the

---

[1] See *The Eagle*, a magazine supported by members of St John's college, Cambridge,
March 1898, pp. 238—43.

world, of culture and of business—and his occupation in later life, at Wotton, the beautiful old Surrey country house, with its woods planted by himself, has formed an appropriate background for his picturesque figure. He was a calm and dignified man, largely taken up by the duties of his family and his social position, for, although peculiarly fitted for the contemplative life, he did not shirk the responsibilities of his station, but consistently carried out in an efficient and thoroughly businesslike manner the important duties undertaken by him. All the many books he produced during his life are of interest; but Evelyn was not a professed author, and his publications were mostly intended to meet some particular want which he had descried. That his judgment was not often at fault is seen by the fact that several of his books went through many editions.

Evelyn's diary really tells the history of his life, and tells it well. The diarist is contented to relate facts and seldom analyses his feelings or gives his opinions; nevertheless, his fine character is exhibited in lifelike proportions. Southey said of him that

> Satire from whom nothing is sacred, scarcely attempted to touch him while living; and the acrimony of political and religious hatred, though it spares not the dead, has never assailed his memory[1].

John Evelyn's father, Richard Evelyn, kept a diary, and the son began to follow the father's example in the year 1631; but the diary we possess cannot have been undertaken until a much later period of his life, although his birth at Wotton on 31 October 1620 begins the record. After some unconnected teaching, which began when he was four years old, he was placed in the free school of Southover in January 1630, where he remained until he was entered, in 1637, as a fellow-commoner of Balliol college, Oxford. In 1640, his father died, and, at the age of twenty, he was left his own master. Richard Evelyn was a man of ample means, his estate being estimated as worth about £40,000 a year; and, when high sheriff of Surrey and Sussex, he distinguished himself by his princely hospitality. John was the second son; but George, the eldest, was attached to his brother and always encouraged him to feel that Wotton was his home. The growing political troubles caused Evelyn to leave England for a time; so he embarked for Holland on 21 July 1641, and made good use of his time in visiting some of the chief continental towns. He returned to England on 12 October and, at Christmas, was appointed one of the comptrollers of the Middle Temple revels; but, wishing to spend the

---

[1] *The Quarterly Review*, xix, 53.

holidays at Wotton, he obtained leave to resign his staff of office.

Evelyn was a cavalier and a hearty royalist; but, as Sir Leslie Stephen says, 'his zeal was tempered with caution.' This may be seen in the instance of the battle of Brentford (12 November 1642) between the royal and parliamentary troops. Evelyn came in with his horse and arms just at the retreat, and he only stayed with the royal army until the 15th, because it was about to march to Gloucester. Had he marched with it, he and his brothers would have been exposed to ruin, without any advantage to the king. So he returned to Wotton, and no one knew that he had been with the royal army.

In spite of his attempts to live in retirement at Wotton, he was forced to leave the country, in order to escape the constant pressure upon him to sign the covenant. Therefore, in November 1643, he obtained from Charles I a licence to travel, and he made an extensive tour on the continent, the particulars of which are recorded in the diary in an interesting narrative. The diarist tells just the things we want to know, and many bits of information given by him help us to form a vivid picture of the places which he visited, both in France and Italy. The galleys at Marseilles and the beauty of malls at Blois and Tours (where 'pall mall' was played) are specially noted. He passed across the Alps from Italy to Geneva, and, after travelling along many miles of level country, came suddenly to the mountains. He remarks that nature seemed to have swept up the rubbish of the earth in the Alps, to form and clear the plains of Lombardy. Bears and wolves abounded in the rocky fastnesses; and, the accommodation for travellers being of the most meagre description, they had some excuse for speaking of 'the horrid mountains' in what is now 'the playground of Europe.'

On Thursday 27 June 1647, Evelyn was married by John Earle (afterwards bishop of Salisbury) to Mary, daughter of Sir Richard Browne, Charles I's resident at the French court, with whom, on his first visit to Paris, Evelyn became very intimate. His newly married wife was a mere child of fifteen, and when, after an absence of four years, he returned to England, he left her 'under the care of an excellent lady and prudent mother.' On 10 October 1647, he kissed the captive king's hand at Hampton court, and gave him an account of certain things he had in charge to tell. He also went to see Sayes court at Deptford, then inhabited by a brother-in-law of its owner, Sir Richard Browne. A little over a year after

this, Evelyn himself took up his residence at Sayes court, which
was associated with him for many years of his life.

About the same time (January 1648—9) appeared his first publication, a translation from the French of an essay by François de la
Mothe Le Vayer, entitled *Liberty and Servitude.* In the preface,
Evelyn was overbold in his reference to the captive king; and, in
his own copy of this little volume, he wrote the following pencil
note: 'I was like to be call'd in question by the Rebells for this
booke, being published a few days before His Majesty's decollation.'
At midsummer of the same year (1649), he left England for a time,
as it was not then a place where a pronounced royalist could
live with comfort. In September 1651, he visited Hobbes of
Malmesbury in Paris, from whose window he saw the procession
of the young king Louis XIV (then in his fourteenth year) to
parliament, where he took upon himself the government. Afterwards, Evelyn accompanied Sir Richard Browne to an audience
with the king and his mother. The news of the decisive battle of
Worcester, fought on 3 September, did not reach Paris until the
twenty-second of the month. This event dashed all the hopes of
the royalists, and Evelyn decided to settle with his wife in England.
He went first, at the beginning of 1652, Mrs Evelyn following in
June. It was an adventurous journey; for, at the time when the
party escaped from Paris, that city was being besieged by Condé.

Thus ended Evelyn's travels abroad, which occupied nearly ten
years of his life, and the account of which takes up more than a
third of the diary. He now quietly settled with his wife in
England. In January 1653, he sealed the writings connected with
his purchase from the commonwealth of Sayes court, for which he
paid £3500. When the property was securely in his own possession
(though, in 1672, the king would only renew the lease of the pastures
for 99 years), Evelyn began to set out the oval garden, which, he
says, was the beginning of all succeeding gardens, walks, groves,
enclosures and plantations. Before he took it in hand, the place
was nothing but an open field of one hundred acres, with scarcely
a hedge in it, so that he had a fine scope for his skill in the art of
horticulture.

There is little to record of his experiences during this comparatively quiet period of his life, besides the birth and death of
some of his children, and the production of the children of his
brain, a notice of which will be found in the bibliography. His
eldest child Richard was born in 1652 and died in 1658. The father
was very proud of his boy, who was so filled with the ardour of

knowledge that, when he was told that Terence and Plautus were too difficult for him, 'he wept for very grief and would hardly be pacified[1].' During these years, Evelyn was in the constant practice of sending abroad intelligence to Charles II; and he mentions, in his diary for 22 October 1657, that he had contracted a friendship with the Dutch ambassador, whose information he found of great use in his correspondence with the king.

We now come to the period when the diaries of Evelyn and Pepys cover somewhat the same ground; thus, there is much about the newly-founded Royal Society in both, for the two men were greatly interested in its proceedings. In December 1660, Boyle, Oldenburg, Denham, Ashmole and Evelyn were elected fellows, and, in the following January, Evelyn was one of those whom the king nominated as members of council. From this time forward, the records of the society prove how constant an attendant he was at the meetings. Pepys did not join the society until 1664. In 1672, Evelyn was elected secretary, in place of his friend Thomas Henshaw; but he only held the office for a single year. Ten years afterwards, he was importuned to stand for election as president; infirmities were, however, growing upon him, and he desired his friends to vote, in his stead, for Sir John Hoskins, who was elected. Eleven years later, he was again importuned to take the presidentship, but he again refused[2]. Pepys was president for two years from 1684; and, after his retirement, he continued to entertain some of the most distinguished fellows.

Immediately after the restoration, Evelyn's public life became a very busy one. He was employed on many important commissions, without slackening in his literary labour. In 1661, he published, by the king's special command, *Fumifugium, or The inconvenience of the Air and Smoke of London dissipated.* Charles was pleased with the book, and commanded the author to prepare a bill for the next session of parliament to make certain provisions for the prevention of evils caused by smoke in London; but the royal interest cooled, and nothing was done.

A curious instance of the value of these diaries in respect to notices of passing events may be found in the narrative of the adoption of a special costume by the king and his court, in opposition to the fashions of the French. The whole story is

---

[1] Diary, 27 January 1657/8; and see Evelyn's translation of *The Golden Book of St John Chrysostom*, 1658.

[2] Cf., as to Evelyn's interest in science, and his connection with the Royal Society, *post*, chap. xv.

amusing, as showing how an international quarrel may arise out of a very small matter. In 1661, Evelyn published a booklet entitled *Tyrannus, or the Mode*, in which he condemns the tyranny of a foreign fashion, and urges Charles II to form a standard for his people, writing, 'we have a Prince whose shape is elegant and perfect to admiration.' Henrietta, duchess of Orleans, was of the same opinion as to her brother doing justice to the costume she suggested. She wrote to him on 8 April 1665:

Madame de Fiennes having told me that you would be glad to see a pattern of the vests that are worn here, I take the liberty of sending you one, and am sure that on your fine figure it will look very well[1].

On 10 October 1666, Evelyn wrote:

To Court. It being the first time His Majesty put himself solemnly into the Eastern fashion of vest, changing doublet, stiff coller, bands and cloake into a comely dress, after the Persian mode, with girdle, or straps and shoe strings and garters into boucles, of which some were set with precious stones: resolving never to alter it.

The courtiers wagered the king that he would not persist in his resolution, and they soon won their bets. Evelyn, in his book, takes credit for having suggested this change of costume. Pepys gives an account (22 November 1666) of the sequel of the story, which is that Louis XIV caused all his footmen to be put into vests like those adopted by Charles II. Pepys adds: 'It makes me angry to see that the King of England has become so little as to have this affront offered to him.'

After the restoration, special attention was paid to the wants of the navy, and the officers of the navy found great difficulty in obtaining the timber required in shipbuilding. There had been a serious destruction of woods caused by the glassworks, the iron furnaces and, partly, by the increase of shipping; and this destruction had culminated during the period of the civil wars. Not only was destruction rampant, but cultivation was neglected. In its difficulty, the navy office propounded certain queries to the Royal Society, who gave them to Evelyn to answer. Thus originated that noble book *Sylva* (1664), which revived the spirit of planting in England, and exerted an enormous influence upon the future of the country. Evelyn was able to say, in his dedication to the king: 'Many millions of timber trees have been propagated and planted at the instigation and by the sole direction of this work.'

Evelyn obtained his first public appointment in May 1662, when he was chosen one of the commissioners for reforming the buildings, ways, streets and encumbrances, and regulating the

[1] Cartwright, Julia (Mrs Henry Ady), *Madame*, p. 210.

hackney coaches, in London. About the same time, he was appointed on a commission for the purpose of enquiring how the revenues of Gresham college had been disposed of, and why the salaries of the professors were not improved. Little came of either of these commissions. He was appointed on others; but he was not in full public employment until 1664, when he was named one of four commissioners for dealing with the sick and wounded in the Dutch war. This was a most onerous duty, which caused him immense anxiety, not only in providing accommodation and food, but as to meeting the difficulty of obtaining money. In May 1665, Evelyn was called into the council chamber before the king, when he explained why the expenses of the commission were not less than £1000 a week. In June, he asked for £20,000, and he obtained the use of Savoy hospital, where he fitted up fifty beds. The plague was then raging in London; and he was left single-handed to deal with the vast business of providing for the sick and wounded prisoners. It is interesting to note that, when others fled, Pepys, as well as Evelyn, remained to do their duty in the plague-stricken city.

On 17 September 1666, Evelyn received news of the defeat of the Dutch by lord Sandwich, and learned that 3000 prisoners had been sent to him to dispose of. He was at a loss how to deal with this great responsibility, but proposed the erection of an infirmary at Chatham, and made an elaborate estimate of the cost, which he sent to Pepys. The commissioners of the navy encouraged the scheme, but they were without money, and the project fell through. At this time, Evelyn required £7000 for the weekly expenses of his charge, but he had great difficulty in obtaining it. Money was still owing to him long after the revolution, and he had to petition for his rights so late as March 1702, when some of his just charges were disallowed. The highest office held by Evelyn was that of one of the commissioners appointed to execute the office of lord privy seal, in September 1685, when the second earl of Clarendon was sent to Ireland as lord lieutenant. Evelyn took the test in February 1686, and went to lodge at Whitehall, in the lord privy seal's apartments. It was not an easy position for him, as he was unable to agree to James II's arbitrary proceedings; and he refused to put his seal to certain documents for purposes forbidden by acts of parliament. In March 1687, the commissioners were relieved of their duties. Evelyn was highly gratified by his appointment as treasurer of Greenwich hospital in 1695, and laid the first stone of the new building on 30 June of the following year. At the time of the great fire of London, he was ready with help; and, like

Christopher Wren and Robert Hooke, he prepared a plan of considerable merit for the improved building of London. To the two great diaries we owe many vivid pictures of this great calamity, which was turned into a blessing by the self-reliant courage of the men and women of London.

Evelyn was in every way admirable in his public life; but our interest in him centres in his private virtues. He was a fast friend, who stood by those he loved through good report and evil report. He was not ashamed to visit those who were in disgrace, and, as bishop Burnet tells us, was always 'ready to contribute everything in his power to perfect other men's endeavours.' His charity was not of the kind which costs nothing; for we find that, when Jeremy Taylor was in want, Evelyn settled an annual allowance upon him. Both his benevolence and his taste were exhibited in his patronage of Grinling Gibbons. The large correspondence which he left behind him shows him to have been in relations of close intimacy with some of the most worthy persons of his time. Clarendon consulted him respecting the magnificent collection of portraits which he gathered together, and Tenison asked his advice when projecting a library for the parish of St Martin in the Fields. A matchless collection of manuscripts which he had once possessed and greatly valued gradually passed out of his custody through the carelessness of borrowers. Some were lent to the duke of Lauderdale, and, as he omitted to return them, were sold with his library. Burnet borrowed others for his *History of the Reformation*, and asserted that they had been lost by the negligence of the printers. Still more were borrowed by Pepys, and these are now in the Pepysian library at Magdalene.

The best known of his friends was the beautiful Margaret Blagge (afterwards Mrs Godolphin), who, in October 1672 (when she was twenty years of age), gave him a signed declaration of 'inviolable friendship.' Evelyn says in the diary (3 September 1678) that she regarded him 'as a father, a brother and what is more a friend....She was most deare to my wife and affectionate to my children.' Her *Life*, which he wrote some years after her death and left in manuscript, first saw the light in 1847, under the editorship of bishop Samuel Wilberforce. This volume has established itself in popular esteem as the revelation of a beautiful soul, by one who knew his subject thoroughly, and who was able, with exquisite taste, to make the purity of a woman's life, lived not in seclusion but in the midst of a vicious court, reveal itself.

Lady Sylvius, to whom Evelyn afterwards addressed his *Life of Mrs Godolphin*, introduced Margaret Blagge to Evelyn.  She was married privately to Sidney Godolphin (afterwards earl of Godolphin), at the Temple church, on 16 May 1675; on which Evelyn remarks, 'Her not acquainting me with this particular of a good while after, occasioned a friendly quarrel between us.' On 3 September 1678, she gave birth to a son, and she died of puerperal fever on the 9th of September following.  Evelyn's expression of his grief occupies some space in the diary; but he adds, 'It is not here that I pretend to give her character, having design to consecrate her worthy life to posterity.'  Her husband was so completely overcome by his grief at her loss that the entire care of the funeral was committed to Evelyn[1].  The two men who loved her best looked over and sorted her papers, and they were astonished 'to see what she had written, her youth considered.'

We have great cause to be grateful for the *Life of Mrs Godolphin*, a book which, written with fidelity and charm, presents to us a portrait of a woman who lived for those around her, and, while always seeking heavenly guidance in her difficult position at court, was never austere, but moved in her proper sphere with an air of bright cheerfulness seasoned with witty speech.  Her life, however, was a great trial, and, when, at last, she was allowed to take leave of the king and queen, her biographer tells us

the moment she sett foote in the coach her eyes sparkled with joy ... the roses of her cheeks were soe fresh and her countenance soe gay as if with the rest of her perfections she had caryed all the beautyes as well as all the virtue of the court away with her too.  As she left the presence chamber a whisper went round the circle—'the court had never such a starre in all its hemisphere.'

Evelyn was a good husband and a fond father, and the most pathetic portions of the diary are devoted to the troubles which came upon him owing to the early deaths of many of his children.  His widow thus testified in her will to her husband's devotion to her:

His care of my education was such as might become a father, a lover, a friend and a husband, for instruction, tenderness, affection and fidelity to the last moment of his life; which obligation I mention with a gratitude to his memory, ever dear to me; and I must not omit to own the sense of my parent's care and goodness in placing me in such worthy hands.

[1] Lady Sunderland, a woman of a different type, wrote to her favourite correspondent Henry Sidney: 'Mr Godolphin, I believe, will best like your saying nothing to him on that subject, for I dare swear there neither is, nor will be, any such thing as his marriage.' *Diary of Henry Sidney*, ed. Blencowe, R. W., vol. I, p. 209.

The publication of Evelyn's diary only increased the fame of the writer, and added a fuller portraiture of one who was well known before the new material appeared. On the other hand, the fame of Pepys had so far escaped recognition at the time of the publication of his diary that it was an entirely new man who was now presented to public notice. The enthralling interest of the diary has had the effect of urging lovers of Pepys to obtain further information respecting him, with the result that we have come to know much more respecting his life-history, and this knowledge has added greatly to our appreciation of the importance of the author. The reputation of Samuel Pepys had much changed at various times. When he died, his great qualities were generally recognised, although he was half forgotten as years rolled by; but it is to the credit of the admiralty that his name has always been honoured there. Thus, his reputation remained the property of an intelligent few until the end of the first quarter of the nineteenth century, when readers were startled by the appearance of a work in which the inner life of the diarist is portrayed in a manner absolutely unique and without either precedent or parallel. Confessions have frequently been made in writing; but their authors wrote them for the public eye, and their disclosures are made in such a manner as to attract the reader's sympathy. This was not so with Pepys's diary, for there can be no doubt that its pages were never intended to be seen by other eyes than those of the writer. Everyone read and was entertained. A new man was added to the circle of our intimate friends—a man whose confessions are ever fresh and can never tire. Can we be surprised that, for a time, little was thought of Pepys outside the diary? With a revived public interest in the history of the navy came the rediscovery of Pepys's great work at the admiralty.

Samuel Pepys went into the navy office without any knowledge of any particular ships or of the navy as a whole; and yet, in a few years, according to high authority, he had become 'the right hand of the Navy,' and not only understood more of administration than all the other officers (some of them brilliantly successful admirals) put together, but, in spite of opposition, was able to carry on the work of his office with no small success. Pepys was a historical character of mark, for he figured in all the most important scenes that occurred during his official life. He acted with vigour during the Dutch war; and, when the Dutch fleet was in the Medway, in 1667, he was among the few who, during a time of national humiliation, deserved credit for their conduct. His

name, too, stands out among those who performed their duty
during the terrible times of the plague and the fire of London.
He suffered during the reign of terror caused by the action of the
promoters of the trials of persons supposed to be involved in
the so-called popish plot. He was committed to the Tower in
May 1679; but, when brought before the privy council to answer
charges against him, he covered his influential enemies with confusion, and his defence was so complete that he was ordered to be
set free without a trial. His last great work, as secretary of the
admiralty, was to reform the navy, which had been brought into a
dangerous state by an incompetent commission.

Samuel Pepys was born on 23 February 1632/3, probably in
London, since he tells us that, as a small boy, he went to school
with his bow and arrows across the fields to Kingsland. Later,
it is fair to suppose that his kinsman and patron through life,
Sir Edward Montagu, first earl of Sandwich, the 'My lord' of the
diary, sent him to school, first to Huntingdon grammar school,
then to St Paul's school, and, afterwards, to the university of
Cambridge. We may take it for certain that John Pepys never
had sufficient money for the satisfactory education of his son.
Samuel seems to have done fairly well at St Paul's, and he always
retained an affection for the school. At Cambridge, he was first
entered at Trinity hall; but, subsequently, he was transferred to
Magdalene college, of which, in after life, he became one of the
best friends[1]. In 1655, he married Elizabeth St Michel, a pretty
girl, the daughter of an impecunious Frenchman and his English
wife. Mr and Mrs Pepys were a young and inexperienced couple,
the bridegroom being twenty-two years old and the bride only
fifteen[2]. The newly-married pair went to live at Sir Edward
Montagu's London house, and Pepys seems to have acted as a
sort of steward or factotum to 'My lord.' On 26 March 1658,
Pepys underwent an operation for the stone, which was removed;
and, afterwards, he kept the anniversary of the operation as a
festival. In the same year, he became clerk (at a salary of £50)
to George Downing (who gave his name to Downing street).

---

[1] See Purnell, E. K., *History of Magdalene College, Cambridge*, chap. IX.

[2] In connection with the date of this marriage, there is a most incomprehensible
confusion. Both Pepys and his wife believed that they were married on 10 October,
and they kept that day as the anniversary of the wedding. The register, however, gives
the date of the marriage as December 1. In the absence of further information on this
curious point, it seems that the only possible explanation is that a religious ceremony
of some sort was performed on 10 October 1655, just before the banns were published,
and that the civil marriage took place, as above stated, on 1 December.

The diary opens on 1 January 1660, when Pepys was no longer living at Sir Edward Montagu's, but in Axe yard, Westminster (which stood on part of the site of the present India office), in a very humble way of life, his family consisting of himself, his wife and one servant named Jane. During the frosty weather, they have not a coal in the house, and Samuel is forced to dine at his father's, or to make himself as comfortable as he can in the garret. That the larder is not very plentifully supplied is seen by the fact that, on 1 February, he and his wife dine on pease pudding—a very different meal from most of those recorded in the diary; but a great change soon occurred in Pepys's condition. He had every reason for welcoming the restoration, as it was through the change of government that he obtained a comfortable income. This was the turning-point of his career, when he became a prosperous man.

Through Montagu's influence, he was appointed secretary to the two generals of the fleet (Monck and Montagu). On 30 March 1660, Montagu and his party went on board the 'Naseby,' the ship in which he had sailed to the Sound, Pepys accompanying him, in the previous year. Things went slowly as well as surely; so the ships remained in the neighbourhood of Deal, and it was not until 3 May that Montagu received the king's declaration, and a letter to the two generals. He dictated to Pepys the words in which he wished the vote of the fleet in favour of the king to be couched. The captains all came on board the 'Naseby,' and Pepys read the letter and declaration to them; and, while they were discoursing on the subject, he pretended to be drawing up the form of vote, which Montagu had already settled. When the resolution was read, it passed at once; and the seamen cried 'God bless King Charles,' a cry that was echoed by the whole fleet. About the middle of May, the English fleet was off the Dutch coast, and, on the 22nd, the dukes of York and Gloucester came on board the 'Naseby.' Pepys took the opportunity to bespeak the favour of the former, and was overjoyed when the duke called him 'Pepys.' This was the beginning of their long friendship.

Again through Montagu's influence, Pepys was appointed clerk of the privy seal (which, for a time, turned out to be a very profitable appointment) as well as clerk of the acts. Montagu told Pepys: 'We must have a little patience, and we will rise together; in the meantime I will do you all the good jobs I can' (2 June 1660). Pepys's salary was fixed at £350 a year; at this time, however, fixed salaries bore little relation to actual income, which was largely obtained from fees. At the opening of the diary, Pepys was only worth £40 and, at one time, found it difficult to pay his rent; but, by June 1667, he had accumulated £6900. Besides his salary, he had the advantage of a house in the navy office, Seething lane, which he found very comfortable after the little home at Westminster. The diary contains many particulars of the new apartments, and of those belonging to his colleagues. He lived here during all the time the diary was being written, and he did not leave until he obtained the more important post of secretary of the admiralty. One of the most interesting passages in the diary relates to the great speech he made at the bar of the House of Commons on 5 March 1667–8. A storm of indignation had been stirred up against the navy office, and this storm burst in parliament when some members demanded that officers should be put out of their places. The whole labour of defence fell upon Pepys, and he presented his case with such success, in a speech which occupied more than three hours in delivery, that the House received it as a satisfactory defence, and his fellow-officers, who were unable to assist him, were naturally overjoyed at the result. The orator was congratulated on every side, and the flattery he received is set down in the diary in all good faith. Sir William Coventry addressed Pepys the next day with the words 'Good morrow Mr Pepys that must be Speaker of the Parliament House,' and the solicitor-general protested that he spoke the best of any man in England. No report of this important speech is known, and *The Commons Journals* merely contain a statement that the principal officers of the navy appeared at the bar, Pepys's name not being mentioned.

This was his first great public achievement; but he had previously (1665) shown what grit was in him. One of the most unsatisfactory divisions of the naval accounts related to the pursers. He was early interested in the victualling department, out of which he afterwards made much money; and, on 12 September 1662, we find him trying 'to understand the method of making Purser's accounts, which is very needful for me, and very hard.' On 22 November 1665, he was pleased to have it demonstrated 'that a Purser without professed cheating is a professed loser twice as much as he gets.' Pepys received his appointment of surveyor general to the victualling office chiefly through the influence of Sir William Coventry; and, on 1 January 1665/6, he addressed a letter and 'New Yeares Guift' on the subject of the pursers to his distinguished friend. He relates, in the diary, how he wrote the letter, and how Sir William praised his work to the duke of York.

Pepys's habit of sitting up late reading and writing by candle-light began to tell upon his eyesight, and, in January 1663/4, he found that his sight failed him for the first time. On 5 October 1664, he consulted the celebrated Edmund Cocker as to the glass which would best suit his eyes at night ; but the weakness of the eyes continued to trouble him, and he proposed to get some green spectacles. How the eyesight became weaker, so that the diary had to be discontinued, we all know to our great cost. On 16 May 1669, Pepys drew up a rough copy of a petition to the duke of York for leave of absence for three or four months. A few days after this entry, the duke took him to the king, who expressed his great regret for the cause of his trouble and gave him the leave he desired. On 31 May 1669, Pepys made his last entry; and the diary ends with these words of deep and subdued feeling:

> And thus ends all that I doubt I shall ever be able to do with my own eyes in the keeping of my Journal. I being not able to do it any longer, having done now so long as to undo my eyes almost every time that I take a pen in my hand; and therefore whatever comes of it I must forbear.... And so I betake myself to that course, which is almost as much as to see myself go into my grave; for which, and all the discomforts that will accompany my being blind, the good God prepare me! S. P.

We know that Pepys did not become blind, and that he lived for over thirty-three years after the closing of the diary; but, having closed the manuscript, he does not appear to have had the courage to continue his record.

The life of Pepys after the finish of the diary must be told in brief, although it forms a most important period of his career. He took advantage of his leave of absence to make a tour with his wife in France and Holland, which seems to have done him permanent good; but it was fatal to Mrs Pepys, who died shortly after their return home on 10 November 1669, at the early age of twenty-nine. Pepys suffered greatly from the death of his wife, to whom he was beyond doubt deeply attached. He returned to the navy office, but only for a short space of time ; for, at the end of the year 1672, he was appointed secretary of the admiralty, the duke of York being suspended and king Charles taking over the office of lord high admiral with the help of a commission. When Pepys entered upon the office of greater honour, he, no doubt, annexed to the admiralty much of the work he had previously done at the navy office, and the latter did not regain the power which it had

possessed when under Pepys's superintendence. He made great
improvements in the *personnel* and business of the office; and,
during six years, he exercised a wise authority, causing officers to
be smart and constant to their duty.

Disaster came suddenly, without fault on Pepys's part, and
his career was closed for a time. In 1678, the popish plot was
invented, and the death of Sir Edmund Berry Godfrey drove the
public mad with alarm, while unprincipled men took the opportunity of compromising their enemies in order to bring about
their condemnation on false issues. Pepys had enemies who
sought to sacrifice him by means, chiefly, of the fictitious evidence
of a miscreant named John Scott (calling himself colonel Scott).
He was first attacked through his clerk Samuel Atkins; but, when
the latter was brought to trial, in December 1678, as an accessory
in the supposed murder of Godfrey, he was able to prove an *alibi*.
Then, his enemies opened fire upon Pepys himself; and, on 22 May,
he and Sir Anthony Deane, his fellow member of parliament for
Harwich, were sent to the Tower on a baseless charge. Pepys,
with his usual thoroughness, set to work to obtain evidence against
Scott and sent agents to the continent and to the plantations in
North America, who returned with a large number of certified
documents proving the untrustworthiness of Scott's evidence and
his general dishonesty. These, when presented to the privy council,
were sufficient to allow the prisoners to be relieved of their bail
and set free on 12 February 1679/80. Scott refused to acknowledge the truth of his original deposition, and John James,
previously a butler in Pepys's service, confessed, on his death-bed
in 1680, that he had trumped up the whole story relating to his
former master's change of religion at the instigation of William
Harbord, member of parliament for Thetford, one of the diarist's
most malignant enemies.

Pepys was now out of office, and remained unemployed for
some time, although he retained the confidence of the king. He
was sent to Tangier with lord Dartmouth, in 1683, and wrote a
diary of his proceedings during his stay there, which gives an
interesting picture of the condition of the place and a vivid
account of its maladministration. In 1684, he was again appointed
secretary to the admiralty, when the greatest undertaking of his
life was begun. The navy had been brought to a most serious
condition of decay by the neglect of an incompetent commission.
When he took office, he determined to reform the administration
and to supply the country with a sufficient number of thoroughly

sound ships, and this intention he carried out with triumphant success. Then came the revolution, and the man who had not spared any pains in his endeavour to place the country in a proper condition of national defence was sent by the new government to the Gatehouse in Westminster as an enemy to the state. After a time, he was released by the help of stalwart friends, and he now entered into a period of honourable retirement, in which all his old friends and his pupils and followers gathered round him, so that, for the rest of his life, he was considered and treated as 'the Nestor of the Navy,' his advice always being respectfully received. He wrote his *Memoires of the Navy* (1690), which book contains full particulars of the great work he had done, and kept up his general interest in intellectual pursuits, for some years holding social gatherings of fellows of the Royal Society at his home on Saturday evenings. In 1700, he removed from York buildings (Buckingham street) to what Evelyn calls his 'Paradisian Clapham.' Here, he lived with his old clerk and friend William Hewer; but his infirmities kept him constantly in the house. On 26 May 1703, he breathed his last in the presence of the learned George Hickes, the non-juring dean of Worcester, who bears witness to the big-mindedness of the man, his patience under suffering and the fervent piety of his end. He died full of honour—a recognition thoroughly deserved by his public conduct through life; but he was shabbily treated by the men in power. The last two Stewart kings were many thousands of pounds—£28,007. 2s. 1¼d., to be exact—in his debt, and the new government did not see that they were called to help him in recovering it. They might, however, have considered how much the country was indebted to him for a strong navy, and remembered that most of the money owing to him had been spent upon the state.

Pepys's diary is so various in its interest that it is not easy in a few words to indicate where its chief distinction lies. The absolute sincerity and transparent truth of the narrative naturally explains much, but the vitality of the man and his intense interest in the pageant of life supplies the motive power. Important events gain by the strength of their presentment, and trivialities delight us by the way in which they are narrated. Here is not only a picture of the life and manners of the time, but, also, the dissection of the heart of a man, and the exposure suggests a psychological problem difficult of solution. We naturally ask how it came to pass that the writer of the diary arrived at a perfection of style suitable to the character of what he had to relate. Is it

possible that he had previously practised the writing of a journal?
We see the man grow in knowledge and power as the diary proceeds; but the narrative is equally good at the beginning and at
the end. Pepys apparently made notes on slips of paper and then
elaborated them without any unnecessary delay. It is remarkable
that there should be few or no corrections in the written manuscript.
He wrote in secret, and, when he unguardedly (at the time of his
detention in the Tower) told Sir William Coventry that he kept a
diary, he was immediately afterwards sorry for his indiscretion.
It is also matter for wonder that he should have trusted a binder
with the precious book. Was the binder brought into the house to
bind the pages under the writer's eye?

The brilliancy of the narrative and the intimacy of the
confessions so thoroughly charm the reader that, in many cases,
he overlooks the fact that, although Pepys was devoted to pleasure,
he was not absorbed by it, but always kept in view the main
object of his life—the perfection of the English navy. Pepys was
not a man of letters in the same way that Evelyn was one. When
the latter was interested in a subject, he wanted to write upon it,
and not only wanted to, but did write, as is shown by the list of
his works in our bibliography. This was not the case with Pepys.
Early in his official life, he proposed to write a history of the navy,
and collected materials for the purpose; but, although he talked
about the project, he never got at all forward with it. His
*Memoires of the Navy* was prepared under an urgent desire to
present his *apologia*, and was only a chapter in the great work
that had long been projected. This little book contains a
thoroughly effective statement of his case; but it is not lively
reading or a work of any literary merit. The question, therefore,
arises why the diary is different, and why it is remarkable as a
literary effort.

The entries are all made with care, and there is no hurry about
any of them; but we must remember that they were written fresh
from the heart, and many hard judgments passed on colleagues
were the result of temporary indignation. He was himself careful,
tidy and methodical, and he was impatient of untidiness and
improvidence in those around him. His wife often irritated him
by her carelessness and want of method; but his poor sister,
Paulina Pepys, comes off as badly as anyone in the diary. She did
not receive much kindness from her brother and sister-in-law,
although Pepys did his best to find her a husband, and, when
the search was followed by success, gave her a handsome

dowry[1]. The pages of the diary are full of particulars respecting Pepys's various servants, and their part in constant musical performances. It is necessary to bear in mind that most of these servants were more properly companions or maids of Mrs Pepys.

Pepys's system of vows and the excuses made for not carrying them out are very singular and amusing. He feared the waste of time that would arise from a too frequent attendance at the theatre, and from his tendency to drink. The fines which he levied upon himself had some influence in weaning him from bad habits. It does not appear that he neglected his work, even when taking pleasure; for, although the working day was often irregular in arrangement, the work was done either early in the morning or late at night, to make up for occasional long sittings after the midday meal. The diary contains a mine of information respecting theatres and music; there is much about the buying of his books and book-cases, but it should be borne in mind that the larger portion of the Pepysian library now preserved at Magdalene college, Cambridge, was purchased after the conclusion of the diary.

It has been said that Pepys knew Evelyn a great deal better than we know that stately gentleman, but that we know Pepys a hundred times better than Evelyn did. In illustration of this dictum, two passages from Pepys's diary come to mind. On 10 September 1665, he joined a party at Greenwich, where Sir John Minnes and Evelyn were the life of the company and full of mirth. Among other humours, Evelyn repeated some verses introducing 'the various acceptations of may and can,' which made all present nearly die of laughing. This is certainly a fresh side of his character. On the following 5th of November, Pepys visited Evelyn at Deptford, when the latter read to the former extracts from an essay he had in hand, also a part of a play or two of his making, and some short poems. 'In fine a most excellent person he is and must be allowed a little for a little conceitedness but he may well be so, being a man so much above others.' So Pepys helps us to know Evelyn better and love him none the less; while, as for Pepys himself, we certainly know him better than Evelyn knew him, though we readily accept Evelyn's noble tribute to his merits. His frailties he has himself recorded; but, even were there no other evidence on the subject than is to be found in the diary itself, it would show him to have been a patriot and a true and steadfast friend.

---

[1] Her descendants—the family of Pepys Cockerell—are now the representatives of Samuel Pepys.

## II. Other Writers of Memoirs and Letters

### A.

The anonymous *Mémoires de la Vie du Comte de Gramont,* published for the first time at Cologne in 1713, is universally acknowledged to be a masterpiece of French literature; in fact, Voltaire went so far as to say that the author was the first to discover the essential genius of the French language. Yet this book was written by an Englishman, and it deals chiefly with the English court of Charles II. It was carelessly translated into English by Abel Boyer (a French Huguenot who settled in England and wrote histories of king William III and queen Anne) and published in the year after that of the appearance of the original work. This translation was touched up by Sir Walter Scott and has generally been used in the various editions of the English version. No first-rate writer has been at the pains of retranslating it and making it a masterpiece of English prose. Some of the blunders made by the original translator have been continued without correction, and have given considerable trouble[1]. The names of persons mentioned in the original French are often wrong, as 'Stwart' for Stewart and 'Hubert' for Hobart, and so forth ; but, in the English translation, they are usually given with an initial followed by a line; this allowed of the publication, at the price of twopence, of a needed *Key to the Memoirs*[2].

The author was Anthony Hamilton, third son of Sir George Hamilton and grandson of the earl of Abercorn. At the end of the first chapter of his book, he wrote 'To himself we owe these Memoirs since I only hold the pen.' Report told how Gramont dictated his *Memoirs* to Hamilton in the year 1701 and sold the manuscript to a publisher for fifteen hundred *livres*. When Fontenelle, then censor of the press, saw the manuscript, he is said to have refused to license the publication, on account of the scandalous conduct of the hero in cheating at cards which is described in the third chapter. There is little authority for this report, and Gramont is only known as a brilliant talker and not as an author.

---

[1] Thus, Elizabeth Davenport, the actress who took the part of Roxolana in Davenant's *Siege of Rhodes*, has been confused with Anne Marshall, who was Roxana in Lee's *Rival Queens*. In the original French, we find the statement '*Le rôle de Roxelane, dans une pièce nouvelle*'; but this is incorrectly translated by Boyer: 'particularly the part of Roxana in the Rival Queens.'

[2] In the modern editions, Mademoiselle is translated as Miss; but even Boyer knew better than this, and always printed Mrs. We know what Evelyn says of the term 'Miss,' and it certainly should not be attached to the names of maids of honour.

The book is divided into eleven unequal chapters, of which the first five are short and relate only to continental adventures. This portion closes with the chevalier Gramont's banishment from the French court owing to his persistent attentions to Mlle La Motte Houdancourt, one of Louis XIV's mistresses. This escapade brought him to England, and chapters VI to XI are devoted to the doings of the English court. Hamilton knew nothing of Gramont's adventures abroad, and this portion has all the marks of having been taken down from Gramont's dictation. The English portion of the book is quite different in mode of treatment, and, here, Gramont does not relate his own adventures as before. In some scenes he does not even appear, and Hamilton evidently wrote from his own intimate knowledge about subjects and persons unlikely to be known so well to Gramont, as a foreigner.

It is most improbable that Hamilton should have handed over his manuscript, upon which he must have spent much time and labour, to be disposed of by Gramont as his own. Moreover, Hamilton waited for six years after Gramont's death in 1707, and then issued the work at Cologne instead of at Paris. No doubt, although many of the actors in the scandalous scenes related were dead, some influential persons still lived, who would use all their influence to prevent the publication. In 1713, however, Hamilton was sixty-seven years of age; and, if he wished to see his beloved book in print, he had to find a publisher with as little delay as possible.

The question as to the truthfulness of the details related by Hamilton is one of the greatest importance. In reply to Lord Hailes's remark that the chronology of the *Memoirs* is not exact, Horace Walpole exclaimed, 'What has that book to do with chronology?' Hallam, likewise, was of opinion that the *Memoirs* 'scarcely challenge a place as historical.' It must be admitted that Hamilton produced a book which is too much a work of art to be entirely trustworthy, and the subject-matter is often arranged for effect, which would scarcely have been allowed if strict accuracy had been the main object[1]

[1] The king and queen with their court made two visits to Tunbridge Wells, one in 1663 and the other in 1666, but the author confuses the incidents and makes the two visits into one. There was good excuse for this in the length of time that had elapsed since the visits were made when the author wrote his book. Several of the adventures described are also recounted by Pepys and, in these cases, we are able to attach a date. Peter Cunningham (appendix to *The Story of Nell Gwyn*, 1852, p. 183) set himself to give some indications of the chronology of the *Memoirs*; but, unfortunately, he made a mistake in the date of Gramont's marriage with *la belle* Hamilton, sister of the author of the book.

Anthony Hamilton became an intimate friend of Gramont immediately after his arrival in England; but he never mentions himself in his book. Moreover, he purposely confuses the circumstances and date of Gramont's marriage with his sister, Elizabeth Hamilton, which actually took place in December 1663[1].

There is evidence that the chevalier de Gramont and his wife left London for France in November 1664, and took up their permanent residence there. They appear to have made frequent visits to the English court in succeeding years; but their settlement in France in itself proves that the later portion of the book, some of the incidents in which seem to have occurred in the year 1669, must have been written by Hamilton without help from Gramont. Therefore, the following passage from the last chapter can hardly be considered to be written in good faith:

> We profess to insert nothing in these Memoirs but what we have from the mouth of him whose actions we transmit to posterity.

The subject of these *Memoirs* was an ill-formed man—it was said that he had the face of an ape—and his character was thoroughly worthless. He does not appear to have possessed even the most elementary feelings of honour, as he is proved to have been a cheat. Doubtless, his attentions had compromised mistress Hamilton, or her brothers would not have been anxious for the marriage, as the lady had had many more eligible suitors. It may be said that Hamilton has performed a feat in making so showy and profligate a man passable as the hero of his book; but even he is not able to speak highly of Gramont as a husband.

[1] This well known story is told in a letter from Lord Melfort to Richard Hamilton (written about twenty-seven years after the marriage). Gramont, being suddenly recalled to France, was on the point of returning without mistress Hamilton (to whom he had made violent love), and had got as far as Dover, when he was overtaken by the lady's two brothers—George and Anthony. They at once put this question to him— '*Chevalier de Gramont, n'avez-vous rien oublié à Londres?*' To which, the chevalier replied, '*Pardonnez-moi, messieurs, j'ai oublié d'épouser votre sœur.*' He then returned to London and the marriage was solemnised.

On 22 December that year, Pepys noted: 'This day I hear for certain that Lady Castlemaine is turned Popish.' In illustration of this entry, Lord Braybrooke printed an extract from a letter of the count d'Estrades to Louis XIV—in which he wrote that the marriage of chevalier de Gramont and the conversion of Madame de Castlemaine were published on the same day. This fact would never be gathered from the statement in the *Memoirs*, that Gramont was recalled to France by his sister, the marchioness de Saint-Chaumont, who told him that the king had given him leave to return. When he arrived, he found that it was all a mistake. His brother, marshal de Gramont, had orders from the king for him to go back again without appearing at court.

ʃSir William Musgrave fixed the date of the occurrences recorded in the *Memoirs* from 1663 to 1665; but Cunningham fixes the longer period of May 1662 to October 1669, supposing, as we have already seen, that Gramont remained in England until the end of the book.

The author certainly had ever before his eyes the great aim of putting his sister in a prominent position, and wiping out of existence any discreditable rumours respecting her. In this he has succeeded, and she stands out as the one woman in the book of whom nothing ill can be said. Many of the women described in the *Memoirs*, such as Castlemaine and Shrewsbury, probably deserved every ill word that could be said of them; but we may hope that some, at least, of the others were less vicious than they are painted; for Hamilton was one of those authors who will not lose a point that adds to his picture to save a reputation, and no scandal was likely to be scrutinised too keenly by him in order to prove it untruthful. We have seen that at least one pure woman —Evelyn's friend Mrs Godolphin—lived for a time in a court which was a hotbed of corruption; but even she, because she was not like other ladies, is treated with contempt in these *Memoirs*[1].

It is not necessary to analyse the contents of so well known a book as the Gramont *Memoirs*. They will always be consulted with interest, for they turn a searchlight upon the inner history of a period, which, indeed, owes the bad reputation it bears largely to their revelations.

*The Memoirs of Sir John Reresby* are the work of an accomplished man who united in himself the qualities of a courtier and those of a country squire. The book contains a pleasing record of the chief events, some of them of very great importance, which came under his notice, as well as of other matters founded on the mere gossip of court circles. The author writes with distinction, and the reader cannot well follow his adventures without a feeling of esteem and sympathy, although it must be confessed that he was somewhat of a self-seeker—indeed, he has been styled[2] 'a cautious time-serving politician.' To those who read his pleasant narrative with interest, this must, however, appear a hard saying. He lived in a difficult period, and, although he was whole-heartedly loyal to Charles II, he does not appear to have approved of the next sovereign, and his protestant feelings prevented him from being troubled with much regret when the revolution was completed; so that he had not any difficulty in deciding to swear allegiance to William III.

---

[1] Miss Hobart is made to say 'Alas! poor Mrs Blague! I saw her go away about this time twelve month in a coach with such lean horses that I cannot believe she is half way to her miserable little castle' (chap. IX).

[2] In the *Dictionary of National Biography*.

Reresby had really small reason for gratitude to Charles II, since, although the king was glad to enjoy his agreeable conversation, and to make use of him generally, all that the courtier obtained from his long attendance at court was

an appointment to be high sheriff of his county, to which his rank alone entitled him, the government of a city that had no garrison, and the command of a fort, which never appears to have been built[1].

Reresby was only 55 years of age when he died in 1689; and it was not until 1734 that his *Memoirs* were first published, the manuscript having, in the interval, passed through several hands. The book was popular, and several editions of it[2] were called for; among which, that of 1813 for the first time printed the author's *Travels*, while that of 1875 printed some of his letters, together with passages of the diary previously omitted. It is well that the diary and the travels—both of them short works—should be united, as, together, they form a connected whole, and the chronology of Reresby's life is thus completed. The scheme of his writings has a certain likeness to that of Evelyn's diary. The same circumstances in the history of the country caused these two men to begin their lives with the experience of foreign travel. Reresby, like Evelyn, felt that to live at home was worse than banishment, and begins his journeyings with these words:

I left England in that unhappy time when honesty was reputed a crime, religion superstition, loyalty treason; when subjects were governors, servants masters, and no gentleman assured of anything he possessed; the least jealousy of disaffection to the late erected commonwealth being offence sufficient to endanger the forfeiture of his estate, the only laws in force being those of the sword.

He took his departure in 1654, and made an extensive tour through Europe. His descriptions of France, Italy, Germany and the Netherlands are valuable, and contain much information of interest as to the state of these countries in the seventeenth century. Reresby spent some time at Saumur (in Anjou), where there was a protestant university. Here, he was able to study the French language, which he found 'the great resort of my countrymen to Paris prevented me from doing satisfactorily there.' After staying again in Paris, which he considered the finest city of Europe (not excepting London), he returned to England, in May 1658, after four years' absence.

He opens his memoirs with a notice of the death of Cromwell, which, he thought, paved the way for the return of the king. This

---

[1] *Retrospective Review*, vol. VIII, p. 346.
[2] As to these and other editions, see bibliography.

was on 23 September 1658, and, in October of the same year, he was back in Paris, where he made himself known to the queen mother, who kept her court at the Palais Royal. He was well received and became very friendly with the charming princess Henrietta (then fifteen years of age), who was the queen's only child living with her. In 1660, hopes arose of the restoration of Charles II, and we are told that now there was a greater resort to the Palais Royal than to the French court. On 2 August, Reresby returned to England, and he took with him a particular recommendation of the queen mother to the king. On 10 August 1669, the queen died, and Reresby describes her as 'a great princess and my very good mistress.' It is interesting to learn that, at one time, he was attracted by *la belle* Hamilton, and there was a chance of his marrying her, although she was a catholic; but, after he had seen mistress Frances Browne (to whom he was married in 1665), he had no inclination for any other choice. He had probably a fortunate escape; but, on the other hand, one feels that, as Lady Reresby, Elizabeth Hamilton would have had a happier life than she was fated to live as the partner of Philibert de Gramont.

Reresby was not a man of letters; but there is a distinction about his writings, which give us pleasure from their liveliness and freshness, indicating the insight and impartiality of a man of the world. By a careful selection of subjects, he manages to furnish a good idea of the period from the restoration to the revolution. He allots much space to his notes on the popish plot, which shows his appreciation of the dangers to be apprehended from the rapid progress of the supposed design, although we see that he was early convinced of the villainy of Oates[1].

The author carefully narrates the transactions which preceded the revolution; but he saw little of the new *régime*, for he died on 12 May 1689.

### B.

Among the memoir- and letter-writers of this period should, also, be mentioned Sir Richard Bulstrode, though, born in 1630, he

---

[1] He relates an interesting meeting with James II, after the arch-conspirator was convicted of perjury. It was proved 'that he was at St Omer the 24th of April 1678 when he swore he was at the White-Horse tavern in the Strand, where Pickering, Groves, and other Jesuits signed the death of King Charles the second.' Reresby was told by James that it was fortunate for him that Oates was ignorant of the place of meeting, for it actually took place in the duke of York's rooms at St James's. The king added 'that Oates being thus convicted, the popish plot was now dead'; to which Reresby answered that it had long been dead, and now it would be buried.

survived till 1711, when he is stated to have died 'not of old age.' He served in arms in the civil war, and, as agent and envoy at the court of Brussels, under Charles II and James II, whom he followed to St Germain. His prose-writings, all of which were published posthumously, include, besides *Original Letters written to the Earl of Arlington,* in 1674, which narrate the principal events in the Low Countries and the adjoining parts of France in that year, *Memoirs and Reflections upon the Reign and Government of King Charles the 1st and King Charles the 2d,* besides a *Life of James II,* stated to have been printed at Rome shortly after the author's death. The earlier of these works, which announces itself as 'a vindication of the characters of both Charles I and Charles II from Fanatical Aspersions,' displays judgment and insight, as well as loyalty. If Charles I is designated 'the best of kings,' while of Oliver Cromwell it is asserted that 'there was certainly never a more wicked man,' the former is shown to have erred in not depending on his own judgment, and the latter is credited not only with self-reliance, but with 'prodigious Address.' The memoir of Charles II is badly constructed, and, after a long account of the popish plot agitation, ends with a series of diplomatic letters of secondary importance.

The *Diary* of Henry Sidney (afterwards earl of Romney and lord-lieutenant of Ireland), which extends from June 1679 to January 1682, during which period the writer held the post of ambassador at the Hague and had in his hand the threads of much important negotiation, public and private, with William III of Orange, possesses no literary qualities; but interspersed with it[1] are a number of letters to and from Sidney which add considerably to its general interest. Foremost among these are the sprightly communications, partly in a very necessary cipher, of the countess of Sunderland, with whom, though her husband's doings and prospects are among her most frequent themes, he was on the very friendliest of terms. They also include letters from the dowager countess, a charming old lady whom, in her younger days, Waller had celebrated as Sacharissa, and from Sir William Temple

---

[1] See the edition by Blencowe, R. W., 2 vols. 1843. The *Sydney Papers: Letters and Memorials of State* (from the reign of queen Mary to that of Charles II), ed. Collins, A., 2 vols. 1746, consist only to a small extent of letters so late as those of lord Lisle and Algernon Sidney. Those written by the latter from abroad (under the commonwealth, he was ambassador to Denmark and Sweden) are full of interest, especially his letters from Rome in 1660/1, in one of which he gives, in the style of the time, a series of characters of cardinals, identified by numerals corresponding to those in a previous letter.

and others[1]. The author of Gramont's *Memoirs* is severe on the difference between Henry Sidney's gifts of intellect and of 'figure'; but, both he and his favourite correspondent played an important part in drawing closer the relations which resulted in seating William of Orange on the English throne; and she deserves a place among the letter-writers of her age, if only for her graphic vignettes of Whitehall and the doings of 'that jade' (in cipher), the double-faced duchess of Portsmouth.

Lady Warwick, the wife of the fourth earl (Charles, who died in 1673), represents, among the 'good women' of the restoration age, the puritan type proper, though, at the same time, she had a very distinct individuality of her own. Lady Mary Boyle was a daughter of the first, sometimes called 'the great,' earl of Cork, and sister of Robert Boyle the natural philosopher and Roger Boyle lord Broghill (earl of Orrery). Her father's ambitious nature had been much vexed by her secret match with an 'insignificant younger son'; but the death of his elder brother made Charles Rich heir to the earldom of Warwick, to which he succeeded in 1659, twenty years after his marriage, so that she became a peeress like six out of her seven sisters. Much of her married life was spent at Little Leighs park in Essex ('delicious Leez,' as her brother Robert called it, in his dedication to her of his treatise entitled *Seraphic Love*, written in 1648). She came from a family accustomed both to think and to write; the religious frame of mind which she maintained during the whole of her later life was, no doubt, largely due to the hospitality extended by her father-in-law (the parliamentary general) to most of the puritan ministers in England, and she ascribes her conversion to a devout life partly to the counsels of one of them, Anthony Walker, partly to archbishop Ussher's preaching against plays, of which she 'saw not two' after her marriage[2]. Her husband seems to have been a warm-hearted man, much attached to his wife and children (on the death of his only son, he sent forth loud cries of grief, though declaring that 'his chief sorrow was that the trouble would kill his wife, who was more to him than a hundred sons'), but very passionate, and addicted to the habit of cursing and swearing,

---

[1] As to Sir William Temple, see *post*, chap. xvi. Concerning Dorothy Sidney, see Cartwright, Julia, *Sacharissa: some Account of Dorothy Sidney, Countess of Sunderland her Family and Friends*, 1693. Other correspondents of her brother Henry were her son the celebrated Robert earl of Sunderland (minister in succession under three kings), Halifax and Lawrence Hyde (earl of Rochester), and there is a letter, in the grand style, from William Penn.

[2] *Autobiography*, p. 22.

very often at his wife. Altogether, his treatment of her seems, notwithstanding his affection, to have been wanting in kindness. Her consciousness that she 'did not remonstrate with him about his sins with sufficient faithfulness' was one of the great troubles of her life; a house, she felt, should be 'perfumed with prayers, not profaned by oaths.' As to herself, solemn thoughts were never far from her: in the midst of a 'great show' in the banqueting-house at Whitehall, a blast of trumpets aroused in her the thought, 'What if the trump of God should now sound,' with a remembrance of the 'glory' of which, in the days of the late king, she had been a witness in the very place whence he was to go forth to his death[1]. Other passages in her *Diary* show that religious feeling, at times, overcame her with mystic force; in a prayer after an outburst with her husband, her 'soul did but breathe after God'; on another page, she records how she had 'all that day great pleasure in thinking upon those happy hours she enjoyed with God in the morning.'

Lady Warwick's *Diary* reaches from July 1666 to April 1672; a further portion, extending to 1677, is now lost, though it existed about the close of the eighteenth century. The whole of it was accessible to Anthony Walker[2], who preached a long biographical sermon at her funeral at Felsted, and published it later under the title Εὕρηκα Εὕρηκα. *The Virtuous Woman Found, her Loss Bewailed and Character Exemplified* (1686). It was annotated by lady Warwick's own domestic chaplain Thomas Woodroffe, who resided with her till the time of her death (1678). Besides this *Diary*, she composed, in the course of three days in February 1671, a short autobiography, to which she subsequently made a few additions bringing down the memoir to 1674[3]. She also left behind her a series of *Occasional Meditations*—the fruit of her solitary hours in the 'Wilderness' at Leighs park, or in her chamber there or at Chelsea. 'Meditation,' says Walker, 'was her master-piece': and her 'short returns to God,' as she calls her hours of pious thought, were to her the luminous points in her life. But,

---

[1] It is significant of the quality of her puritanism that, to the end of her life, she never failed to keep 30 January as a solemn fast.

[2] Author of *A true Account of the Author of a Book called* Εἰκὼν Βασιλική (1692). Walker was John Gauden's curate at Bocking, and they were both intimates in the house of lady Warwick's father-in-law, to whom, as well as to his son, Walker was chaplain.

[3] It was edited by Croker, T. Crofton, for the Percy Society in 1848. The *Diary* and *Occasional Meditations*, together with some simple *Rules for a Holy Life in a letter written to George Earl Berkeley* were published in 1847. The whole of this material is utilised with much skill in Miss Charlotte Fell Smith's *Mary Rich, Countess of Warwick (1625—1678): her Family and Friends* (1901).

from an early date, she was also in the habit of expressing her
thoughts in the form of apophthegms intended to have an effect
upon others, and formulating what might be called witty religious
sayings, with which she fell into the habit of winding up her discourse.
They were something in the manner of the *Pensées* of Pascal and
similar collections, chiefly by French writers, with none of which
she can have been acquainted when she set about this style of
composition; moreover, Miss Fell Smith has discovered that the
example actually followed by lady Warwick was the *Occasional
Meditations* of bishop Joseph Hall, of which a third edition appeared
in 1633. Altogether, her epigrammatic thoughts number nearly two
centuries (182), being unevenly distributed over the years in which
they were set down (1663—78). 'The true measure of loving God
is loving him without measure' is one of them; another (scarcely
original): 'Why are we so fond of that life which begins with a cry
and ends with a groan?' Many are suggested by the experiences
—even the trivial incidents—of every day life: 'upon feeding the
poor at the gate'; 'upon children playing,' and then quarrelling,
'in the streets'; 'upon my looking in a looking-glass in the morning
to dress myself'; 'upon my taking a great deal of pains to make a
fire'; others arise out of events of deep personal interest, such as
her husband's death, and her own impending farewell to her loved
country home. But all are characterised by the combination of
spiritual depth and literary ingenuity which was her note.

Though the *Memoirs of Lady Fanshawe* remained unpublished
in full till 1829/30, they challenge comparison both as to the
interest of their matter and as to the high spirit informing them,
and also as to clearness and vivacity of style, with any memoirs of
the age to which they belong—including, as has been justly said,
even those of Mrs Hutchinson. Unlike Lucy Apsley, Ann Harrison
was, according to her own account, 'a hoyting girl in her youth,'
though we may well believe her asseveration that she was 'never
immodest but skipping.' Her mother's death awakened the serious
side of her nature, which, henceforth, in the great crises of her life,
showed itself forth in words of almost impassioned prayer—ordinarily, however, in deeds rather than in words. The first sixteen
years of her married life (from 1644) were a period of incessant
struggle and sacrifice, through which she passed with unfailing and,
at times, heroic courage. Sacrifice for the sake of the royal cause
might have been called the badge of her husband's as well as of
her father's family, which were closely connected with one another;
she reckoned their revenues 'engaged and sequestered for the

crown in the time of the late rebellion' at near eighty thousand pounds a year. Nothing could be more stirring than the personal courage which she displayed by her husband's side—as when she crept to his side on deck, disguised in a cabin-boy's 'thrum-cap' and tarred coat, while their ship was facing the approach of a 'Turk's man of war'; or when, night after night, she stood beneath his prison window on the bowling green at Whitehall. Nor could any devotion have surpassed that which she showed to him during his long absences in the king's service—including the perpetration of a most ingenious forgery of a pass to Calais for herself and her children. All these things she tells in a style of delightful directness and freshness; and the interest of the narrative (which is diversified by one or two thrilling ghost stories) only slackens (as is common in biographies) when prosperous times at last came to her husband and herself with the restoration. It was, to be sure, a modified prosperity, owing to the king's way of keeping his promises (of which she says very little) and to Clarendon's real or supposed malice (of which she says a good deal). After serving as ambassador in both Portugal and Spain, concerning which country his lady has many favourable particulars to relate, Sir Richard Fanshawe died at Madrid, shortly after receiving his recall (1666); his widow had to bring his body to England and there live for the survivors among her many children, as she had lived for him whose story she set down for the benefit of his heir[1].

In this great distress I had no remedy but patience.... Neither did these circumstances following prevail to mend my condition; much less found I that compassion I expected upon the view of myself, that had lost at once my husband and fortune in him, with my son of but twelve months old in my arms, four daughters, the eldest but thirteen years of age, with the body of my dear husband daily in my sight for near six months together, and a distressed family, all to be by me in honour and honesty provided for; and to add to my afflictions, neither person sent to conduct me, neither pass or ship or money to carry me a thousand miles, but some few letters of compliment from the chief ministers bidding 'God help me' as they do to beggars—and they might have added 'they had nothing for me,' with great truth. But God did hear and see and help me, and brought my soul out of trouble....

---

[1] The circumstances of Sir Richard Fanshawe's recall from Spain are discussed at length in the voluminous and valuable notes to the edition of the *Memoirs of Ann Lady Fanshawe* published in 1907 by a descendant. Lady Fanshawe was offered a very large sum of money if she would remain in Spain and become a catholic.— Sir Richard Fanshawe, it may be noted, was a man of strong literary tastes, to some extent inherited. In 1647, he printed a translation of Guarini's *Pastor Fido* (which, thirty years later, Elkanah Settle adapted for the stage, apparently without acknowledgment); in 1652, translations from Horace; and, in 1655, a version of the *Lusiads* of Camoëns, composed in Yorkshire during an interval of rest. His last publication was a Latin translation, entitled *La Fida Pastora*, of Fletcher's *Faithfull Shepheardesse*.

The *Letters of Rachel Lady Russell*, the devoted widow, as she had been the faithful wife, of William lord Russell, virtually begin with the death of her husband (of whose last paper, delivered to the sheriffs on the scaffold, a letter to king Charles II vindicates the genuineness) and with that of her only son, Wriothesley duke of Bedford. She survived him and her daughter the duchess of Rutland (who died a few months later) for twelve years, retaining to the last the clearness of mind and serenity of spirit which are characteristic of all her writing. Through all her troubles, she preserved a keen interest in public affairs, as well as in the extensive business of her private estate. Her chief correspondents were divines, more especially her father's chaplain and her own tutor John Fitzwilliam, whom she consulted on all subjects, together with Burnet and Tillotson; but she was also in frequent correspondence with leading statesmen and ladies of high rank. Her tone throughout is that of a self-possession at the same time devout and reasonable, to which the even calm of her style corresponds. She is not, however, without moments of wrath as well as of tenderness—the former being, on occasion, directed against the archfoe of civil and religious liberty both within and beyond his dominions—Louis XIV. She died in 1723, in her eighty-seventh year. Her *Letters* were first published in 1773.

Although small in bulk, the *Memoirs of Queen Mary II*, published in 1886 from the Hanover archives, and extending from nearly the beginning of her reign to the year before that of her death, should not be overlooked. No reasonable doubt as to their genuineness can remain, if they are compared with the autobiographical fragments given to the world by countess Bentinck in 1880, and with the indisputably genuine letters of the good queen. Written in English, while the fragment of 1880 was in French (she possessed both languages, as well as Dutch), they were guarded with great care by the writer, who, in 1691, burnt nearly the whole of the 'meditations' which, according to the custom of her day, she also indited. Her record of often trying experiences attests her innate modesty and her sense of duty, upheld by a deep piety, which was at all times ready to translate itself into good works. The story of the anxious years of her reign, which is further illustrated by a short series of letters from her hand, is full of interest—partly of a pathetic kind.

# CHAPTER XI

## PLATONISTS AND LATITUDINARIANS

It was, apparently, after a short visit to Cambridge, in 1663, that Gilbert Burnet, in his *History of my Own Times*—after describing the degeneracy of the episcopal order which followed upon the failure of the Savoy conference—proceeded to declare that the English church herself would have 'quite lost her esteem over the nation, had it not been for the appearance of a new set of men of another stamp' at that crisis. 'These,' he goes on to say, 'were generally of Cambridge, formed under some divines the chief of whom were Drs Whitchcote, Cudworth, Wilkins, More and Worthington.' And, passing on to a brief characterisation of each, he describes Whichcote as 'much for liberty of conscience,' and one who, 'being disgusted with the dry systematical ways of those times,' 'studied to raise those who conversed with him to a nobler set of thoughts,' and, with this aim, 'set young students much on reading the ancient philosophers, chiefly Plato, Tully, and Plotin, and on considering the Christian religion as a doctrine sent from God both to elevate and sweeten human nature.' This passage, while it supplies additional evidence of Burnet's habitual sympathy with whatever was enlightened in conception and generous in sentiment, affords, at the same time, another instance of what Macaulay, in his shrewd estimate of his distinguished countryman, describes as his 'propensity to blunder.' The Cambridge Platonists, as they are often termed, although generally inclined to latitudinarianism, appear to have had their origin independently of the latter movement, and Whichcote's claim to rank as one of their number must be pronounced as at least doubtful; but of latitudinarianism itself he is one of the earliest examples and, certainly, the most conspicuous. As regards his philosophy, if such it may be termed, it was that of Bacon, while his distinctive religious belief was largely the outcome of his own observation and personal convictions, and continued to survive long after the Platonic school with which his name is associated had ceased to exert any perceptible influence.

A member of a good Shropshire family, Benjamin Whichcote entered as a pensioner at Emmanuel college in October 1626 ; but where he received his previous education is not recorded. In 1634, he was elected a tutor of the society, where, as his biographer informs us, 'he was famous for the number, rank, and character of his pupils, and the care he took of them.' Two years later, he was appointed afternoon lecturer at Trinity church, Cambridge, an office which he continued to hold for twenty years—from the time, that is to say, when Laud's administration of ecclesiastical affairs was at its height to that of Cromwell's *Proclamation,* whereby equal and complete religious freedom was established throughout the realm—those malcontents alone being excepted whose opinions were avowedly and manifestly prejudicial to the maintenance of law and order. In the preparation of this great measure, Whichcote, together with Cudworth and others of his party, was especially consulted by Cromwell as to the expediency of extending toleration to the Jews. In his discourses at Trinity church, he had made it his chief object, his biographer tells us, to counteract the 'fanatic enthusiasm and senseless canting' then in *vogue*—an expression in which the term 'enthusiasm' must be understood in its original sense, as implying the assumption by any individual, whether educated or uneducated, of the right to interpret, at his own discretion, not merely the meaning of Scripture, but, also, to decide upon its applicability to existing social and religious conditions, in short, to be himself inspired.

In 1644, Whichcote was installed by Manchester in the provost-ship of King's college, where he was able to exercise a marked influence over a community differing considerably from Emmanuel, and, at the same time, himself to assume a more independent tone. In the academic year 1650—1, he was elected to the office of vice-chancellor, and his commencement oration, delivered in that capacity, was marked by a freedom and significance of expression which involved him in a noteworthy correspondence with Tuckney, his former tutor at Emmanuel. Tuckney, with other seniors of the university, had been in the habit of attending the afternoon lectures at Trinity church, and their apprehensions were already excited by what they had there heard. Whichcote, as Tuckney understood him, had said 'that *all* those things wherein good men differ, may not be determined from Scripture,' inasmuch as Scripture itself 'in some places seems to be for the one part

and in some other places for the other,' which, says his critic,
'I take to be unsafe and unsound.' Still 'more dangerous,' as
it appeared to him, had been the advice given by the preacher,
that Christians, when seeking a common ground of agreement,
should be willing to restrict the language of belief solely to
'Scripture words and expressions,' and 'not press other forms
of words, which are from fallible men.' 'Christ by his blood,'
wrote Tuckney, who discerned the drift of such a limitation, 'never
intended to purchase such a peace, in which the most orthodox,
with Papists, Arians, Socinians, and all the worst of heretiques,
must be all put in a bag together.' To this, Whichcote's rejoinder
(had he thereupon expressed his whole mind) would, doubtless,
have been, that, as he himself lays it down in his *Aphorisms,*
'Determinations beyond Scripture have indeed enlarged faith,
but lessened charity and multiplied divisions.' In the first instance,
however, he contented himself with a purely defensive affirmation
of his view—namely, that the devout Christian was entitled to
advance as his own individual conviction, whatever 'upon search
he finds cause to believe, and whereon he will venture his own
soul.' In his next letter, however, he made bold to assert his
position in the following pregnant terms: 'Truth is truth, who-
soever has spoken it, or howsoever it hath been abused: but if
this liberty may not be allowed *to the university,* wherefore do we
study? We have nothing to do, but to get good memories, and to
learn by heart.'

There can be little doubt that his equable nature was at this
time being roused to unwonted indignation, as he marked the
unsparing severity with which, in 1651, the *Engagement* was being
pressed home throughout the university, and especially at King's
college, by the presbyterian party; and, before his correspondence
with Tuckney closed, we find him roundly denouncing those 'who
indeed profess some zeal,' for that 'happie point,' of justification
by faith, but 'yet are sensiblie degenerated into the devilish nature
of malice, spite, furie, envie, revenge.' His final words to Tuckney,
contained in a short letter, written in the after-part of the day on
which he laid down his office of vice-chancellor, are as follows:
'Sir, wherein I fall short of your expectation, *I fail for truth's
sake,* whereto alone I acknowledge myself addicted.'

The difficulties in which the broadminded provost of King's
thus found himself involved were precisely those which Bacon,
to some extent, had succeeded in evading, by his candid avowal,
that he considered all articles of faith to lie beyond the province

of his new method of induction—although, indeed, his personal sentiments were so far surmised by others that he did not escape the unenviable imputation of being the real author of the notorious *Christian Paradoxes*. Whichcote, however, determined otherwise. Firmly convinced of the truth of Christianity, and fully persuaded in his own mind that its principles—wherever accepted in their spirit rather than subscribed to in the letter—were capable of conferring priceless benefits on mankind, he argued that the more clearly they were understood, the greater would be the mental assurance they would carry with them. And, towards the bringing about of such an understanding, he held the inductive method to be eminently favourable, and calculated to prove as effectual in allaying theological contention as it had been, in the hands of Galileo, in proving beyond dispute the rotation of the earth on its own axis, or, in the hands of Harvey, in demonstrating the circulation of the blood. But, in those cases where there were differences of opinion with respect to interpretation, he advised the suspension of dogmatism. 'We must not,' he was heard to say, 'put Truth into the place of a Means, but into the place of an End[1]'—holding that, even if the 'end' seemed unattainable, the path pursued was not necessarily the wrong one.

Another passage in the above-mentioned correspondence, which occurs in Tuckney's second letter, must not be left unnoticed. He had been discussing Whichcote's discourses with other seniors of the university, and writes to the following effect:

'Some are readie to think that your great authors, you stear your course by are Dr Field, Dr Jackson, Dr Hammond,—all three very learned men, the middle sufficiently obscure; and both he and the last, I must needs think, too corrupt. Whilst you were fellow here, you were cast into the companie of very learned men, who, I fear,—at least some of them,—studied other authors more than the Scriptures, and PLATO and his schollars, above others: in whom, I must needs acknowledge, from the little insight I have into them, I finde manie excellent and divine expressions; and as we are wont more to listen to and wonder at a parrot, speaking a few words, than a man, that speaks manie more and more plainlie; so, whilest we find such gemmes in such dunghills (where we least expected them), and hear some such divine things from them, we have been too much drawn away with admiration of them. And hence, in part, hath run a veine of doctrine which divers very able and worthy men, whom from my heart I much honour, are, I fear, too much knowen by,—the power of Nature in morals, too much advanced, reason, too much given to it, in the mysteries of Faith,—a *recta ratio* much talked of, which I cannot tell where to find[2].'

The drift of the above passage is unmistakable. Tuckney believed that Whichcote, when at Emmanuel, had come under

---

[1] *Aphorisms*, cent. VIII, no. 795.　　　[2] *Eight Letters*, p. 38.

the influence of certain students and admirers of Plato, not that he had influenced them; had he done so, indeed, it is difficult to understand how the fact could have failed to attract the notice of his former tutor, and the latter have omitted to make any reference to the same in the above controversy.   As it is, his conjectures may be said to be fairly disposed of by Whichcote's reply, in which he complains that Tuckney is under a complete misapprehension; it was true, indeed, he admits, that he had once read the treatise, *Of the Church*, by Richard Field (an Oxford divine much admired by James I), but that was ten years ago; while, as regarded Thomas Jackson, a former president of Corpus Christi college, and Henry Hammond of Magdalen college, in the same university, a former chaplain of Charles I, chiefly known as the author of *A Practical Catechism*, he says, 'I have a little looked into them here and there, a good while since, but have not read the hundredth part of either of them.'

'Trulie,' he goes on to say, 'I shame myselfe to tell you, how little I have been acquainted with bookes; while fellow of Emmanuel Colledge, employment with pupils took my time from me.   I have not read manie books, but I have studied a fewe; meditation and invention hath bin rather my life than reading, and trulie I have more read Calvin, Perkins, and Beza, than all the bookes, authors, or names you mention.   I have alwaies expected reason, for what men saye; less valuing persons or authoritie, in the stating and resolving of truth; and therefore have read them most where I have found it[1].'

If, to this explicit statement, we add the internal evidence supplied by Whichcote's own manuscript notes of the *Aphorisms* and the *Sermons* (neither of which was published until after his death), the theory which numbers him among the Platonists, and would even recognise him as their leader, would seem to be altogether inadmissible.   Neither Plato nor Plotinus finds a place among his cited authorities, while the latter is not even mentioned —although, in addition to the Greek text of the New Testament, he quotes both Aristotle and Origen; and, among Latin writers, Lucretius and Marcus Antoninus.   But mysticism and recondite philosophy were foreign to his genius; and the divine with whom he was in fullest sympathy, after the restoration, was, probably John Wilkins of Oxford, who, after acquiring eminence by his labours as a teacher at Wadham college, was, also, for rather less than a twelvemonth, master of Trinity college, Cambridge. Wilkins was further distinguished by the interest with which he regarded the scientific investigations of the Royal Society, and his toleration in dealing with dissenters.   The evidence, accordingly,

[1] *Eight Letters*, p. 54.

would lead us to conclude that the statement of Burnet, in his *History*—which, it is to be borne in mind, was not published until eight years after his death—was simply the inaccurate impression derived by a young man of twenty during a hurried visit to the university, and not placed on record until long after ; while it is certain that what he says about 'Plato, Tully, and Plotin,' is perfectly applicable to Henry More of Christ's college, who was Whichcote's junior by only four years and, about the time of Burnet's visit, at the height of his reputation.

It would seem, however, that even More is not to be regarded as the originator of the Platonist movement at Cambridge. So early as the year 1641, there had appeared, printed at the University Press, a collection of *Commonplaces*[1], delivered in the chapel of Trinity college, by John Sherman, a fellow of the society and bachelor of divinity, in which the following noteworthy sentences occur:

Nature's light is a subcelestiall star in the orb of the microcosme; God's Voice, man's usher in the school of the world. As truths supernaturall are not contradicted by reason, so neither surely is that contradicted by Scripture which is dictated by right reason[2].

I know not how it cometh to pass, but too many Christians have too much of heathen talk; and so also, in a reciprocation, some heathen have very much of that which seemeth correspondent unto sacred Scripture[3].

The teacher of the Gentiles instructeth us Christians not to disembrace goodnesse in any, nor truth in any. Plato's rule is good,—Οὐ τίς, ἀλλὰ τί. Let us not so much consider who saith, as what is said; who doeth, as what is done[4].

The above quotations may be said both to indicate the point beyond which Whichcote and his followers are to be regarded as making a distinct advance upon the Baconian philosophy, by the recognition of Christian doctrine as in harmony with the voice of nature ; and, further, by the acceptance of pagan philosophy as lending additional force to both; while the author's references to Aristotle, as maintaining the theory of the immortality of the soul (p. 75), and his belief in the indebtedness of 'Pythagoras, Trismegist and Plato' to Scripture (p. 30), afford almost equally strong presumption of an intimacy with Henry More. The title of Sherman's volume, *A Greek in the Temple*, suffices to indicate that his appeal is from the traditions of the Latin church to that pagan philosophy from which he, and those with whom he was in

---

[1] The term 'Commonplace,' as there used, is defined in Samuel Clarke's *Lives*, p. 115, as 'a college-exercise in divinity, not different from a sermon, but in length.'

[2] p. 1.          [3] p. 25.          [4] p. 21.

sympathy, derived much of their inspiration; and it is at least open to question, as he was slightly Whichcote's senior in academic *status*, whether his published *Commonplaces* may not have contributed, to a far greater degree than is on record, to promote the movement the origin of which has been generally attributed, almost exclusively, to the (as yet unprinted) discourses of the provost of King's.

The second son of a gentleman of fair estate at Grantham, the genius of Henry More ran counter alike to parental admonitions and to the bias which his home education was designed to impart, for his father was a rigid Calvinist. He tells us, however, that the latter would often in winter evenings read aloud Spenser's *Faerie Queene* to his elder brother and himself; while, in his conversations with the two lads, he frequently 'commended philosophy and learning.' At the age of 14, Henry was sent to Eton—'for the perfecting of the Greek and Latin tongue,' as Richard Ward, his biographer, tells us; who also states that the boy's master would, 'at times, be in admiration at his exercises.' Such language, in relation to the Eton of the seventeenth century, can only be interpreted as implying a special facility in Latin verse composition, varied, occasionally, by translations from Latin authors, and may be regarded as affording an explanation of the fact of More's superiority as a classical scholar over the rest of the 'Platonists'; when in advanced years, he turned this to account by translating his English treatises into Latin, fondly anticipating that they were destined to as wide a popularity on the continent as they had met with in England. From Eton, he went up to Cambridge, where, in his seventeenth year, he was admitted a pensioner of Christ's college. This was in December 1631; and it was in the following July, that John Milton, having proceeded M.A., finally quitted Cambridge. Brief as was the period of their joint residence in college, More can hardly fail to have heard a good deal of his illustrious compeer, as one of the most notable students of the society, and already famed as the writer of some exceptionally clever occasional verses; but whether they became personally acquainted must be considered doubtful. During the next quarter of a century, however, Christ's college became distinguished by the enthusiasm with which some of its fellows embraced the doctrines of Descartes; and, in 1654, the celebrated Ralph Cudworth was elected master of the society. More himself, who was three years Cudworth's senior, succeeded, in due course, both to a fellowship and a tutorship, and continued to reside in

college to his death. 'His pupils,' says Ward, 'much admired the
excellent lectures he would deliver to them, of Piety and Instruction,
from the chapter that was read on nights in his chamber'; his
seniors recognised the value of the example he set, by his
regular attendance at chapel and at 'the publick ordinances' of
the church; while the persistent refusals with which he put aside
all offers of preferment disarmed the criticism of those who might
otherwise have been his rivals in the unceasing pursuit of pelf or
place in the wider world without. Ultimately, however, he became
essentially a recluse and an ascetic, although he fully understood
'the benefit of exercise and the fresh air,' and paid particular
attention to his diet; and, as a fish diet did not suit his constitution, he, during Lent, often dined in his own chamber. When
no longer occupied as a tutor, the monotony of his life was relieved, to some extent, by visits to the country seat of one of his
former pupils, Edward, viscount Conway. Ragley, retired from
the ordinary haunts of men, with its woods and shady walks, was
an ideal retreat for one of More's highly imaginative temperament;
and in its recesses, he tells us, 'the choicest theories' of one of his
most noteworthy treatises, that entitled *The Immortality of the
Soul,* were conceived. Lady Conway also became his pupil, of
whom his biographer gives us the following account:

> She was of incomparable parts and endowments,...and between this
> excellent person and the Doctor there was, from first to last, a very high
> friendship; and I have heard him say, that he scarce ever met with any
> person (man or woman) of better natural parts than the lady Conway. She
> was mistress of the highest theories, whether of philosophy or religion, and
> had, on all accounts, an extraordinary value and respect for the Doctor,—I
> have seen abundance of letters that are testimonies of it....And as she
> always wrote a very clear style, so would she argue sometimes, or put to
> him the deepest and noblest queries imaginable[1].

On his father's death, More found himself in fairly affluent
circumstances, and, when writing to lady Conway, on one occasion, he observes, that it is 'the best result of riches,' that,
'finding ourselves already well provided for, we may be fully
masters of our own time.' Notwithstanding, however, his ample
leisure, it is undeniable that a certain precipitancy in pronouncing
judgment was one of his most serious defects, and one which offers
a marked contrast to the habitual deliberation of Cudworth, which
was itself, in turn, perhaps carried to excess. Another point of
difference between the master of Christ's and its distinguished
fellow is to be noted in the fact that the former was not a public

---

[1] *Life of Dr Henry More*, p. 193.

school man. Cudworth had been educated at home by his father-in-law, Dr Stoughton, and had been admitted a pensioner of Emmanuel at the age of thirteen. It is probable, therefore, that he never attained to the facility in Latin, either colloquially or in composition, which More appears to have acquired at Eton; and he consequently preferred to write in English. Throughout his life, moreover, he was much busied with official duties. In 1645, when only twenty-eight years of age, he had been elected master of Clare, besides being appointed to fill the chair of Hebrew in the university; and, on migrating, in 1654, from Clare to assume the mastership of Christ's college, he found himself called upon to undertake the office of bursar; he was also a frequent preacher. Notwithstanding, therefore, his reputation both for learning and ability, his leisure was scanty and mainly bestowed on Hebrew and cognate studies. But Cudworth was intimate with Whichcote, and, in their frequent conversations, could hardly fail to become familiar with the views of the latter on the subject of morality. 'The moral part of religion,' Whichcote was wont to say, 'is the knowledge of the Divine Nature, and it never alters. Moral laws are laws of themselves, without sanction of will, for the necessity of them arises from the things themselves[1].' Cudworth, in the course of his varied reading, and especially in connection with the literature of the *Cabala*, had met with evidence which appeared to him strongly corroborative of such a theory, and he had intimated to his friends his design of publishing, before long, a treatise entitled *Moral Good or Evil, or Natural Ethics.* It was a subject, however, which demanded not only very wide research, but, also, that careful suspension of judgment which he was wont to exercise in arriving at his conclusions; and his friends were already beginning to entertain misgivings whether his profound speculations would ever result in actual accomplishment, when he was himself taken by surprise, and not a little ruffled, on learning that Henry More, living within the precincts of Christ's college, was about to publish a manual on the same subject, and this, too, in Latin, thereby appealing to a wider circle of readers than any English philosophical treatise could possibly command! The master was naturally inclined to surmise that some, at least, of the views which he had formed on the subject and had often talked over with his friends had been appropriated by More. He protested warmly against such apparently disingenuous conduct, in a letter to Worthington—

[1] *Aphorisms*, cent. I, no. 99; cent. III, no. 221.

formerly master of Jesus college and their common friend—and, through his intervention, More was induced to profess his perfect willingness to wait until Cudworth should have put forth his own elaborate disquisitions. But publication, so far as the master was concerned, was still remote; and, eventually, More's *Enchiridion Ethicum* made its appearance in 1667. It was in Latin; and (as described by the author himself) merely 'a portable little volume,' designed 'for the instruction of beginners,' and setting forth 'in lucid and connected fashion the elements of Ethics, so as to render the methods of the recognised teachers on the subject more easily intelligible.' Cudworth's profound *Treatise concerning Eternal and Immutable Morality,* on the other hand, remained in manuscript for another sixty-four years, when—long after the author's death—it at last appeared, under the editorship of Edward Chandler, the learned bishop of Durham.

But, long before *Enchiridion Ethicum* appeared, More was already a voluminous author, and as conspicuous for his daring as was the master for his caution. Taking for his maxim the heroic sentiment of Cicero—*rationem quo ea me cunque ducet, sequar*—he proposed that, in order to counteract alike the scepticism hatched in Paris and the 'enthusiasm' rampant in Rotterdam, the Christian teacher should call in the aid both of the pagan philosopher of the past and of the scientific philosopher of the present. But nothing, he held, could be of worse augury for the Christian faith than that its recognised expounders should be seen rallying to the support of what the voice of reason had demonstrated to be untrue. So early, accordingly, as 1647, in his *Song of the Soul,* he had openly confessed himself the disciple of Plato and Plotinus, as restorers of oriental traditions of a remote and probably inspired philosophy, boldly proclaiming that

> ...if what's consonant to Plato's school
> (Which well agrees with learned Pythagore,
> Egyptian Trismegist, and th' antique roll
> Of Chaldee wisdome, all which time hath tore
> But Plato and deep Plotin do restore)
> Which is my scope, I sing out lustily;
> If any twitten me for such strange lore,
> And me, all blamelesse, brand with infamy,
> God purge that man from fault of foul malignity[1].

Although, consequently, the fate of Galileo was still a warning to the scientific world, the poet's conviction that the Ptolemaic

[1] *Philosophicall Poems,* p. 155.

theory was destined ultimately to give place to the Copernican was no less candidly expressed. After apostrophising those

> Blest souls first authours of Astronomie!
> Who clomb the heavens with your high reaching mind,
> Scaled the high battlements of the lofty skie,
> To whom compar'd this earth a point you find,

he proceeds to compare their assailants to those 'fabled Giants,' who, piling Pelion upon Ossa, themselves, in turn, strove, 'with raging wind,' 'to clamber up to heaven.'

> But all in vain, they want the inward skill.
> What comes from heaven only can there ascend.
> Not rage nor tempest that this bulk doth fill
> Can profit aught; but gently to attend
> The soul's still working, patiently to bend
> Our mind to sifting reason, and clear light
> That strangely figur'd in our soul doth wend,
> Shifting its forms, still playing in our sight,
> Till something it present that we shall take for right.

And, finally, the following rebuke of the persecutors of Galileo probably went home to the consciences of not a few readers who were still, perhaps, hesitating to express their open assent:

> O you stiff-standers for ag'd Ptolemee,
> I heartily praise your humble reverence
> If willingly given to Antiquitie;
> But when of him[1] in whom's your confidence,
> Or your own reason and experience
> In those same arts, you find those things are true
> That utterly oppugne our outward sense,
> *Then are you forc'd to sense to bid adieu,*
> *Not what your sense gainsayes to holden straight untrue*[2].

*The Song of the Soul* (the poem from which the above extracts are taken) is in five books, each prefaced by an 'Address to the Reader,' wherein the author discusses, in plainer prose, that phase of his subject with which the book itself is especially concerned, thus successively dealing, though very briefly, with those several problems which suggest themselves in connection with the theory of the soul's independent existence—its life, immortality, sleep, unity and (in opposition to the theory of the fabled Lethe) its memory after death.

Taken as a whole, More's poem is entitled to the praise of being a highly ingenious series of arguments, adorned by fancy and clothed in poetic diction, in support of his several theories. When compared with the *Psyche* of Joseph Beaumont, which

---

[1] Galileo.    [2] *Philosophicall Poems*, pp. 155—6.

appeared in the following year, it must be pronounced altogether superior ; and, in fact, the difference between the two compositions is such that a comparison is almost impossible. Beaumont was a native of Hadleigh in Suffolk and had received his education at the grammar school in that town. He subsequently entered at Peterhouse, Cambridge, where he gained a fellowship, from which he was ejected in 1644. On his ejection, he retired to Hadleigh, where, 'for the avoiding of mere idleness,' and being 'without the society of books,' as he himself tells us, he began the composition of his poems—an endeavour to represent 'a soule led by Divine Grace and her Guardian Angel through the assaults of lust, pride, heresie, and persecution.' This singular production, conceived in imitation of Spenser, but written in the six-line stanza, extends to twenty cantos, or some thirty thousand lines, and, although it is said to have been commended by Pope, produces in the modern reader little else than wonderment. Even the author's son (himself a fellow of Peterhouse), when re-editing it for the press in 1702, deemed it so far capable of improvement that he left hardly a stanza unaltered. Genius itself, indeed, in essaying to depict the career of a pure and devout nature, assailed at every stage by temptations designed to effect the ruin alike of its earthly and of its spiritual happiness, might well fail in the attempt to impart variety to the incessant recurrence of doleful circumstance or impending peril. But Beaumont was neither an Edmund Spenser nor a John Bunyan; and the latter, when, a quarter of a century later, he wrote *The Pilgrim's Progress*, may unhesitatingly be acquitted of having borrowed anything from the pages of *Psyche*. Few readers have ever felt disposed to nod over Bunyan's masterpiece, while Beaumont's poem belongs very much to that order of literature which induces the slumber not infelicitously described by its author in the following stanza:

> In this soft calm, when all alone the Heart
> Walks through the shades of its own silent Breast,
> Heaven takes delight to meet it, and impart
> Those blessed Visions, which pose the best
> Of waking eyes, whose beams turn all to night,
> Before the looks of a spiritual sight[1].

If, however, Beaumont cannot be numbered among those poets of whom Cambridge is proud, he was a master to whom Peterhouse has reason to be grateful. He was not only a 'painful' regius professor of divinity, but he also approved himself an industrious and

---

[1] Cant. viii, 11.

careful guardian of the college archives, which he reduced to order, indexing the register of admissions, and compiling a volume of personal memoranda useful as illustrating the college life of the period.

In the meantime, Henry More was acquiring a brilliant reputation by his untiring literary activity, and, in 1652, brought out his *Antidote against Atheism.* In the following year appeared his *Conjectura Cabbalistica*, and, in 1656, his *Enthusiasmus Triumphatus*, a skilful exposure of the pretensions of the 'enthusiasm' which was then at its apogee. In 1659, he re-wrote, in an expanded and connected form, the dissertations prefixed to the several books of his *Song of the Soul*, and, along with the argument of *The Song* itself, reduced to plainer prose, published his treatise entitled *The Immortality of the Soul.* In 1660 appeared his *Grand Mystery of Godliness*, which Beaumont was imprudent enough to take upon himself to criticise. The prosaic poet was incapable of appreciating the poetic philosopher, and blundered sadly. The underlying design of More's treatise would appear, indeed, to have been unintelligible to him, and his attack recoiled disastrously on himself. In 1662, More published a collected edition of his prose works up to that date, including his correspondence with Descartes. It is in the preface to this volume that More appears at his best, still adhering to his original standpoint, when he asks, 'what greater satisfaction can there be to a rational spirit than to find himself able to appeal to the strictest rules of reason and philosophy?'

'I conceive,' he goes on to say, 'the Christian religion rational throughout, ... and every priest should endeavour, according to his opportunity and capacity, to be also, as much as he can, a rational man or philosopher, for which reason, certainly, Universities were first erected, and are still continued to this very day,... for take away reason, and all religions are alike true; as, the light being removed, all things are of one colour[1].'

It is here, also, that he refers to the service which he had rendered in 'interweaving' Platonism and Cartesianism—'making use of these Hypotheses as invincible bulwarks against the most cunning and most mischievous efforts of Atheism[2]'—this, it is to be noted, being the last occasion on which he alludes with complacency to the doctrines of Descartes.

After the collapse of the Savoy conference, however, his avowed sentiments and whole tone (in common with those of not a few other writers) underwent a radical change. Worthington suggested

[1] pp. iv, v.　　　　[2] p. vi.

to him to throw over Cartesianism, and he did so—his *Enchiridion Metaphysicum*, which appeared in 1668, being especially designed as an exposition of a science of spiritualism, in opposition to the Cartesian doctrines.

In 1664, his *Mystery of Iniquity* aroused afresh the public interest in past history by its denunciation of the claims of popery, while it also excited gloomy forebodings as regarded the future, by its discussions on the fulfilments of prophecy under the reign of anti-Christ. The interest aroused by these arbitrary interpretations of past historical events was further stimulated by his returning to the subject in his *Divine Dialogues*, published in 1668, the most popular of all his works. Here, in the fifth *Dialogue*, he took upon himself to point out that the occurrence of the calamities which the soundings of the six trumpets in *The Revelation* were successively to usher in was clearly to be discerned in certain recognised historic epochs, from the fall of the Roman empire to the invasion of the Turks. Such, indeed, was his confidence in the interpretation of past church history which he thus put forward that he ventured to assert that its outlines, before long, would become as 'common and ordinary' a subject of instruction in Christian schools as the children's catechism itself. The appearance, in 1665, of two portly folios—the *Works* of Joseph Mede, edited by Worthington, a task on which that eminent scholar, now resident in London, had expended an amount of labour and research which excited high encomiums—proved a further incentive to such studies; while *Clavis Apocalyptica*, more especially, attracted fresh attention. The popular interest, accordingly, rose almost to a fever of expectancy, when one Israel Tongue of Oxford, the associate of Titus Oates and a notorious charlatan, proclaimed that he had ready for the press certain 'Apocalyptical Expositions' which would supersede all that had hitherto been written on that absorbing theme. As, however, his lucubrations never saw the light, More continued to take rank as the most advanced and authoritative writer on a subject in connection with which his fervid imagination might find scope for its employment almost without a check; although, in other relations, it is evident that he was already beginning to incline to a more guarded declaration of his opinions. In common with Cudworth and other leading theologians at Cambridge, he had become, since the restoration, an avowed supporter of the doctrines of the church of England, and he regarded with undisguised alarm the growing progress of infidelity, especially as represented by Hobbes.

In other respects, the points of contrast between the master and the fellow of Christ's college are strong and marked, for Cudworth's reputation as an author was almost entirely posthumous, the chief noteworthy exception being a sermon preached before parliament in 1647, when he was only in his thirtieth year. In this remarkable discourse, he had given distinct evidence of his sympathy with the party of academic reform by a candid avowal of his dissatisfaction with the prevailing dialectics, on the one hand, and of his sense of the advantages to be derived from the study of nature, on the other. In the endeavour to arrive at a clearer understanding of natural laws, he urged that man was really only discharging a universal religious duty, the neglect of which was, in itself, a violation of the homage due from mankind to its Creator.

Naturally disposed to weigh evidence and carefully to ponder over each conclusion, Cudworth was as deliberate as More was unquestionably precipitate in his judgments; and, at his death, a pile of unpublished manuscripts mostly unfinished, gave evidence of a vast amount of patient toil, the results of which were not destined ever to be given to the world. His great masterpiece, *The true Intellectual System of the Universe*, was not published until 1678, when it was fated to meet with a reception, for the most part, unsympathetic, and, in some quarters, distinctly hostile, according as it ran counter to the prevailing scientific cynicism or to the growing religious formalism; while, to quote the language of Martineau, 'it laid itself open to the rebuke of scholars, for reading the author's favourite ideas, without adequate warrant, into the Greek text of Plato, Aristotle, and Plotinus.' The whole treatise, indeed, according to the same eminent critic,

conceded too much to the Pagan philosophers, recognizing among them the essence of Christian wisdom, to suit the assumptions of either the rising High Churchmen or the retiring Puritans. It placed too little value on the instituted observances of religion for the former, and on its niceties of dogma for the latter.

With regard, however, both to More and Cudworth, there is evidence, other than that afforded by their writings, which must not be overlooked. If we revert to the aspect of affairs a quarter of a century before *The Intellectual System* appeared—the time, that is to say, when More published his *Antidote to Atheism* (1652)—we find our attention arrested by the appearance from among the number of their disciples of two remarkable writers, who, like two genii responding to their call, had risen and vanished with equal suddenness. In 1651 died Nathaniel Culverwel, to be

followed, the next year, by John Smith of Queens'; in the latter
year appeared Culverwel's *Light of Nature*, and, in 1660, Smith's
*Select Discourses*, edited by Worthington. These two writers were
both natives of Northamptonshire, who entered at Emmanuel
college during the period of Whichcote's tutorship—the former in
1633 (when he was probably about sixteen), the latter in 1636,
when already eighteen years of age. In 1642, Culverwel was
elected to a fellowship at Emmanuel; but the restrictions then
existing in the college with regard to counties made it necessary
for Smith to migrate to Queens', in order to obtain like preferment,
although not before he had become well known both to Whichcote
and to Worthington. The former, discerning Culverwel's genius,
gave him not only valuable advice, but, also, pecuniary aid; while
the latter, whose age was the same as Smith's, but who had entered
at Emmanuel four years earlier, lived to be his lifelong friend, and
wrote the notice of him in the 1660 edition of his *Discourses*.
According to Worthington, Smith 'studied himself into a consumption,' and the extraordinary attainments of which the
*Discourses* give evidence lend support to the statement—especially
if we consider that he had to discharge the duties of dean and also
to lecture on Hebrew in his college and on mathematics in the
schools. The testimony of Simon Patrick, afterwards president of
Queens' college and bishop of Ely, is to the same effect, as he bore
witness to the merits of his departed friend in the same chapel
in which the latter had often discoursed—'his sharp and piercing
understanding,' 'his Herculean labours day and night from his
first coming to the University' and, especially, his communica-
tiveness with respect to what he knew and the clearness of his
language when imparting it,

wherein he seems to have excelled the famous philosopher, Plotin, of whom
Porphyry tells us, that he was something careless of his words, ἀλλὰ μόνον τοῦ
νοῦ ἐχόμενος, but was wholly taken up into his mind.

As Smith, like More, wrote on the immortality of the soul, their
merits, as authors, admit of a certain comparison, although the
former, when he wrote, was not yet thirty, and directs his argument
mainly against the scepticism of the ancients, such as Epicurus and
Lucretius, while the latter was in his fifty-fifth year and concerns
himself mainly with the philosophy of Hobbes. Notwithstanding,
however, the ingenuity of More's speculations and the remarkable
range of reading displayed throughout his pages, his readers can
hardly fail to experience a certain disappointment at finding that,
after a variety of questions have been mooted, with rather vague

conclusions, the author is firm in his opinion that the belief in the soul's immortality necessarily involves a recognition of the existence of ghosts, and that all that can with certainty be predicated respecting its condition in a future state, is that it will be an entity not needing food and not casting a shadow.

Very different is the impression left upon the mind by John Smith's less discursive treatment of his subject and skilful compression of his well reasoned generalisations. To him, it appears that the main argument in support of the soul's immortality is that derived from the *universality* of the belief—a certain *consensus gentium*, discernible throughout pagan times, fondly cherished by the multitude, and no less firmly maintained by philosophers such as Plotinus, Proclus and Aristotle. And this belief, he points out, is, in turn, clearly involved in a yet grander conception, revealing itself to the sanctified human intellect as an inevitable corollary from the belief in the Divine beneficence. Over and above 'the Epicurean herd,' he distinguishes four grades of spiritual existence on earth, of which the ἄνθρωπος θεωρητικός, the true metaphysical and contemplative man, represents the final and the highest—in whom the soul has already attained to communion with the Divine Nature, and regards its confinement in this material body as but the period of its infancy.

In order to realise the conditions under which Culverwel's *Light of Nature* was conceived, we must bear in mind that, although not published until 1652, it had been written six years before, when the author was probably less than thirty years of age. As regards general literary excellence, he may be said to divide with John Smith the claim to rank foremost among Platonists. It is evident, from his opening chapter, that he did not conceal from himself the magnitude of the task upon which he had embarked, and which he defines as that of 'giving to reason the things that are reason's and unto faith the things that are faith's'; it requires, he adds, 'our choicest thoughts, the *exactest discussion* that can be, to give faith her full scope and latitude, and to give reason also her just bounds and limits.' 'Reason is the first-born, but the other has the blessing.' Such is the assumption which underlies the whole treatment of his subject, namely, that the function of faith is superior to that of reason. 'Reason discerns the existence of a God, the eye of faith, a Trinity of Persons; the former recognises the immortality of the soul, faith spies out the resurrection of the body.' 'Revealed truths are never against reason, they will always be above reason.'

It was Culverwel's design to embody in a second treatise the evidence and the arguments whereby he proposed to prove, first, that all moral law is founded in natural and common light—*i.e.* in the light of reason ; and, secondly, that there is nothing in the mysteries of the Gospel contrary to reason, nothing repugnant to the light that shines from 'the candle of the Lord.' But he was never able to carry into effect this great design, which would have admirably supplemented the vast researches of Cudworth. So far, indeed, as it is possible to discern the facts, it would appear that, for at least five years before his death, Culverwel's labours were altogether suspended ; while a singular mystery involves his life during that time. It may, perhaps, be conjectured, that his outspoken language in his college *Commonplaces*, together with his generally independent attitude as a thinker, brought upon him the disfavour of certain seniors at Emmanuel (where Whichcote was no longer fellow), and, under the combined effects of anxiety with respect to his future prospects and the strain involved in his literary labours, his health, mental as well as physical, completely gave way. He died in 1651, when, probably, not more than thirty-two years of age.

With regard to both Smith and Culverwel, it is also not a little remarkable that, although none of their contemporaries can have possessed a closer personal knowledge of them than More or Cudworth, in the pages of neither of these do we find any reference either to them or to their writings. It is possible, indeed, that Culverwel's depreciatory language as to Descartes may have offended More at the time when he was still in the first flush of his admiration for the great French philosopher; but, on the whole, it seems most probable that both the newly installed master of Christ's and its most distinguished fellow were alarmed by the confidence with which these new theories were advanced, especially when viewed in connection with the widespread tendency (already apparent at this time) to repudiate all dogmatic teaching, of whatever school. It was certainly no reassuring note that was sounded in 1655, when George Rust, another member of the same society—who had been elected to a fellowship from St Catharine's, in 1649—deemed it incumbent on him to call attention to the impending peril. In terms remarkable for their vigour and precision, the future bishop of Dromore, preaching from St Mary's pulpit in Cambridge, declared that the very foundations on which 'men had so long built their opinions and faith' were 'shaken and staggered in this sceptical age':

Every one, upon a particular and several sect, is in quest of Truth; and so foolish and full of vain affectation is the mind of man, that each one confidently believes himself in the right, and, however others call themselves, that he and those of his party are the only Orthodox. Should we go abroad in the world, and ask as many as we meet, *What is* Truth?, we should find it a changeable and uncertain notion, which every one cloath's his own apprehensions with. Truth is in every sect and party, though they speak inconsistences among themselves and contradictions to one another. Truth is the Turkish Alcoran, the Jewish Talmud, the Papists' Councils, the Protestants' Catechisms and Models of divinity,—each of these in their proper place and region. Truth is a various uncertain thing, and changes with the air and the climate,—'tis Mahomet at Constantinople, the Pope at Rome, Luther at Wittemberg, Calvin at Geneva, Arminius at Oldwater[1], Socinus at Cracow; and each of these are sound and orthodox in the circuit of their own reign and dominion.

The spirit of compromise in regard to this conflict of beliefs, combined, however, with a maintenance of personal individuality, is exemplified in Joseph Glanvill, of Exeter college, Oxford, afterwards fellow of the Royal Society and chaplain-in-ordinary to Charles II. In the main, he was in agreement with Cudworth and More—his *Lux Orientalis* being chiefly a reproduction of the theory held by the latter as to the prior existence of souls, a doctrine which he held to be all the more defensible in that it appeared never to have been formally condemned by any Christian church, while its acceptance serves to vindicate the Divine Being from the charge of injustice, since suffering in the present life may be punishment for sins committed in a previous state of existence. In his *Sadducismus Triumphatus* (1681), Glanvill defends the belief in witchcraft—a defence pronounced by Lecky 'the ablest ever published' of that superstition.

An excellent illustration of the points at issue among educational writers subsequent to the restoration is afforded by the controversy between Glanvill and Henry Stubbs, a retired physician at Warwick. Glanvill, in his *Plus Ultra*, had been led, by his sympathy with the progressive tendencies of the Royal Society, to pass a rather indiscriminate censure on the scholastic Aristotle. This evoked from Stubbs a reply, *The* Plus Ultra *reduced to a Non Plus*, setting forth the '*Advantages* of the *Ancient Education* in *England* over the *Novel* and *Mechanical.*'

In the meantime, we find the principles of the latitudinarians—

> Whether the Church inspire that eloquence,
> Or a Platonic piety confined
> To the sole temple of the inward mind—

spreading widely, although often rudely assailed. 'I can no more look back,' Whichcote had written to Tuckney, 'than St Paul, after

---

[1] Oudewater in Holland, the birthplace of Arminius.

Christ discovered to him, could return into his former strayne,' and his influence continued to extend long after his ejection from King's college in 1660; while his death took place when he was a guest of Cudworth's at Christ's college lodge in 1683. But, after the restoration, the tenets of the party seem frequently to have been confused with those of the Arminians. Among their number, Hezekiah Burton of Magdalene college, Cambridge—styled by Anthony Wood, 'that great trimmer and latitudinarian'—was a prominent figure, and, together with him, his friend, Richard Cumberland, of the same society, afterwards bishop of Peterborough, who, in his *De Legibus Naturae*, (writing in opposition to Hobbes) applied to the observance of the moral law and the natural rewards resulting therefrom very much the same theorisation as that which it had been Culverwel's aspiration to set forth and which Cudworth succeeded in expounding. Another distinguished representative of the same principles was Thomas Burnet, who, as an undergraduate, had followed Cudworth from Clare hall to Christ's, and was afterwards master of the Charterhouse[1]. Simon Patrick, Edward Stillingfleet and Tillotson—all three members of the episcopal order, while the lastnamed was, perhaps, the most popular preacher in his day[2]—contributed powerfully to the whole movement. At the same time, there is to be noted a corresponding change taking place in the pulpit oratory of the church itself—a change compared by Lecky to that which

had passed over English poetry between the time of Cowley and Donne and that of Dryden and Pope; and over English prose between the time of Glanvil and Browne and that of Addison and Swift[3].

As regards the subsequent influence of latitudinarianism— whether on the pulpit oratory of the Church of England or on the teaching of its divines—widely different estimates have, from time to time, been formed by those writers whose sympathies have been with the movement, and by those whose endeavour it has been to elaborate and define with increased clearness the doctrinal belief of the Church; for, while the former, in agreement with Montesquieu, have recognised in an habitual abstention from dogmatism one of the most effective means of promoting unity and concord within her communion, the latter have no less emphatically deprecated such a policy as the main cause of the 'deadness, carelessness and apathy' in relation to religious questions which largely characterised the eighteenth century[4].

[1] As to Thomas Burnet see p. 347, *post*.
[2] As to these divines see also *ante*, chap. VI.
[3] *Hist. of England in the Eighteenth Century*, I, 85.
[4] *Ibid.* I, 314—815; Perry, G. G., *Hist. of the English Church*, 514—515, 587—8.

# CHAPTER XII

## DIVINES OF THE CHURCH OF ENGLAND
### 1660—1700

WITH the restoration of the church came a vociferous out-burst of loyalty to the king, which threatened to engraft upon the style of the pulpit not a little of the extravagance of the puritan manner, adapted to other themes than those of its origin. But the influence of the older tradition of restraint proved too strong. The leaders of the restored church were men trained in the school of Laud; disciples, in the second generation, of Andrewes, and, in the first, of Hammond; scholars in whom the classical habit was still strong, but who had learnt a severer simplicity of expression. The divines to whom men listened, and whom they read and copied, were, in literature, of the type rather of Sanderson and Hammond than of Donne or even Jeremy Taylor; and, before long, their language was deeply affected by Bunyan and Izaak Walton. Pedantry, crabbed conceit, elaboration of metaphor or illustration, gave way to advanced directness, and the English language was made to show of what it was capable when it was not strained: style, casting off imitation, became direct and plain. During the forty years which followed the return of Charles II, English divines, in their treatment of serious themes, laid the foundations on which Addison based his mastery over the language of his day.

The transition was gradual. There were no startling moments in the development. Progress was not attained by new departures, by sudden originalities, or by deliberate leadership on new ways. Thus, we find among the divines of the restoration and the revolution but few writers that stand out among their contemporaries. The religious writers, for the most part, accepted the manner of their time rather than influenced it. Bunyan, Walton and Dryden had no peers among the professional writers on religion. In the ecclesiastical writers of the time, with an occasional exception, we find a high level of careful excellence, but nothing that recalls the conspicuous individuality of Andrewes, or Mountague or Jeremy Taylor. Nor can we say that the theological writing of the period can be divided into definite literary schools. The style is very much a matter of date; yet not always that—for there are survivals, and a few anticipations, of other days. The later Caroline divines may be said almost exactly to cover, among them, the seventeenth century; for they include George Morley, who was born in 1597, and Herbert Thorndike, born in the next year; while few of their conspicuous representatives survived the reign of William III.

Herbert Thorndike is important rather for his opinions than for his literary merits. He was a catholic anglican of the most convinced and complete kind. He was a learned scholar, an important contributor to Brian Walton's *Polyglot Bible*, finished in 1657, and an influential, though not self-assertive, member of the Savoy conference. His position in English theology is, perhaps, best expressed in the book he published in 1670: *The Reformation of the Church of England better than that of the Council of Trent.* He advocated, for example, the practice of confession, using language so strong as

in my judgement no Christian Kingdom or State can maintain itself to be that which it pretendeth more effectually than by giving force and effect to the law of private confession once a year by such means as may seem both requisite and effectual to enforce it;

the reservation of the sacrament for the sick, in both kinds, and not, after the Roman fashion, only in one; and the appeal to Scripture as interpreted in the primitive church. In his *Epilogue to the Tragedy of the Church of England* (1659), he had desired the restoration of the episcopate as in ancient times, the use of prayer for the dead and the introduction into the English communion service of the *Epiklesis* before the consecration. He was a student of liturgies, at a time when they were not well known; and his studies were reflected in a repeated use of quotations from the Fathers which reminds the reader of Andrewes and his contemporaries.

John Cosin, who, born in 1594, died in the same year as Thorndike (1672), was also a liturgiologist, and, as early as 1627, published *A Collection of Private Devotions*, at the request of Charles I, to supply an English antidote to the Roman devotions of queen Henrietta Maria's ladies. Cosin, in many respects, resembles Thorndike: in the nature of his interests, in the main principles of his theology, in the character of his influence. But he was a much more attractive writer of English, and has, at times, a touch of Jeremy Taylor; he had an ear for the music of prose, though he did not always take pains to be in tune himself; but he was certainly not, as Aubrey tells us, though unconvincingly, that Thorndike was, 'a good poet,' though his compressed translation of *Veni Creator* has merit.

Side by side with these two writers may be placed George Morley, the 'honest doctor' of the exiled court, who wrote little and that rather in the antique style, but was as witty as he was pious, the friend of Walton and Clarendon, and yet a Calvinist as men were when he learnt his theology. Thorndike was a prebendary of Westminster; Cosin, chaplain to Charles I and master of Peterhouse, became bishop of Durham under Charles II; Morley died as bishop of Winchester. A greater writer than any of these, Isaac Barrow, lived only to be forty-seven, but rose to the mastership of Trinity college, Cambridge, and left a mark of originality upon the theology of his age. Charles II, who had the means of learning which are at the disposal of kings, said that he was 'the best scholar in England'; but, though Aubrey tells us that he was 'pale as the candle he studied by,' his writings show little of the wearisome preciseness of the pedant. He had spent five years, from 1655 to 1659, abroad, and, at Constantinople, he had made a longer stay than, in those days, was dared by most Christians who were not on an embassy or a trading venture: when he lay dying, 'the standers-by could heare him say softly " I have seen the glories of the world." ' It was this width of experience, as well as the extent of his learning—he said that he used tobacco to 'regulate his thinking'—which gave him the mingled strength and richness that made him greatly admired by critics of taste so different as were the elder Pitt and Henry Hallam. His manner of writing, which has been considered hasty and almost extemporaneous, has been shown to have been elaborated with the most extraordinary care, his manuscripts being revised, rewritten and subjected to continual addition or correction. The ease with which he appears to write is the result of prolonged labour; the sentences are smooth, if often lengthy; the meaning is direct in reaching the reader, and, behind all, there is unquestionable strength. Throughout, his appeal is to the reason rather than the heart or the ear ; but, though he argues like a mathematician, he writes like a classical scholar. He is never extravagant; he does not aim at beauty or search for conceits ; his characteristic merits are completeness, coherence, consecutiveness ; and, thus, his chief influence was exercised upon those who wished to argue or to think—upon Locke and Warburton and the elder and the younger

Pitt. It is not easy to find a passage which satisfactorily illustrates his style, for he treats every subject which he approaches so lengthily that it is difficult to disentangle a few sentences from the web of argument or exposition. But a few sentences from his sermon on the beauty of thankfulness (occupying nearly a hundred octavo pages in his *Works*) may afford an example of the clearness and simplicity which, under his influence, began to mark the prose of the later seventeenth century.

> And verily could we become endowed with this excellent quality of delighting in others good, and heartily thanking God for it, we needed not to envy the wealth and splendour of the greatest princes, nor the wisdom of the profoundest doctors, nor the religion of the devoutest anchorets, no, nor the happiness of the highest angels; for upon this supposition, as the glory of all is God's, so the content in all would be ours. All the fruit they can conceive of their happy condition, of what kind soever, is to rejoice in it themselves, and to praise God for it. And this should we do then as well as they. My neighbour's good success is mine, if I equally triumph therein: his riches are mine, if I delight to see him enjoy them: his health is mine, if it refresh my spirit: his virtue mine, if I by it am bettered, and have hearty complacence therein. By this means a man derives a confluence of joy upon himself, and makes himself, as it were, the centre of all felicity; enriches himself with the plenty, and satiates himself with the pleasure, of the whole world; reserving to God the praise, he enjoys the satisfaction of all good that happens to any[1].

In this, there are touches which recall the writers of the earlier Caroline age; but the general manner of writing is an anticipation of Addison, and even suggests something of the style of Butler.

In his sermons, Barrow avoided controversy and preached morals; but he was also a controversial writer of great weight, and that chiefly against the papacy, whose followers, according to his biographer Abraham Hill, he had seen 'militant in England, triumphant in Italy, disguised in France.' His treatise *On the Pope's Supremacy*, published by his executor Tillotson in 1680, was a masterpiece, in the manner of the time, seeking logic rather than bitterness and completeness rather than venomous polemic. Side by side with this may be placed Cosin's *Historia Transubstantionis Papalis*, which was also published posthumously, in 1675, but was based on

> a Declaration of the Ancient Catholic Faith and Doctrine of the Fathers Concerning the Real Presence ... showing that the doctrine of Transubstantiation (as it was first set forth by Pope Innocent III ... and afterwards by Pope Pius the Fourth), was not the faith or doctrine in the Catholic Church in any age before them,

written by him in 1647[2]. Cosin had experience of endeavours

---

[1] *Works*, ed. 1859, vol. I, p. 390.
[2] Published in *Cosin's Correspondence* (Surtees Society), part I, 1869, pp. 233 ff.

to convert Englishmen to Roman Catholicism in Charles I's time and, in consequence, had studied theology with a special bent. Barrow, with similar experience abroad, and knowledge of the Greek church to confirm his resistance to Rome, saw that a period of acute controversy was imminent in England. His *Exposition of the Creed, Decalogue and Sacraments* may be regarded as a dogmatic support for his fellow churchmen ; but its influence was eclipsed by the work, on rather different lines, of his contemporary John Pearson, whom he succeeded as master of Trinity. Pearson was a notable preacher and an accurate scholar : he vindicated the authenticity of the *Epistles* of St Ignatius, anticipating the labours of later scholars : he was an active bishop at Chester from 1673 to 1686. But his chief fame is due to his *Exposition of the Creed*, published on the eve of the restoration, which, till the last generation, remained the standard work of English theology on the subject. The character of Pearson's writing is its learning : he was critical, elaborate, closely argumentative, replete with quotations. But his writing is never clear or flowing; he is encumbered by the weight of his knowledge, and precedent has stifled originality alike in his exposition and in his style.

The earlier period of the reign of Charles II was closely linked to the days before the war. The chief writers had experience of earlier times and bore the marks of puritan or anti-puritan training. Besides those whom we have named, it may be convenient to remember that Richard Baxter, who preached in London after the restoration, began to write his *Life and Times* in 1664, and did not die till 1691 ; that Jeremy Taylor survived the return of the king by seven years ; and that Benjamin Whichcote lived till 1683. John Wilkins (who preceded Pearson as bishop of Chester), a scientific writer of eminence, an experimentalist and philosopher, and a man of humour to boot, was a link between these times and those of the later latitudinarians. He gave his stepdaughter in marriage to Tillotson, telling her, as an attraction, that he was ' the best polemicall Divine this day in England.' He contrasted his own position, as theologian and bishop, with Cosin's.

'While you,' he said, 'are for setting the top on the picqued end and downwards, you won't be able to keep it up any longer than you keep whipping and scourging; whereas I am for setting the broad end downwards, and so 't will stand of itself;'

and his funeral sermon, by William Lloyd, afterwards bishop of St Asaph and one of the famous seven bishops, speaks of the 'vehemence of his desire to bring the Dissenters off their pre-judices and reduce them to the unity of the Church.'

In this aim, many eminent men concurred; few of them, how-ever, occupy a position of eminence in English literature. Yet some of those who were, or may be, called latitudinarians, or who were, if not 'men of latitude,' men of charity, left a distinct mark, as writers, upon their times. While Gilbert Sheldon, in his youth the friend of Falkland and a member of the liberal circle of Great Tew, was too much occupied as primate of all England to be able to make any contribution even to the theological literature of his age, Leighton and Burnet, Sancroft, Patrick, Beveridge, Stilling-fleet, in different ways combined writing with practical work.

Robert Leighton, who was ordained priest at the age of thirty and became a famous preacher, was principal of Edinburgh university from 1653, and professor of divinity there. In 1661, he became bishop of Dunblane; in 1669, archbishop of Glasgow. By the simple beauty of his life, he gave visible expression to the idea of true tolerance, which no one in all the seventeenth century more sincerely advocated and more fully exemplified. He was, at the same time, one of the great preachers of his day. His style is simple and dignified, abounding in aphorism rather than in epigram, powerful yet not rhetorical: its excellence is the reflection of the spirit within, of the inspiration which filled the writer's heart. To Coleridge, it seemed that Leighton's writings, beyond anything outside the Bible, suggested 'a belief of inspiration, of something more than human'; they were 'the vibration of that once-struck hour remaining on the air.' And Burnet's description of his preaching conveys, with remarkable fidelity, what the student of English literature may recognise as the secret of his influence and, also, as the note of his prose:

His preaching had a sublimity both of thought and expression in it; and, above all, the grace and gravity of his pronunciation was such that few heard him without a very sensible emotion: I am sure I never did. It was so different from all others, and, indeed, from everything that one could hope to rise up to, that it gave a man an indignation at himself and all others. It was a very sensible humiliation to me, and for some time after I heard him I could not bear the thought of my own performances, and was out of coun-tenance when I was forced to think of preaching. His style was rather too fine, but there was a majesty and a beauty in it that left so deep an impression that I cannot yet forget the sermons I heard him preach thirty years ago.

If Leighton was a Scot, he had assimilated the English manner, as he had the English theology, and, when he resigned the arch-bishopric, he retired to a little village in Sussex where he preached and ministered. If he would not say, writes Burnet, that the

English was 'the best constituted church in the world, he thought it was truly so with relation to the doctrine, the worship, and the main parts of our government.' George Herbert, most typical of anglicans, was his favourite poet. He died at an inn in London, under the shadow of St Paul's, in the arms of Burnet, his fellow countryman and disciple, who learnt from him what was best in his own religious thought and work.

With Leighton, indeed, Burnet is naturally coupled, for both were Scotsmen of liberal opinions who rose to high place in an episcopal church. As a historian, Burnet, whose labours in this kind extend beyond the general range of the present volume, will receive notice later[1]; but he was a man of boundless activity, and it must not be forgotten that he said with truth that his thoughts had 'run most, and dwelt longest, on the concerns of the Church and religion.' As a theological writer, Burnet, who lived to witness in the Hanoverian succession the triumph of his party, and died on the day when George I met his first parliament, had a distinct position and a considerable influence. He was intimately conversant with ecclesiastical matters during something like half a century, and set a conspicuous example—to be largely followed—of how it was possible to be at the same time a latitudinarian, a whig and an energetic bishop. Born in the land of presbytery and Calvinism, he became an episcopalian and an anglican. He was a convinced supporter of episcopacy as the original order from which the others derive. But his interest lay in personal religion more than in theology. He regarded 'the function of the pastoral call as the highest on earth.' Of him, more, perhaps, than of any other writer of his age, is it true that *le style c'est l'homme*. He was an energetic Scot, of intense and perpetual vigour and vivacity, irrepressible and, at all times, without the slightest doubt as to the truth of his own opinions or the folly of other people's. He was a glorified 'man in the street,' always aware of, and intensely impressed by, what partisan laymen were saying; exceedingly afraid of seeming to have 'a clerical mind'—a fear which often prevented his own views from being received as an expert judgment; and always ready to show that great statesmen were right and great ecclesiastics were wrong. He was a keen student, a man who read quickly and formed conclusions clearly, yet not a great scholar or endowed with a scholar's mind; a kind, generous, enthusiastic man, a genuine patriot as well as a strong partisan, but not at all a deep thinker;

[1] See *post*, vol. IX.

changeable in opinions, and one who changed generally with the party in power, or with the popular voice; a man who bulked large in the public eye, too large for his judgment to have the same weight with the wise or with posterity. He was extraordinarily deficient in taste, and, indeed, in real distinction of mind or feeling. His manner of writing about ecclesiastical questions reflects all this. He is omniscient, unsympathetic and narrow; and his judgment of the religion of his own day is often strangely distorted. He is typical of a certain side of English churchmanship. His *Exposition of the Thirty-Nine Articles* (1699) was, for more than a century, as famous as Pearson's *Exposition of the Creed.* Leibniz described it as 'a system of theology in brief, extremely vigorous and profound, and, what is better, extremely temperate and logical.' Indeed, it represents the moderation of the English church, without any nebulousness or lack of vigour. As literature, it is remarkable chiefly for its clearness and the lucid compression of details into a coherent summary. The merits of his more spiritual writing are much more conspicuous. His ministration to the dissolute Rochester, who died a believer and a penitent, is one of the most touching memories of his life, and he has preserved it, as *Some passages in the Life and Death of the right honorable John Earl of Rochester,* 1680, in language of almost perfect piety, reticence and true charm. And his admirable book *The Pastoral Care,* 1692, is as straightforward and sensible in manner as it is in matter and opinion. Had he never written a word of history, he would still deserve a permanent place among English writers.

With Burnet, may, not unfairly, be associated the name of another divine, who was his antithesis in character, Edward Stillingfleet, bishop of Worcester. His personal attractiveness gave him wide popularity; men called him 'the beauty of holiness.' His *Irenicum* (1659), which, though directed against nonconformity, regards the system of church government as unimportant, gave him a place among 'latitude men'; but one of his earlier works was a defence of Laud's *Relation* of his controversy with the Jesuit John Fisher against the *Pretended Answer of T. C.* (1664). Burnet commended him to William III as 'the learnedst man of his age in all respects'—a description justified by his *Origines Sacrae* (1662), and *Origines Britannicae* (1685). Stillingfleet's writing has no exceptional merit as literature. It reflected, without enriching, the manner of his time; and, when his learning became obsolete, his books passed out of use. Though his reputation as a man of letters during his life was higher than any of those yet mentioned, his style entirely lacked the distinction which could make it permanent. Another friend of Burnet was Simon Patrick, bishop, successively, of Chichester and Ely, who, commended at the revolution to the new king's notice, afterwards became one of the commission through which the royal patronage was exercised in the interests of latitudinarians and whigs. Patrick was much influenced by the Cambridge Platonists and preached the funeral sermon of John Smith. He was a voluminous writer, controversial, exegetical, homiletic; but his chief excellence lay in his sermons. Burnet called him 'a great preacher' and he was said to be an example to all bishops, and all dissenters, in 'sermonising.' What he did at St Paul's, Covent Garden, William Beveridge did at St Peter's, Cornhill: churches were filled and multitudes were influenced by the earnestness of the preacher. Robert Nelson, himself a writer of importance as well as a leading lay churchman, said of Beveridge that he had 'a way of touching the consciences of his hearers which seemed to revive the spirit of the Apostolic age.' This, indeed, is the character of his writings—eminently emotional, tender, full of feeling and pathos. He was ranked among the churchmen whom a later age called evangelical, but he was as emphatic in stating the doctrines of the church as any member of the school of Andrewes or Laud.

The age of sermons was not yet over. If laymen no longer found their chief theological instruction in sermons, they still crowded to hear a great preacher, and the preaching of a sermon, in a very great number of cases, involved, sooner or later, in some form or another, its appearance in a book. The list of theologians which we have given might be very greatly extended if we were to add those who were primarily preachers. The *Diary* of Evelyn, who exemplifies the high standard of a devout anglican gentleman, and that of Pepys, who must be ranked, for the greater part of his life at least, among the worldly, supply constant illustrations of the interest taken by Londoners of the later Stewart age in fashionable preachers. Anthony Horneck, for example, a German who was incorporated at Oxford and, after serving a cure there, became preacher at the Savoy and was made king's chaplain at the revolution, was—says Anthony à Wood—'a frequent and florid preacher, very popular in London and Westminster'; and Evelyn thought his eloquence most pathetic. His popularity shows that a reaction against the learned and lengthy style of Barrow and his school was setting in. Quotation from the classics and the

Fathers was, indeed, becoming less common: a volume of Beveridge
may be read through without meeting a single quotation except
from the Bible; early in the eighteenth century, Swift could
declare that he had outlived the custom of learned quotation.
But, during the last forty years of the seventeenth, a variety of
styles survived. Much controversy was compressed into the
pulpit hour, and occasionally extended it. The literature of the
Popish plot, of the anti-nonconformist controversy, of the Roman-
ising movement under James II, is well represented in sermons.
There were 'plain, honest, good, grave' discourses such as Pepys
heard from Stillingfleet, whom he declared to be, in the opinion
of the archbishop of Canterbury, and the bishop of London, and
another, 'the ablest young man to preach the Gospel since the
Apostles.' Archbishop Dolben, described by Dryden as

> [He] of the Western Dome, whose mighty sense
> Flow'd in fit words and heavenly eloquence,

was equally eloquent and direct in his appeal. The language of
both these preachers is simple and unaffected, and their argument
clear and coherent: they would have agreed with Horneck that
the object of the preacher should be 'to convert souls and not to
paint them.' For the most part, however, it would still be true to
say that English sermons, in this period—though at no other time
were they ever more popular or effective—were rather expository
and argumentative than descriptive or hortatory.

A special style belonged to a class of discourse which had
become very common. Now that prayers for the departed were
no longer publicly said, their place was taken by the pomp, gloomy
but inferior, of the funeral sermon, where solemn language fell
rapidly into a convention like the nodding plumes on the heads of
the horses which drew the coffin, or the customary cloak of solemn
black which disguised the mourners into a pattern of imposing
grief. The mass of extant funeral sermons is enormous: hardly a
country squire was suffered to be buried without a eulogium which
found its way into print; and, on the deaths of great personages,
the chief preachers used the opportunity for impressing a wide
circle with the solemnity of mortal things. Extempore preaching
was beginning to be popular. Burnet encouraged, and Charles II,
apparently, admired, it; but, all through the seventeenth century,
the written composition was much the more common. Whether it
were written out or not, there can be no doubt of the sermon's
influence or popularity; it still remained the sole class of literature with which everyone was, or might be, brought into contact;

and it affords a constant parallel to the literary work of secular writers. During the period of the later Stewarts, there gradually ceased to be a 'pulpit style' pure and simple; the preachers were ordinary men and wrote ordinary English. Thus, after Jeremy Taylor, they ceased to lead in the development of prose. No one of them had the charm of Fénelon, nor anything of the dignity and splendour of Bossuet, Massillon or Bourdaloue. They were typically, and almost exclusively, English. Foreign influence hardly touched them.

This is clearly seen when we turn to the most popular of all the preachers of the revolution period, John Tillotson, a 'latitudinarian' who rose as much through the pulpit as through politics to be archbishop of Canterbury. It was said of him that 'his sermons were so well heard and liked, and so much read, that all the nation proposed him as a pattern and studied to copy after him'; and, after his death, two thousand five hundred guineas were given for the copyright of two volumes of his discourses. Little more than a century later, they could be bought for waste paper; and it is in the last degree unlikely that they will ever be reprinted or studied again. Here, public taste can unhesitatingly be said to have formed a sound judgment. Tillotson's style is simple and easy, in comparison with much that was written in his day; but it is utterly without charm, or distinction, or interest. The thought is commonplace, and the language matches it. A comparison of Tillotson with Addison shows at once how differently a simple style can be used, how effectively the general aim of goodness can be expressed in prose, and how unexpected touches can redeem the exposition of thoughts which are the common stock of intelligent men.

But, before we have done with sermons, we must touch on the striking contrast, at once to the ornate and the commonplace, to Taylor and to Tillotson, noticeable in the work of Robert South, who was twenty years younger than the former and died twenty-two years after the latter. South, before all things, was original. He rejected the flowers of Taylor, and followed the simple way before Tillotson. But he followed it with a difference. If he delights not in tropes or figures, he abhors the commonplace and the dull. He revels in humour: he continually shoots shafts of ridicule against vice, be it pride or hypocrisy, ingratitude or anger. He had fixed orthodox opinions and considered orthodoxy important, unlike Tillotson. But he knew how to make beliefs effective without being venomous; he could make home truths stick, though the wound did not fester. His writing is as sincere as Tillotson's, but of quite different quality: while the one maintains a level of plainness from which it is difficult to detach a passage of interest, the other is always vivacious, and the difficulty in quoting from South is to find a passage which will not lose by its separation from a context equally vigorous and emphatic. Many an epigram could be set down by itself; but there was never a time when English prose lacked a maker of epigrams. Part of a longer passage, chosen almost at random, may illustrate at once the characteristic merits of South and the ordinary unaffected language of Charles II's day. It is from a sermon preached before the university of Oxford, at the beginning of the October term of 1675, on ingratitude. The preacher is approaching his 'consequences,' and, after advising that friendships should not be made with the ungrateful, he continues:

> Philosophy will teach the Learned, and Experience may teach all, that it is a thing hardly sensible. For, Love such an one, and he shall despise you. Commend him, and, as occasion serves, he shall revile you. Give to him, and he shall but laugh at your easiness. Save his life; but when you have done, look to your own. The greatest favours to such an one, are but like the Motion *of a Ship upon the Waves; they leave no trace, no sign, behind them;* they neither soften nor win upon him; they neither melt, nor endear him, but leave him as hard, as rugged, and as unconcerned as ever. All *Kindnesses* descend upon such a Temper, as Showers of Rain, or Rivers of fresh Water falling into the Main Sea: the Sea swallows, but is not at all changed, or sweetened by them. I may truly say of the Mind of an Ungratefull person, that it is *Kindness-proof.* It is impenetrable; unconquerable; Unconquerable that which conquers all things else, even by Love itself. Flints may be melted (we see it daily) but an Ungrateful heart cannot; no, not by the strongest and noblest Flame. After all your Attempts, all your Experiments, for any doing that Man can doe, *He that is Ungratefull, will be Ungratefull still*[1].

Style such as this was well employed in controversy. South's *Animadversion on Mr Sherlock's Book entituled a Vindication of the Holy and ever-blessed Trinity* is the liveliest piece of theological criticism of the time. Sherlock himself (master of the Temple and, ultimately, dean of St Paul's) wrote well. His *Practical Discourse concerning a Future Judgment* (1691) is a piece of sound and sober prose, and there is a touch of interest in almost everything that he wrote. But he will not be read today, and will be remembered only for the witty remarks on his short sojourn among the non-jurors, and for having undergone the criticism of a writer far abler and more lucid than himself.

South affords an agreeable diversion to the student of later seventeenth century religious writing. Under Charles II, James II

---

[1] *Sermons*, vol. I, 1697, pp. 512—514.

and William III, theologians seem more concerned to be serious than to be attractive, and it was natural that they should seek rather to convince than to entertain. Among those who attained distinction by writing sharply, Samuel Parker, whom James II made bishop of Oxford, in his *Discourse of Ecclesiastical Polity*, merits attention, because he shows (as, indeed, do not a few theologians by affinity or contrast) the marked influence of Hobbes. He was a clever satirist, too, and he had views on toleration which were in advance of his age. But he did not leave any permanent impression on letters.

Among the mass of literature called forth by the controversies of the time may, perhaps, be noted the little known *Episcopalia, or Letters of . . . Henry* [Compton] *Lord Bishop of London to the Clergy of his Diocess* 1686. These show that 'conferences' with the London clergy were no modern invention; and they are written in the plain straightforward style, without affectation or obscurity, which was becoming the property of all educated men. On another side were a number of Roman Catholic, and especially Jesuit, writings, ranging from the ephemeral treatises of Obadiah Walker to the vigorous polemic of Andrew Pulton. Pulton's opponent was Thomas Tenison, Sheldon's successor at Canterbury, of whose manner of writing Swift said that he was 'hot and heavy like a tailor's goose.' But in none of these, their imitators and their followers, is there anything which arouses interest. Apart from them, yet still winning fame chiefly through controversial works, is the solitary and dignified figure of George Bull (who died as bishop of St David's), perhaps the one English ecclesiastic of the period who attained to European fame. Robert Nelson's eulogy of his sermons shows that they had a distinction which most sermons of the time lacked; and they amply justified the praise. 'He had a way of gaining people's hearts and teaching their consciences, which bore some resemblance to the apostolical age.' But Bull's sermons, in the eyes of his own age, were the least of his works. Nelson sent his *Judicia Ecclesiae Catholicae* to Bossuet, by whom it was presented to the French episcopate; and the great French theologian returned the congratulations of 'the whole clergy of France' for his defence of the Divinity of Christ. His *Harmonia Apostolica*, and, of his sermons, that on the Fall, were, also, titles to high fame. But it is the matter rather than the manner which places Bull among the glories of the Caroline age.

So far, we have considered writers who were closely allied with the national life. The church of England, in the years which followed the restoration, was the institution round which most affection, and most controversy, gathered; and its representatives were prominent in the public eye. Nonconformist writers, whether Roman Catholic or protestant, had very little influence; they were not conspicuous for learning, and their defective education left them without a valuable literary weapon. It was different with another body which came into existence at a crisis in the national history.

When William and Mary were called to the throne by the convention parliament, there was a large number of clergy who thought it impossible to take the oath of allegiance anew, the sovereign to whom they had already taken it being still alive. The doctrine of the Divine right of kings, Hobbism, the theory of passive obedience, united to confirm their refusal. And a large number of conscientious men, with the primate of all England at their head, went into voluntary exile from the main current of national life. It was natural that among such men should be some of the leaders of the learning and literature of the age. Sancroft himself had ceased to contribute to literature or learning; but, in his day, he had wielded the pen adroitly. His *Fur Praedestinatus*, a delightful satire on Calvinism, was an early work; but archbishops cannot afford to be satirical in print, and, when he became a non-juror, Sancroft refrained from all written works. His chaplain Henry Wharton did not long remain attached to the party; but his sympathies were certainly with the high church and high tory theory. The testimony of a great historian of the nineteenth century to Wharton's greatness cannot be passed over. 'This wonderful man,' wrote bishop Stubbs, 'died in 1695 at the age of thirty, having done for the elucidation of English Church History more than anyone before or since[1].' But his eminence is that of the scholar and investigator rather than of the man of letters. Among the definite members of the non-juring body were several who combined these characteristics. No survey of this chapter of English literature would be complete which did not mention the work of Ken and Kettlewell, of Dodwell and Hickes.

Thomas Ken was one of those religious writers in whom a beautiful soul shines through the words which express the sincerity of their appeal. The motto of his writings might well be the words which he set at the head of all his letters—'All glory be to God.' He wrote only when he felt deeply. *Ichabod* tells of his disappointment with the church after the recovery of 1660. Of

[1] Preface to *Registrum Sacrum Anglicanum*, 2nd edition.

three sermons, the best is that for 'the Funeral of the Right Hon.
the Lady Margaret Mainard, at Little Easton, in Essex, June 30,
1682.' In it, he commemorated a 'gracious woman' whose goodness he knew from an intimate acquaintance of twenty years, and
through the confessional, as that of one who 'never commited any
one mortal sin.' Here, sorrow was chastened by the delightful
memory of virtue: the charm of which he wrote gave a lightness
to his style, and a felicity of touch, which greater writers might
have envied. But all his writing, it is easy to see, was unstudied
in form. His poetry, simple and flowing, came readily from his
pen; his prose, which often embodies anxious thought, is still
an excellent example of the prose which educated men naturally
wrote in his day. And, if he could write tenderly, he could
also write severely, as his letter to archbishop Tenison shows
(written because, as he thought, the deathbed of queen Mary
had not been made to bring her to repentance for her un-
dutifulness towards her father). John Kettlewell, himself a saint,
had a natural affinity with Ken: his work was essentially practical
and devotional; almost all his books treat of Christian duty and
privileges, sacrament and creeds, and their manner is of a piece
with their matter. George Hickes, on the other hand, and Henry
Dodwell, were scholars first and men of piety afterwards. The
former was a student from his youth, a collector of manuscripts
and antiquities: he learnt Hebrew that he might discuss rabbinical
learning with the extraordinary duke of Lauderdale; and 'Anglo-
Saxon and Meso-Gothic,' it seems, for his own pleasure; and his
*Linguarum veterum septentrionalium thesaurus grammatico-
criticus et archaeologicus* is a marvel of erudition and industry.
Hickes's style is sharp in controversy; in general literature—concerned, chiefly, with the burning questions of nonconformity and of
the oaths—it is coloured by the diversity of his learning; and he
shows, like several of his friends among the non-jurors, the influence
of the early liturgies in which he was thoroughly at home. If Hickes
was the most learned clerk, Henry Dodwell was the most learned
layman, among those who refused the oath to William and Mary.
His friend Francis Brokesby preserved his memory in a *Life*
published in 1715, in which the 'Accomplishments and Attainments' of the 'lay-dictator' are profusely eulogised in a style of
crabbed pedantry from which the subject of the biography had
quite escaped. Dodwell is not an easy writer; but, then, his
subjects are not easy. He is mathematical and theological, eager
to quote and overwhelm with authority. Were the literary work

of the non-jurors, in both divisions—those who returned to communion with the national church and those who abstained—to be estimated by the writings of those we have named, its value to literature, apart from its services to learning, would be adjudged small. But Robert Nelson, in his *Companion for the Festivals and Fasts* (1704), produced one of the most popular of all religious books, and the success which he achieved was deserved by the sincerity of his writing. Nelson did for the church of England in prose, what Keble, more than a century later, did in poetry. He showed the romance of its past, the nobility of its ideal, the purity of its forms of prayer. His book, though it is not more than good, certainly not great, literature, had an influence which good work does not always achieve. It caught exactly the religious tone of honourable men trained in the traditions of anglicanism, such as Clarendon or Evelyn, or of typical characters, imaginary but very real, like Sir Roger de Coverly or Sir Charles Grandison. The religion which Nelson represented was that which Herbert has immortalised, the religion of an English gentleman; and his writing has the quietness and confidence which belongs to the character.

The period of the later Caroline divines, from 1660 to 1700, has no conspicuous literary merit: it is a period of learning and commonsense rather than of conspicuous originality. Moreover, it may be observed how little it was associated with European culture or indebted to foreign influence. Ken read Spanish and may very likely have been influenced by the holy life of Pavillon a model French bishop. Many English ecclesiastics treated French ecclesiastics with courtesy. But English preachers did not take the French for their model, and English theologians seemed to pay little heed to what was being said over sea. There could be no greater contrast than that between the attitude of the Elizabethans and the later Carolines towards foreign literature—between Hooker, for example, and Barrow or Bull. Interest in the church abroad, in the east among the oppressed Christians in Turkey, and in the assertion of Gallican liberties, began, it is true, to grow at the end of the century, and it was fostered by the non-jurors; but, for the most part, English theology remained apart from the current of European thought. Its expression was becoming more simple, more direct, more typically national.

# CHAPTER XIII

## LEGAL LITERATURE

### I

In order to treat at all adequately the subject of legal literature in the seventeenth century, it seems necessary to make a rapid survey of the writings of the earlier periods—indeed, to go back to the very *origines juridicales,* and that for two reasons. First, because English law, even more than English liberty, had 'broadened down from precedent to precedent'; so that the key to the legal literature of the seventeenth century has to be sought among the records of its predecessors. Secondly, because the great law-writers of the Stewart era—whether, as in the case of Selden, drawn by the spirit of science, or whether, as in that of Coke, driven by the condition of the system of law which they were administering, and by the exigencies of party politics—were antiquaries, whose works consisted largely of commentaries upon the legal scriptures of their patriarchal forerunners. Hence, if we desire to understand either the principles of Stewart law or the nature of the legal literature of the seventeenth century, we must go back to the sources.

English legal literature may be said to have had its beginning when, about A.D. 600, king Ethelbert of Kent, newly converted to Christianity, put into writing the dooms of his folk *juxta exempla Romanorum*[1]. The influence that moved him came from the Roman church, the model that guided him was furnished by the Roman empire; but—and this is the remarkable fact—both the substance and the language of the laws of Ethelbert were Kentish. They stand unique in legal history as 'the first Germanic laws that were written in a Germanic tongue[2].' Further, they typify the

---

[1] Bede, *Hist. Eccles.* Bk. II, c. 5.
[2] Pollock and Maitland, *Hist. of English Law,* vol. I, p. 11 ; Brunner, *Deutsche Rechtsgeschichte,* vol. I, p. 283.

general relation of English law to Roman law through many succeeding centuries. English law owes much to Rome—both civil and ecclesiastical Rome—in respect of unifying principles, general ideas, logical arrangement and symmetrical form; but, in substance, it is of native growth. The lead given by Ethelbert of Kent, and his successors, was followed, after the lapse of a hundred years, by Ine of Wessex, and, towards the close of the eighth century, by Offa of Mercia. With the codification of the laws of Mercia, the first era of the history of English legal literature was closed. It had seen the embodiment of ancient tradition in writing.

It was succeeded by the era of the capitularies, which add to, and amend, the previous codes; and here, again, England stands apart from the continent of Europe. On the continent, during the three centuries of chaos that followed the break up of the Carolingian empire, general legislation ceased. But, in England, a long and almost continuous line of strong kings—Alfred, Edward, Athelstan, Edmund, Edgar, Canute—issued administrative ordinances, which reveal the activity of a resolute central government. Taken as a whole, they constitute a very notable body of primitive Teutonic law.

The Norman conquest, however, led to complications. The administration of the English law fell into the hands of persons, mainly clerics, who were ignorant not merely of the law itself, but even of the language in which it was promulgated. The English people clamoured for *Laga Eadwardi*, that is, for the law as it had been observed during the reign of the Confessor. The Normans, for their part—those who were rulers, by means of formal inquests, and private persons, from such sources as were available—made sincere efforts to find out what *Laga Eadwardi* was, and to render it accessible to the clerical mind through the medium of Latin translations. The works that resulted mark the third period of the history of legal literature in England (1066—1166). The most important among such of them as have survived to the present time are *Rectitudines Singularum Personarum, Leges Willelmi I* (also in a French version *Les Leis Williame*), *Liber Quadripartitus, Leges Henrici 1*, and the late Norman and half apocryphal *Leges Edwardi Confessoris*. The main fact which emerges from these compilations is that, during the century which followed the Norman conquest, there was no common law in England. 'The division of the law of England is threefold,' say *Leges Henrici*; 'there is the law of Wessex, the law of Mercia,

and the Danelaw[1].' It was the task of the Angevins, and especially
of Henry II, not only to weld the peoples of England together and
to amalgamate the institutions of conquerors and conquered, but,
also, to create the common law.

The common law of England, in the twelfth century, was a new
creature. There were in it elements taken from the old West
Saxon, Mercian and Danish law ; there were also elements derived
from Norman custom; but the most important elements were
novel, and were introduced by the authoritative over-ruling of the
king's court[2]. *Hoc tremendum regiae majestatis imperium,* as
*Leges Henrici* call it, was immensely extended by the Angevin
kings and their ministers. By means of royal writs, issuing from
chancery, they called such cases as they would before the *curia
regis* or its itinerant justices ; and these cases they treated with
equitable freedom, drawing their law eclectically from many
sources, of which, perhaps, at any rate in the sphere of public law,
the Frankish were more important than the English[3]. But, though
the elements were taken from many sources, the basis of the
system was the royal writ. Accordingly, from the reign of
Henry II, when the law of the king's court began to be, in
fact, a common law, we get legal writings of a wholly new type.
They consist, primarily, of registers of writs, of commentaries on
writs, of directions for pleading in cases originated by writs, of
records of decisions given in cases adjudged upon writs[4]. First
and foremost of these writings is *Tractatus de Legibus et
Consuetudinibus Regni Angliae,* commonly attributed to Ranulf
de Glanvil, Henry II's chief justiciar during the last ten years of
his reign, but more probably written *c.* 1189 by Hubert Walter
Glanvil's nephew. The object of this treatise is to describe the
procedure of the king's courts ; more, it does not attempt[5]. Its
peculiar value consists in its collection of writs, the first, so far
as we know, ever made ; and, since the making of this collection
was almost certainly the work of Glanvil, the treatise is not

---

[1] *Legis eciam Anglie trina est particio, alia enim Westsexie, alia Mircena, alia
Danelaga est. Leg. Hen.* VI, 2. See, also, Pollock and Maitland, *Hist. of Eng. Law,*
vol. I, p. 106, and Holdsworth, *Hist. of Eng. Law,* vol. I, p. 3.

[2] Cf. Glasson, *Histoire du Droit,* vol. I, p. xv.

[3] Cf. Sohm, *Fränkisches Recht und römisches Recht,* p. 69, quoted by Maitland,
*English Law and the Renaissance,* p. 68. As an example of Frankish elements may
be mentioned the jury system, the writ process and the idea of tenure.

[4] Cf. Holdsworth, *Hist. of Eng. Law,* vol. II, p. 421, and especially the following
quotation from *Diversité des Courtes,* p. 17: *Nota que les briefs sont les principals et
premiers choses en nostre ley.*

[5] See Glanvil, prologue to the *Tractatus.*

inappropriately called by his name, even if he did not himself write it[1].

The form and the language of Glanvil show very clearly the influence of the new school of Roman law, with which the name of Irnerius of Bologna is identified; and that influence is even more evident throughout the next classical work on English law, namely, Bracton's treatise *De Legibus et Consuetudinibus Angliae* (c. 1256). Bracton wrote, it will be observed, at a date which marks, approximately, the very zenith of the great legal renascence of the thirteenth century. The study of Roman civil law—the common law of the universal empire—and the study of Roman canon law—the *jus commune* of the catholic church—then shared with the study of theology the intellectual empire of Europe. Bracton, although apparently he never sat at the feet of the famous doctors of Bologna, was familiar with *Corpus Juris* and with the works of Azo, as well as with the *Decretum* of Gratian and the Decretals of Gregory IX. His knowledge of these sources of civil and canon law determined, to a large extent, the mould and the character of his treatise. It gave him general conceptions; it revealed to him fundamental principles; it enabled him to take a large outlook upon the legal world which he set himself to portray, and to construct an intelligible system on the basis of native customary law[2].

It is worthy of remark, in this place, that the victory of common law over the royal prerogative in the seventeenth century was largely the triumph of Bracton. The cantankerous Coke was always appealing to him; he was called as a witness on behalf of John Hampden; he was quoted by Bradshaw when he delivered judgment on Charles I; Milton appealed to him in *Defensio Pro Populo Anglicano*. It is difficult to conceive that English common law could have survived the attacks of its many enemies during the Tudor and Stewart periods, if it had not been cast into the form, alike logical and literary, of Bracton's treatise. The work at once had a great vogue, and it was a fruitful source of

---

[1] So early as the thirteenth century it was described as *Summa quae vocatur Glanvile*. Pollock and Maitland, *Hist. of Eng. Law*, vol. I, p. 164.

[2] How far the substance, as well as the form, of Bracton's treatise was directly derived from Roman sources is a disputed point. Sir William Jones states an extreme view when he says, 'I am perfectly aware that he copied Justinian almost word for word.' Sir Henry Maine is more moderate in claiming (*Ancient Law*, p. 82) that only a third of the contents were directly borrowed from *Corpus Juris*. The view now commonly held, however, is that Bracton's direct borrowings were quite inconsiderable. See Carl Güterbock, *Henricus de Bracton und sein Verhältniss zum römischen Rechte*, and Maitland, *Bracton and Azo*.

other works, which, in the main, were summaries of Bracton compiled for the use of the legal practitioners. Foremost among these
were two—both of date about 1290—the one known as *Fleta*,
written in Latin, and the other, *Britton*, written in French (of the
Stratford-atte-Bowe order), which was the language of the courts
at that time[1].

In this same provincial French were composed the next series
of works in legal literature which demand mention, namely, the
*Year Books*. English common law—in striking contrast to
Roman law—has been developed by cases adjudged. Each un-
reversed judicial decision forms a precedent to be followed in all
subsequent cases of a similar kind. Hence, the necessity for law
reports; and the strange thing is that their provision has always
been left to private enterprise. We have a more or less complete
series of reports from 1292 to the present day[2].

Those of the period from 1292 to 1534 are known as the *Year
Books*. These *Year Books* rank with the Old English *Chronicle*
and the *Domesday Book* among England's unique historical
treasures. 'They should be our glory,' say Pollock and Maitland,
'for no other country has anything like them.' The same writers
are, however, compelled to add that 'they are our disgrace, for no
other country would have so neglected them[3].' Beginning as mere
students' note books, they rapidly developed into regular reports
of the proceedings in court[4]. Though their arguments are sometimes inconclusive, they are full of human interest, giving, as they
do, the *ipsissima verba* of the old-world lawsuits. Humour and
passion often manifest themselves beneath the formalities of
procedure, as when John de Mowbray, in a burst of irritation, tells
the bishop of Chester to 'go to the great devil[5].' It is difficult to
say whether the *Year Books* are more valuable to the lawyer, the
historian, or the philologer. To the lawyer, they reveal the
material out of which, on the foundation of writs, the structure
of common law was raised—that common law by which the lives

---

[1] To this period belongs that apocryphal work *The Mirror of Justices*, which, mainly
through the influence of Coke, was long regarded as a serious authority on law. Cf.
preface to Coke's 9th and 10th reports, Maitland's Introduction to the Selden Society's
edition of *The Mirror*, and Holdsworth's *Hist. Eng. Law*, vol. II, pp. 284—290.

[2] In 1895 there were over 1800 volumes. Pollock, *First Book of Jurisprudence*,
p. 308.

[3] Pollock and Maitland, *History of English Law*, vol. I, p. xxxv.

[4] This is particularly true of the *Year Books* for 40—50 Edward III, known to
lawyers as *Quadragesms*.

[5] See Holdsworth's *Hist. of Eng. Law*, vol. II, pp. 444—462, where an admirable
account of the *Year Books* is given.

of both Britons and Americans are conditioned to this very day. To the historian, they supply first-hand sources for the social life of the later middle ages. To the philologer, they furnish rich mines of information (as yet little worked) concerning a remarkable and originally uncorrupted French dialect. As the number of the *Year Books* increased, it became convenient to make classified abridgments of their leading cases. The first of these was made, about 1470, by Nicholas Statham, baron of the exchequer under Edward IV.

The same reign saw two other notable additions to legal literature, viz. Sir John Fortescue's *De Laudibus Legum Angliae*, and Sir Thomas Littleton's *Tenures*. Fortescue's well known work was written (*c.* 1470) in France, where the author was living in exile with the Lancastrian court. It was written to instruct the young prince Edward in the laws which, it was hoped, he would one day be called to administer. In form, it is a dialogue between the prince and the author; its language is Latin[1]. Having been composed for the edification of a non-legal person, it is full of information—commonplace then, but extraordinarily valuable today—concerning the legal profession, the training of lawyers, the constitution of the inns of court and the elements of jurisprudence. Throughout, it praises and magnifies English common law, pointing out in detail its superiority to Roman civil law. It was for this quality that Sir Edward Coke extolled it as ' worthy of being written in letters of gold.' The same enthusiastic common lawyer used even larger terms of appreciation in respect of Littleton's *Tenures*. He described it as 'the most perfect and absolute work that was ever written in any human science.' Yet it is a wholly different sort of book from that of Fortescue. It is a highly technical work on feudal land law intended for the professional student and practitioner. But it so well sums up the development of what had then become the most important branch of medieval common law, it is so lucid and well arranged, its language—the law French of the period—is so forceful and well chosen, that it has deservedly attained the rank of a classic. It was written shortly after 1475, and Littleton himself is supposed to have been in the act of seeing it put into print by Lettou and Machlinia when he was overtaken by death in 1481. It was the first English law book to pass through the newly invented press ; and so popular did it become that when, in 1628, Coke published his

---

[1] Cf. vol. ii, pp. 296—9 as to this and other writings by Fortescue.

commentary upon it, it had already appeared in more than seventy editions.

The advent of the printing press effected a great, though silent, revolution in law, as it did in every department of learning. It widely disseminated legal knowledge ; it greatly facilitated the standardising of justice throughout the country ; it provided politicians with an armoury of those juristic weapons with which they fought the battle of English liberty in the seventeenth century. The first hundred years, however, of the era of the printing press did not witness the production and publication of any new work in English legal literature to be compared in merit or importance with either Fortescue or Littleton. Lawyers seemed to be content if they received from the press a steady supply of old authorities—registers of writs, books of entries, year books, abridgments, statutes and court keepers' guides.

This literary sterility may have been due to the fact that English common law was out of favour in high places. The Tudors leaned towards courts like the Star chamber, in which not common law but something very different was administered. English common law, indeed, was during the first half of the sixteenth century, in almost as grave danger of losing its supremacy as was the English parliament. It was saved, however, by the inns of court, and by the weapons which the printing press put into the hands of these organised champions of precedent.

Of the new works which issued from the press during this century perhaps the most important—or least unimportant—was Saint German's *Doctor and Student* (1523—30), a dialogue between a doctor of the civil and canon law and a student of the common law, composed with the main object of contrasting the relations between equity and common law, but incidentally affording a good introduction to the principles of both. It passed through twenty-two editions before, in the eighteenth century, it was superseded by Blackstone's *Commentaries.* Mention should also be made of Perkins's *Profitable Book* (1532), a treatise on conveyancing, 'acceptable and preciouse to young students'; of two *Abridgments of the Year Books,* prepared, the one by Sir Anthony Fitzherbert (1516), the other by Sir Robert Brooke (1568); and of Lambarde's *Eirenarcha* (1581), a manual for justices of the peace, written in a style which, says a contemporary, 'runneth like a temperat stream.' The same writer's *Archeion* (1591) and *Archaionomia* (1568) are valuable, the one as showing the Tudor view of the relation between the common law **courts** and their various rivals, the other as a treatise on legal antiquities. Gentili's *De Jure Belli* (1588—9) was a pioneer work in international law, to which, a generation later, Grotius was much indebted in the compilation of his more famous book with a similar title. Finally, we note three great collections of *Law Reports*, the successors of the *Year Books*, and, like the *Year Books*, in French, namely, those of Plowden (1571), Dyer (1585) and Coke (1600).

With the name of the notable lawyer and politician Sir Edward Coke, we enter the seventeenth century. We may divide that century for the purpose of study into three periods : the first, that of the struggle between king and parliament ; the second, that of the commonwealth ; the third, that of the restoration and revolution. It will be seen that this classification corresponds to the main political division of the Stewart era. This is as it should be ; for never were law and politics more closely bound together than they were at this time. When James I came to the throne, the great unsettled constitutional question was whether the country should be governed by *rex* or *lex*. On the side of the royal prerogative ranged themselves generally the equity lawyers and the civilians ; over against them were the common lawyers led by Coke. Foremost among equity lawyers was Coke's life-long rival and personal enemy, Francis Bacon (lord chancellor 1618—21). But Bacon's fame rests rather on his philosophical achievements than on his legal writings. It is true that it cannot be said of him, as it was said later of lord Brougham, that, if only he had known a little law, he would have been omniscient; for he knew a good deal of law, although he still remained fallible. He was, indeed, eager to attain legal celebrity.

'I am in good hope,' he wrote, 'that when Sir Edward Coke's reports and my rules and decisions shall come to posterity, there will be—whatsoever is now thought—question who be the greater lawyer.'

But he dissipated his energies ; he did not carry out his great project, that of making a complete digest of the laws of England[1]; and he died leaving legal writings of no greater bulk than admits of their inclusion in a single volume of his collected works. Of these writings, the most important, apart from several arguments in important cases, are the tracts entitled *Maxims of the Law*, and *A Reading on the Statute of Uses*. The former contains materials collected for the never completed digest ; while the

---

[1] For Bacon's view as to the need of a revision and digest of the law of England, see the aphorisms appended to his treatise *De Augmentis Scientiarum*.

latter discusses, with remarkable subtlety and philosophic insight, a highly technical department of equitable jurisdiction. Bacon's scanty legal writings kept fairly clear of political controversy. Such, however, was not the case with the works of his contemporary, the civilian John Cowell, regius professor at Cambridge. In 1605, he published his *Institutiones Juris Anglicani ad Methodum Institutionum Justiniani Compositae et Digestae*, an attempt to codify English law under Roman rubrics; in 1607, he issued his more famous *Interpreter*, a dictionary of law terms, in which, under such words as 'king,' 'parliament,' 'prerogative,' 'subsidy,' he maintained the theory of absolute monarchy. The champions of common law took alarm, caused Cowell to be reprimanded by the council, and his book to be burned by the hangman. Other notable civilians of the period who were to be found on the same political side were Sir Arthur Duck and Richard Zouche, both of them men whose writings on Roman law gave them European note. On the other side was the formidable Sir Edward Coke (chief justice of the king's bench 1613—16), a host in himself. He produced many legal books; but his fame, as a writer, rests fundamentally upon two, namely, his *Reports* and his *Institutes*. In his political zeal he was not always scrupulous as to historical accuracy. To him was largely due the legend of *Magna Carta*, the acceptance of *The Mirror of Justices* as a serious legal authority, the fiction of the official nature of the early *Year Books*, and many imaginary rules of law. 'I am afraid,' said chief justice Best, 'we should get rid of a good deal of what is considered law in Westminster Hall, if what Lord Coke says without authority is not law.' Nevertheless, he did a great and useful work for English law, and, therefore, for England. In his *Reports* (eleven volumes, 1600—15), which are models of terse and vigorous expression, a highly authoritative and almost complete statement of contemporary common law is given. In his *Institutes* (four volumes, 1628—44), a mass of antique learning is brought to bear upon the explanation and defence of the English legal system[1]. Coke's title to fame is that he adapted the medieval rules of common law to the needs of the modern state, and recast these rules in an intelligible form, collecting and condensing the obscure and chaotic dicta of the *Year Books* and

[1] The contents of the four volumes of Coke's *Institutes* are as follows: vol. I, Littleton's *Tenures*; vol. II, *Magna Carta*, and subsequent statutes; vol. III, Criminal Law; vol. IV, Jurisdiction of Courts. As to the style, G. P. Macdonell remarks (*Dict. Nat. Biog.*), 'He often reaches a perfection of form, exhibiting that freedom from flabbiness and that careful use of terms which is essential to a good legal style.'

the abridgments. But, in political cases, his learning is always to be looked upon with suspicion or, at least, with caution. His search for truth was merely monocular. He kept one eye steadily fixed on the interests of his party. There was, however, living at the same time a group of men who were whole-heartedly devoted to research, men who are rightly called the fathers of the scientific study of legal history. Foremost among them was John Selden— but with him should be remembered Camden, Cotton, Spelman and Dugdale.

Selden was admittedly the most erudite Englishman of his day. To a wide classical scholarship he added a remarkable knowledge, based, largely, upon original research, of archaeology, history, philology and legal antiquities. He was endowed, moreover, with a mind free from prejudice, a well balanced judgment, a calm judicial temperament. 'I sought only truth,' he said in one of his works, and the expression might well be applied as a motto to them all. In 1610, before he was called to the bar, he published a discourse on the laws and customs of the Britons, English and Danes under the title *Jani Anglorum Facies Altera*. In 1616, he issued an annotated edition of Fortescue. Two years later, he wrote—though for diplomatic reasons it lay unpublished till 1636— his treatise *Mare Clausum*, an attempt to vindicate, on the basis of international law, England's claim to sovereignty over the narrow seas against the destructive attack which Grotius had made upon it in his *Mare Liberum*. Finally, in 1647, he gave to the world his edition of *Fleta*, and, in a prefatory dissertation, condensed the results of a lifelong study of the origins of English law. By his work, he established that tradition of scholarly research into legal antiquities which, at the present day, is maintained by the society called by his name[1].

When Selden's *Fleta* was published, the tragedy of Charles I's career was drawing to its close. Two years later, it was finished, and the commonwealth was established. During the period of this rule, when all institutions were in the melting-pot, few matters received more anxious consideration than did the laws of England. There was, indeed, abundant need of reform. The delays of litigation were proverbial; the expenses of the courts were inordinately heavy, legal procedure was a maze of technicalities amidst which justice frequently lost itself. Everywhere was felt

---

[1] See *Selden as Legal Historian*, by Hazeltine, H. D., in Brunner's *Festschrift* (Weimar, 1910), and, also, in *Harvard Law Review*, 1910. As to Selden's *Table Talk*, see below (II).

the pressure of the dead hand of the Middle Ages. On 22 October 1650, a committee was appointed to consider the matter of legal reform, and, three days later, parliament resolved that one thing, at any rate, should be done—English should be made the language of the law. A bill was accordingly brought in and passed on 22 November 1650. Till then, Latin had remained the language of the records, and French the language of pleadings in court. But, in the seventeenth century, what Latin and what French! This is no place to enter into the subject, great as is its literary interest, and it must suffice to mention, as a specimen of the Latin, the indictment of a man in the Savoy, *quia tetheravit vaccam apud watermill*, and, as a specimen of the French, the report of an incident at the Salisbury assizes in 1631, when chief justice Richardson *fuit assault per prisoner la condemne pur felony que puis son condemnation ject un brickbat a le dit Justice que narrowly mist*[1]. The resolution of the House that these jargons should cease led to a good deal of activity in translation. But, apart from this desirable concession to commonsense in the matter of language, very little was accomplished. When discussion turned to questions of substantial reform, the would-be reformers could not agree. Hugh Peters, for instance, would have liked to introduce the laws of Holland, while John Rogers would have preferred the Mosaic code: 'The body of laws,' he said, 'lies ready before you in the Word of God.' In vain did Matthew Hale, one of the ablest of English lawyers, in conjunction with a select committee, draft not less than nineteen bills embodying practicable improvements. Not one was carried into effect, and, before long, the establishment in the country of a military despotism, with the enforcement of martial law, threw into the background the whole problem of legal reform. Apart, then, from translations, there are few works in legal literature to chronicle during the commonwealth period. The most important were numerous volumes of *Reports*—very poor in quality—mainly of cases of the reigns of James I and Charles I; Matthew Hale's *London's Liberties* (1650); Thomas Hobbes's *Elements of Law* (1640); and, finally, William Prynne's *Collection of Fundamental Liberties and Laws* (1654—5).

The restoration of 1660 heralded a notable revival of the common law, and with it came back its old languages, Latin and French, which it was not able wholly to discard till near the middle of the eighteenth century. One of the signs of this

[1] See, more fully, Pollock, *First Book of Jurisprudence*, p. 295.

revival was the publication, in 1668, of a new *Abridgment des plusiers Cases et Resolutions del Commun Ley.* It was the work of Henry Rolle, once chief justice of the king's bench and a friend of Selden. Its compiler had died in 1656, and it fell to Sir Matthew Hale to see it through the press. Hale himself was a voluminous writer on legal themes; but he seemed to have little desire for the renown of authorship. His valuable introduction to Rolle is anonymous, and the bulk of his writings were still in manuscript at the time of his death (1676) ; indeed, a good deal remains even now unpublished, stored in the libraries of the British Museum and Lincoln's inn. His most notable works were his fragmentary *History of the Common Law of England* (printed 1713), and his *Historia Placitorum Coronae* (printed 1739). Both these books deal, to some extent, with legal antiquities. A much more thorough survey, however, of the field of early law and the institutions connected with it was made by Sir William Dugdale in his *Origines Juridicales* (1666). This valuable work was all but lost to the world ; for the whole of the first edition perished in the fire of London. Fortunately, however, a few presentation copies had been sent out beforehand, and, from these, a second edition was prepared. The zeal for the study of antiquity may, in some measure, account for the issue of a collected edition of the *Year Books* in 1679—the largest edition of the *Year Books* that has yet appeared, and still the standard edition. But this was more than an enterprise of antiquarian zeal, for the *Year Books* were still in constant demand on the part of practising lawyers, and many of the volumes had attained to scarcity prices. The old law, in fact, had come back in force at the restoration. But it did not remain without its critics and assailants. Prominent among these was the irreconcilable William Prynne. We read in Pepys's diary (25 April 1666): 'Mr. Prin...did discourse with me a good while in the garden about the laws of England, telling me the main faults in them.' In 1669, Prynne published his *Animadversions on the Fourth Part of Coke's Institutes*; and these, perhaps, include some of the remarks which their author made to Pepys in the garden. A much more formidable critic, however, both of Coke and of the laws of England, was Thomas Hobbes. ' Truly,' he said, ' I never read weaker reasoning in any author on the law of England than in Sir Edward Coke's *Institutes.*' In his *Dialogue between a Philosopher and a Student of the Common Laws* (published posthumously in 1681) he assails with vigorous dialectic the fundamental legal and political principles inherent in the works of

Coke and the other opponents of the Stewart autocracy. But the mention of Hobbes confronts us with a new age, and warns us that we have reached our time limit. Though an Elizabethan by birth, he is in outlook very modern. As a writer on law, indeed, he has not even yet come by his own. His ideas, couched in severe and exact terminology, have not, it is true, directly reached the popular mind. But, indirectly, through the works of other men, they have made their sovereign entry, and they hold a commanding place in present day legal theory. They ushered in the era of Blackstone, Bentham and Austin.

## II

To the preceding summary of the progress of English legal literature, through the great days of Bacon and Coke, to those of Hale and Selden, may be added a few words concerning a publication which has served to keep the last of these famous names green in popular remembrance, and which, so far as English books are concerned, stands virtually by itself in the century of its origin. *Table-Talk: being the Discourses of John Selden, Esq. Being His Sense of various Matters of Weight and high Consequence; relating especially to Religion and State* was first published in 1689, thirty-five years after Selden's death, and nine years after that of his sometime amanuensis, Richard Milward (afterwards rector of Great Braxted and canon of Windsor). Milward was responsible for the collection and 'digestion' of the utterances which compose the little book. Its title and general plan were manifestly taken from what is, perhaps, the most famous of all anthologies of this particular sort—the *Tischreden* of Martin Luther, otherwise called his *Colloquia*, which were first edited, in 1566, by John Aurifaber from the remembrance of himself and others. Here, too, the 'discourses' are arranged according to subject rather than chronologically, and, as in Milward's alphabetical disposition, the series of sayings is thus deprived of not a little of its biographical interest and significance[1]. Yet the reporter of Selden's *Table-Talk* chooses, as the motto of his collection, the words *Distingue tempora*! In the latter part of the sixteenth, and during the course of the seventeenth, century, were put forth not a few collections of the sayings or conversations of eminent French scholars, from the redoubtable younger Scaliger down to Gilles Ménage, renowned alike as a not very laborious

---

[1] Cf. Köstlin, J., *Martin Luther, sein Leben und seine Schriften*, 3rd ed. Elberfeid, 1883, vol. ii, pp. 487 ff.

lexicographer and as a devotee to the pleasures of the great world[1]. In England, on the other hand, the era proper of *ana* had not yet been reached, although collections of the sayings of kings and magnates had become popular from the middle of the seventeenth century onwards[2], and although great wits and profound scholars of the succeeding generations continued to unbend in occasional converse in coffee-house or common-room, as they had indulged their humour at the Mermaid in the days of Ben Jonson and of Selden himself, or as Jonson had (if the phrase be permitted) let himself go in his harangues—called *Conversations*—addressed to Drummond at Hawthornden. The golden era of this species was inaugurated by Boswell's *Life of Johnson*; but Johnson himself, whose conversations, like Martin Luther's colloquies, cover a far wider ground and possess a far wider, as well as more intimately human, interest than can be ascribed to Selden's *Table-Talk*, pronounced this English collection superior to any of its French rivals[3].

Unfortunately, the original manuscript of *Table-Talk* is lost, so that some passages of the printed texts are of composite origin or actually uncertain; but the authenticity of the whole may be regarded as established, notwithstanding the cavils of Wilkins, the editor of Selden's *Works* (1726). The period during which Milward stated that he had collected his materials from the lips of his patron extended over twenty years—clearly the last two decades of Selden's life, for, in the section *Tithes*, Selden speaks of himself as having written his *History of Tythes* (published in 1618) 'about forty years ago.' Milward neither says nor implies that his manuscript was in any way revised or approved by Selden. There is not any need, it may be added, for calling in the evidence of style in order to determine the date of the utterances recorded in *Table-Talk*. Aubrey, no doubt, refers to Selden's writings when stating that he quite left off the obscurity which he affected in his younger years; and Clarendon, whose character of Selden is one of the earliest, as it is one of the most generous, tributes of friendship enshrined in the *Life* of the great historian[4], while noting that

[1] For a list of these French *ana* see preface to *The Table-Talk of John Selden*, ed. Irving, David, Edinburgh, 1854, pp. xxii—xxv.

[2] See for some earlier English collections of *ana*, bibliography to the present section.

[3] See Boswell's *Life of Johnson*, ed. Hill, G. B., vol. v, p. 311. Boswell, when, in self-defence, discussing publications of a kind similar to his own, also mentions Spence's *Anecdotes*, which, however, is rather different in scheme and remained in manuscript till 1820.

[4] Vol. I, p. 35, ed. 1827.

his friend's style, in all his writings, seemed 'harsh and sometimes obscure,' was careful to add that 'in his conversation he was the most clear discourser, and had the best faculty of making hard things easy, and of presenting them to the understanding, of any man that hath been known.' The essential qualities, and the supreme merit, of the style of *Table-Talk* could not have been more admirably summarised, though Clarendon's intimacy with Selden must have dated from about seven years before that (1642) which saw it end with the great lawyer's definitive resolution to cast in his lot with the parliament rather than with the king.

On the whole, the references in *Table-Talk* to the political events and transactions in which Selden had borne part, even before he became a member of Charles I's second parliament in 1626, are but few. It is only incidentally that he mentions either 'the imprisoning of the parliament men,' of whom he was one, '3° Caroli[1],' or any of the proceedings of the Long parliament (except the removal of bishops 'out of the house[2]'). He is less reticent concerning the doings of the Westminster assembly of divines, of which, in common with other parliament men, he was chosen a member, and in whose debates Whitelock[3] states him to have taken active part, at times 'totally silencing' some of the divines by comparing their biblical quotations with the original Greek and Hebrew texts. But the times were manifestly not such as to invite individual comment on the action of public bodies; for, during practically the whole of the period which can be supposed to be covered by *Table-Talk*, peace seemed as far off as ever, and, 'though we had peace, yet 'twill be a great while ere things be settled; though the wind lie, yet after a storm the sea will work a while[4].' Thus, 'the wisest way for men in these times is to say nothing[5].' Personal references or allusions, such as light up the hearthside or tavern talk of Luther or Johnson, are, therefore, scanty in Selden's observations—save for a few seasonable illustrations from the sayings of king James, or references to eccentrics like Sir Kenelm Digby or Sir Robert Cotton.

The distinctive characteristics of Selden's deliverances at his

---

[1] See 'LX. Incendiaries.'

[2] See 'VII. Bishops in the Parliament.'

[3] *Memorials*, p. 71, cited by Reynolds, S. H., in the introduction to his edition of *Table-Talk*, p. xviii. In 'CXV. Presbytery,' Selden speaks with some satisfaction of the suspicious delay of the divines in the assembly in answering the queries of parliament as to the proofs of the presbytery's possession of the *jus divinum*. 'Their delaying to answer makes us think there's no such thing there.'

[4] See 'O. Peace.'          [5] *Ibid.*

hospitable board are of a different, and, perhaps, of a higher, order. We have described them as deliverances rather than conversations; the truth being that, in these communings, the speaker, quite consciously, lays down the law, while it is only here and there that room is found for objections offered by interlocutors or, more probably, suggested by the autocrat of the table himself, and, in any case, always supplied with a satisfactory answer. These deliverances reveal to us the rapid working of a powerful intellect, putting forth, without any effort of full exposition or sustained argument, but with perfect frankness and freedom of expression, opinions on subjects with which, however difficult or abstruse they may at times seem, it is invariably found to be at home. To occasional discourse of this sort, Selden, in the first instance, brought an equipment of immense learning in law and legal history, together with the habit, which he indulged even in his writings on legal history[1], of illustrating his discourse from nonlegal, as well as legal, sources. It must, however, be allowed that the reporting powers of Milward (who was not a lawyer)—and, perhaps, his powers of memory—were but limited; for *Table-Talk* not only contains few if any 'quotations from poetical writings in various languages' such as 'embellish many of' Selden's written 'pages[2],' but it displays little interest in literature; indeed, the section on 'Poetry' (CV) is not so much disappointing as flatly paradoxical[3]. However cautiously Selden, even among trusty friends, may have abstained from an application of his analytical powers to 'burning' questions of the day, it is clear that, in his later years, his intellectual interests came more and more to concentrate themselves upon matters of state and church. On the former head, he was steadily and sturdily opposed to any encroachment upon popular rights, when those rights had once found expression in the existing law, and he disliked change in the institutions, popular or other, whose growth had been a legal process. The longlived theory which, about the time of the publication of *Table-Talk*, was to assume control over the political philosophy of a series of generations—the conception of a contract between governor and governed—pervaded Selden's views as to the political conflict

---

[1] Cf. Hazeltine, H. D., *Selden as Legal Historian*, p. 599.  [2] *Ibid.*

[3] The Crashaw whom Selden states he converted from writing against plays, was, of course, William Crashaw, the puritan preacher and poet and not (as one of the editors of *Table-Talk* has assumed) his more celebrated son. Selden entertained a strong feeling against 'lecturers,' as being another sort of friars (see 'LXXXIX. Lecturers'); and it was in the former capacity that the elder Crashaw seems to have begun his ministrations.

of which he had witnessed the development. At the bottom of all political doubts and disputes lay to his mind the question: 'Have you agreed so? If you have, then it must remain till you have altered it[1].' A clear consequence was that a breach of the contract on the one side justified resistance on the other:

> To know what obedience is due to the prince, you must look into the contract betwixt him and his people.... Where the contract is broken, and there is no third person to judge, then the decision is by arms. And this is the case between the prince and the subject[2].

Hence, Selden's advocacy of the right of resistance, and his opposition to conceptions, like those of Hobbes, which upheld the duty of passive obedience on the part of the subjects to the monarch. In its very bases, his system of political thought is irreconcilable with the excesses against law that had been the real beginnings of the English revolution. Without mentioning names, he points at the 'incendiaries of the state[3],' who first set it on fire by swerving from the path of legality, and, in order to provide the sovereign with money, 'outran the constable[4].' But, though he reverences an act of parliament as law[5], he is without any superstitious reverence for parliament itself as an acting machine of government; and no censure of an omnipotent chamber could be more severe than that which he passes on the action of 'the parliament party,' though he does not make any pretence of questioning the authority of the assembly under its control[6].

On religious subjects, Selden delivered himself with more expansiveness. It must be allowed that, like many of his contemporaries, he found it difficult to speak of the clergy, even of his own church, without an impatience not far removed from dislike. This prejudice, as he freely confesses, was a remnant of times when it was not easy to find a 'parson' who was a 'gentleman' by birth and breeding[7]. But, of course, Selden's antipathy went deeper than this. Though an advocate, in his own way, of 'set forms[8],'

---

[1] 'CII. People.'

[2] 'CXLVII. War.' See, also, 'XXVIII. Contracts,' where, however, there is a touch of irony in the concluding 'epitome.'

[3] 'LX. Incendiaries.'    [4] 'LXXXIX. Money.'

[5] 'XCVII. Parliament.' This section concludes with a very seasonable protest against pressure of any sort for the purpose of carrying a vote in parliament, winding up with the odd assertion that a man is sent there, not to persuade others, but 'to speak his own heart.' Selden was suspicious of rhetoric, and, though he could not rule its power out of court, declared that it 'is either very good, or stark naught' ('CX. Preaching').

[6] See 'XCVII. Parliament.'    [7] See 'LXXXVIII. Minister Divine.'

[8] See the rather paradoxical, but extremely interesting, 'CIX. Prayer.'

what irritated him in the clergy was the mixture which they presented of religious form and worldly motive—'every religion,' he could bring himself to say, 'is a getting religion[1].' Yet, morality and religion, to his mind, were inseparable, nor could the former stand without the latter[2]. Selden also disliked the clergy because of the incompleteness of their intellectual equipment; theology was a study to which, from this point of view also, he had given much thought[3], and he says—in words of which the humour may have been heightened by the delivery: 'There is all the reason you should believe your minister, unless you have studied divinity as well as he or more than he.' At the same time, he could be just to the position of English churchmen, at a time when it was denounced as illogical and hypocritical[4], and, on historical grounds, could defend both them and the bishops against unfounded charges[5]. The *jus divinum* claim for presbyteries, as has been seen, he derided[6]. But his protestantism was outspoken and deeprooted, and one of the most incisive things in these discourses is the little dialogue on the foundations of the contending forms of faith[7]. His attitude towards the Bible may be described as frankly Erasmian[8]; and, in general, his religious standpoint is an enlightened acceptance of the creed and church of his fathers, equally removed from fanaticism and from faithlessness.

The real fascination of Selden's utterances in *Table-Talk* lies neither in the legal learning of which it furnishes constant evidence, nor in the historical judgments which it pithily supplies or, by means of a pregnant word or phrase, suggests, nor, again, in its incidental illustrations of contemporary currents of opinion or tendencies of feeling[9]. Its charm lies in the play of mind, which, passing from subject to subject, familiar to the speaker in its depths as well as in its more superficial aspects, illuminates them all in turn. Selden's wit has many varieties, and more than one of these, half imperceptibly, reveals itself as true wisdom. By the side of some instances of a coarse kind of wit, which still found ready acceptance in Selden's age—especially in the form of anecdotal illustrations, with which he evidently took pleasure in

---

[1] See 'CXVIII. Proverbs.'   [2] See 'XC. Moral Honesty.'
[3] See 'LXXXVIII. Minister Divine.'   [4] See 'CVII. Popery.'
[5] See 'VI. Bishop before the Parliament.'   [6] See 'CXV. Presbytery.'
[7] See 'CXXI. Religion.'   [8] See 'V. Bible, Scripture.'
[9] Such as the rather sophistical 'CL. Witches.' It is amusing that even Selden should not have escaped the impression common with elderly people that manners are deteriorating, though he can hardly have been an old man when he gave utterance to 'LXXI. King of England.'

clinching an argument—there are others of a trenchant wit, too
rough in flavour to suit the modern palate, and others, but not so
many, of a cynicism which tends, hardly less than coarseness, to
mar table-talk. But there are others of a pleasant wit betokening
a genial apprehension of the humorous side of things[1], besides
yet others where the speaker manifests that kind of insight
into the real nature of men and affairs which only the constant
application of the mind to prompt treatment of intricate problems
is capable of producing[2]. Finally, there are to be found in *Table-
Talk* illustrations of that highest kind of wit which, by a winged
word, makes plain an everlasting truth—that gnomic wisdom
which is as pellucid as it is profound. Here, humility and per-
spicacity join hands, as in the plain moral which ends a homely
argument on Vows[3]: 'He that vows can mean no more in sense
than this; to do his utmost endeavour to keep his vow.'

Thus, a simple sheaf of sayings apprises us, were there nothing
else to show it, how, for this great lawyer and deeply read scholar,
the light of reason shone with the same clearness, calm rather than
cold, whether it fell upon the ancient tomes in his library, or lit up
the chambers of political or religious debate, or burnt in the lamp
hanging in the sanctuary.

[1] A single instance may be cited from 'LXXXVI. Measure of things.' We cry
down a rotten pear, and approve a rotten medlar; 'and yet, I warrant you, the pear
thinks as well of itself as the medlar does.'
[2] By way of example, see the explanation of the custom of painting terrific
Saracens' heads as signs on inns in 'CXLVIII. War.'
[3] CXLIV.

# CHAPTER XIV

## JOHN LOCKE

JOHN LOCKE may be regarded as, on the whole, the most important figure in English philosophy. Others excelled him in genius; he had not the comprehensive grasp of Hobbes, or the speculative originality of Berkeley, or the subtlety of Hume; but he was surpassed by none in candour, sagacity and shrewdness. These qualities recommended him to his countrymen, and the width of his interests reconciled them to his philosophy. He was a physician, always on the outlook for new knowledge, an adviser of statesmen, a sufferer in the cause of freedom and an amateur theologian. His writings on economics, on politics and on religion expressed the best ideas of the time—the ideas that were about to become dominant. He was the philosopher of the revolution settlement; and, when the settlement was made, he came home to publish the books which he had prepared in exile. Even his great work, *An Essay concerning Human Understanding*, may have seemed only to show the grounds in the human mind for the lessons of honesty, liberty and toleration which he constantly inculcated. It is almost with a shock of surprise that one realises that this same *Essay*, by its 'historical plain method,' gave a new direction to European philosophy, and provided a new basis for the science of psychology.

Locke was born at Wrington, a village in Somersetshire, on 29 August 1632. He was the son of a country solicitor and small landowner who, when the civil war broke out, served as a captain of horse in the parliamentary army. 'I no sooner perceived myself in the world than I found myself in a storm,' he wrote long afterwards, during the lull in the storm which followed the king's return. But political unrest does not seem to have seriously disturbed the course of his education. He entered Westminster school in 1646, and passed to Christ Church, Oxford, as a junior student, in 1652; and he had a home there (though absent from it for long periods) for more than thirty years—till deprived of his studentship by royal mandate in 1684. The official studies of the university were uncongenial to him; he would have preferred to have learned philosophy from Descartes instead of from Aristotle; but, evidently, he satisfied the authorities, for he was elected to a senior studentship in 1659, and, in the three or four years following, he took part in the tutorial work of the college. At one time, he seems to have thought of the clerical profession as a possible career; but he declined an offer of preferment in 1666, and, in the same year, obtained a dispensation which enabled him to hold his studentship without taking orders. About the same time, we hear of his interest in experimental science, and he was elected a fellow of the Royal Society in 1668. Little is known of his early medical studies. He cannot have followed the regular course, for he was unable to obtain the degree of doctor of medicine. It was not till 1674 that he graduated as bachelor of medicine. In the following January, his position in Christ Church was regularised by his appointment to one of the two medical studentships of the college.

His knowledge of medicine and occasional practice of the art led, in 1666, to an acquaintance with lord Ashley (afterwards, from 1672, earl of Shaftesbury). The acquaintance, begun accidentally, had an immediate effect on Locke's career. Without severing his connection with Oxford, he became a member of Shaftesbury's household, and seems soon to have been looked upon as indispensable in all matters domestic and political. He saved the statesman's life by a skilful operation, arranged a suitable marriage for his heir, attended the lady in her confinement, and directed the nursing and education of her son— afterwards famous as the author of *Characteristics*. He assisted Shaftesbury, also, in public business, commercial and political, and followed him into the government service. When Shaftesbury was made lord chancellor in 1672, Locke became his secretary for presentation to benefices, and, in the following year, was made secretary to the board of trade. In 1675, his official life came to an end, for the time, with the fall of his chief.

Locke's health, always delicate, suffered from the London climate. When released from the cares of office, he left England in search of health. Ten years earlier, he had had his first experience of foreign travel, and of public employment, as secretary to Sir Walter Vane, ambassador to the elector of Brandenburg during the first Dutch war. On his return to England, early in 1666, he declined an offer of further service in Spain, and settled again in Oxford, but was soon induced by Shaftesbury to spend a great part of his time in London. On his release from office, in 1675, he sought milder air in the south of France, made leisurely journeys, and settled down for many months at Montpellier. The journal which he kept at this period is full of minute descriptions of places and customs and institutions. It contains, also, a record of many of the reflections that afterwards took shape in the *Essay concerning Human Understanding*. He returned to England in 1679, when his patron had again a short spell of office. He does not seem to have been concerned in Shaftesbury's later schemes; but suspicion naturally fell upon him, and he found it prudent to take refuge in Holland. This he did in August 1683, less than a year after the flight and death of Shaftesbury. Even in Holland, for some time, he was not safe from danger of arrest at the instance of the English government; he moved from town to town, lived under an assumed name and visited his friends by stealth. His residence in Holland brought political occupations with it, among the men who were preparing the English revolution. It had at least equal value in the leisure which it gave him for literary work, and in the friendships which it offered. In particular, he formed a close intimacy with Philip van Limborch, the leader of the Remonstrant clergy, and the scholar and liberal theologian to whom *Epistola de Tolerantia* was dedicated. This letter was completed in 1685, though not published at the time; and, before he left for England, in February 1689, the *Essay concerning Human Understanding* seems to have attained its final form, and an abstract of it was published in Leclerc's *Bibliothèque universelle* in 1688.

The new government recognised his services to the cause of freedom by the offer of the post of ambassador either at Berlin or at Vienna. But Locke was no place hunter; he was solicitous, also, on account of his health; his earlier experience of Germany led him to fear the 'cold air' and 'warm drinking'; and the high office was declined. But he served less important offices at home. He was made commissioner of appeals in May 1689, and, from 1696 to 1700, he was a commissioner of trade and plantations at a salary of £1000 a year. Although official duties called him to town for protracted periods, he was able to fix his residence in the country. In 1691, he was persuaded to make his permanent home at Oates in Essex, in the house of Sir Francis and lady Masham. Lady Masham was a daughter of Cudworth, the Cambridge Platonist; Locke had manifested a growing sympathy with his type of liberal theology ; intellectual affinity increased his friendship with the family at Oates ; and he continued to live with them till his death on 28 October 1704.

With the exception of the abstract of the *Essay* and other less important contributions to the *Bibliothèque universelle,* Locke had not published anything before his return to England in 1689; and, by this time, he was in his fifty-seventh year. But many years of reflection and preparation made him ready now to send forth books from the press in rapid succession. In March 1689, his *Epistola de Tolerantia* was published in Holland ; an English translation of the same, by William Popple, appeared later in the same year, and, in a corrected edition, in 1690. The controversy which followed this work led, on Locke's part, to the publication of a *Second Letter,* and then of a *Third Letter,* in 1690 and 1692 respectively. In February 1690, the book entitled *Two Treatises of Government* was published, and in March of the same year appeared the long expected *Essay concerning Human Understanding,* on which he had been at work intermittently since 1671. It met with immediate success, and led to a voluminous literature of attack and reply; young fellows of colleges tried to introduce it at the universities, and heads of houses sat in conclave to devise means for its suppression. To one of his critics Locke replied at length. This was Edward Stillingfleet, bishop of Worcester, who, in his *Vindication of the Doctrine of the Trinity* (1696), had attacked the new philosophy. It was the theological consequences which were drawn from the doctrines of the *Essay* not so much by Locke himself as by Toland, in his *Christianity not mysterious,* that the bishop had chiefly in view ; in philosophy for its own sake he does not seem to have been interested. But his criticism drew attention to one of the least satisfactory (if, also, one of the most suggestive) doctrines of the *Essay*—its explanation of the idea of substance ; and discredit was thrown on the 'new way of ideas' in general. In January 1697, Locke replied in *A Letter to the Bishop of Worcester.* Stillingfleet answered this in May ; and Locke was ready with a second letter in August. Stillingfleet replied in 1698, and Locke's lengthy third letter appeared in 1699. The bishop's death, later in the same year, put an end to the controversy. The second edition of the *Essay* was published in 1694, the third in 1695, and the fourth in 1700. The second and fourth editions contained important additions. An abridgment of it appeared in 1696, by John Wynne, fellow of Jesus college,

Oxford; it was translated into Latin and into French soon after the appearance of the fourth edition. The later editions contain many modifications due to the author's correspondence with William Molyneux, of Trinity college, Dublin, a devoted disciple, for whom Locke conceived a warm friendship. Other correspondents and visitors to Oates during these years were Sir Isaac Newton and Anthony Collins, a young squire of the neighbourhood, who afterwards made his mark in the intellectual controversies of the time[1].

Other interests also occupied Locke during the years following the publication of his great work. The financial difficulties of the new government led, in 1691, to his publication of *Some Considerations of the Consequences of the Lowering of Interest, and Raising the Value of Money*, and of *Further Considerations* on the latter question, four years later. In 1693 he published *Some Thoughts concerning Education*, a work founded on letters written to a friend, and, in 1695, appeared *The Reasonableness of Christianity*, and, later, *A Vindication* of the same against certain objections; and this was followed by a second vindication two years afterwards. Locke's religious interest had always been strongly marked, and, in the later years of his life, much of his time was given to theology. Among the writings of his which were published after his death are commentaries on the Pauline epistles, and a *Discourse on Miracles*, as well as a fragment of a fourth Letter on Toleration. The posthumously published writings include, further, *An Examination of Father Malebranche's Opinion of Seeing all things in God, Remarks on Some of Mr Norris's Books*, and—most important of all—the small treatise on *The Conduct of the Understanding*, which had been originally designed as a chapter of the *Essay*.

Locke opened a new way for English philosophy. Stillingfleet saw dangers ahead in that way; but its discovery was Locke's title to fame. It was no new thing, certainly, to lay stress upon method. Herein, he followed the example of Bacon and Hobbes and other pioneers of modern philosophy. Bacon had done more: he had found dangers and defects in the natural working of men's minds, and had devised means to correct them. But Locke went a step further, and undertook a systematic investigation of the human understanding with a view to determining something else —namely, the truth and certainty of knowledge, and the grounds

---

[1] The productions of Collins, Toland, and the other deistical writers will be dealt with in the next volume of this work.

of belief, on all matters about which men are in the habit of
making assertions. In this way he introduced a new department,
or a new method, of philosophical enquiry, which has come to be
known as theory of knowledge, or epistemology; and, in this
respect, he was the precursor of Kant and anticipated what Kant
called the critical method.

We have Locke's own account of the origin of the problem
in his mind. He struck out a new way because he found the
old paths blocked. Five or six friends were conversing in his
room, probably in London and in the winter of 1670—1, 'on a
subject very remote from this'; the subject, as we learn from
another member of the party, was the 'principles of morality
and revealed religion'; but difficulties arose on every side, and
no progress was made. Then, he goes on to say,

it came into my thoughts that we took a wrong course, and that before we
set ourselves upon inquiries of that nature, it was necessary to examine our
own abilities, and see what objects our understandings were, or were not,
fitted to deal with.

At the request of his friends, Locke agreed to set down his
thoughts on this question against their next meeting; and he
expected that a single sheet of paper would suffice for the purpose.
So little did he realise the magnitude of the issues which he raised
and which were to occupy his leisure for nearly twenty years.

Locke's interest centres in the traditional problems—the nature
of self, the world and God, and the grounds of our knowledge
of them. We reach these questions only in the fourth and last
book of the *Essay*. But to them the enquiry of the first three
books is preliminary, though it has, and Locke saw that it had,
an importance of its own. His introductory sentences make this
plain :

Since it is the understanding that sets man above the rest of sensible
beings, and gives him all the advantage and dominion which he has over
them; it is certainly a subject, even for its nobleness, worth our labour to
inquire into. The understanding, like the eye, while it makes us see and
perceive all other things, takes no notice of itself; and it requires art and
pains to set it at a distance and make it its own object. But whatever be the
difficulties that lie in the way of this inquiry; whatever it be that keeps us so
much in the dark to ourselves; sure I am that all the light we can let in upon
our minds, all the acquaintance we can make with our own understandings,
will not only be very pleasant, but bring us great advantage, in directing our
thoughts in the search of other things.

Locke will not 'meddle with the physical consideration of
the mind'; he has no theory about its essence or its relation
to the body ; at the same time, he has no doubt that, if due pains

be taken, the understanding can be studied like anything else : we can observe its objects and the ways in which it operates upon them. All the objects of the understanding are described as *ideas,* and ideas are spoken of as being in the mind[1]. Locke's first problem, therefore, is to trace the origin and history of ideas, and the ways in which the understanding operates upon them, in order that he may be able to see what knowledge is and how far it reaches. This wide use of the term 'idea' is inherited from Descartes. The term in modern psychology which corresponds with it most nearly is 'presentation.' But presentation is, strictly, only one variety of Locke's idea, which includes, also, representation and image, percept, and concept or notion. His usage of the term thus differs so widely from the old Platonic meaning that the danger of confusion between them is not great. It suited the author's purpose, also, from being a familiar word in ordinary discourse as well as in the language of philosophers. Herein, however, lay a danger from which he did not escape. In common usage 'idea' carries with it a suggestion of contrast with reality ; and the opposition which the 'new way of ideas' excited was due to the doubt which it seemed to cast on the claim of knowledge to be a knowledge of real things.

The *Essay* is divided into four books; the first is a polemic against the doctrine of innate principles; the others deal with ideas, with words, and with knowledge respectively. The first book is remarkable for the way in which the author brings to bear upon the question all the facts that could then be ascertained regarding the ideas and beliefs of primitive and savage races. He points to the variety of human experience, and to the difficulty of forming general and abstract ideas, and he ridicules the view that any such ideas can be antecedent to experience. It is in its most extreme form that the doctrine of innate ideas is attacked ; but he cannot see any alternative between that form and his own view that all ideas have their origin in experience.

Locke wishes to avoid any presupposition about matter, or mind, or their relation. It is not difficult to see that the notions which he has expelled often re-enter unbidden. But the peculiar value of his psychology consists in his attempt to keep clear of them. He begins neither with mind nor with matter, but with ideas. Their existence needs no proof: 'everyone is conscious of them in himself, and men's words and actions will satisfy him that they are in others.' His first enquiry is 'how they come into the

[1] Cf. *Essay*, introduction, sec. 2; bk. II, chap. I, sec. 5; bk. II, chap. VIII, sec. 8.

mind'; his next business is to show that they constitute the whole material of our knowledge. In his answer to the former question we discover the influence of traditional philosophy, or, rather, of ordinary commonsense views of existence, upon his thought. All our ideas, he says, come from experience. The mind has no innate ideas, but it has innate faculties: it perceives, remembers, and combines the ideas that come to it from without; it also desires, wills, and deliberates; and these mental activities are themselves the source of a new class of ideas. Experience is, therefore, twofold. Our observation may be employed either about external sensible objects, or about the internal operations of our minds. The former is the source of most of the ideas which we have, and, as it depends 'wholly upon our senses,' is called 'sensation.' The latter is a source of ideas which 'every man has wholly in himself,' and it might be called '*internal* sense'; to it he gives the name 'reflection.'

Hence, the peculiarity of Locke's position. There are no innate ideas 'stamped upon the mind' from birth; and yet impressions of sense are not the only source of knowledge: 'the mind,' he says, 'furnishes the understanding with ideas.' No distinction is implied here between 'mind' and 'understanding,' so that the sentence might run, 'the mind furnishes itself with ideas.' As to what these ideas are, we are not left in doubt: they are 'ideas of its own operations.' When the mind acts, it has an idea of its action, that is, it is self-conscious. Reflection, there-fore, means self-consciousness, and, as such, is assumed to be an original source of our knowledge. Afterwards both Hume and Condillac refused to admit reflection as an original source of ideas, and both, accordingly, found that they had to face the problem of tracing the growth of self-consciousness out of a succession of sensations. According to Locke, reflection is an original, rather than an independent, source of ideas. Without sensation, mind would have nothing to operate upon, and, there-fore, could have no ideas of its operations. It is 'when he first has any sensation' that 'a man begins to have any ideas[1].' The operations of the mind are not themselves produced by sensation, but sensation is required to give the mind material for working on.

The ideas which sensation gives 'enter by the senses simple and unmixed[2]'; they stand in need of the activity of mind to bind them into the complex unities required for knowledge. The complex ideas of substances, modes and relations are all the

---

[1] Bk. II, chap. I, sec. 23.     [2] Bk. II, chap. II, sec. 1.

product of the combining and abstracting activity of mind operating upon simple ideas, which have been given, without any connection, by sensation or reflection. Locke's doctrine of knowledge has thus two sides. On the one side, all the material of knowledge is traced to the simple idea. On the other side, the processes which transform this crude material into knowledge are activities of mind which themselves cannot be reduced to ideas. Locke's metaphors of the *tabula rasa*, 'white paper[1],' and 'dark room' misled his critics and suggested to some of his followers a theory very different from his own. The metaphors only illustrate what he had in hand at the moment. Without experience, no characters are written on the 'tablets' of the mind; except through the 'windows' of sensation and reflection, no light enters the understanding. No ideas are innate; and there is no source of new simple ideas other than those two. But knowledge involves relations, and relations are the work of the mind; it requires complex ideas, and complex ideas are mental formations. Simple ideas do not, of themselves, enter into relation and form complex ideas. Locke does not, like Hobbes before him and Hume and Condillac after him, look to some unexplained natural attraction of idea for idea as bringing about these formations. Indeed, his treatment of 'the association of ideas' is an afterthought, and did not appear in the earlier editions of the *Essay*.

Starting from the simple ideas which we get from sensation, or from observing mental operations as they take place, Locke has two things to explain: the universal element, that is, the general conceptions with which knowledge is concerned or which it implies, and the reference to reality which it claims. With the former problem Locke deals at great length; and the general method of his exposition is clear enough. Complex ideas arise from simple ideas by the processes of combination and abstraction carried out by the mind. It would be unfair to expect completeness from his enterprise; but it cannot be denied that his intricate and subtle discussions left many problems unsolved. Indeed, this is one of his great merits. He raised questions in such a way as to provoke further enquiry. Principles such as the causal relation, apart from which knowledge would be impossible, are quietly taken for granted, often without any enquiry into the

---

[1] The same metaphor is used by Hooker, *Ecclesiastical Polity*, bk. I, chap. VI: 'The soul of man being therefore at the first as a book, wherein nothing is, and yet all things may be imprinted.'

grounds for assuming them. Further, the difficulty of accounting for universals is unduly simplified by describing certain products as simple ideas, although thought has obviously been at work upon them. At the outset of his enquiry, simple ideas are exemplified by yellow, white, heat, cold, soft, hard, and so forth; but, towards the close of the second book, a very different list is given, which includes space, time, solidity, motion, power. Having arrived at this latter point, he seems to forget his view that all knowledge begins with the particular, with something 'simple and unmixed.' Indeed, his whole doctrine of modes may be said to be based on oblivion of the fact that a simple idea must be really simple. Instead of showing how the idea of space is built up out of many particular sensations (or simple ideas) of particular spaces, he regards particular spaces as modes of the simple idea space; instead of showing how the idea of time is evolved from our experience of particular durations, he calls the latter modes of the simple idea duration; and so on. Unwittingly, he generalises the particular. He professes to begin with the mere particulars of external or internal sense, and to show how knowledge—which is necessarily general—is evolved from them. But, instead of doing so, he assumes a general or universal element as already given in the simple idea, and then treats the particular experience as one of its modes.

Having gone so far, he might almost have been expected to take a further step and treat the perceptions of particular things as modes of the simple idea substance. But this he does not do. Substance is an idea regarding which he was in earnest with his own fundamental theory; and the difficulties in which his theory involved him on this head were both provocative of criticism and fruitful for the progress of thought. He admits that substance is a complex idea; that is to say, it is formed by the mind's action out of simple ideas. Now, this idea of substance marks the difference between having sensations and perceiving things. Its importance, therefore, is clear; but there is no clearness in explaining it. We are told that there is a 'supposed or confused idea of substance' to which are joined (say) 'the simple idea of a dull whitish colour, with certain degrees of weight, hardness, ductility and fusibility,' and, as a result, 'we have the idea of *lead.*' A difficulty might have been avoided if substance could have been interpreted as simply the combination by the understanding of white, hard, etc., or some similar cluster of ideas of sensation. But it was not Locke's way thus to ignore facts. He sees that something more is needed than these ideas of sensation. They are only *joined to* 'the supposed or confused idea of substance,' which is there and 'always the first and chief.' He holds to it that the idea is a complex idea and so made by the mind; but he is entirely at a loss to account for the materials out of which it is made. We cannot imagine how simple ideas can subsist by themselves, and so 'we accustom ourselves to suppose some substratum wherein they do subsist,' and this we call substance. In one place, he even vacillates between the assertions that we have no clear idea of substance and that we have no idea of it at all. It is 'a supposition of he knows not what.' This uncertainty, as will appear presently, throws its shadow over our whole knowledge of nature.

The 'new way of ideas' is thus hard put to it in accounting for the universal element in knowledge; it has even greater difficulties to face in defending the reality of knowledge. And, in the latter case, the author does not see the difficulties so clearly. His view is that the simple idea is the test and standard of reality. Whatever the mind contributes to our ideas removes them further from the reality of things; in becoming general, knowledge loses touch with things. But not all simple ideas carry with them the same significance for reality. Colours, smells, tastes, sounds, and the like are simple ideas, yet nothing resembles them in the bodies themselves; but, owing to a certain bulk, figure and motion of their insensible parts, bodies have 'a power to produce those sensations in us.' These, therefore, are called 'secondary qualities of bodies.' On the other hand, 'solidity, extension, figure, motion or rest, and number' are also held by Locke to be simple ideas; and these are resemblances of qualities in body; 'their patterns do really exist in the bodies themselves,' and, accordingly, are 'primary qualities of bodies[1].' In this way, by implication if not expressly, Locke severs, instead of establishing, the connection between simple ideas and reality. The only ideas which can make good their claim to be regarded as simple ideas have nothing resembling them in things. Other ideas, no doubt, are said to resemble bodily qualities (an assertion for which no proof is given and none is possible); but these ideas have only a doubtful claim to rank as simple ideas. Locke's prevailing tendency is to identify reality with the simple

---

[1] A similar distinction between qualities of body was formulated by Galileo, Hobbes and Descartes; its origin may be traced to Democritus; and the words 'primary' and 'secondary' were occasionally used in this connection by Robert Boyle, *Origine of Formes and Qualities* (1666), pp. 10, 43, 100—1; cp. *Tracts* (1671), introduction, p. 18.

idea, but he sometimes comes within an ace of the opposite view
that the reference to reality is the work of thought.

In the fourth book of his *Essay*, Locke proceeds to apply these
results so as to determine the nature and extent of knowledge. As
ideas are the sole immediate object of the mind, knowledge can be
nothing else than 'the perception of the connexion of and agreement, or disagreement and repugnancy of any of our ideas.' This
agreement or disagreement is said to be of four sorts: identity
or diversity; relation; co-existence or necessary connection; real
existence. Each of these kinds of knowledge raises its own
questions; but, broadly speaking, one distinction may be taken
as fundamental. In the same paragraph in which he restricts
knowledge to the agreement or disagreement of our ideas, he
admits one kind of knowledge which goes beyond the ideas
themselves to the significance which they have for real existence.
When the reference does not go beyond the ideas 'in the mind,'
the problems that arise are of one order; when there is a further reference to real things, another problem arises. The preceding books
have prepared the way for the solution of both sets of problems.

When ideas are together in the mind, we can discover their
relations to one another; so long as they are not taken to
represent archetypes outside the mind, there is no obstacle to
certainty of knowledge: for 'all relation terminates in, and is
ultimately founded on, those simple ideas we have got from sensation or reflection.' In this way, Locke vindicates the certainty
of mathematics: the science is merely ideal, and its propositions
do not hold of things outside the mind. He thinks, also, that
'morality is capable of demonstration as well as mathematics.'
But, in spite of the entreaties of his friend Molyneux, he never
set out his ethical doctrine in detail. In the second book he had
reduced moral good and evil to the pleasure and pain which—as
reward and punishment—come to us from some lawgiver; thus
they point to a source outside the mind. But his ground for
maintaining the demonstrative character of morality is that moral
ideas are 'mixed modes' and, therefore, mental products, so that
their 'precise real essence ... may be perfectly known.' He
ventures upon two examples only of this demonstrative morality;
and neither of them is more than verbal or gives any information
about good or evil. Yet the doctrine is significant as showing the
influence upon Locke of another type of thought, of which there
are many traces, both in the *Essay* and in his other works.

The real existences to which knowledge extends are self, God, and the world of nature. Of the first we have, says Locke, an intuitive knowledge, of the second a demonstrative knowledge, of the third a sensitive knowledge. This view he proceeds to explain and defend. Locke holds that the existence of the self is known by immediate intuition. Like Descartes, he thinks that doubt on this head is excluded. But he fails to point out how self can be an idea and thus belong to the material of knowledge. An idea of self cannot come from sensation; and the simple ideas of reflection are all of mental operations, and not of the subject or agent of these operations. On the other hand, when he had occasion to discuss personal identity, he followed his new way of ideas, and made it depend on memory. His proof of the existence of God belongs to the order called by philosophers cosmological. It starts with the existence of a thinking self or mind, and argues from this position to the necessity for an intelligent first cause. Locke assumes, without question, the validity of the causal principle even beyond the range of possible experience. It was left for David Hume to take the momentous step of questioning this principle. Regarding self and God, therefore, Locke does not show any special originality of view. It is when he faces the question of the real existence of external bodies that his doctrine of ideas as the sole immediate object of the understanding comes into play, and casts uncertainty upon the propositions of natural science. He does not, indeed, question the transition from the presence of an idea of sensation to the existence 'at that time' of a thing which causes the idea in us[1]. Here, he thinks, we have 'an assurance that deserves the name of knowledge[2],' although he admits that it is 'not altogether so certain as our intuitive knowledge, or the deductions of our reason employed about the clear abstract ideas of our own minds.' Knowledge of this sort is merely sensitive; it does not extend beyond 'the present testimony of our senses employed about particular objects that do then affect them[3].' Necessary connection here is beyond our reach. Any assertion about things, except in respect of their immediate presence to the senses—all the generalisations of natural science, therefore—fall short of knowledge strictly so called. 'God has set some things in broad daylight[4]'; but the science of nature is not one of them; there, as in many other matters, we have only 'the twilight of probability'; but probability is sufficient for our purposes. This sober practical note marks the outcome of the whole enquiry:

---

[1] Bk. IV, chap. XI, sec. 2.
[2] Bk. IV, chap. XI, sec. 3.
[3] Bk. IV, chap. XI, sec. 9.
[4] Bk. IV, chap. XII, sec. 1.

our faculties being suited not to the full extent of being, nor to a perfect, clear, comprehensive knowledge of things free from all doubt and scruple; but to the preservation of us, in whom they are; and accommodated to the use of life[1].

In his other works Locke's practical interests find ample scope; he deals with most of the questions that attracted the mind of the day, and he left upon them the mark of his thought. In *Two Treatises of Government* he has two purposes in view: to refute the doctrine of absolute power, as it had been put forward by Sir Robert Filmer, and to establish a theory which would reconcile the liberty of the citizen with political order. The criticism of Filmer is complete. His theory of the absolute sovereignty of Adam, and so of kings as Adam's heirs, has lost all interest; and Locke's argument has been only too effective: the exhaustive reply to so absurd a thesis becomes itself wearisome. There is little direct reference to the more enduring work of Hobbes; but this work seems to have been in Locke's mind when he argued that the doctrine of absolute monarchy leaves sovereign and subjects in the state of nature towards one another. The constructive doctrines which are elaborated in the second treatise became the basis of social and political philosophy for many generations. Labour is the origin and justification of property; contract or consent is the ground of government, and fixes its limits. Behind both doctrines lies the idea of the independence of the individual man. The state of nature knows no government; but in it, as in political society, men are subject to the moral law, which is the law of God. Men are born free and equal in rights. Whatever a man 'mixes his labour with' is his to use. Or, at least, this was so in the primitive condition of human life in which there was enough for all and 'the whole earth was America.' Locke sees that, when men have multiplied and land has become scarce, rules are needed beyond those which the moral law or law of nature supplies. But the origin of government is traced not to this economic necessity, but to another cause. The moral law is always valid, but it is not always kept. In the state of nature, all men equally have the right to punish transgressors: civil society originates when, for the better administration of the law, men agree to delegate this function to certain officers. Thus, government is instituted by a 'social contract'; its powers are limited, and they involve reciprocal obligations; moreover, they can be modified or rescinded by the authority which conferred them. Locke's theory is thus no

[1] Bk. IV, chap. XI, sec. 8.

more historical than the absolutism of Hobbes. It is a rendering of the facts of constitutional government in terms of thought, and it served its purpose as a justification of the revolution settlement in accordance with the ideas of the time.

Locke's writings on economic subjects do not rank in importance with his treatises on government. They deal with particular questions raised by the necessities of the political situation. No attempt had yet been made to isolate the fact of wealth and make it the subject of a special science[1]. The direction of industry and commerce was held to be part of the statesman's duty; but, in the seventeenth century, it began to be carried out with less thoroughness than before; and at the same time new problems were opened up by the growth of the national life. The American colonies, the enterprise of the East India company, the planting of Ireland, the commercial rivalry with Holland and with France, as well as questions regarding the rate of interest and the currency, occupied the attention of a crowd of writers in the second half of the century. Sir William Temple's career had made him familiar with the economic condition both of Holland and of Ireland, and he wrote on both (1672 and 1673), praising highly the industrial methods of the Dutch[2]. Sir Josiah Child, also, a great merchant who became chairman of the East India company, admired the commercial conditions of Holland, specially the low rate of interest so favourable to traders. This, he thought, was the true cause of the greatness of the Dutch; in like manner, cheap money would stimulate the enterprise of English merchants, and he urged that a low rate should be fixed by law. After the revolution, the economic policy of the whig House of Commons was criticised by several writers of whom the most important were Charles Davenant and Sir Dudley North. Davenant was the author of *An Essay on the East India Trade* (1697), besides other works, and North wrote *Discourses upon Trade* (1691). They were not free traders in the modern sense, but they argued against the restrictions and regulations adopted by the government for the encouragement of English trade.

Of all the economists contemporary with Locke, Sir William Petty was, in many ways, the most remarkable. Circumstances made him acquainted with France, Holland and Ireland. He studied medicine in Holland; in France he became intimate with

---

[1] Cf. Cunningham, *Growth of English Industry and Commerce*, sec. 206.

[2] See *post*, chap. XVI, as to Temple's writings.

Hobbes; an appointment as army physician in Ireland, under the lieutenant-governorship of Henry Cromwell, led to his undertaking the 'Down survey' of forfeited lands, and thus determined both his own fortunes and the character of his literary work. His type of mind inclined him to experimental work and to the exact sciences; and, as experiment is seldom possible in economic affairs, he found a substitute for it in what is now called statistics. This he himself styled 'political arithmetic': 'instead of using only comparative and superlative words, and intellectual arguments,' he states his intention to 'consider only such causes as have visible foundations in nature,' and to express himself 'in terms of number, weight, or measure.' Thus he adopted the quantitative method, and applied it to a variety of topics. At the time, there were many complaints of national decay; *Britannia languens* was vocal; rents (it was said) were falling; money was scarce; trades were disappearing; the country was underpeopled; and the people underemployed and overtaxed. Petty did not sympathise with these complaints; he distrusted vague generalities, and asked for exact statements of the resources of England as compared with those of her rivals. The net results of his own enquiry into the matter are given in his *Political Arithmetic.* It was characteristic of Petty to look facts in the face, without being too much overawed by the prevalent assumptions of statesmen and men of business. He did not share the fears of the mercantilists regarding the danger of exporting the precious metals: the country, he thinks, is not always the poorer for having less money. On the subject of money, he gives two definitions which are worth quoting. Interest is 'a reward for forbearing the use of your own money for a term of time agreed upon'; similarly, Exchange is 'local interest, or a reward for having your money at such a place where you most need the use of it.' The sentence 'labour is the father and active principle of wealth, as lands are the mother' occurs in his *Treatise of Taxes,* but is not introduced as original on the author's part.

Locke's own contributions to economics were occasioned by the financial problems which faced the new government after the revolution. His reflections on the rate of interest show the growing disfavour with which appeals for state interference were beginning to be met. He points out the obstacles to trade that are caused when the rate of interest is fixed by law, and he argues in favour of freedom for what he calls, in words which suggest Adam Smith, 'the natural interest of money.' Money 'turns the wheels of trade';

therefore its course should not be stopped. At the same time, he holds no general brief against the interference of the state in matters of commerce; nor is the language of the mercantilists foreign to him. Riches consist in plenty of gold and silver, for these command all the conveniences of life. Now, 'in a country not furnished with mines, there are but two ways of growing rich, either conquest or commerce.' For us commerce is the only way; and Locke condemns 'the amazing politics of some late reigns' which had 'let in other competitors with us for the sea.' In the concluding portion of *Some Considerations,* dealing with the currency, Locke laid stress on the importance of a uniform and stable measure of values; four years later, in his *Further Considerations,* he defended his view against the proposals, involving a depreciation of the standard, which William Lowndes, secretary of the treasury, had set forth in *An Essay for the amendment of the silver coins* (1695).

Locke's plea for toleration in matters of belief has become classical. His Common-Place Book shows that his mind was clear on the subject more than twenty years before the publication of his first Letter. The topic, indeed, was in the air all through his life, and affected him nearly. When he was a scholar at Westminster, the powers of the civil magistrate in religious matters were the subject of heated discussion between presbyterians and independents in the assembly of divines that held its sessions within a stone's throw of his dormitory; and, when he entered Christ Church, John Owen, a leader of the independents, had been recently appointed to the deanery. There had been many arguments for toleration before this time, but they had come from the weaker party in the state. Thus Jeremy Taylor's *Liberty of Prophesying* appeared in 1646, when the fortunes of his side had suffered a decline. For Owen the credit is claimed that he was the first who argued for toleration 'when his party was uppermost[1].' He was called upon to preach before the House of Commons on 31 January 1649, and performed the task without making any reference to the tragic event of the previous day; but to the published sermon he appended a remarkable discussion on toleration. Owen did not take such high ground as Milton did, ten years later, in his *Treatise of Civil Power in Ecclesiastical Causes*—affirming that 'it is not lawful for any power on earth to compel in matters of religion.' He abounds in distinctions, and, indeed, his position calls for some subtlety. He holds that the

[1] Orme, W., 'Memoirs of John Owen,' prefixed to the latter's *Works,* 1826, vol. I, p. 76.

civil magistrate has duties to the church, and that he ought to give facilities and protection to its ministers, not merely as citizens, but as preachers of 'the truth'; on the other hand he argues that civil or corporal penalties are inappropriate as punishments for offences which are purely spiritual. The position ultimately adopted by Locke is not altogether the same as this. He was never an ardent puritan; he had as little taste for elaborate theologies as he had for scholastic systems of philosophy; and his earliest attempt at a theory of toleration was connected with the view that, in religion, 'articles in speculative opinions [should] be few and large, and ceremonies in worship few and easy.' The doctrines which he held to be necessary for salvation would have seemed to John Owen a meagre and pitiful creed. And he had a narrower view, also, of the functions of the state.

> The business of laws is not to provide for the truth of opinions, but for the safety and security of the commonwealth, and of every particular man's goods and person. And so it ought to be. For truth certainly would do well enough, if she were once left to shift for herself. She seldom has received, and I fear never will receive, much assistance from the power of great men, to whom she is but rarely known, and more rarely welcome. She is not taught by laws, nor has she any need of force, to procure her entrance into the minds of men. Errors, indeed, prevail by the assistance of foreign and borrowed succours. But if truth makes not her way into the understanding by her own light, she will be but the weaker for any borrowed force violence can add to her.

A church, according to Locke, is 'a free and voluntary society'; its purpose is the public worship of God; the value of this worship depends on the faith that inspires it: 'all the life and power of true religion consist in the inward and full persuasion of the mind'; and these matters are entirely outside the jurisdiction of the civil magistrate Locke, therefore, (to use later language) was a voluntary in religion, as he was an individualist on questions of state interference. There is an exception, however, to his doctrine of the freedom of the individual in religious matters. The toleration extended to all others is denied to papists and to atheists; and his inconsistency, in this respect, has been often and severely blamed. But it is clear that Locke made the exception not for religious reasons but on grounds of state policy. He looked upon the Roman Catholic as dangerous to the public peace because he professed allegiance to a foreign prince; and the atheist was excluded because, on Locke's view, the existence of the state depends upon a contract, and the obligation of the contract, as of all moral law, depends upon the Divine will.

Locke's theological writings exhibit the characteristic qualities which his other works have rendered familiar. The traditions of theologians are set aside in them much as philosophical tradition was discarded in the *Essay*. He will search the Scriptures for religious doctrine just as he turned to experience for his philosophy, and he follows a method equally straightforward. Locke does not raise questions of Biblical criticism, such as Hobbes had already suggested and some of his own followers put forward soon afterwards, and the conclusions at which he arrives are in harmony with the Christian faith, if without the fulness of current doctrine. At the same time, his work belongs to the history of liberal theology, and was intimately connected with the deism which followed; it treats religion like any other subject, and interprets the Bible like any other book; and, in his view of the nature of religion, he tends to describe it as if it consisted almost entirely in an attitude of intellectual belief—a tendency which became more prominent in the course of the eighteenth century.

Locke's *Thoughts concerning Education* and his *Conduct of the Understanding* occupy an important place in the history of educational theory, though only a scanty reference can be made to them here. The subject had a right to prominence in his thought. The stress he laid on experience in the growth of mind led him to magnify, perhaps overmuch, the power of education. He held that 'the minds of children [are] as easily turned, this way or that, as water itself.' He underrated innate differences: 'we are born with faculties and powers, capable almost of anything'; but, 'as it is in the body, so it is in the mind, practice makes it what it is.' Along with this view went a profound conviction of the importance of education, and of the breadth of its aim. It has to fit men for life—for the world, rather than for the university. Instruction in knowledge does not exhaust it; it is essentially a training of character.

Locke had the gift of making philosophy speak the language of ordinary life. As a consequence, his writings were followed by a whole literature of attack and defence. Of his critics Stillingfleet was the most prominent; he breathed an atmosphere of controversy, and his powers were displayed on many fields; he was not Locke's equal in intellectual fence; but he was a formidable opponent, and the difficulties in Locke's doctrine were pressed home by him with no little power. Among Locke's other critics were John Sergeant (who asserted *Solid Philosophy* 'against the fancies of the Ideists'),

Henry Lee, William Sherlock, archbishop King, John Broughton, and Thomas Burnet (author of *Sacra telluris theoria*). Another Thomas Burnet, of Kemnay, in Aberdeenshire, was the intermediary through whom Locke received the *Reflexions* of Leibniz upon the *Essay*. The *Nouveaux Essais* of Leibniz, in which the doctrines of the *Essay* were criticised, section by section, were ready for publication when Locke's death occurred, but, owing to this event, their appearance was postponed indefinitely. Amongst the writers who sided with Locke were Samuel Bold, Vincent Perronet, and Mrs Catherine Cockburn. Two other writers of the period deserve further mention on their own account. These are Richard Burthogge and John Norris.

Burthogge had no great reputation in his own day, and was almost entirely forgotten afterwards, till recent historians drew attention to his merits. His chief work, *An Essay upon Reason and the Nature of Spirits*, was published in 1694 and dedicated to Locke 'as to a person... acknowledged by all the learned world for one of the greatest masters of reason.' But he cannot be counted either as a follower or as a critic of Locke. His characteristic doctrines had been expressed in an earlier work, *Organum vetus et novum*, published in 1678. He had come into contact independently with the Cartesian reform; he was acquainted (though he did not sympathise) with the work of Malebranche; and he may have been influenced directly by Geulincx, who was lecturing in the university of Leyden when Burthogge studied medicine there and, in 1662, graduated M.D. Burthogge's object was to reconcile the experimental or mechanical with the scholastic method. His most striking doctrine, however, concerns the subjective factor in knowledge, and this led to his assertion of the relativity of all knowledge. What Descartes and Locke had said of the secondary qualities is generalised. The understanding apprehends things only by its own notions: these are to it what colours are to the eye or sounds to the ear; whole and part, substance and accident, cause and effect are but 'entities of reason conceived within the mind,' and 'have no more of any real true existence without it, than colours have without the eye, or sounds without the ear.' With this radical doctrine of relativity, Burthogge combined a neoplatonic metaphysic. He held that there is one spirit that actuates and acts in all, in men as well as in nature, and that the spirit of nature is not (as Henry More taught) an incorporeal substance, but simply the 'plastic faculty' of the spirit of God.

John Norris, fellow of All Souls, and rector of Bemerton, was a man of much greater and more enduring reputation. He was also a voluminous author of discourses, letters, and poems, as well as of the longer and more systematic work on which his fame depends, *An Essay towards the Theory of the Ideal or Intelligible World*, the first part of which was published in 1701, and the second in 1704. In temper of mind, Norris may be regarded as the antithesis of Locke. He represents mysticism as against the latter's critical empiricism. But it would be a mistake to regard him as lacking in clearness of logical faculty. He was diffuse, and his argument would sometimes break off into devotional reflection, or into verse; but, from these digressions, he would return to the argument refreshed and ready to abide by its logic. Different as he is from Locke, both exhibit the powerful influence that swept over European thought from the mind of Descartes. But Locke was critical of the more speculative elements in the philosophy of Descartes, whereas these were the thoughts that appealed most strongly to Norris. The course of his studies, especially in Plato and St Augustine, and the tone of his mind, made him welcome the speculative, if mystical, development of Cartesianism due to Father Malebranche. Malebranche had a number of followers in England at this time; and two translations of the *Recherche de la Vérité* appeared in the year 1694; but Norris was the only writer of note who adopted his views; and his importance is due to the fact that he was no mere follower. He had thought out—one may even say, he had lived— the theory for himself. In his work, he considers the ideal theory, first, as it is in itself, and then, in its relation to our knowledge. He holds that the very nature or essences of things (as distinguished from their existence) are Divine ideas or 'degrees of being in the Divine nature[1]'; and by the same theory he explains our perception of things. "'Tis generally allowed that the things without us are not perceived immediately by themselves, but by their ideas. The only question is, by what ideas, or what these ideas are?' His answer to this question is, that they are the Divine ideas, or, in the words of Malebranche, that we 'see all things in God[2].'

---

[1] *Ideal or Intelligible World*, vol. i, p. 232.　　　[2] *Ibid.* vol. ii, pp. 442—3.

# CHAPTER XV

## THE PROGRESS OF SCIENCE

WITH one or two exceptions—astronomy on the physical side, human anatomy on the biological—the reawakening in science lagged a century or more behind the renascence in literature and in art. What the leaders of thought and of practice in the arts of writing, of painting and of sculpture in western Europe were effecting in the latter part of the fifteenth and throughout the sixteenth century began to be paralleled in the investigations of the physical laws of nature only at the end of the sixteenth century and throughout the first three quarters of the seventeenth.

Writing broadly, we may say that, during the Stewart time, the sciences, as we now class them, were slowly but surely separating themselves out from the general mass of learning, segregating into secondary units; and, from a general amalgam of scientific knowledge, mathematics, astronomy, physics, chemistry, geology, mineralogy, zoology, botany, agriculture, even physiology (the off-spring of anatomy and chemistry) were beginning to assert claims to individual and distinct existence. It was in the Stewart reigns that, in England at any rate, the specialist began to emerge from those who hitherto had 'taken all knowledge to be' their 'province.'

Certain of the sciences, such as anatomy, physiology and, to a great extent, zoology and botany, had their inception in the art of medicine. But the last two owed much to the huntsman and the agriculturist. During the preceding century, the great Belgian anatomist Vesalius had broken loose from the bond of the written word which had strangled research for a thousand years, and had looked at the structure of the human body for himself; he taught what he could himself see and what he could show to his pupils. Under him, anatomy was the first of the natural sciences to break loose from the scholastic domination which had hitherto ever placed authority above experiment.

As anatomy on the biological side, so astronomy on the physical, led the way. Copernicus had claimed that the sun was the centre of our system; but it was not until the following century, when the truth of his views was mathematically proved, that, first, men of science, and, later, the world at large, abandoned the views of Ptolemy, which, like those of Aristotle, of Galen and of Hippocrates, had obsessed the learned world since classical times.

The great outburst of scientific enquiry which occurred during the seventeenth century was partly the result, and partly the cause, of the invention of numerous new methods and innumerable new instruments, by the use of which advance in natural knowledge was immensely facilitated. Early in the century (1614), Napier of Merchiston had made known his discovery of logarithms, and logarithmic tables were first published in 1617. Seven years later, the slide rule, which today plays a large part in physical and engineering science, was invented by Edmund Gunter. Decimals were coming into use and, at the close of the sixteenth century, algebra was being written in the notation we still employ. William Gilbert, physician to queen Elizabeth, published his experiments on electricity and magnetism in the last year of the sixteenth century. Galileo was using his newly constructed telescope; and, for the first time, Jupiter's satellites, the mountains in the moon and Saturn's rings were seen by human eye. The barometer, the thermometer and the air pump, and, later, the compound microscope, all came into being at the earlier part of our period, and by the middle of the century were in the hands of whoever cared to use them. Pepys, in 1664, acquired

a microscope and a scotoscope. For the first I did give him £5. 10. 0, a great price, but a most curious bauble it is, and he says, as good, nay, the best he knows in England. The other he gives me, and is of value; and a curious curiosity it is to discover objects in a dark room with.

Two years later, on 19 August 1666 'comes by agreement Mr Reeves, bringing me a lantern'—it must have been a magic lantern—'with pictures in glass, to make strange things appear on a wall, very pretty.'

As we pass from Elizabethan to Stewart times, we pass, in most branches of literature, from men of genius to men of talent, clever men, but not, to use a Germanism, epoch-making men. In science, however, where England led the world, the descent became an ascent. We leave Dr Dee and Edward Kelly, and we arrive at Harvey and Newton.

The gap between the medieval science which still obtained in queen Elizabeth's time and the science of the Stewarts was bridged by Francis Bacon, in a way, but only in a way. He was a reformer of the scientific method[1]. He was no innovator in the inductive method ; others had preceded him, but he, from his great position, clearly pointed out that the writers and leaders of his time observed and recorded facts in favour of ideas other than those hitherto sanctioned by authority.

Bacon left a heritage to English science. His writings and his thoughts are not always clear, but he firmly held, and, with the authority which his personal eminence gave him, firmly proclaimed, that the careful and systematic investigation of natural phenomena and their accurate record would give to man a power in this world which, in his time, was hardly to be conceived. What he believed, what he preached, he did not practise. 'I only sound the clarion, but I enter not into the battle'; and yet this is not wholly true, for, on a wintry March day, 1626, in the neighbourhood of Barnet, he caught the chill which ended his life while stuffing a fowl with snow, to see if cold would delay putrefaction. Harvey, who was working whilst Bacon was writing, said of him : 'He writes philosophy like a Lord Chancellor.' This, perhaps, is true, but his writings show him a man, weak and pitiful in some respects, yet with an abiding hope, a sustained object in life, one who sought through evil days and in adverse conditions 'for the glory of God and the relief of man's estate.'

Though Bacon did not make any one single advance in natural knowledge—though his precepts, as Whewell reminds us, 'are now practically useless'—yet he used his great talents, his high position, to enforce upon the world a new method of wrenching from nature her secrets and, with tireless patience and untiring passion, impressed upon his contemporaries the conviction that there was 'a new unexplored Kingdom of Knowledge within the reach and grasp of man, if he will be humble enough, and patient enough, and truthful enough to occupy it.'

The most sublime of English poets survived into our period by a few years. A comparison between Dante's and Milton's great epics affords some indication of the advance in knowledge of this world and in the outlook on a future state which measures the progress made between the Middle Ages and the seventeenth century. As a poet (and, indeed, often in other activities of his life) Milton stood above, or at least, outside, the stream of tendency of the times through which he lived. Yet, in his poems (not in his

[1] Cf. as to Bacon and ' the new method,' *ante*, vol. IV, pp. 278 ff.

political tractates—the most ephemeral of all literature) we see effects of the rising tide of science on literature.

Milton, one must never forget—and indeed, it is not easy to do so—was, for some years, a schoolmaster. He took a view of his profession which even now would be thought liberal; he advocated the teaching of medicine, agriculture and fortification, and, when studying the last of these, remarked that it would be 'seasonable to learn the use of the Globes and all the maps.' Like lord Herbert of Cherbury, he held that the student should acquire some knowledge of medicine, he should know 'the tempers, the humours, the seasons and how to manage a crudity.' Himself, a sufferer from gout, he learnt, at any rate, the lesson of moderation. Mathematics, in his curriculum, led to the 'instrumental science of Trigonometry and from thence to Fortification, Architecture, Enginry or Navigation.'

At the time of the writing of *Paradise Lost*, the learned had accepted the theory of Copernicus, although the mathematical proof afforded a few years later by Newton was still lacking. But the world at large still accepted the Ptolemaic system, a system which, as a schoolmaster, Milton taught. Mark Pattison has pointed out that these two

systems confront each other in the poem, in much the same relative position which they occupied in the mind of the public. The ordinary, habitual mode of speaking of celestial phenomena is Ptolemaic[1]; the conscious or doctrinal exposition of the same phenomena is Copernican[2].

But the incongruity between these two statements is no greater than will be found today in authors writing of subjects still *sub judice*. Further, we must not forget that Milton never saw either of his great epics in writing or in print. His power of impressing his visions on the world was, however, such that Huxley held that it was not the cosmogony of *Genesis* but the cosmogony of Milton which had enthralled and misled the world.

More distinctly than in his epics, Milton, in his history, showed a leaning to the scientific method. Firth has lately told us that 'his conclusions are roughly those of modern scholars, and his reasoning practically that of a scientific historian.' In one respect, however, he was less than lukewarm. He had no sympathy with antiquarian researches and sneered at those 'who take pleasure to be all their lifetime raking the foundations of old abbeys and cathedrals.'

[1] Mark Pattison cites *Paradise Lost*, vɪɪ, 339—356; ɪɪɪ, 420, 481. And yet, in 1639, Milton had visited Galileo.

[2] See *ibid.* vɪɪɪ, 77, 122—140.

To turn to other evidence, the better diaries of any age afford us, when faithfully written, as fair a clue as do the dramatists of the average intelligent man's attitude towards the general outlook of humanity on the problems of his age, as they presented themselves to society at large. The seventeenth century was unusually rich in volumes of autobiography and in diaries which the reading world will not readily let die. Some account has been already given[1] of the autobiography of the complaisant lord Herbert of Cherbury; it is again noticed here as giving an interesting account of the education of a highly-born youth at the end of the sixteenth and the beginning of the seventeenth century. Lord Herbert seems to have had a fair knowledge of Latin and Greek and of logic when, in his thirteenth year, he went up to University college, Oxford. Later, he 'did attain the knowledge of the French, Italian and Spanish languages,' and, also, learnt to sing his part at first sight in music and to play on the lute. He approved of 'so much logic as to enable men to distinguish between truth and falsehood and help them to discover fallacies, sophisms and that which the schoolmen call vicious arguments'; and this, he considered, should be followed by 'some good sum of philosophy.' He held it also requisite to study geography, and this in no narrow sense, laying stress upon the methods of government, religions and manners of the several states as well as on their relationships *inter se* and their policies. Though he advocated an acquaintance with 'the use of the celestial globes,' he did 'not conceive yet the knowledge of judicial astronomy so necessary, but only for general predictions; particular events being neither intended by nor collected out of the stars.' Arithmetic and geometry he thought fit to learn, as being most useful for keeping accounts and enabling a gentleman to understand fortifications.

Perhaps the most characteristic feature of lord Herbert's acquirements was his knowledge of medicine and subjects allied thereto. He conceived it a 'fine study, and worthy a gentleman to be a good botanic, that so he may know the nature of all herbs and plants.' Further, 'it will become a gentleman to have some knowledge in medecine, especially the diagnostic part'; and he urged that a gentleman should know how to make medicines himself. He gives us a list of the 'pharmacopaeias and anechodalies' which he has in his own library and certainly he had a knowledge of anatomy and of the healing art—he refers to a wound which penetrated to his father's 'pia mater,' a membrane for a mention

[1] See *ante*, vol. VII, pp. 204—5.

of which we should look in vain among the records of modern ambassadors and gentlemen of the court. His knowledge, however, was entirely empirical and founded on the writings of Paracelsus and his followers; nevertheless, he prides himself on the cures he effected, and, if one can trust the veracity of so self-satisfied an amateur physician, they certainly fall but little short of the miraculous.

John Evelyn, another example of a well-to-do and widely cultivated man of the world[1], was acquainted with several foreign languages, including Spanish and German, and took interest in hieroglyphics. He studied medicine in 1645 at Padua, and there acquired those 'rare tables of veins and nerves' which he afterwards gave to the Royal Society; attended Le Felure's course of chemistry at Paris in 1647, was skilled in more than one musical instrument, learned dancing and, above all, devoted himself to horticulture.

When travelling abroad, he made a point of visiting the 'cabinets' of collectors, for, at that time, public museums, which, in fact, grew out of these cabinets, were non-existent. The following quotation records the sort of curiosities at which men marvelled in the year 1645:

Feb. 4th. We were invited to the collection of exotic rarities in the museum of Ferdinando Imperati, a Neapolitan nobleman, and one of the most observable palaces in the citty, the repository of incomparable rarities. Amongst the naturall herbals most remarkable was the Byssus marina and Pinna marina; the male and female cameleon; an Onacratulus; an extraordinary greate crocodile; some of the Orcades Anates, held here for a great rarity; likewise a salamander; the male and female Manucodiata, the male having an hollow in the back, in wch 'tis reported the female both layes and hatches her egg; the mandragoras of both sexes; Papyrus made of severall reedes, and some of silke; tables of the rinds of trees written wth Japoniq characters; another of the branches of palme; many Indian fruites; a chrystal that had a quantity of uncongealed water within its cavity; a petrified fisher's net; divers sorts of tarantulas, being a monstrous spider with lark-like clawes, and somewhat bigger.

But Evelyn's chief contribution to science, as already indicated, was horticultural. He was devoted to his garden, and, both at his native Wotton, and, later, at Sayes court, Deptford, spent much time in planting and planning landscape gardens, then much the fashion.

In the middle of the sixteenth century, the fact that 'nitre' promoted the growth of plants was beginning to be recognised. Sir Kenelm Digby and the young Oxonian John Mayow, experimented *de Sal-Nitro*; and, in 1675, Evelyn writes: 'I firmly believe that where saltpetre can be obtained in plenty we should not need to find other composts to ameliorate our ground.' His

---

[1] See *ante*, chap. x.

well known *Sylva*, published in 1664, had an immediate and a widespread effect, and was, for many years, the standard book on the subject of the culture of trees. It is held to be responsible for a great outbreak of tree-planting. The introduction to Nisbet's edition gives figures which demonstrate the shortage in the available supply of oak timber during the seventeenth century. The charm of Evelyn's style and the practical nature of his book, which ran into four editions before the author's death, arrested this decline ('be aye sticking in a tree ; it will be growing, Jock, when ye're sleeping' as the laird of Dumbiedykes counselled his son), and to the *Sylva* of John Evelyn is largely due the fact that the oaken timber used for the British ships which fought the French in the eighteenth century sufficed, but barely sufficed, for the national needs.

Pepys[1], whose naïve and frank self-revelations have made him the most popular and the most frequently read of diarists, was not quite of the same class of student to which lord Herbert of Cherbury or John Evelyn belonged. But, gifted as he was with an undying and insatiable curiosity, nothing was too trivial or too odd for his notice and his record ; and, being an exceptionally able and hard-working government servant, he took great interest in anything which was likely to affect the navy. He discoursed with the ingenious Dr Kuffler 'about his design to blow up ships,' noticed 'the strange nature of the sea-water in a dark night, that it seemed like fire upon every stroke of the oar '—an effect due, of course, to phosphorescent organisms floating near the surface—and interested himself incessantly in marine matters. His troubled eyesight and his love of music account for the attention he paid to optical appliances, the structure of the eye, musical instruments of every kind and musical notation; for this last, he seems to have invented a system which is still preserved at Magdalene college, but which no one now understands.

Physiology and mortuary objects had, for him, an interest which was almost morbid. He is told that 'negroes drounded look white, and lose their blackness, which I never heard before,' describes how 'one of a great family was... hanged with a silken halter... of his own preparing, not for the honour only' but because it strangles more quickly. He attended regularly the early meetings of the Royal Society at Gresham college, and showed the liveliest interest in various investigations on the transfusion of blood, respiration under reduced air pressure and many other ingenious experiments

and observations by Sir George Ent and others.   On 20 January
1665, he took home *Micrographia*, Hooke's book on microscopy—
' a most excellent piece, of which I am very proud.'

Although Pepys had no scientific training—he only began to
learn the multiplication table when he was in his thirtieth year,
but, later, took the keenest pleasure in teaching it to Mrs Pepys—
he, nevertheless, attained to the presidentship of the Royal Society.
He had always delighted in the company of 'the virtuosos' and, in
1662, three years after he began to study arithmetic, he was
admitted a fellow of their—the Royal—Society.   In 1681, he was
elected president. This post he owed, not to any genius for science,
or to any great invention or generalisation, but to his very exceptional powers as an organiser and as a man of business, to his
integrity and to the abiding interest he ever showed in the cause
of the advancement of knowledge.

If we pass from the interest taken in scientific progress by men
of superior intelligence to the obstacles opposed to it by popular
ignorance and superstition, we are brought face to face with the
long-lived crew of witches, wizards and alchemists.   It is often
said that the more rationalistic outlook of the seventeenth century,
due to Hobbes and others, did much to discredit these practitioners.
But the observant dwellers in our cities or remote country villages,
pestered as they are with advertisements of those who practise
palmistry, and of those who predict the future by crystal-gazing
or by the fall of sand, of followers of the sporting prophet,
and of far more presumptuous and more dangerous impostors,
or confronted by the silent, indomitable belief of the rustic in
the witchery of his ancestors, may well hold the opinion that the
stock of superstition is a constant stock and permeates now, as it
did in Elizabeth's time, every class of society.   What improvement
there was in the seventeenth century, and it is extremely doubtful
if there was much, was largely due to the advent of James I and
the later rise of puritanism, associated as they were with the most
cruel and most inhuman torture of sorcerers.   When the alchemist
and the astrologer ran the risk of suffering as a sorcerer or a
warlock, he paused before publicly embarking on the trade.

Under the Tudors, the laws against witchcraft were milder than
those of other countries, but, under James I, these laws were
repealed and he himself took—as he had done before in Scotland—
an active part in this cruel and senseless persecution.   During the
first eighty years of the seventeenth century, no less than 70,000
men and women are said to have been executed for alleged offences

under the new act. The king even wrote a book on demonology, attacking the more sensible and reasonable views of Scot and Wier. It must be remembered, however, that, in these times, the generality of learned and able men believed in the maleficent effects of sorcery and the black art. The bench of bishops and the bench of judges alike took part in what seems to us a hideous and wanton brutality. Even so great a writer as Sir Thomas Browne, who tells us, 'for the sorrows of others he has quick sympathy,' gave evidence against two unhappy women charged before Sir Matthew Hale at Bury St Edmunds, and his evidence helped to secure their iniquitous conviction.

Browne, like many of his day, was a firm believer in horoscopes— 'I was born in the planetary hour of Saturn and I think I have a piece of that leaden planet in me.' He was, however, perhaps a little in advance of some of his contemporaries; at any rate, he recognised that foretellings based on star-gazing do not always 'make good.' 'We deny not the influence of the stars but often suspect the due application thereof.' During the civil war, both sides used astrologers and acted on their prognostications; but, on the whole, the firm belief that future events could be foretold by a study of the planetary system was waning. 'They' (*i.e.* the stars) 'incline but do not compel... and so gently incline that a wise man may resist them; *sapiens dominabitur astris :* they rule but God rules them[1].' This was said by Robert Burton, and it probably represents the average opinion of the more educated in our period.

The part played by alchemy in the life of the times can be judged by Ben Jonson's *Alchemist,* first acted in 1610[2], which affords a true insight into the fashionable craze of the time. The play was constantly presented from that date until the closing of the theatres and, on the restoration, was one of the first plays to be revived. Jonson certainly had mastered the jargon of this form of quackery, and showed a profound knowledge of the art of its professors. In *Epicoene, or the Silent Woman,* he refers to the love philtres of one Forman, a most flagrant rascal who was mixed up with the Overbury trial.

It has been said that a competent man of science should be able to put into language 'understanded of the people' any problem, no matter how complex, at which he is working. This seems hardly possible in the twentieth century. To explain to a trained histologist

---

[1] *Anatomy of Melancholy,* part 1, sec. II, Mem. 1, sec. IV.
[2] Cf. *ante,* vol. VI, chap. I, pp. 22—23.

double $\theta$ functions or to a skilled mathematician the intricacies of karyokinesis would take a very long time. The introduction in all the sciences of technical words is not due to any spirit of perverseness on the part of modern *savants*; these terms, long as they usually are, serve as the shorthand of science. In the Stewart times, however, an investigator could explain in simple language to his friends what he was doing and the advance of natural science was keenly followed by all sorts and conditions of men.

Whatever were the political and moral deficiencies of the Stewart kings, no one of them lacked intelligence in things artistic and scientific. The pictures at Windsor and at Buckingham palace which the nation owes to Charles I and Charles II are only approached by those it owes to the knowledge and taste of queen Victoria's consort. At Whitehall, Charles II had his 'little elaboratory, under his closet, a pretty place[1],' and was working there but a day or two before his death, his illness disinclining him for his wonted exercise. The king took a curious interest in anatomy; on 11 May 1663, Pierce, the surgeon, tells Pepys 'that the other day Dr Clerke and he did dissect two bodies, a man and a woman before the King with which the King was highly pleased.' Pepys also records, 17 February 1662/3, on the authority of Edward Pickering, another story of a dissection in the royal closet by the king's own hands.

It has, I think, seldom been pointed out that Charles II's ancestry accounts for many of his qualities and especially for his interest in science. He was very unlike his father, but his mother was the daughter of a Medici princess, and the characteristics of that family are strongly marked in the 'merry monarch.' His gaiety and wit and his skill in money matters when he chose to apply himself, all bring to mind the Italian family from which he sprang[2].

Another royal personage, prince Rupert, 'full of spirit and action, full of observation and judgement,' about this time invented his 'chemical glasses which break all to dust by breaking off a little small end: which is a great mystery to me[3].' He had,

---

[1] Pepys, 15 Jan. 1669.

[2] Even the swarthy complexion of Charles II was probably due to his Italian blood, and his fondness for outdoor sports is another trait which is often observed in the Medici themselves. There is an old engraving of a portrait of Lorenzo (d. 1648), the brother of Cosimo II, which shows an astonishing resemblance to Charles II; and it is interesting to remember that Cosimo II earned his chief claim to the gratitude of posterity by his courageous encouragement, protection and support of Galileo, who owed to him the opportunity and means of making his famous astronomical discoveries.

[3] Pepys, 13 Jan. 1662.

says Gramont, *quelques talens* for chemistry and invented a new
method for making gunpowder, for making 'hails hot' and for
boring cannon.  His traditional invention of the almost lost art of
mezzotint is probably due to the fact that, at an early date, the real
inventor, Ludwig von Siegen, explained to him his process and that
prince Rupert demonstrated with his own hands this new method
of engraving to Evelyn.

Another aristocratic inventor, Edward Somerset, second marquis
of Worcester, has received more credit than he deserved.  He was
interested in mechanics and employed a skilled mechanician, one
Kaltoff, in his laboratory, but his claims to have invented a steam-
engine do not bear critical investigation, and his well known *Century of Inventions* does not rise to the level of *The Boy's Own
Book* of the last century.  Many of his suggestions, though ingenious,
are based on fallacies, and comparatively few of them were practical.

A curiously versatile amateur in science was Sir Kenelm Digby,
of whom mention has already been made elsewhere[1].  Like most
prominent men of his time, he intervened in theological questions,
besides playing an active part in public affairs.  He was an original
member of the Royal Society, but, although he is reported to have
been the first to record the importance of the 'vital air'—we now
call it oxygen—to plants, and although he had gifts of observation,
his work lay largely in the paths of alchemy and astrology, and he
seems to have had recourse to a lively imagination in estimating
the results of his experiments.  He trafficked in the transmutation
of metals, and his name was long associated with a certain 'powder
of sympathy' which, like the 'absent treatment' of the twentieth
century practitioners of Christian science, 'acted at a distance.'
Evelyn looked on him as a quack, 'a teller of strange things,' and
lady Fanshawe refers to his infirmity of lying ; he was certainly a
great talker.  Still, other men of his epoch spoke well of him and
his conversation was doubtless stimulating if profuse.

In mathematics, John Wallis was, to some extent, a forerunner
of Newton.  At Felsted school and at Emmanuel college, he received the curiously wide education of his age.  He was a skilled
linguist ; although he had taken holy orders, he was the first of
Francis Glisson's pupils to proclaim in public Harvey's discovery
of the circulation of the blood, but his bent was towards mathematics, and he possessed an extraordinary memory for figures.  His
*Arithmetica Infinitorum* is described as 'the most stimulating

[1] See *ante*, vol. VII, chap. IX, pp. 222—3.

mathematical work so far published in England.' It contained the germs of the differential calculus, and it suggested to Newton, who 'read it with delight,' the binomial theorem. In it $\pi$ was evaluated, and it must not be forgotten that to Wallis we owe the symbol for infinity, $\infty$. Living in troublesome times, under many rulers, he contrived, not without some loss of popularity, to remain on good terms with all. His services were, indeed, indispensable to a succession of governments, for he had a power of deciphering which was almost miraculous. Cromwell, who seems to have had a great respect for his powers, appointed him Savilian professor of geometry at Oxford in 1649.

Another mathematical ecclesiastic was Seth Ward, bishop of Exeter and afterwards of Salisbury. Ward was educated at Sidney Sussex college and. in 1643, was chosen as mathematical lecturer to the university at Cambridge. But, like Wallis, he was appointed, and in the same year, to a Savilian professorship, that of astronomy—another instance, not, uncommon at the time, of men educated at Cambridge but recognised and promoted at Oxford. He took the place of the ejected John Greaves, who magnanimously used his influence in his successor's favour. Ward was renowned as a preacher; but his later fame rested chiefly on his contributions to the science of astronomy, and he is remembered in the world of science mainly for his theory of planetary motion. Ward and Wallis—but the burden of the attack was borne by the latter—laid bare Hobbes's attempted proof of the squaring of the circle; there was also a little controversy 'on the duplication of the cube,' and mixed up with these criticisms in the realm of pure reason were political motives. Hobbes had not begun to study Euclid until he was forty; and, after Sir Henry Savile had founded his professorships at Oxford, Wood says that not a few of the foolish gentry 'kept back their sons' in order not 'to have them smutted by the black art'—so great was the fear and the ignorance of the powers of mathematics. Ward was a pluralist, as was the manner of the times, and Burnet tells us 'he was a profound statesman but a very indifferent clergyman.' Yet, what money he got he lavishly spent on ecclesiastical and other purposes[1].

---

[1] As bishop of Exeter, he restored, at the cost of £25,000, the cathedral; repaired the palace; considerably increased the value of the poorer benefices of his diocese and of the prebends of his cathedral; and gave a considerable sum of money towards the cost of making the river navigable from his cathedral city to the sea. He founded the Seth Ward almshouses at Salisbury, and he gave certain farms and fee-farm rents for scholarships at Christ's college, Cambridge.

Like the distinguished mathematicians just mentioned, Isaac Newton took a keen interest in certain forms of theology current in his day; but in his intellectual powers he surpassed not only them but all living mathematicians and those who lived after him. His supreme genius has ensured him a place in the very small list of the world's thinkers of the first order. He, too, exercised a certain influence in affairs, and, during his later years, he took a keen interest in theological speculations; but his activities in these fields are completely overshadowed by the far-reaching importance of his great discoveries as a natural philosopher and a mathematician. As the discoverer of the decomposition of white light in the spectrum, he may be regarded as the founder of the modern science of optics. His discovery of the law of gravitation, and his application of it to the explanation of Kepler's laws of planetary motion and of the principal inequalities in the orbital motion of the moon made him the founder of the science of gravitational astronomy. His discovery of the method of fluxions entitles him to rank with Leibniz as one of the founders of mathematical analysis. All these great discoveries gave rise to long and sometimes acrimonious controversies among his contemporaries, relating both to the subjects themselves and to priority of discovery. In a letter to Halley referring to one of these disputes, Newton writes:

Philosophy is such an impertinently litigious lady, that a man has as good be engaged in lawsuits, as have to do with her. I found it so formerly, and now I am no sooner come near her again, but she gives me warning.

His chief work, *Principia*, has been described by dean Peacock as 'the greatest single triumph of the human mind[1].'

The second man of outstanding genius in British science in the seventeenth century was Harvey, who, like Newton, worked in one of the two sciences which, in Stewart times, were, to some extent, ahead of all the others. Harvey, 'the little choleric man' as Aubrey calls him, was educated at Cambridge and at Padua and was in his thirty-eighth year when, in his lectures on anatomy, he expounded his new doctrine of the circulation of the blood to the college of Physicians, although his *Exercitatio* on this subject did not appear till 1628. His notes for the lectures are now in the British Museum. He was physician to Charles I; and it is on record how, during the battle of Edgehill, he looked after the young princes as he sat reading a book under a hedge a little removed from the fight.

In the chain of evidence of his convincing demonstration of the

[1] Newton held the office of president of the Royal Society for the last twenty-five years of his life, a period exceeded only in the case of one president, Sir Joseph Banks.

circulation of the blood, one link, only to be supplied by the invention of the compound microscope, was missing. This, the discovery of the capillaries, was due to Malpighi, who was amongst the earliest anatomists to apply the compound microscope to animal tissues. Still, as Dryden has it,

> The circling streams once thought but pools of blood—
> (Whether life's fuel or the body's food),
> From dark oblivion Harvey's name shall save [1].

Harvey was happy in two respects as regards his discovery, It was, in the main and especially in England, recognised as proven in his own lifetime, and, again, no one of credit claimed or asserted the claim of others to priority. In research, all enquirers stand on steps others have built up; but, in this, the most important of single contributions to physiology, the credit is Harvey's and almost Harvey's alone. His other great work, *Exercitationes de Generatione Animalium*, is of secondary importance. It shows marvellous powers of observation and very laborious research; but, although, to a great extent, it led the way in embryology, it was shortly superseded by works of those who had the compound microscope at their command. Cowley, a man of wide culture, wrote an *Ode on Harvey* in which his achievement was contrasted with a failing common to scientific men of his own time, and, so far as we can see, of all time:

> *Harvey* sought for Truth in Truth's own Book
> The Creatures, which by God Himself was writ;
>    And wisely thought 'twas fit,
> Not to read Comments only upon it,
> But on th' original it self to look.
> Methinks in Arts great Circle, others stand
>    Lock't up together, Hand in Hand,
>    Every one leads as he is led,
>    The same bare path they tread,
> A Dance like Fairies a Fantastick round,
> But neither change their motion, nor their ground:
> Had *Harvey* to this Road confin'd his wit,
> His noble Circle of the Blood, had been untroden yet.

Harvey's death is recorded in a characteristic seventeenth century sentence, taken from the unpublished pages of Baldwin Harvey's *Bustorum Aliquot Reliquiae* :

Of William Harvey, the most fortunate anatomist, the blood ceased to move on the third day of the Ides of June, in the year 1657, the continuous movement of which in all men, moreover he had most truly asserted ...

Ἐν τε τροχῷ πάντες καὶ ἐνὶ πᾶσι τροχοί [2].

---

[1] Epistle to Dr Charleton.

[2] The writer is indebted for this quotation to Dr Norman Moore's *History of the Study of Medicine in the British Isles*, Oxford, 1908.

Among other great physiologists and physicians, Sir Theodore Turquet de Mayerne (godson of Theodore Beza), who settled in London in 1611, has left us *Notes* of the diseases of the great which, to the medically minded, are of the greatest interest. He almost diagnosed enteric, and his observations on the fatal illness of Henry, prince of Wales, and the memoir he drew up in 1623 on the health of James I, alike leave little to be desired in completeness or in accuracy of detail.

Before bringing to a close these short notices of those who studied and wrote on the human body, whole or diseased, a few lines must be given to John Mayow of Oxford, who followed the law, 'especially in the summer time at Bath.' Yet, from his contributions to science, one might well suppose that he had devoted his whole time to research in chemistry and physiology. He it was who showed that, in respiration, not the whole air but a part only of the air breathed in takes an active part in respiration, though he called this part 'by a different name, he meant what we now call oxygen[1].'

Thomas Sydenham was one of the first physicians who was convinced of the importance of constant and prolonged observation at the bedside of the patient. He passed by all authority but one—'the divine old man Hippocrates,' whose medicine rested also on observation. He, first in England, 'attempted to arrive at general laws about the prevalence and the course and the treatment of disease from clinical observation.' He was essentially a physician occupied in diagnosis, treatment and prognosis. When he was but 25 years old, he began to suffer from gout, and his personal experience enabled him to write a classic on this disease, which is even now unsurpassed.

Francis Glisson, like Sydenham, was essentially English in his upbringing, and did not owe anything to foreign education. His work on the liver has made 'Glisson's capsule' known to every medical student, and he wrote an authoritative book on rickets. He, like Harvey, was educated at Gonville and Caius college, and, in 1636, became regius professor of physic at Cambridge, but the greater part of his life he spent at Colchester. We must perforce pass by the fashionable Thomas Willis and his more capable assistant Richard Lower, with Sir George Ent, and others.

Great as were the seventeenth century philosophers in the biological and medical sciences, they were paralleled if not surpassed by workers on the physical and mathematical side. Robert Boyle was, even as a boy of eighteen, one of the

[1] Foster, Sir Michael, *The History of Physiology*, Cambridge, 1901.

leaders in the comparatively new pursuit of experimental science. His first love was chemistry, 'Vulcan has so transported and bewitched me as to make me fancy my laboratory a kind of Elysium,' thus he wrote in 1649. A few years later (1652—3), in Ireland, where he was called to look after the family estates, he found it 'hard to have any Hermetic thoughts,' and occupied his mind with anatomy and confirming Harvey's discovery of the circulation of the blood. A year later, he settled at Oxford, where he arranged a laboratory and had as assistant Robert Hooke. Meetings were held alternately at Boyle's lodgings and at John Wilkins's lodge at Wadham, and were frequented by Seth Ward and Christopher Wren and by many others.

Stimulated by Otto von Guericke's contrivance for exhausting air from a vessel, Boyle, aided by Hooke, invented what was called the 'machina Boyliana,' which comprised the essentials of the air-pump of today. At this time, Boyle busied himself with the weight, with the pressure and with the elasticity of air—the part it played in respiration and in acoustics. Like Newton, he took a deep interest in theology, and not only spent considerable sums in translating the Bible into foreign tongues, but learnt Greek, Hebrew, Syriac and Chaldee so that he might read it at first hand. He was, indeed, a very notable character. Suffering under continued ill-health, with weak eyes, a slight stammer, and a memory treacherous to the last degree, he was yet one of the most helpful of friends and universally popular alike at the court of three kings, and in the society of men of letters, men of business and men of science. In spite of the fact that he was the first to distinguish a mixture from a compound, to define an element, to prepare hydrogen, though he did not recognise its nature, he had in him the touch of an amateur, but an amateur of genius. His style in writing was unusually prolix and he seldom followed out his discoveries to their ultimate end.

It was men such as these that reestablished the Royal Society in 1660. Exactly a century earlier, the first scientific society, the *Academia Secretorum Naturae* of Naples had its origin. This was followed by several others, most of them but shortlived, in Italy and in France. Among English or Teutonic folk, the Royal Society was the earliest to appear, and, even if we include the scientific societies of the world, it has had the most continuous existence. Indeed, before its birth, it underwent a long period of incubation, and its inception was in reality in 1645. At that date, a society known as the Philosophical, or, as Boyle called it, the

'Invisible,' college came into being, which met from time to time at Gresham college and elsewhere in London. During the civil war, this society was split in two, some members meeting in London, some at Oxford, but the meetings, wherever held, were at irregular intervals. On the restoration, the meetings were resumed in London and, in 1662, the society received the royal charter.

Of all the poets of the time, Cowley took, perhaps, the greatest interest in science. He had, indeed, like Evelyn and at about the same date, developed a plan for the institution of a college of science. Evelyn explains his scheme in a letter addressed to Robert Boyle, dated 3 September 1659 from Sayes court, which contains minute details as to the buildings, the maintenance, and the government of his college, the inmates of which were to 'preserve science and cultivate themselves.' Cowley's scheme was also elaborately thought out, and had the original and admirable suggestion that, out of the twenty salaried professors, sixteen should be always resident and four always travelling in the four quarters of the world, in order that they might 'give a constant account of all things that belong to the learning and especially Natural Experimental Philosophy, of those parts.' To his 'Philosophical Colledge' was to be attached a school of two hundred boys. Both these schemes, according to bishop Sprat, hastened the foundation of the Royal Society, of which both projectors were original members.

Cowley's poems were greatly admired during his lifetime, later critics have considered him affected, perhaps because, like Donne, he understood, and was not afraid to use the technical language of the schools. We have quoted some of his lines on Harvey, and may add a few from the ode with which he greeted the birth of the Royal Society :

> From . . . . . . all long Errors of the way,
> In which our Praedecessors went,
> And like th' old *Hebrews* many years did stray
>     In Desarts but of small extent,
> *Bacon*, like *Moses*, led us forth at last
>     The barren Wilderness he past,
>     Did on the very Border stand
>     Of the blest promis'd Land,
> And from the Mountains Top of his Exalted Wit,
>     Saw it himself, and shewed us it.
> But Life did never to one Man allow
> Time to Discover Worlds, and Conquer too;
> Nor can so short a Line sufficient be
> To fadome the vast depths of Natures Sea :

The work he did we ought t' admire,
And were unjust if we should more require
From his few years, divided 'twixt th' Excess
Of low Affliction, and high Happiness.
For who on things remote can fix his sight,
That's alwayes in a Triumph, or a Fight?

Donne, who, like Cowley, indulged in quaint poetical conceits and who founded a new school of poetry, abjuring classical conventions and classical characters, and treating of topics and objects of everyday life, was not afraid of realism. 'Upon common objects,' Dr Johnson tells us, he was 'unnecessarily and unpoetically subtle.' Space limits us to one quotation:

Marke but this flea, and marke in this,
How little that which thou deny'st me is;
It suck'd me first, and now sucks thee,
And in this flea, our two bloods mingled bee.

Donne did not of course foresee the appalling part that these insects, by the habits he mentions, play in the spread of such diseases as bubonic plague and many epizootics in animals.

The dramatists of the Stewart period hardly afford us the help we need in estimating the position occupied by science and by men of science in the world of the seventeenth century. The astrologer and the alchemist were then stock characters of the drama of everyday life, just as the company promoter is now. 'The Gentlemen of Trinity Colledge' presented 'before the King's Majesty' a comedy entitled *Albumazar*, which takes its name from the chief character, an astrologer, a very arrant knave, and the type of the false man of science. This play, originally printed in 1615, was soon forgotten, but it was revived in 1668 and met with great success.

Samuel Butler, who was not a fellow of the Royal Society, for some reason difficult to explain, spent much time in attacking it. He wrote his entertaining satire on the *virtuosi* entitled *The Elephant in the Moon* in short verse, and was so pleased with it that he wrote it over again in long verse[1]. Though this 'Satire upon the Royal Society' remains a fragment, enough of it is extant to show Butler did not appreciate what even in these days is not always appreciated, that the minute investigation of subjects and objects which to the ordinary man seem trivial and vain often lead to discoveries of the profoundest import to mankind.

Ben Jonson, with his *flair* for presenting what zoologists call 'type species,' showed, as has been seen, in his *Alchemist*

---

[1] Cf. *ante*, chap. II.

an unusual, but a thorough, mastery of the half scientific and half quack jargon of the craft, so that this play is a quarry for all interested in the history of chemical and physical studies. To the play-writer of the time, the man of science or of pseudo-science was a vague, peevish pedant, much occupied with physiognomies, dreams and fantastic ideas as to the properties and powers of various substances. But there seems to have been a clear distinction drawn between a real and a false astrology, as is shown in Dryden's *An Evening's Love* (1668)[1].

The political economists of the seventeenth century

were greatly influenced by the Baconian enthusiasm for empirical study; they were eager to accumulate and interpret facts, and to apply inductive methods to political phenomena. They therefore concerned themselves with the anatomy of the body politic, and with numerical observations which served as the best available substitute for experiment. They followed the analogy of the biological rather than of the mathematical science of their day; hence, their mode of thought has a close affinity with that which has become current since the decline of the classical school of Political Economy[2].

Sir William Petty and the philosopher Locke are the best known names in this group of political economists. Locke, in particular, was interested in questions concerning the currency and the rate of interest. Sir William Petty, who was among the first to state clearly the nature of rent, wrote a celebrated *Treatise of Taxes and Contributions*[3]. Captain John Graunt's *Natural and Political Observations* marked the beginning of that interest in statistical data concerning health and population which is a distinguishing feature of modern economic research. Another writer, Samuel Fortrey, followed Petty in his endeavour to go behind the mere art of taxation and analyse the ultimate sources of national wealth in the land and labour of the country. In general, it may be said that, in the seventeenth century, political economy was still an art rather than a science. Between these writings and Adam Smith's *Wealth of Nations* (1776), there was a great gap; but the practical observations of the seventeenth century were not without use in supplying material for his scholarly and impartial analysis.

---

[1] Cf. *ante*, chap. I.
[2] Cunningham, *Growth of English Industry and Commerce*, vol. II, p. 880.
[3] Cf. *ante*, chap. XIV.

# CHAPTER XVI

## THE ESSAY AND THE BEGINNING OF MODERN ENGLISH PROSE

PERHAPS the most important literary achievement that falls within the period covered by this volume is the creation of a prose style, which, in structure if not in vocabulary, is essentially the same as that of today. Caroline prose, the prose of Milton and Taylor, of Browne and Clarendon, had produced, in the hands of genius, some of the noblest passages in our literature. But, at the restoration, men began to feel the need of an instrument upon which the everyday performer might play—an instrument suited to an age of reason, possessing, before all things, the homely virtues of simplicity, correctness, lucidity and precision. These qualities, indeed, were not unknown to English prose before the restoration. They are to be found in private letters, not meant for the public eye. Above all, they are to be found in the writings of the veteran Hobbes, who, like Bacon and Ben Jonson, with both of whom he had literary relations, disdained all superfluity of ornament, and was content to make his prose a terse and pregnant expression of a clear and vigorous intellect. But even Hobbes is by no means free from the besetting sins of the older prose—careless construction and trailing relative clauses.

The new prose was the work of a multiplicity of causes, all more or less reflecting the temper of the age. One of these was the growing interest in science, and the insistence of the new Royal Society on the need of a clear and plain style for scientific exposition.

There is one thing more about which the *Society* has been most solicitous; and that is the manner of their *Discourse*: which, unless they had been only watchful to keep in due temper, the whole spirit and vigour of their *Design* had been soon eaten out by the luxury and redundance of speech.... And, in few words, I dare say that of all the Studies of men, nothing may be sooner obtain'd than this vicious abundance of *Phrase*, this trick of *Metaphors*, this volubility of *Tongue*, which makes so great a noise in the *World*.... It will suffice my present purpose to point out what has been done by the *Royal*

*Society* towards the correcting of excesses in *Natural Philosophy*, to which it is of all others, a most profest enemy. They have therefore been most vigorous in putting in execution the only Remedy that can be found for this *extravagance*, and that has been a constant Resolution to reject all amplification, digressions, and swellings of style; to return back to the primitive purity and shortness, when men deliver'd so many *things* almost in an equal number of *words*. They have exacted from all their members a close, naked, natural way of speaking, positive expressions, clear senses, a native eas'ness, bringing all things as near the Mathematical plainness as they can, and preferring the language of Artizans, Countrymen, and Merchants before that of Wits or Scholars.

So writes Sprat, the first historian of the Royal Society. Almost at the same time, in December 1664, his colleagues gave effect to their views by appointing a committee for the improvement of the English language, which included, besides himself, Waller, Dryden and Evelyn[1]. Doubtless, it was out of this committee that the idea arose of founding an English academy for the 'improvement of speaking and writing' on the model of the French one. This idea was discussed at three or four meetings held at Gray's inn, where, in addition to the above, Cowley and the duke of Buckingham, also members of the Royal Society, were present. But, in consequence of the plague and 'other circumstances intervening,' the plan 'came to nothing[2].'

The same need for greater plainness and simplicity of language was felt in pulpit oratory so far back as 1646, when Wilkins, afterwards bishop of Chester, one of the founders of the Royal Society, and its first secretary, had recommended, in his popular *Ecclesiastes or the Gift of Preaching*, that the style of preaching should be plain and without rhetorical flourishes[3]. After the restoration, these views found an adequate exponent in his friend John Tillotson, whose sermons at Lincoln's inn and St Lawrence Jewry attracted large congregations[4]. His St Paul's sermon, preached before the lord mayor, in March 1664, and printed by request under the title *The Wisdom of being religious*, is, in its perfect plainness and absence of rhetoric, an instructive contrast to the brilliantly imaginative discourse which Jeremy Taylor delivered, only eight months earlier, at the funeral of archbishop Bramhall. But the reformation of pulpit oratory was not the work of one

---

[1] Evelyn embodied his views in a letter to the chairman, Sir Peter Wyche, which is printed in J. E. Spingarn's *Critical Essays of the Seventeenth Century*, vol. II, pp. 310 ff.

[2] Evelyn to Pepys (*op. cit.* vol. II, pp. 327 ff.). As to the origin of the Royal Society see, also, *ante*, chap. XV.

[3] Cf., as to the change in the style of pulpit oratory, *ante*, chap. XII.

[4] See *ante*, *ib.*

sermon or one man. Both Stillingfleet, reader at the Temple, who was even more popular than Tillotson, and South, public orator at Oxford, who was made a prebendary of Westminster in 1663, belonged to the modern school. In a sermon preached on Ascension day 1667, the latter divine commended apostolic preaching for its plainness and simplicity:

nothing here of the finger of the North-star...nothing of the door of angel's wings or the beautiful locks of cherubims: no starched similitudes, introduced with a 'thus have I seen a cloud rolling in its airy mansion,' and the like.

This ungenerous hit at Jeremy Taylor, who was lately dead, well marks the antithesis between the new age and the old, between wit and poetry, between reason and imagination.

Dryden's statement that 'if he had any talent for English prose it was owing to his having often read the writings of the great archbishop Tillotson' must be regarded as a piece of generous exaggeration. At the most, he can only have learnt from him the virtues of clear and logical statement, and of short, well coordinated sentences. In the epistle dedicatory of *The Rival-Ladies* (1664), and in the earlier part of the *Essay of Dramatick Poesie* written in the summer of 1665, his management of the clause is still somewhat uncertain. It is not till Neander, who represents Dryden, joins in the discussion that we recognise our first master of modern prose.

In the *Essay of Dramatick Poesie*, the conversational character of Dryden's style is, also, already apparent. This, of course, is due, in part, to the dialogue form, but we may also trace in it the influence of Will's coffee-house, where, though he was 'not very conversible[1],' he was listened to as an oracle. The statement suggests a man who talked with unusual deliberation and precision, and with a nice choice of words, and whose written style was thus a more exact copy of his talk than is ordinarily the case. Moreover, that style is always refined and well bred, reflecting, in this, the tone of the court and, particularly, that of the king. 'The desire,' says Dryden in his *Defence of the Epilogue* (1672), 'of imitating so great a pattern loosened' the English 'from their stiff forms of conversation, and made them easy and pliant to each other in discourse.' And, of Charles II, Halifax says that his wit 'consisted chiefly in the quickness of his apprehension.' It was a trait which he inherited—with others—from his grandfather Henri IV, and he gave expression to it with a refinement of language and a

[1] Pope on Spence, sec. VII, p. 261 (Singer's ed.).

conversational ease natural to one who had spent five years in Paris society.

The influx of French fashions at the restoration has become a commonplace with historians; but, so far as regards literature, it had begun at least as early as the reign of Elizabeth. The marriage of Charles I with Henrietta Maria (1625) gave a fresh impulse to the movement, and it was under the queen's auspices, if not by her actual command, that an English version of Corneille's *Cid* was put on the stage in 1638, little more than a year after its publication in French. In the same year, three volumes of Balzac's *Letters* appeared in an English translation, one of them in a second edition. The *vogue* of a rhetorician like Balzac, whose style is more important than his thought, is a striking testimony to the high estimation in which the language and literature of France were then held. It must be remembered that Richelieu's great design of making France the first power in Europe was just beginning to be successful, and that it was partly in furtherance of this that, in 1634, he had founded the *Académie française.* Though the civil war (1642—8) checked, for a time, the French studies of Englishmen, it ultimately contributed to their diffusion. For it sent most leading English men of letters to Paris. In 1646, Hobbes, 'the first of all that fled,' Waller, D'Avenant, Denham, Cowley and Evelyn were all gathered together in the French capital. Cowley remained there till 1656; D'Avenant returned, a prisoner, in 1650, the others in 1652.

In 1651, D'Avenant published his unfinished heroic poem *Gondibert,* which he had written at Paris, and which, in general conception and tone, shows the influence of the heroic romances[1]. Their popularity in England is well known[2]. Gomberville's *Polexandre* appeared in an English dress in 1647 but 'so disguised' that Dorothy Osborne, that ardent reader of romances, 'hardly knew it.' A translation of La Calprenède's *Cléopâtre*, and two translations of his *Cassandre,* began to appear in 1652 (Sir Charles Cottrell's translation of the former was published in 1676). English versions of Madeleine de Scudéry's *Ibrahim, Le Grand Cyrus* and *Clélie* followed in 1652, 1653—5 and 1656—61. There was a subsequent version of the last named in 1678, and translations by John Phillips of La Calprenède's *Pharamond* and of Madeleine de Scudéry's *Almahide* in the previous year. English imitations also appeared, such as lord Broghill (Orrery)'s *Parthenissa* (first

---

[1] See, as to *Gondibert, ante,* vol. VII, chap. III, and cf. p. 9 of the present volume.

[2] Cf. *ante,* chap. I, as to their influence upon the English drama, and upon heroic plays in particular.

part) in 1654, with which, in spite of its 'handsome language,' Dorothy Osborne was not very much taken, and Sir George Mackenzie's *Aretina or the Serious Romance* in 1661. A complete edition of *Parthenissa* in three volumes was published in 1665 and 1667. The most active translator at this time was John Davies of Kidwelly. Besides *Clélie* (1652) and the last four parts of *Cléopâtre* (1658—60), he translated novels by Scarron (1657—67); Voiture's *Letters* (1657), which soon eclipsed Balzac's in favour and are recommended by Locke as a pattern for 'letters of compliment, mirth, railery or conversation'; Sorel's *Le Berger extravagant* (1653); and Scarron's *Nouvelles tragi-comiques* (1657—62). The same author's *Don Japhet d'Arménie* and *Les trois Dorothées* were translated in 1657, and his *Roman comique* in 1676. But it was his burlesques which had the greatest *vogue* in this country and produced numerous imitators. Charles Cotton led the way with his *Scarronides*, a burlesque of the first book of Vergil, in 1664, and followed it up with the fourth book in 1665. Other writers burlesqued Homer and Ovid, all outdoing Scarron in coarseness and vulgarity. In the words of Dryden, Parnassus spoke the cant of Billingsgate.

But, to return to the days of the commonwealth, there appeared, in 1653, the translation of a more famous work, which, in one sense, was a burlesque. This was Sir Thomas Urquhart's remarkable version of the first two books of Rabelais's great romance. It apparently fell flat, for the third book was not published till forty years later[1]. Greater success attended the translation of another monument of French prose, Pascal's *Lettres Provinciales*, which, under the title *The Mysterie of Jesuitisme, discovered in certain letters*, was published in 1657, the year in which Pascal wrote the last of the letters, a new edition being called for in the following year. And a translation of Descartes's *Traité des passions de l'âme* (1650) testifies to an interest in that psychological analysis which was to be a brilliant feature of the new school of French writers.

At the restoration, there was a decided falling off in this work of translation. In fact, all the translations from the French produced during the twenty-five years of Charles II's reign hardly surpass in number those which appeared during the last eight years of the commonwealth. The first decade after the restoration was marked chiefly by a fairly successful attempt to acclimatise

---

[1] Cf. vol. IV, p. 8; and see, as to Urquhart, vol. VII, pp. 253 ff. As to Butler and Rabelais, see *ante*, chap. II.

Corneille, the details of which have been given in a previous chapter[1]. The psychological tragedies of Racine were less to the taste of English audiences, and it was not till nearly the close of queen Anne's reign that they secured a footing on the English stage with Ambrose Philips's *Distrest Mother* (*Andromaque*). The unparalleled debt to Molière has been pointed out in an earlier chapter[2]. It need only be said here that, of all his thirty-one plays, only about half-a-dozen escaped the general pillage[3]. La Fontaine was not translated into English till the next century; but he was read and admired by the English wits, and it was only his growing infirmities which, towards the end of his life, prevented him from accepting an invitation sent by some of his English admirers, who 'engaged to find him an honourable subsistence' in London.

To Boileau, the remaining member of this illustrious group of friends, Dryden refers in 1677, three years after the publication of *L'Art Poétique*, as one of the chief critics of his age; while, in the *Discourse concerning the Original and Progress of Satire* (1693), he pays a splendid tribute to him, as 'the admirable Boileau, whose numbers are excellent, whose expressions are noble, whose thoughts are just, whose language is pure, whose satire is pointed and whose sense is close.' His *Lutrin* appeared in English in 1682; his *Art Poétique*, translated by Sir William Soames and revised by Dryden, in 1683; and, about the same time, Oldham imitated two of his satires, the fifth and the eighth. The second had been already translated by Butler, and the third by Buckingham and Rochester. Bossuet is represented by some of his controversial writings, such as his *Exposition de la Doctrine de l'Église Catholique* and *Conférence avec M. Claude*, and by his great *Discours sur l'Histoire Universelle*, which was translated in 1686. Malebranche's *Recherche de la Vérité* and La Rochefoucauld's *Maximes* both appeared in English in 1694, and, of the latter, there had been an earlier translation by Mrs Aphra Behn. Pascal's *Pensées* and La Bruyère's *Caractères*, which Dryden couples together as 'two of the most entertaining books that modern French can boast of,' were translated in 1688 and 1699 respectively; in 1688, too, appeared an English version of Mme de la Fayette's *Princesse de Clèves*. But a mere record of translations from a

---

[1] See *ante*, chap. VII. *Le Menteur* was acted and printed in London under the title *The Lyer* in 1671. It was rptd with the first title *The Mistaken Beauty* in 1685.

[2] See *ante*, chap. V.

[3] See Jacob, Giles, *Poetical Register*, vol. I, p. 292; Ward, A. W., *History of English Dramatic Literature*, vol. III, p. 315 n.

foreign literature is far from constituting a measure of its influence. The real influence which French literature exercised upon our own between the restoration and the close of the seventeenth century may be classified under four heads: that of Corneille and the heroic romances upon tragedy, that of Molière upon comedy, that of Montaigne upon the essay and that of French criticism upon English criticism. Neither the first nor the second of these influences is really important: for the fashion of the riming heroic play soon passed away; and, though our comedy borrowed its materials from Molière, it took over little of his form, and nothing of his spirit. The influence of Montaigne upon the essay will be discussed later. But it may be well, in the first instance, to consider the influence which is the most important of all, because it affected our whole literature and not merely some special department of it.

The debt of English literature to French criticism begins with D'Avenant's laboured and longwinded preface to *Gondibert*, written in Paris and there published, with an answer by Hobbes, in 1650. It was, no doubt, suggested by Chapelain's turgid and obscure preface to Marino's *Adone* (1623). In 1650, Chapelain was at the height of his authority as a critic, and the whole tone of this piece of writing, with the talk about nature and the insistence on the need of criticism as well as inspiration in poetry, is thoroughly French. Dryden, in his *Essay of Dramatick Poesie*, is perfectly independent in his views; but he must have written it with a copy of the 1660 edition of Corneille's plays, which contain his *Examens* and *Discours*, by his side[1]. Among the French critics of the next generation, Boileau stands out prominent, but his authority in England during the last quarter of the seventeenth century was balanced by that of Rapin, whose *Réflexions sur la poétique d'Aristote* was translated by Rymer in the same year in which it appeared in French (1674), and of whom Dryden says that he 'is alone sufficient, were all other critics lost, to teach anew the rules of writing[2].' Le Bossu and Dacier were also highly esteemed. Dryden speaks of Le Bossu as 'the best of modern critics,' and the greater part of his *Discourse concerning the Original and Progress of Satire* (1693) is little more than an adaptation of Dacier's *Essai sur la Satire*. A translation of this treatise, which consists of only a few pages, was printed in an appendix to one of Le Bossu's, *Du poème épique*, in 1695. 'I presume your Ladyship has read

---

[1] Cf. *ante*, p. 23.

[2] *Apology for Heroick Poetry* (1677) (*Essays*, ed. Ker, W. P., vol. i, p. 181).

Bossu,' says Brisk to lady Froth, in Congreve's *Double-Dealer* (1693)[1]. 'O Yes, and Rapin and Dacier upon Aristotle and Horace'; and, in Dennis's *The Impartial Critic*, produced in the same year as Congreve's play, frequent appeals are made to Dacier's translation of Aristotle's *Poetics*, which he had published, *avec des Remarques*, in the previous year.

Of these three Frenchmen, all of whom have now passed into oblivion, it may be said that, like Boileau, they express in their literary criticism the absolutist ideas of their age. But their outlook is narrower, and their attitude towards the ancients less independent, than Boileau's. Conform to 'the Precepts of Aristotle and Horace and to the Practice of Homer and Virgil,' is the summary of Le Bossu's longwinded treatise. Rapin says that 'to please against the rules is a bad principle,' and he defines art as 'good sense reduced to method.' In Thomas Rymer, who prefixed to his translation a characteristic preface, he found an interpreter who, with equal respect for Aristotle, laid even greater emphasis on commonsense. He aspired to be 'the Plain Dealer' of criticism, and, having examined modern epic poems in the preface to Rapin, proceeded, four years later (1678), to 'handle' *The Tragedies of the Last Age* 'with the same liberty.' He was answered in verse by Butler (*Upon Critics who judge of modern plays by the rules of the Ancients*), and in prose by Dryden, who, in his preface to *All for Love*, the play in which he renounced rime, rebels against the authority of 'our Chedreux critics,' and, while he admits that 'the Ancients as Mr Rymer has judiciously observed, are and ought to be our masters,' qualifies his admission with the remark that, 'though their models are regular, they are too little for English tragedy.' The earl of Mulgrave (afterwards marquis of Normanby and duke of Buckinghamshire), in his much admired *Essay upon Poetry* (1682), drew largely from Boileau's *Art Poétique*; and, in 1684, the authority of 'the rules' was reinforced by a translation of the abbé d'Aubignac's *Pratique du théâtre*:

> Then, 'tis the mode of France; without whose rules
> None must presume to set up here as fools[2].

Rymer's *Short view of Tragedy* (1693), with its famous criticism of *Othello*, roused Dryden to another spirited defence of English tragedy[3]. But the authority of Rymer continued to stand high,

---

[1] Act II, sc. 2.

[2] Dryden, Prologue to *Albion and Albanius* (1685).

[3] *Dedication of Examen Poeticum* (vol. III of *Miscellany Poems*) (1693). As to Rymer, cf. *ante*, chaps. VI and VII.

even with Dryden. It was well, therefore, for English literature that there were critics in France who paid little or no respect to the rules, and who believed that individual taste was a better criterion than Rymer's 'common-sense of all ages.' Such were the chevalier (afterwards marquis) de Méré, whose letters, containing a good deal of scattered criticism, were published in 1687 ; the *père* Bouhours, whose *Manière de penser sur les ouvrages de l'esprit* appeared in the same year; and La Bruyère, whose *Caractères*, with the admirable opening chapter *Des Ouvrages de l'esprit*, followed at the beginning of the next. All these three writers, of whom the second and third were known in England before the close of the century, may be said to belong to the school of taste, when taste was still a matter of individual judgment, and had not yet stiffened into the narrow code of an oligarchy.

But there was another critic of the same school who exercised a far greater influence on writers, for he was living in our midst. This was Saint-Évremond, who, exiled from his own country, made England his home from 1662 to 1665 and, again, from 1670 to his death in 1703. He was on intimate terms with the English wits and courtiers, with Hobbes, Waller and Cowley, with Buckingham, Arlington and St Albans, and his conversational powers were highly appreciated at Will's and other places of resort. His occasional writings were translated from time to time into English, the first to appear being a small volume of essays on the drama, including one on English comedy (1685). Regarded as an oracle on both sides of the Channel, he had a marked influence on English literary criticism. But, though he had a real critical gift, he was neither catholic nor profound. He clung to the favourites of his youth, to Montaigne, Malherbe, Corneille, Voiture, and, having been exiled from France at the close of *la bonne Régence*, he had little sympathy for the age of Louis XIV. Molière and La Fontaine barely found favour in his eyes; he was unjust to Racine, and he detested Boileau. Yet much should be pardoned in a man who ventured to say, in the year 1672, that 'there is nothing so perfect in the *Poetics* of Aristotle that it should be a rule to all nations and all ages.'

It was possibly owing to Saint-Évremond that Montaigne's popularity in this country, which had lain dormant for a season, blossomed afresh after the restoration, and gave a new stimulus to the literary essay, which owed to him its name and original inspiration. For, after 1625, the year in which Bacon's *Essays* received their final form, the essay began to lose its popularity.

Then, at the beginning of the commonwealth, a versatile writer, named Thomas Forde, produced a volume of essays, *Lusus Fortunae* (1649), the common topic of which, the mutability of man and human affairs, strongly suggests Montaigne; and, on the eve of the restoration, Francis Osborne published *A Miscellany of Sundry Essayes Paradoxes and Problematical Discourses, Letters and Characters* (1659), of which the style has all the faults, and none of the virtues, of the older prose[1]. The author, who was master of the horse to Shakespeare's patron William Herbert, earl of Pembroke, is best known for his *Advice to a Son*, which, first published in 1656, went through numerous editions. It is a strange admixture of platitude and paradox, much of which might have come straight from the lips of Polonius. The style, when it is not terse and apophthegmatic, as of one trying to imitate Bacon, is stiff with conceits and longwinded sentences.

It was Abraham Cowley, a friend of Saint-Évremond, who gave a new turn to the essay. Cowley has often been called a transitional writer; but he is one in the sense, not that he dallied in a halfway house, but that, both in prose and verse, he made a complete transit from the old school to the new. It is particularly interesting to trace this progress in his prose writings. In the earliest of these, the preface to the 1656 edition of his poems, his sentences are at first cumbrous and involved, and though, when he warms to his work, they become shorter and better balanced, there remains a certain stiffness in the style quite unlike the conversational ease of his later essays. It is nearer to Jeremy Taylor (who was only five years Cowley's senior, and who died in the same year) than to Dryden. To the older school also belongs the *Discourse by way of Vision concerning the Government of Oliver Cromwell* (1661), of which the latter part is a fine example of rhetorical prose. Even in the preface to *Cutter of Coleman-Street*[2] (1663), though the sentences, as a rule, are short and well coordinated, Cowley has by no means shaken himself free from the old mannerism. The essays proper, eleven in number, were all written during the last four or five years of his life, and, to most of them, a more approximate date can be assigned. In 1663, having been disappointed of the mastership of the Savoy hospital, he accomplished his design of withdrawing himself from 'all tumults and business of the world,' by retiring to Barn Elms on the Thames, then a favourite resort of Londoners. Before this,

---

[1] Cf. *ante*, vol. VII, chap. VIII.

[2] As to Cowley's poetry, see *ante*, vol. VII, chap. III, pp. 61 ff.

he must have written the essay entitled *The danger of Procrastination*, in which he refers to his 'design' as only in contemplation. It is not without charm, but long sentences still occur. Transitional in style, also, is the essay *Of Agriculture*, in which he proposes that 'one college in each University should be erected and appropriated to this Study,' and the short essay entitled *The Garden*, dedicated to his friend Evelyn, which was written in 1664, between the publication of Evelyn's *Kalendarium Hortense* and that of his *Gardening*. Cowley speaks of himself as 'sticking still in the inn of a hired house and a garden.' In April 1665, he moved to the Porch House, Chertsey, and there he died two years later. To these last two years of his life belong the essays *Of Obscurity*, *Of My Self* and that entitled *The dangers of an Honest man in such Company*; and to the same period we may with all probability assign *Of Solitude*, *Of Greatness* and *The Shortness of Life and uncertainty of Riches*. In these six essays, Cowley has found his style and his method. The influence of Montaigne is unmistakable. In the two essays in which he is mentioned by name, *Of Solitude* and *Of Greatness*, not only the titles, but some of the contents, are borrowed from him. Of those chief characteristics which mark the *essai* of Montaigne in its final phase of development—the examples from classical and other authors, the personal element and the artistic workmanship—none is wanting in Cowley. Yet he is no mere satellite of Montaigne. He is saved from this by the personal element in his writings. In the words of his biographer, his essays are 'a real chronicler of his own thoughts upon the point of his retirement.' In spite of *The Spectator's* sneer that 'he praised solitude when he despaired of shining in a court,' there is no reason to doubt his earnest affection for obscurity and retirement. We can see, too, in his essays, the other qualities ascribed to him by Sprat—his lack of affectation, his modesty and humility, and, above all, the pleasant gravity of his speech. The essay *Of Greatness* may be taken as an example of his method. Here we find, not the solitary self-communing of a Burton or a Browne, but a friendly interchange of confidence between author and reader—an anecdote freely translated from the elder Seneca, a few examples from Suetonius of the foibles of the Roman emperors; a pointed reference to 'the late giant of our nation'; a quotation or two from the Latin poets; and a few lines of the author's own. There is no disdain of commonplaces; but they are dressed up as 'ridiculous paradoxes,' before being stripped and presented to the reader as brand-new truths. As for the style, it is neither stiff nor slovenly; neither a court suit, nor a dressing gown and slippers. The choice of words is fastidious, without being affected; the use of metaphor is restrained; sentences are well turned, but not all cut to the same pattern. The artist, in short, has concealed his art. Cowley, we are told, intended to publish a discourse upon style. It would have been agreeable reading; but it would doubtless have revealed as little of his secret as have similar treatises by later masters of the art of prose.

Cowley's essays were first printed, under the title *Several Discourses, by way of Essays, in Verse and Prose*, in 1668, the year after his death. In the same year, his friend Thomas Sprat (afterwards bishop of Rochester) wrote an 'elegant' account of his life and writings, which, unfortunately, is as sparing of facts as the same writer's *History of the Royal Society*. Worse than this, having told us that Cowley excelled in his letters to his private friends— as we can well believe from the one letter of this sort which has escaped destruction[1]—Sprat declines to publish them on the ground that 'in such letters the souls of men should appear undressed; and in that negligent habit, they may be fit to be seen by one or two in a chamber, but not to go abroad into the street.'

Happily, one collection of private letters of this period has been preserved, which reveals a 'native tenderness and innocent gaiety of mind' equal to Cowley's. These are the letters of Dorothy Osborne, niece of Francis Osborne, written to her future husband, Sir William Temple, between the autumn of 1652 and that of 1654. She not only writes delightful letters, full of good sense, penetration and humour, but she has views of her own about the epistolary style. 'All letters, methinks, should be free and easy as one's discourse: not studied as an oration, not made up of hard words like a charm.' This criticism she does not consider applicable to the letters of her lover.

Nothing is more pleasant than to trace through the records of Temple's political life the services rendered to him, and, through him, to the public interest, by this most devoted of women, though the title has been held to be disputable on behalf of Temple's sister, lady Giffard, whom he commemorated with his wife and himself on his tombstone. Lady Giffard gave up the whole of her long widowhood to the companionship and service of her beloved brother, and wrote anonymously the brief *Life* and

---

[1] A letter to Sprat is printed in Johnson's *Life of Cowley*. The letters written to Henry Bennet (afterwards earl of Arlington), from Paris, in 1650, which are printed in *Miscellanea Aulica*, contain only public news.

admirable character of him, afterwards prefixed to the folio edition of his works (1750). But, although, at times, it was more convenient for lady Giffard to be the companion of her brother's journeys than it was for his wife, the latter was by no means, as has been suggested, thrown into the shade by her, and a complete harmony of purpose and feeling seems to have existed among the trio. Lady Temple was taken into her husband's confidence as completely in his public, as in his private, business, except when he was under obligations of absolute secrecy; when left behind at the Hague, she was able to give him trustworthy information as to Buckingham's negotiations with France ; and she had the principal share in the confidential enquiries as to what 'concern'd the Person, Humour and Dispositions' of the young princess Mary of York whose hand William of Orange thereupon made up his mind to ask in marriage[1]. Lady Giffard's own letters, which have been recently published[2], lack the rare charm which attaches to those of her sister-in-law, after, as well as before, marriage, even at seasons when, according to lady Temple's own description, she felt 'as weary as a dog without his Master.' The greatest tragedy of her life, the death by his own hand of the son of whom, in his babyhood, she had written as 'the quietest best little boy that ever was borne,' seems to school her into a calm solemnity of expression which has a pathos of its own, unlike that which mingles with the humour of her earlier writing.

Temple's own letters—not including those to Dorothy—were published after his death by his *quondam* secretary Swift (whose reverence for his patron certainly did not go deep), the first two volumes appearing in 1700, and the third in 1703[3]. This correspondence, which includes many letters from Arlington, lord keeper Bridgeman, and others (with Clifford, notwithstanding their connection through lady Temple, her husband was quite out of touch

[1] See Temple's *Memoirs* (ed. 1692), p. 155; and cf. the volume cited in the next note, pp. 129—130.

[2] By Miss Julia Longe (1911). The collection includes, besides a few letters from lady Temple to her husband, several letters by lady Giffard and her correspondents, extending over the long period of years from 1664 to 1722. Among these correspondents are Mrs Katherine Philips ('the Matchless Orinda') in a rather longwinded letter, Sir William Godolphin (an admirer of Sacharissa), the mad lord Lincoln, lady Berkeley (afterwards countess of Portland), the duchess of Somerset and Edward Young (author of *Night Thoughts*). The length of time covered by this correspondence deprives it of value as characteristic of any particular period; but the collection, as a whole, s an interesting supplement to the Dorothy Osborne series.

[3] The volume of letters of 1668 and 1669, published in 1699 by Jones, D., was unauthorised; but there is no reason for doubting the authenticity of its contents. See Courtenay, T. P., *The Life of Sir William Temple*, vol. II, p. 142.

from the first), fails to warrant the statement of its title-page, that it contains 'an account of the most Important Transactions that pass'd in Christendom' during the period which the earlier volumes cover (1665—72)[1]; but it furnishes a lucid survey of unusual interest. In his *Letters*, even more conspicuously than in his *Memoirs*, Temple's style is wholly unaffected and unambitious, and the early letter to his father in Ireland, giving an account of his visit to the slippery bishop of Münster, is an admirable specimen of lively narrative. It is worth noticing that not only Temple but most of the men of affairs who correspond with him write in the same straightforward and simple style—it was a period when much importance had begun to be attached in France to the clearness and readableness of diplomatic despatches, and it was natural that the same habit should have become more common in English diplomatic correspondence. In 1666, Temple was, as he says, 'Young and Very New in Business'; but it was not long before he was engaged in the negotiations of which the result was a diplomatic masterpiece, the famous Triple Alliance of 1668, and in those which accompanied its break-up. A considerable number of Temple's letters and other papers are in French, Latin or Spanish, in all of which tongues he was a proficient; but he naturally finds few opportunities for a display of literary taste as well as of linguistic ability[2]. The personal interest of some of his letters is, however, considerable; not only his trust in his wife, but his modest and unaffected estimate of the value of his own public services, even in so exceptional an instance as the carrying through of the Triple Alliance, and bringing 'Things drawn out of their Center' back 'to their Center again,' cannot fail to engage the sympathy of the reader.

The distinctive qualities of Temple as a writer of clear and agreeable prose are even more distinctive of his *Memoirs*, which are concerned with the later years of his career—from 1674, when the conclusion of peace with the Dutch and the general

---

[1] Swift makes a similar criticism of the title originally given to Temple's *Memoirs* when published without his authority. See *Preface* to part III (ed. 1709).

[2] In a letter dated August 1667 (vol. I, p. 117), Temple expresses a wish that Cowley could sing the heroic death of captain Douglas in his burning ship at Chatham, and, generally, that something could be done 'to turn the Vein of Wits,' and 'to raise up the Esteem of some Qualities, above their real value, rather than bring everything,' even the poetry of Mr Waller, 'to Burlesque.' As it is, he says, in offering this curious though unconscious contribution to the 'heroic' tendency in contemporary literature, we 'neither act Things worth Relating, nor relate Things worth the Reading.' It would almost seem as if Temple's absence from home had left him in ignorance of the appearance, in this very year 1667, of *Annus Mirabilis*.

desire of inducing the French government to follow the example of the English brought him again to the front, to the conclusion of the peace of Nymegen, in 1678, and thence to his final withdrawal, at the very height of political agitation at home, from all further open share in public affairs. The second part professes to begin in 1672 (though it cannot really be said to go back beyond 1674), and was preceded by a first part beginning with 1665, which, at some unknown period of his life, and for reasons which can only be conjectured[1], was destroyed by the author himself. Thus, only the second part, published without authority in 1691 and republished by Swift in 1692, and the third part, published by him on his own motion, remain to us. But they are among the best examples of a class of literature which was as yet new in England—memoirs of affairs, as well as of personal experiences, conveying the information and instruction which they are designed to impart in a thoroughly readable and often highly attractive style. It would not be easy to find a more lucid account of the political results of the declaration of war by England against the Dutch, with which the narrative opens, or of the *impasse* to which the selfishness of party purposes and personal interests had reduced English politics when Temple bade them a long farewell. On the other hand, few memoirs or diaries of the time succeed better in suggesting a lifelike, and, at the same time, reasonable, conception of both the ways of talking and the ways of thinking of two princes so different from one another as were Charles II and William III (before his accession to the English throne). It is not a little to Temple's credit as a diplomatist that he should have been able, in a very uncommon degree, to gain the confidence of both; it is hardly less to his credit as a writer that, especially in the case of Charles II, to none of whose weaknesses he was blind, he should have been able to show what there was in him that fitted him for his destiny.

In the preface to part III of these *Memoirs*, Swift is at pains to refute the objections taken against them 'first, as to the Matter; that the Author speaks too much of himself; next, as to the Style; that he affects the Use of French Words, as well as some Turns of Expression peculiar to that Language.' Temple's nature, no doubt, was, in a sense, self-centred, but his *Memoirs* preserve a due

---

[1] See Courtenay, *u.s.* vol. II, p. 110; and *ibid.* pp. 242—3 as to the protest of lady Giffard against the publication of part III and Swift's angry rejoinder. The whole story of Swift's relations with the Temple family, and, more especially, with lady Giffard, whom he hated, is discussed by Miss Longe, *u.s.* pp. 179 ff., but belongs to the history of Swift rather than to that of his patron.

balance between egotism and a reticence about himself which would
have detracted from the impression of veracity conveyed by them,
besides depriving them of much of the human interest without
which many valuable political memoirs have become virtually closed
books. Temple's Gallicisms of vocabulary and expression Swift
seeks to excuse by more or less ingenious pleas; but, to modern
English readers, Temple's style will not seem to stand in need of
defence, whether or not there were many French words which he
blotted out, as Swift states, in order to put English in their place.
On the other hand, if we may ourselves be guilty of the fault
imputed to him, he was an excellent *raconteur*; and his good
stories are all the better because they are neither too long nor too
numerous. They often point a characteristic trait in princes or
statesmen or, like the anecdote of Richelieu's wrathful outburst
against Charles I, illustrate the genesis of a whole Iliad of truths;
occasionally, they are merely amusing 'problems,' like the story of
the old count of Nassau and the parrot. But the writer is at
his best in the lighthanded analysis of character and conduct
(including his own) which shows the influence of French example
far more notably than does his choice of words or phrases. Yet,
even when speaking of himself, he could write with force, when it
seemed in place:

> I have had in Twenty Years Experience, enough of the Uncertainty of
> Princes, the Caprices of Fortune, the Corruption of Ministers, the Violence
> of Factions, the Unsteddyness of Counsels, and the Infidelity of Friends;
> Nor do I think the rest of my Life enough to make any new Experiments.

Temple's general judgment of the political and social characteristics of a people whom he learnt to know well, not only by
long sojourns among them, but because, as he relates with pardon-
able pride, his visits were welcomed by them as are those of the
swallow in the spring, is laid down in his sympathetic but unpre-
judiced *Observations upon the United Provinces of the Netherlands* (1672). They present themselves as the expansion of a
summary of the condition of the country, sent in, according to
custom, at the close of an ambassador's stay there; but they are
put together under the impression of the great and, as it seemed
to Temple, decisive catastrophe, which had suddenly brought to the
brink of destruction a state, 'the Envy of some, the Fear of others,
and the Wonder of all' its neighbours. It is the growth of that
polity's greatness, due to moral, as well as physical, causes—to the
principle of tolerance as well as the control of the sea—which this
admirable essay demonstrates with equal lucidity and conviction.

During the same period of leisure, he produced, in 1667 or 1668, *An Essay upon the present State and Settlement of Ireland,* which, though censuring the process of the late settlement, advises no remedy for existing results beyond that which had been commended by Spenser. In 1673, Temple published *An Essay upon the Advancement of Trade in Ireland,* which asserts 'the true and natural ground of Trade and Riches' to be the 'Number of People in proportion to the Ground they inherit,' but proposes some useful developments of the export trade suggested to him by his own residence in Leinster.

Part I of the *Miscellanea* contains *A Survey of the Constitution and Interests of the Empire* and other principal European countries, *with their Relations to England in the Year* 1671, presented in that year to Arlington: a clear exposition of the political situation and of the reasons for and against England's joining France against the Dutch, with a specially luminous account of the general history of Spanish politics and of the rise of the United Provinces to the rank of a firstrate power. It will be noted that this diplomatic summary, clear as it is, opens with sentences of almost Clarendonian length. To a later period seems to belong *An Introduction to the History of England* (published in 1695), which may possibly have been intended as an introduction to Kennett's *History,* the editors of which, however, proposed to use Milton for the period before the Norman conquest. Temple shows a characteristic contempt for mythology, and treats no part of his subject very assiduously till he comes to the reign of William the Conqueror, whom he holds to have been unjustly censured by ecclesiastical writers. Like all Temple's writings, this abridgment is very readable, though, unlike most of them, the work of a *dilettante.* Of much greater interest is his *Essay upon the Original and Nature of Government* (written about 1672), which is noticeable as arguing, in direct contravention of the theory of a social contract elaborated by Hobbes and Locke, that state government arose out of an extension of paternal and patriarchal authority. It is not too much to say that, in this argument, Temple was before his times; Locke takes no notice of his speculations[1].

Temple's essays, or, as they were called, *Miscellanea,* appeared in three parts; the first in 1680 the second in 1690 and the third, two years after the author's death, in 1701. The most widely read

[1] See Herriott, F. I., *Sir William Temple on the Origin and Nature of Government* (Johns Hopkins University Diss.), Baltimore, n.d.

of these essays, *Upon Ancient and Modern Learning* (1690), was
inspired by that quarrel between the ancients and the moderns
which, for more than two years, had divided the literary world of
Paris, and was, in its turn, the origin of the celebrated controversy on the *Letters of Phalaris* between Bentley and Charles
Boyle. But neither in this nor in the companion essay, *Upon
Poetry*, does Temple show to much advantage. His knowledge is
too superficial for his task. He has a bowing acquaintance with
many authors, but he is not on intimate terms with any. He has
sauntered through the outer courts of literature, but he has never
penetrated to the sanctuary. It is interesting, however, to note
his opinions on French literature. In poetry, he only mentions
two names, Ronsard for the past and Boileau for the present.
For prose, he names Rabelais, Montaigne, and, among the moderns,
Voiture, La Rochefoucauld and Bussy-Rabutin, whose *Histoire
Amoureuse de Gaule* (1665) had a *succès de scandale* in this country
as well as in France[1]. Of the French language, Temple justly
observes that, as it 'has much more Finess and Smoothness at
this time, so I take it to have had much more Force, Spirit, and
Compass in Montaigne's Age'; while, of Rabelais, he says that
he 'seems to have been Father of the Ridicule, a man of universal learning as well as wit.' Was it this praise which led to
the publication, in the following year (1693), thirty-three years
after the author's death, of Sir Thomas Urquhart's translation of
the third book of *Pantagruel*[2], followed, in 1708, by that of the
fourth and fifth books from the pen of Pierre-Antonius Motteux,
one of the 84,000 refugees whom the revocation of the edict of
Nantes sent to this country? The most agreeable of Temple's
essays are those *Upon the Cure of the Gout* (part I), *Upon the
Gardens of Epicurus, or Of Gardening* (part II) and *Upon Health
and Long Life* (part III). The latter is especially interesting for
the light that it throws upon the notions of the age as to health
and longevity, and the specifics in use for the cure of ordinary
ailments. Thus, we learn that alehoof or ground-ivy is 'most
sovereign for the eyes' and 'admirable in Frenzies' and that the
constant use of alehoof ale is a 'specifick Remedy or Prevention
of the Stone'; that 'the Spirit of Elder is sovereign in Cholicks,
and the use of it in general very beneficial in Scurvies and

---

[1] Pepys read it in 1666.

[2] Urquhart's translation of books I and II was first printed in 1653; it was again
published, with his translation of book III and a life of Rabelais by the editor, Motteux,
in 1693—4, and with books IV and V translated by Motteux, in 1708.

Dropsies'; and that 'for Rheums in the Eyes and the Head a leaf of Tobacco put into the Nostrils for an Hour each Morning is a Specifick Medicine.'

In the essay *Of Gardening*, written in 1685, Temple gives an agreeable account of his own garden at Sheen, which was renowned for its fruit trees, discoursing of his grapes and figs, his peaches and apricots, with that complacent sense of superiority which is the foible of most gardeners. The essay entitled *Gout*, written in 1677, gives much information as to various cures for that malady of statesmen, and, incidentally, introduces us to several of Temple's diplomatic colleagues in a new and entertaining light. Temple's style was highly thought of in his own day. 'It is generally believed,' said Swift, 'that this author has advanced our English tongue to as great perfection as it can well bear.' But this is the exaggerated praise of an editor. Lamb's 'plain, natural, chit-chat' is nearer the mark. Temple writes like a fine gentleman at his ease, without any affectation, but with considerable negligence. His syntax is sometimes faulty, and his expression does not always fit his thought. Though his sentences are kept, as a rule, within convenient bounds, they straggle occasionally and leave trailing ends. To agree wholly with Johnson that 'Temple was the first writer who gave cadence to English prose,' is to forget Browne and Taylor; but Temple has a true feeling for cadence; in this alone he is Cowley's superior. It is largely through this quality that he rises at times beyond the level of 'natural chit-chat,' as in the fine passage in praise of poetry and music which concludes the essay *Upon Poetry* and ends with the often quoted comparison between human life and a froward child.

Like Cowley, Temple came under the spell of Montaigne. In the essay *Of Gardening*, he borrows from him the story of Heraclitus playing with the boys in the porch of the Temple, and he refers to him in two later essays, *Upon Popular Discontents* and *Upon Health and Long Life*. Moreover, two essays, heads for which were found among his papers, *Upon the different conditions of life and fortune* and *Upon Conversation*, suggest, not only in the titles, but in the subjects themselves, frequent intercourse with the father of the essay. There were other Englishmen of letters, too, who kept the same excellent company. Dryden quotes from 'Honest Montaigne' in the preface to *All for Love*[1], while, according to Pope, Montaigne and La Rochefoucauld were among the *livres de chevet* with which Wycherley was wont to 'read himself

[1] Cf. *ante*, chap. I, p. 28.

to sleep.' In 1685, Montaigne was popular enough in England to warrant the publication of a new translation of his essays from the pen of Charles Cotton. Cotton sometimes misses his author's meaning, but he does not write sheer nonsense, as Florio sometimes does. On the other hand, his style lacks the glamour and quaint individuality of the Elizabethan translation, and, though sound on the whole, is somewhat unequal. His work is dedicated to George Savile, marquis of Halifax, who, in acknowledging the dedication, says that 'it is the book in the world I am best entertained with.'

Halifax's own *Miscellanies*, first collected in 1700, are, for the most part, political pamphlets, but a few words concerning them may, perhaps not inappropriately, find a place here. For his finest piece of writing is his praise of truth in *The Character of a Trimmer*—a passage worthy of Montaigne, whom Halifax also resembles in his bold and happy use of metaphor. Although this famous pamphlet, which, notwithstanding its substantial length, must have circulated largely between the date of its composition (early in 1685) and that of its first publication (April 1688), was then ascribed on the title-page to Sir William Coventry, there can be no doubt that it was by Halifax, who 'owned it to his friends[1].' The title was suggested to him by a paper by his subsequent adversary L'Estrange; but the use made of the term 'trimmer,' and the lesson read to the nation on the ever old and ever new truth that there are times when the ship of state has to be steadied against the excesses of each of 'the two extremes,' must alike be placed to the credit of Halifax himself. Few publications of the kind, intended to allay, not to heighten or inflame, the changes of an important crisis, have exercised a more direct effect.

The death of Charles II put an end to the trimmer's plan of inducing the king to free himself from an overbearing influence which had now become sovereign authority. Halifax appears to have consoled himself by composing his admirable *Character of King Charles the Second*, which was not published, with an appendix of *Political, Moral and Miscellaneous Thoughts and Reflections*, till 1750. The literature of characters, which the circumstances of the times and the art of both historians and satirists had brought to a great height of perfection, received a notable addition in this admirable portrait, by a man of the world, of a prince whom he thoroughly understood and for whom

---

[1] See quotation from *Saviliana ap.* Foxcroft, H. C., *The Life and Letters of Sir George Savile, Bart., first Marquis of Halifax* (1898), vol. II, p. 277.

he did not care to conceal a liking which was not all loyalty. 'The thing called *Sauntering* is a stronger Temptation to Princes than it is to others.' In this vein of easy philosophy, he delivered a judgment far nearer the truth than many more incisive censures[1].

Halifax's second political pamphlet of importance, *A Letter to a Dissenter Upon Occasion of His Majesties late Gracious Declaration of Indulgence*, was first printed, with the signature 'J. W.,' in 1687. It is much shorter than *The Character of a Trimmer*, but not less notable; for it may unhesitatingly be described as one of the pithiest and most straightforward productions of its kind, abounding in homethrusts and exhibiting throughout the clear candour of a writer sure of his ground and convinced of the necessity of his conclusions. It is wholly directed against the dangerous, indeed suicidal, policy of an alliance between nonconformity and an unlawful strain of the prerogative, and, on the face of it, is written by a loyal patriot possessed by complete distrust of Rome[2]. *The Anatomy of an Equivalent* (probably printed without an author's name in 1688, certainly in 1689) is a tract of considerable subtlety of argument on a cognate subject[3].

Of the collection of aphoristic *Thoughts and Reflections*, published with the *Character of King Charles the Second*, the political section is characterised by much wit, at times thoroughly cynical, as is shown by the trimmer's assertion that 'the best Party is but a kind of a Conspiracy against the rest of the Nation,' and by several of the aphorisms under the head 'Religion.' But not a little wisdom as well as wit is to be found both in these, and in the 'Moral' and 'Miscellaneous' sayings; and, on the whole, there is no unfairness, though there is some severity, in the 'reprisals' made by this shrewd philosopher upon the generation which had grown up under his observant eye.

More in the nature of an essay than any of his other productions, was Halifax's *A Lady's Gift, or Advice to a Daughter* (by which latter name it is generally known). First printed in 1688, it went through many editions. This little book, addressed to his own daughter (mother of lord Chesterfield, author of perhaps the most

---

[1] It must be remembered that the *Character* was written immediately after the king's decease. 'He had Sicknesses before his Death, in which he did not trouble any Protestant Divines; those who saw him upon his Death, saw a great deal.' Halifax possessed in perfection the art of hinting.

[2] Roger L'Estrange published *An Answer to a Letter to a Dissenter*, etc. in the same year, which is clever in its way and rightly makes good use of the 'Popish plot' frenzy.

[3] 'Equivalent' was the current political term for a government offer of something as valuable as the 'Oaths and Tests,' if these were abolished.

celebrated *Letters* ever addressed to a son), shows much knowledge
of the human, especially of the feminine, heart, and much of it is still
so appropriate that one may wonder why it has not been reprinted
in modern times. Aphorisms like 'Love is a passion that hath
friends in the garrison,' and 'You may love your children without
living in the nursery,' and, of an 'empty' woman, 'such an one is
seldom serious but with her tailor,' have lost none of their force.
The chapter on vanity and affectation contains a character of
a vain woman quite in the manner of La Bruyère. The chapter
on a husband is full of worldly wisdom, and good sense, and is
based on a frank recognition of the 'inequality in the sexes,' and
the imperfection of husbands. The treatment of religion is just
what you might expect from a man who, in religion as well as in
politics, had 'his dwelling in the middle between the two extremes.'
If it is a little cold and unspiritual, it is tolerant, cheerful and
reasonable; it breathes the temper of his contemporaries Barrow
and Tillotson. Halifax's style is thoroughly individual. It is the
style not of an essayist communing with his readers for his own
pleasure in the seclusion of his study, but of a man of the world
who takes up the pen for the practical purpose of convincing
others. He had a great reputation as an orator, and this is easy
to believe, for, in his written speech, he often rises to real
eloquence.

There is no trace of Montaigne in the *Reflections upon several
Christian Duties, Divine and Moral, by way of Essays*, which
Clarendon wrote, for the most part, at Montpellier, during the
years 1669 and 1670[1]. It is true that, in at least six of them,
notably those *Of Contempt of Death, Of Friendship* and *Of
Repentance,* he deals with themes also treated by Montaigne. But
the treatment is quite independent; indeed, the essay *Of Repentance*, with its definitely Christian doctrine, forms a striking
contrast to Montaigne's famous essay on the same subject. The
style is that of the *History*, diffuse and unequal—pregnant phrases
of high imaginative beauty alternating with sentences a page long—
but always that of a sincere and serious thinker, of one who is
learned, high-minded and conversant with affairs. Alike in thought
and in style, Clarendon's essays belong to the Caroline age.

Thus, the essay, with its near allies, the literary preface and
the political pamphlet, played a large part in the formation of the
new prose. We have seen that it was in the same year (1665)
that Cowley and Dryden achieved independently the mastery of

[1] Cf. *ante*, vol. VII, chap. IX.

their instruments. Cowley only played on his for a brief moment, but Dryden's mastery became more and more perfect, till, in the last year of the century, he produced his masterpiece in 'the other harmony of prose'; the *Preface to the Fables.* In its numerous digressions—'the nature of a Preface,' he says, 'is rambling'—and in the pleasant intrusion of his own personality, it reminds one happily of Montaigne[1]. But the style is all Dryden's own—short and well balanced sentences, restraint, lucidity and precision, a tone of friendly intercourse with the reader, an ease which never becomes familiarity, and a dignity which never stiffens into pomposity. When, nine years later, Steele wrote the first number of *The Tatler,* he found an instrument ready to his hand. Steele's style suggests Dryden, just as Addison's model in the first paper which he contributed to the same journal is, obviously, Cowley. Steele and Addison addressed themselves to a wider audience than Dryden, not only to scholars and wits and courtiers, but to ordinary middle-class citizens; they made the essay lighter, and introduced into it humour and a spice of malice. But they were not the creators either of the essay or of modern prose. The foundations of most of the literature of the first half of the eighteenth century were already laid down in the seventeenth. Dryden not only dominates his own age, but throws his shadow over the next.

[1] Cf. *ante,* chap. I, p. 52.